PREPARING TO DIE

Preparing to Die

*Practical Advice and Spiritual Wisdom from
the Tibetan Buddhist Tradition*

Andrew Holecek

Snow Lion
Boston & London
2013

Snow Lion
An imprint of Shambhala Publications, Inc.
Horticultural Hall
300 Massachusetts Avenue
Boston, Massachusetts 02115
www.shambhala.com

9 8 7 6 5 4 3 2 1

First Edition
Printed in the United States of America

⊚ This edition is printed on acid-free paper that meets the American National Standards Institute z39.48 Standard.
♻ This book is printed on 30% postconsumer recycled paper.
For more information please visit www.shambhala.com.

Distributed in the United States by Random House, Inc., and in Canada by Random House of Canada Ltd

Designed by Gopa & Ted2, Inc.

Library of Congress Cataloging-in-Publication data

Holecek, Andrew, 1955–
Preparing to die: practical advice and spiritual wisdom from the Tibetan Buddhist tradition / Andrew Holecek.
    pages   cm
ISBN 978-1-55939-408-6 (pbk.)
    1. Death—Religious aspects—Buddhism. 2. Death—Handbooks, manuals, etc. I. Title.
BQ4487.H65 2013
294.3'423—dc23
2012049001

This book is dedicated to the Venerable Thrangu Rinpoche
and Khenpo Tsültrim Gyamtso Rinpoche,
who showed me that death is an illusion.
And to my parents, whose deaths showed me
the heartbreak of illusion.

CONTENTS

Foreword by Tulku Thondup Rinpoche   1

Introduction   3

Part One: Spiritual Preparation

1. WHAT TO DO FOR YOURSELF BEFORE YOU DIE   15
   Living a Good Life, Learning to Let Go   15
   Practices and Teachings to Prepare You for Death   18
        Shamatha Meditation   18
        Vipashyana Meditation   21
        The Four Reminders   22
        Doctrinal Preparation   26
        Tonglen   28
        Reverse Meditations   29
        Pure Land Practice   33
        Preparation for Sudden Death   37
        Noble Truths   38
        Devotion   42
        The Bardos and the Trikaya   44
        Mind Leads All Things   53
        Phowa   54
        Shitro and Vajrasattva Practice   57
        Working with Passion   58
        Insurance Dharma   59

Dharma Wills and the Dharma Box   61
Final Advice   63

2. WHAT YOU CAN DO FOR OTHERS BEFORE THEY DIE   65

3. WHAT TO DO FOR YOURSELF AS YOU DIE   67
Letting Go   68
Dissolution and Signs   70
Outer Dissolution   73
What Is Happening?   76
Inner Dissolution   78
Tukdam   82
The Peaceful and Wrathful Visions   83
The Hourglass   85
Conclusion   89

4. WHAT TO DO FOR OTHERS AS THEY DIE   91
The View   91
Sacred Listening   94
Hopes and Fears of the Dying   96
Holding Environments   97
Creating the Environment   100
Looking Forward   101
Advice from Sogyal Rinpoche   102
  Telling the Truth   105
  Fears about Dying   106
  Unfinished Business   107
  Giving Hope and Finding Forgiveness   107
  Saying Goodbye   108
  Toward a Peaceful Death   109
  By the Bedside of the Dying   110
  Dedicating Our Death   111
  Letting Go of Attachment   112

The Grace of Prayer at the Moment of Death 113

The Atmosphere for Dying 113

Esoteric Practices 115

5. WHAT TO DO FOR YOURSELF AFTER YOU DIE 117

The View 117

First Step 121

After Remembering 123

Other Practices 127

Advice from *The Tibetan Book of the Dead* 127

    Blocking 129

    Bright and Soft Lights 132

    Choosing 133

6. WHAT TO DO FOR OTHERS AFTER THEY DIE 139

The View 139

When to Help 142

The Power of Merit 144

Reading *The Tibetan Book of the Dead* 148

Sur Offering 149

Commissioning Monasteries 150

Monastic Rituals and Ceremonies for the Dead 151

Gelugpa Rituals 156

Summary 158

Part Two: Practical Preparation

7. BEFORE DEATH APPROACHES 161

Legal Issues 163

More on Living Wills and Advance Directives 169

Legal Concerns Before, During, and After Death,
by Alex Halpern, JD 173

    Wills 175

Disposition of Property   178

Trusts   178

The Living Will and the Medical Power of Attorney   180

Demystifying Hospice: An Underused Service at End of Life,
by Beth Patterson, MA, LPC, JD   184

The History of the Hospice Movement   184

The American Hospice Movement and the
Medicare Hospice Benefit   185

Buddhism and the Hospice Movement   186

The Services of Hospice   187

What Does Hospice Care Look Like?   188

The Importance of Managing Pain   189

Conclusion   190

8. CARING FOR THE DYING   191

The Needs of the Dying, by Christine Longaker   191

The Five Psychological Stages of Dying and Medical Issues
Around Death, by Mitchell Gershten, MD   197

The Five Psychological Stages of Dying   198

The Five Stages in Loved Ones   200

Biological Changes   200

Hydration, Nutrition, and Pain Control   203

Physical Signs and Symptoms of Dying, by Andrew Holecek   206

Spiritual Matrix   217

Empty the Disease   219

9. AFTER DEATH   223

After-Death Care, by Karen Van Vuuren   223

Caring for Our Own Dead—Is it Legal?   224

Funeral Directors   225

First Steps Following an Expected Death   226

Care of the Body After Death   227

Rigor Mortis   227

Don't Do It Alone   228

A Sacred Space   228

A Suggested Checklist of Items for Physical Care of the Body   228

Bathing   229

Dressing   230

Temporary Preservation Methods   230

Dry Ice   231

Caskets   232

Unexpected Death   232

Odors and Changes at Death   233

Options for Final Disposition—Cremation or Burial   234

Burial at a Conventional Cemetery   234

Green Burial in an Established Conventional Cemetery   234

*Green Burial at a Conservation Burial Site
or Green Burial Preserve*   235

Home Burial   235

Cremation in a Conventional Crematory   236

Open-Air Cremation   237

What to Do with the Cremains   238

Other Options for Final Disposition   238

Donation   239

Exposing Children to Death   239

Working with Grief, by Kim Mooney   241

Working with Grief from a Buddhist Perspective,
by Andrew Holecek   246

The Relative Approach   246

The Power and Peril of Pain   248

Anticipatory Grief   250

Compassion and Devotion   251

The Absolute Approach   252

The Joy of Inter-being   255

Conclusion   257

10. DIFFICULT ISSUES   259

    Organ Donation   261

    Euthanasia   262

    Suicide   265

    Abortion and Miscarriage   268

    Death of a Pet   270

    Conclusion   271

Part Three: Heart Advice from Spiritual Masters

HEART ADVICE FROM SPIRITUAL MASTERS   275

    Anam Thubten Rinpoche   275

    Anyen Rinpoche   277

    Bardor Tulku Rinpoche   277

    Chökyi Nyima Rinpoche   279

    Dilyak Drupon Rinpoche   280

    Dzigar Kongtrul Rinpoche   283

    Dzongsar Khyentse Rinpoche   286

    Jetsun Khandro Rinpoche   287

    Khenpo Karthar Rinpoche   288

    Lama Tharchin Rinpoche   289

    Mingyur Rinpoche   291

    Namkha Drimed Rinpoche   292

    Dzogchen Ponlop Rinpoche   297

    Tenga Rinpoche   299

    Tenzin Wangyal Rinpoche   300

    Thrangu Rinpoche   302

    Tsoknyi Rinpoche   303

    Tulku Thondup Rinpoche   306

Acknowledgments   309

Appendix 1: Checklists   311
  Spiritual Checklist   311
  Farewell Checklist   312
  Bardo Package   314
  Practical Checklist   315
  Other Contacts to Be Made After Someone Dies   318
  Financial Responsibilities After Death   319
  In the Event of Sudden Death   320
  Be Aware   321

Appendix 2: Things You Can Write to Prepare for Death   325
  Letters of Forgiveness, and Saying Goodbye   325
  Writing Your Own Eulogy and Obituary   325

Appendix 3: Depression and Grief   327
  Symptoms That Suggest a Bereaved Person Is Also Depressed   327
  Who Is at Risk for Depression After a Loss?   328
  Treatment for Grief and Depression   328
  Depressive Grief vs. Depression   329
  What Might I Expect When I Am Grieving?   330

Notes   333

Selected Bibliography   397

Contributors   407

Index   409

Illustrations

Figures

1. Amitabha Buddha   36
2. The Peaceful and Wrathful Deities   50
3. The Hourglass   86
4. The Wheel of Life   88

Tables

1. The three kayas and opportunities for liberation
   in the three bardos   44
2. Stages of the outer dissolution and their correspondences   77

Foreword

L IFE IS a revolving wheel of existence—a chain of endless birth, life, death, and rebirth. If we can train our minds to be peaceful and loving, then whatever we say and do will naturally turn into healthy and beneficial words and deeds for ourselves and others. And then when we die, the experiences that we will have in the bardo and in our next life will, according to Buddhism, also be the same. This is because our experiences are the fruits of the habitual seeds we have sown in our mental soil of the past.

Therefore, while we are alive, we must train our mind with prayers, meditations, and caring for others. Visualize, feel, and believe that we are in front of the Buddha of Loving-Kindness, with his all-knowing wisdom and unconditional love, in a heavenly world of light, peace, and joy. Then sing prayers with devotion—with the energy of joy and trust—to the Buddha. Sing with loving-kindness—wishing joy for all sentient beings. The result will be that after death, and in our next life, the world that will appear to us will be a pure land of peace and joy. It will be the manifestation of the positive habits that we implanted in our mind stream during our meditations. For after death, no physical objects follow us. It's only our minds—our mental habits—that follow us.

According to Buddhist esoteric teachings, if we are highly accomplished meditators, at death and in the bardo we will see and realize the intrinsic awareness, the true enlightened nature of our own mind, nakedly, as it is. This intrinsic awareness is the primordial wisdom with its fivefold aspects and five Buddha Families with their pure lands. All these are the natural radiance and innate power of the intrinsic awareness itself, appearing nondually, dwelling indivisibly, functioning effortlessly, and remaining boundlessly. If we can realize and maintain it, we will attain buddhahood. Although all of us will see the intrinsic awareness during death, the true nature of our mind, the experience is so brief that most of us will not even notice it, let alone maintain it.

Many important Buddhist texts on death, such as the *Tibetan Book of the Dead,* put a premium on realizing the luminous bardo of dharmata. However, most of us are not serious meditators, let alone highly accomplished adepts. So most of us, rather than expecting to realize the wisdom of intrinsic awareness during the most turbulent times of death and the bardo, should focus on training our familiar dualistic thoughts, emotional flames, and sensational experiences into positive qualities through prayers and meditations on devotion, light, and loving-kindness. Such training will be highly beneficial—and easier to do.

Preparing to Die is such a timely gift for all of us, as we are all zooming toward the crucial moment of death. There are no exceptions. Everyone will die. The book is filled with nectar-like religious and practical wisdom on how to make the best of the most profitable time of our lives. It is packed with clear and practical details and adorned with great love and care. This handbook is for anyone who will die, and who wishes to journey with the joyful blessing light of Dharma.

Tulku Thondup
January 2013

INTRODUCTION

If we are duly prepared, I can promise that the moment of death
will be an experience of rejoicing. If we are not prepared, it will
surely be a time of fear and regret.
—ANYEN RINPOCHE

Be still prepared for death—and death or life shall
thereby be the sweeter.
—WILLIAM SHAKESPEARE

DEATH IS one of the most precious experiences in life. It is literally a
once-in-a-lifetime opportunity. The karma that brought us into this
life is exhausted, leaving a temporarily clean slate, and the karma that will
propel us into our next life has not yet crystallized. This leaves us in a unique
"no man's land," a netherworld the Tibetans call "bardo," where all kinds of
miraculous possibilities can materialize.[1] At this special time, with the help
of skillful friends, we can make rapid spiritual progress and directly influence where we will take rebirth. We can even attain enlightenment.

Buddhist masters proclaim that because of this karmic gap, there are
more opportunities for enlightenment in death than in life. Robert Thurman, who translated *The Tibetan Book of the Dead*, says, "The time of the
between [bardo] . . . is the best time to attempt consciously to affect the
causal process of evolution for the better. Our evolutionary momentum is
temporarily fluid during the between, so we can gain or lose a lot of ground
during its crises."[2]

But even for spiritual practitioners, death remains a dreaded event. We
dread it because we don't know about it. We do not look forward to death
because we don't know what to look forward to. For most of us, it's still the
great unknown. Death is the ultimate blackout, something to be avoided at

all costs.³ So we have a choice. We can either curse the darkness, or turn on the light.

Death is not the time for hesitation or confusion. It is the time for confident and compassionate action. Lama Zopa Rinpoche says, "This is when people MUST do something for the person who has died; this is the most crucial time for the person."⁴ *The Tibetan Book of the Dead* says, "This is the dividing-line where buddhas and sentient beings are separated. It is said of this moment: In an instant, they are separated; in an instant, complete enlightenment."⁵

This book will help you prepare. It is based on the richness of Tibetan thanatology (the study of death and dying) and includes many references for those who want to study the complexities of the bardos in more detail. But it is meant as a practical guide, a hands-on manual culled primarily from the abundant resources of Tibetan Buddhism.

The moment of death, like that of birth, is our time of greatest need. The beginning and the end of life are characterized by vulnerability, bewilderment, and rich opportunity. In both cases we are stepping into new territory—the world of the living or the world of the dead. The person who is dying, and his or her caretakers, have an opportunity to create the conditions that will make the best of this priceless event. We will explore what these opportunities are, what it means to make the best use of this time, and learn how to approach death with confidence. We will learn what to do and when to do it.

While all these guidelines are helpful, they are not meant to restrict the sacred experience of death. The map is never the territory. Even though death and rebirth are described in extraordinary detail by the Tibetans, dying is never as tidy as the written word. It is important for the dying, and their caregivers, to study and prepare. But preparation only goes so far. Fixating on the idea of a "good death" can paradoxically prevent one. If we think that our death will follow a prescribed order, and that perfect preparation leads to a perfect death, we will constrict the wonder of a mysterious process.

Surrender is more important than control. A good death is defined by a complete openness to whatever arises. So don't measure your death against any other, and don't feel you have to die a certain way. Let your life, and your death, be your own. There are certain things in life that we just do our own way.

The vast literature about conscious dying is therefore a blessing and a curse. At a certain point we have to leap into death with a beginner's mind and a spirit of adventure. Visions of the perfect death create expectations, a model that we feel we have to match. If experience doesn't match expectation, we might panic. "This isn't how it's supposed to be," "I didn't plan on it ending this way." Death is about letting go. That includes letting go of any expectations. The danger in learning too much about death is that we end up prepackaging the experience, forcing reality into the straightjacket of our concepts.

The best approach is that of the middle way. Learn as much as you can. Study, practice, and prepare. Then drop everything and let this natural process occur naturally. Throw away the map and fearlessly enter the territory. It's like preparing for a big trip. We want to pack properly, review our checklists, and ensure we have enough money and gas. But when the trip starts we just enjoy it. We don't worry about doing it perfectly. Some of our greatest travel adventures happen when we take a wrong turn or get lost. Having thoroughly prepared, we relax in knowing we have everything we need.

Getting out of the way and letting death take its natural course is often the best thing to do. Death will always take care of itself. As a friend once told me, "Dying is no big deal. Living is the trick." But there are times when it helps to step in and act with confidence. Death is an emotional time, and confusion is a common companion. Appropriate guidance can be of great benefit. It is the aspiration of this book to help provide that guidance. Refer to it; then, as with death itself, let it go.

OVERVIEW

This book presents the process of dying, death, and rebirth from the Tibetan Buddhist perspective. It assumes the immutable laws of karma. Understanding karma, which is one of the most complex topics in Buddhism, leads to an understanding of reincarnation. It is beyond our scope to thoroughly explore karma and reincarnation. We simply take them as givens.It's up to the reader to choose how to view these teachings.[6]

Tibetan Buddhism is not the only Buddhist tradition that teaches the bardos, but it is the most complete. Other faith traditions have different views of what happens after death. Even within Buddhism, the views differ from one school to the next. While this book is directed to students of Tibetan Buddhism, it can benefit anyone interested in penetrating the mysteries of death from the Buddhist perspective.[7]

The central orienting view in the Tibetan world, and a doctrine that provides the template for this book, is that of the three death bardos: the painful bardo of dying, the luminous bardo of *dharmata*, and the karmic bardo of becoming. They relate respectively to the "before, during, and after" structure of this book. As a brief overview: the painful bardo of dying begins with the onset of a disease or condition that ends in death. In the case of sudden death, this bardo occurs in a flash. It is called "painful" because it hurts to let go. The luminous bardo of dharmata begins at the end of the bardo of dying. For most of us it passes by unrecognized. "Dharmata" means "suchness," and refers to the nature of reality, the enlightened state. It is fantastically brilliant, hence "luminous." It is so bright that it blinds us and we faint. We then wake up dazed in the karmic bardo of becoming. Suchness is gone, and confusion re-arises as karma returns to blow us into our next life. The entire process takes about forty-nine days, and will be described in detail below.

Not everyone goes through the bardos the same way. Only a few teachers assert that the journey is universal and that everyone will, for example, experience the deities of the bardo of dharmata in a similar way. Most teachers say that cultural differences and personal idiosyncrasies generate a variety of experiences.[8] Why would a Christian or Muslim, with very different beliefs, experience death the same way as a Buddhist?

As we will see, the journey through the bardos is a journey through the mind. In the Buddhist view, the essence of mind is the same for all sentient beings. But the surface structures that cover that essence are different. Hence the journey through the surface structures (bardo of dying), into the essence of mind (bardo of dharmata), and then out of it (bardo of becoming) is not the same. But the general pattern of this three-stage process is universal, at least according to the Buddhist view.

While the Tibetans have breathtaking resources that easily translate from their tradition into our own, modern masters admit to instances of cultural insularity and peculiarity. For example, the ancient texts state that it's best not to cry out in distress when someone is nearing death, as this can adversely affect the mind of the dying person. Tibetan teachers familiar with our Western ways realize this instruction doesn't apply as readily to us. Tibetans are emotionally reserved. They don't express themselves like we do. For us, not only is emotion permissible, it's expected. So while it's not so good to grasp frantically after the dying person, as we will discuss, it's also not healthy to completely repress our feelings.

The issue of universal truth vs. cultural vicissitude is present any time teachings migrate from an ancient culture into a modern one. This is something each reader has to wrestle with when entering the bardo literature.[9] Even the Tibetans didn't categorically accept Indian Buddhism without adapting it to their culture. For example, the "hot hells" of Indian Buddhism (where it gets hot as hell) were supplemented with the "cold hells" of Tibetan Buddhism (where it gets cold as hell). Buddhist scholar Carl Becker writes: "The important point here is that the Tibetans, like the Chinese before them, did not adopt Buddhism in its entirety merely out of political or aesthetic considerations. They accepted Buddhism insofar as it clarified processes that they already knew and as it illustrated new truths that they had not yet verbalized."[10]

On a personal note, my conviction about the importance of presenting these remarkable teachings is born from glimpses of experience. I have been meditating for thirty-five years and have completed the traditional three-year retreat. I have engaged in most of the practices presented below, under the guidance of some of the greatest masters in Tibetan Buddhism. I'm still a beginner, but spending so much time penetrating the mysteries of my own mind has shown me the truth of these mind-bending bardo teachings. Most of what follows can be proven by each of us—if we're willing to make these discoveries for ourselves.

My conviction is also reinforced by twenty years of experience with many masters in India, Tibet, and Nepal. These extraordinary individuals display a fearlessness around death that is as contagious as it is awe-inspiring. They are absolutely unshakable. I marvel at the confidence, almost playfulness, they bring to the formidable topic of death. They know something we don't. In the following pages I hope to convey some of what they know, through the lens of my own understanding. I will share what this gentle but fearless tradition has offered as a cherished gift to humanity.

WHY I WROTE THIS BOOK

Fifteen years ago the director at my meditation center asked me to teach a class on death. I knew enough to realize the complexity of the bardos, so I asked him for time to prepare. I began reading every book in print on the topic, attending every seminar, and doing the meditations associated with death.

Six months into my study I received a phone call that would change my life. A woman from rural Colorado, Susan, got my number from the meditation center and called me in a state of panic. Her beloved husband of forty years was dying. The doctors said he had only a few days left. Susan had no idea what to do and was beside herself. She told me that while neither she nor her husband had much faith in religion, they shared an interest in Buddhism. Susan heard that I was an expert on the Buddhist view of death. I had read some books, but was far from an authority. The problem was there were no experts in the area—no one but me.

I listened to her heartbreaking story. She spoke of their beautiful years together, and her desperation at not knowing how to help him in his greatest hour of need. Over the next few days we spent many hours on the phone. Between calls I crammed information from my books, then tried to convey it with confidence. I don't know how much I helped, but she kept calling because there was no one else. As we spoke she would often whisper something that struck me like a thunderbolt: "I should have prepared earlier. If only I had prepared earlier."

Susan's husband died within a few days, and we lost contact. But I have not forgotten her heartache and her remorse in not being prepared. Before talking to Susan I had an intellectual interest in death. After her call I began to pull these teachings off the page and into my heart. I was so moved by her regret that I resolved to do whatever I could to prevent others from experiencing it, and to prepare for my own death.[11] This book is the product of that resolve.

The Renaissance statesman Montaigne wrote:

> Men come and they go and they trot and they dance, and never a word about death. All well and good. Yet when death does come—to them, their wives, their children, their friends—catching them unawares and unprepared, then what storms of passion overwhelm them, what cries, what fury, what despair! . . .
>
> To begin depriving death of its greatest advantage over us, let us adopt a way clean contrary to that common one; let us deprive death of its strangeness, let us frequent it, let us get used to it; let us have nothing more often in mind than death. . . . We do not know where death awaits us: so let us wait for it everywhere.
>
> To practice death is to practice freedom. A man who has learned how to die has unlearned how to be a slave.[12]

I have been at the side of many who have died—from my own loved ones, to spiritual friends, to strangers who have become my friends. For the past eight years I have presented a series of seminars on the Tibetan views of death and beyond, and have written numerous articles. The Tibetan teachings and the meditations associated with them have instilled a conviction that enables me to enter end-of-life situations with ease. I am no longer afraid of death nor swayed by the painful events that surround it. The information in the following pages has given me this certitude, my experience in being around death has strengthened it, and the blessings of my teachers have given me the confidence to share it.

How to Use This Book

This book is a comprehensive reference manual, an encyclopedia of death. The subject matter is given in a condensed and direct style, which accords with the concentrated intensity of experience at death. It is a gathering of information you can turn to when you need it the most. This book does not offer many personal stories and anecdotes that, while helpful in making a text more readable, can seem superfluous in times of need. The theoretical aspects of the bardos, which are formidable and extensive, are beyond the scope of the present volume. The aim here is to be simple and practical.

Even though the material is concentrated, I have worked to make it as user-friendly as possible. I realize that few people in this busy age have time to read a tome of this size from cover to cover—just as people today are too busy and don't really have the time to die mindfully. Death is so inconvenient. But being unprepared is even more inconvenient.

To make this book more accessible, it is divided into two principal parts: spiritual preparation and practical preparation. Each of these is further divided into what to do before, what to do during, and what to do after death. And each of these subdivisions first describes what to do for yourself and then describes what to do for others. This provides a framework that can be easily referenced during any stage of the dying and rebirth process. A final section contains heart-advice from Tibetan masters actively teaching in the West, pearls of wisdom to take refuge in during death. Each section is clearly defined to help you find the information you need. The material is cross-referenced and thoroughly indexed to help you locate other parts of the book that relate to your interests. There are a number of Sanskrit and Tibetan words that are defined on their first occurrence. For any unfamiliar term, you can check its first entry in the index, which will direct you to its definition.

There are therefore a number of ways to read this book. If you are interested in what to do for yourself, read those sections. If you are interested in what to do for others, then refer to those sections. Some people are interested in spiritual preparation, others in the practical aspects. The beginning of each main section is more general and exoteric, then progresses into increasingly specific and esoteric material. If you bog down in the litany of practices presented in any section, then skim or skip to the next section.

Part 1, on spiritual preparation, and part 3, heart-advice, are specifically directed to Buddhists. Most of part 2, on practical preparations, is directed to anyone interested in death. I have attempted to clarify terms and offer suggestions for further reading in the endnotes; a selected bibliography is also provided.

FAMILIARITY

The key to smoothly negotiating the difficulties of death is familiarity. This book is based on the seminars I have taught, in which we practiced the meditations discussed below as a way to become familiar with death by becoming familiar with our own mind. We visited funeral homes and crematoriums. We took walks in cemeteries, and went to anatomy labs to spend time with corpses. We took the mystery—and therefore much of the misery—out of death by spending time with it.

During these seminars I observed the initial resistance to the meditations and field trips. Participants stepped into the cadaver lab with trepidation, and they stepped into their own minds in meditation with similar apprehension. They were nervous because they didn't know what to expect. But they trusted me because I had been to these external and internal places before. When they walked out of the anatomy lab, or the funeral home, or a long meditation session, I saw how much they had relaxed. Through the process of familiarity, they discovered that while death may not be easy, it's also no big deal. They learned how to smile at death.

If one is unprepared, dealing with the details and intensity of death— the emotional impact, preparing for the funeral, handling friends and loved ones, dealing with medical and legal issues—is like preparing for a big wedding in one day. It's overwhelming. If you deal with some of the details now you can relax at the time of death, and relaxation is the best instruction for how to die. Relaxation is born from familiarity.

You may find yourself referring to this guidebook when the crunch of death is upon you, but reading it in advance of this deadline will prepare you for it. Sogyal Rinpoche summarizes the aspiration of this book:

> It is crucial now that an enlightened vision of death and dying should be introduced throughout the world at all levels of education. Children should not be "protected" from death, but introduced, while young, to the true nature of death and what they can learn from it.
>
> Why not introduce this vision, in its simplest forms, to all age groups? Knowledge about death, about how to help the dying, and about the spiritual nature of death and dying should be made available to all levels of society; it should be taught, in depth and with real imagination, in schools and colleges and universities of all kinds; and especially and most important, it should be available in teaching hospitals to nurses and doctors who will look after the dying and who have so much responsibility to them.[13]

PART ONE

Spiritual Preparation

1. What to Do for Yourself Before You Die

Even if you are going to die tomorrow, you train tonight.
—Sakyong Mipham Rinpoche

For someone who has prepared and practiced, death comes
not as a defeat but as a triumph, the crowning and most
glorious moment of life.
—Sogyal Rinpoche

Living a Good Life, Learning to Let Go

THE MOST IMPORTANT spiritual preparation for death is to lead a genuinely spiritual life. We will die much the same way that we live. As the poet Kabir said of death, "What is found then, is found now." A good life generates good karma that will then run its natural course, leading to a good death. The maxim "karma will take care of you" applies most directly to death. But there's a difference between "I'll take care of it" coming from Mother Theresa or from the Mafia. Good karma will take good care of us when we die, bad karma will take bad care of us. The Dalai Lama says:

> In day-to-day life if you lead a good life, honestly, with love, with compassion, with less selfishness, then automatically it will lead to nirvana. We must implement these good teachings in daily life. Whether you believe in God or not does not matter so much; whether you believe in Buddha or not does not matter so much; as a Buddhist, whether you believe in reincarnation or not does not matter so much. You must lead a good life. In my simple religion, love is the key.[1]

Karma is basically habit. It's the momentum of repeated actions that become habitual. It's in our best interest to develop as many positive habits as we can. In the *Mahanama Sutta*, the Buddha said, "Just as oil rises to the top of a pot submerged in water, your virtue, your goodness, your faith, or generosity will rise to the top, and that is what will carry you to your next destination."

Practicing the good heart, or *bodhichitta*, is the essence of a good life and the best possible habit.[2] Bodhichitta, which is a heart filled with love and compassion, is also the essence of a Buddha. It purifies negative karma and accumulates positive karma. Lama Zopa Rinpoche says, "The main thing is to practice bodhichitta. Dying with bodhichitta is the best way to die."[3]

Try to get to the point where your emotional default is into bodhichitta. In other words, what is your automatic reflex to life situations, especially difficult ones? Do you think about yourself, and how you might profit or escape from a situation? Or do you think about others, and how you can help? Progress on the path, and a sign that you're well prepared for death, is when the former changes into the latter, when you default not into selfishness but into selflessness. If you're uncertain about what to do in a situation, just open your heart and love. This is training in bodhichitta.

Being a good person, and helping others, creates the momentum that will carry you gracefully through the bardos. This is important because most of the practices we will discuss are meditations that non-Buddhists would never encounter. Buddhists aren't the only ones who can have a good death or prepare properly. Anyone who lives with genuine goodness will be taken care of by the force of that goodness. Tenga Rinpoche says, "Even though it may appear to be a worldly activity, if you have the attitude of bodhichitta, then it is the practice of dharma."[4] And it will prepare you for death. Bodhichitta lays down a red carpet for you in the bardos.

The Dalai Lama says, "While I live, I shall meditate on bodhichitta. This is what gives meaning to my life. At the moment of death, I will meditate on bodhichitta. It will help me continue on my way to enlightenment." His Holiness continues:

> If one cultivates spiritual qualities such as mental harmony, humility, nonattachment, patience, love, compassion, wisdom, and so forth, then one becomes equipped with a strength and intelligence able to deal effectively with the problems of this life; and because the wealth one is amassing is mental rather than

material, it will not have to be left behind at death. There is no need to enter the after-death state empty-handed.[5]

In addition to living a good life, the next task is learning how to let go. If we can cut our attachments we will live and die with ease. In many ways, the entire spiritual path is about letting go and is therefore a preparation for death. If we're walking a genuine path we will be prepared. Sakyong Mipham Rinpoche says, "[P]eople say that practicing dharma is preparation for death, that all Buddhism does is prepare you for death. We *are* preparing ourselves—very much."[6] We will have a great deal to say about letting go throughout this book.

The following practices, many of which are daily meditations, are the most beneficial for death. They are presented in a spectrum, going from more common to increasingly esoteric. The point is not that every meditation must be practiced, but to show how much you can do to prepare. These practices also point out how daily meditations are already helping you prepare.

If a practice seems too mystical, don't worry. The esoteric practices are not necessarily more effective than those done by a beginner, especially if they are done wholeheartedly. As the practices get more advanced they often get simpler. The most advanced practice for death is simply relaxing into it. What is important is the quality of your practice and your faith in it, not the number of practices.

Graham Coleman, the principal editor of the first complete translation of *The Tibetan Book of the Dead*,[7] writes about the esoteric practices: "At the heart of these meditative skills are the sophisticated practices through which the masters of these meditative traditions simulate the process of the dissolution of consciousness at the moment of death. . . . [T]he ultimate source of these teachings [is] a direct, complete, and sustained experiential understanding of the ultimate nature of mind."[8] Once again, the journey through the bardos is a journey through the mind, so any meditation that allows you to become familiar with your mind will prepare you for death.

Newcomers may be intimidated by the wealth of meditations available. All these different practices are mentioned because the bardo experience is challenging. Like any intense trip, things may not always go as planned. If Plan A doesn't work during the bardo of dying, we have Plan B for the bardo of dharmata, and Plan C for the bardo of becoming. With so many meditations at our fingertips, we can pull something out of our emergency kit and turn a bad trip into a good one. The most important thing is to prepare. As Chagdud Tulku Rinpoche said of death, "When you have to go to the bathroom, it's too late to build a latrine."

The Dalai Lama summarizes the spirit of our journey in this way:

> [S]ince death is the state when all the gross levels of energy and consciousness have been dissolved, and only the subtle energies and consciousnesses remain, it is possible for an advanced yogin to meditatively induce a state which is almost identical to the actual experience of death. This can be achieved because it is possible to meditatively bring about the dissolution of the gross levels of energy and consciousness. When such a task is accomplished, the meditator gains an enormous potential to progress definitively in his or her spiritual practice.
>
> Normally in our lives, if we know that we are going to be confronted by a difficult or unfamiliar situation, we prepare and train ourselves for such a circumstance in advance, so that when the event actually happens, we are fully prepared. The rehearsal of the processes of death, and those of the intermediate state, and the emergence into a future existence, lies at the very heart of the path in Highest Yoga Tantra. These practices are part of my daily practice also, and because of this I somehow feel a sense of excitement when I think about the experience of death.[9]

PRACTICES AND TEACHINGS TO PREPARE YOU FOR DEATH

Shamatha Meditation

There are two central themes repeated throughout *The Tibetan Book of the Dead*, the most important guidebook in Tibetan Buddhism. The first theme is "do not be distracted." This relates to *shamatha*, which is the ability to rest your mind on whatever is happening (the second, the practice of insight meditation, is discussed below). The stability gained through shamatha enables you to face any experience with confidence. In life, and especially in death, distraction is a big deal. The French philosopher Blaise Pascal wrote, "Distraction is the only thing that consoles us for our miseries, and yet it is itself the greatest of our miseries." Shamatha removes the misery.

Shamatha, or calm abiding meditation, is a fundamental form of mind-fulness meditation. Mindfulness is a powerful preparation because it does not disintegrate at death.[10] If we cultivate proficiency in this one practice alone, it will act as a spiritual lifeline that we can hold on to during the bar-dos, and that will guide us through their perilous straits.

One of the best preparations for death is learning to accept it and to be fully present for it. Being fully present is the essence of mindfulness, which is developed through shamatha. Because death isn't comfortable, it's diffi-cult to be with. As Woody Allen said: "I'm not afraid of death, I just don't want to be there when it happens." Most of us aren't there for our deaths and therefore make it more difficult. To get a feel for this, recall how hard it is to be fully present when you're sick. Most of us just want out.

Even for an advanced practitioner, it can hurt when the life force sepa-rates from the body. Resistance to this hurt, to death, or to any unwanted event, is what creates suffering.[11] We can prepare to embrace the discomfort of death by embracing every moment with mindfulness now. Replace oppo-sition with equanimity. As Dzogchen Ponlop Rinpoche says, when we are a dying person we should be a dying person fully. Don't try to be a living person when living is not what's happening.

Mindfulness is initially cultivated by practicing "shamatha with form," or *referential* shamatha. This type of shamatha uses the reference of the body, breath, or an object to steady the mind. The idea is to use a stable form—while we still have one—as a way to stabilize the mind. When physical sta-bility disappears at death, mental stability becomes our primary refuge.

When we die, the anchor of the body is cut away and the mind is set free. If we're not prepared for this freedom we may panic. Imagine being tossed out of a rocket into outer space. The ensuing freak-out impels us to grasp at anything that can reestablish a sense of ground. Like catching ourselves just before taking a bad spill on a patch of ice, we reflexively reach out to grab on to anything that keeps us from falling. This grasping reflex can spur us to take on an unfortunate form—and therefore an unfortunate rebirth.

The fruition of shamatha is the ability to rest your mind on any object for as long as you wish, and to do so without distraction. Wherever you plop your awareness it stays there, like a bean bag hitting the ground. Shamatha with form develops into formless shamatha. This is the ability to rest your mind on *whatever* arises, not just a specified form. You take off the training wheels and ride smoothly on top of anything.

Formless, or *nonreferential*, shamatha is important because when the body drops away at death, we no longer have any stable forms upon which to place our mindfulness. There's nothing steady to refer to. At this groundless point, instead of mentally thrashing about trying to find a form to grasp, formless shamatha allows us to rest on any experience without being swept away. It's not a problem if we don't have a body to come back to. We simply place our mind on whatever is happening and gain stability from that. The "reverse meditations" and "insomnia yoga" discussed below are helpful in developing this proficiency. Formless shamatha is a lifesaver that keeps us from drowning in a bewildering ocean of experience.

The simplicity of mindfulness belies its profundity. It is the gateway to immortality. The philosopher Ludwig Wittgenstein said, "If by eternity is understood not endless temporal duration but timelessness, then he lives eternally who lives in the present." Trungpa Rinpoche and Padmasambhava agree. They taught about the four ways to relate to the experience of time, emphasizing the *fourth moment.* The first three "moments" relate to the conventional experiences of past, present, and future. The fourth moment is timeless, and therefore immortal. It's beyond the first three. The fourth moment is the immediate experience of the bardo of dharmata, which as we will see, transcends time and space. We don't have to die to experience the deathless dharmata. It lies quietly between each thought—not just between each life.[12]

Even though it transcends the first three moments, the only way to enter the fourth moment is through the inlet of the present. *Nowness,* in other words, is the funnel into eternity. B. K. S. Iyengar, the modern yoga master, says, "The yogi learns to forget the past and takes no thought for the morrow. He lives in the eternal present."[13]

If you can't see this in the gap between your thoughts, you can get a feel for it when you're immersed in an activity. If you're one hundred percent present, whether it's playing with your kids, being at a great concert, or engrossed in work, time seems to stand still. You may come out of such an experience, look at the clock, and be startled by how much time has flown by. This is a concordant experience of the fourth moment—the entry into the realm where time, and therefore *you,* disappears.[14]

These magical states, akin to what psychologists call the state of "flow," and athletes refer to as the "zone," don't have to be accidental. The zone of the fourth moment can be cultivated by training the mind to be present. In this regard, as Zen teacher Baker Roshi puts it, mindfulness makes you "accident prone." The more you practice mindfulness the more you stumble into the zone. Those who achieve shamatha can rest their minds in meditative absorption, or *samadhi*, and taste immortality. They have tripped into the deathless zone of total presence.[15]

Despite the complexity of the bardos, the meditations which prepare us for them don't need to be complex. *Simplicity* and *relaxation* are two key instructions for the bardos. Don't underestimate the power of mindfulness. The Indian master Naropa said, "Since the consciousness [in the bardo] has no support, it is difficult to stabilize mindful intention. But if one can maintain mindfulness, traversing the path will be trouble-free. Meditating for one session in that intermediate state may be liberating."[16]

Vipashyana Meditation

The second main theme in *The Tibetan Book of the Dead* is that "recognition and liberation are simultaneous." This relates to *vipashyana*, the practice of insight meditation. Shamatha pacifies the mind, vipashyana allows us to see it. By seeing our mind more clearly, we're able to recognize how it works. This helps us relate to it skillfully. In the bardos we're "forced" to relate to our mind simply because there's nothing else. Outer world is gone, body is gone, so mind becomes reality. Through insight meditation we discover that whatever arises in the bardos is just the display of our mind. That recognition sets us free.

Just as recognizing that we're dreaming while still in a dream (lucid dreaming) frees us from the suffering of the dream, recognizing that we're in the bardos frees us from the suffering of the bardos. Before we became lucid, the dream tossed us to and fro like Styrofoam bobbing on turbulent waters. But once we wake up to the dream—while still being in it—the tables are suddenly turned. We now have complete control over an experience that just controlled us. Whether in dream or death, this level of recognition, and ensuing liberation, is cultivated with vipashyana, or "clear seeing."

Instead of taking the terrifying visions of the bardo to be real, and getting caught in the resulting nightmare, we can wake up in the bardos. We do this by *recognizing all the appearances to be the display of our own mind.* This recognition is exercised in meditation. The meditation instruction is to label whatever distracts us as "thinking." For example, a thought pops up of needing to buy some milk. We mentally say, "thinking," which is recognizing that we have strayed, and then return to our meditation. Our *clear seeing* melts the distracting thought on contact. Labeling and liberation are simultaneous.[17]

Unrecognized thought is the daytime equivalent of falling asleep. Each discursive thought is a mini-daydream. Drifting off into mindless thinking is how we end up sleepwalking through life—and therefore death. Saying "thinking" in our meditation is therefore the same as saying "wake up!" We wake up and come back to reality—not to our dreamy visions (thoughts) about it. If we can wake up during the day and be mindful, we will be able to wake up in the bardo after we die. This is what it means to become a buddha, an "awakened one." And this is the fruition of shamatha-vipashyana.

Earlier we said that in the bardos, mind (thought) becomes reality. What do you come back to if there is only mind? You come back to just that recognition. As in a lucid dream, you realize that whatever arises is merely the play of your mind. This allows you to witness whatever appears without being carried away by it. Since you no longer have a body, or any other material object to take refuge in, you take refuge in recognition (awareness) itself. From that *awakened* perspective it doesn't matter what happens. It's all just the display of the mind.[18]

The Four Reminders

The *four reminders*, or *four thoughts that turn the mind*, are an important preparation for death because they turn the mind from constantly looking outward to finally looking within.[19] As with mindfulness, they provide another way to work with distraction. They bring the key instruction "do not be distracted" to a more comprehensive level. The four reminders show us that it's not just momentary distraction that's problematic but distraction at the level of an entire life. If we're not reminded, we can be mindless and waste our whole life.[20]

Trungpa Rinpoche presented them this way:
1. Contemplate the preciousness of being so free and well favored. This is difficult to gain, easy to lose, now I must do something meaningful.
2. The whole world and its inhabitants are impermanent. In particular, the life of beings is like a bubble. Death comes without warning, this body will be a corpse. At that time the dharma will be my only help. I must practice it with exertion.

3. When death comes, I will be helpless. Because I create karma, I must abandon evil deeds and always devote myself to virtuous actions. Thinking this, every day I will examine myself.
4. The homes, friends, wealth, and comforts of samsara are the constant torment of the three sufferings. Just like a feast before the executioner leads you to your death, I must cut desire and attachment, and attain enlightenment through exertion.[21]

How long should we contemplate these reminders? Until our mind turns. Until we give up hope for samsara, and realize the folly of finding happiness outside.[22]

Most of us spend our lives looking out at the world, chasing after thoughts and things. We're distracted by all kinds of objects and rarely look into the mind which is the ultimate source of these objects. If we turn our mind and look in the right direction, however, we will find our way to a good life—and a good death. Instead of being carried along with the external constructs of mind, we finally examine the internal blueprints of mind itself.

It is often said that the preliminaries are more important than the main practice. The significance of these four reminders, as a preliminary practice, cannot be overstated. Chökyi Nyima Rinpoche said that if we could truly take them to heart, fifty percent of the path to enlightenment would be complete. These contemplations develop revulsion to conditioned appearances, point out their utter futility, and cause awareness to prefer itself rather than outwardly appearing objects. They turn the mind away from substitute gratifications and direct it toward authentic gratification—which can only be found within.

The four thoughts remind us of the preciousness of this human life; that we are going to die; that karma follows us everywhere; and that samsara is a waste of time that only supplies suffering. Memorize them. They will reframe your life, focus your mind, and advise you in everything you do. As Samuel Johnson, the author of the first English dictionary, said, "When a man knows he is to be hanged in a fortnight, it concentrates his mind wonderfully."

What would you do if you had six months to live? What would you cut out of your life? What would you do if you had one month, one week, one day? The Indian master Atisha said, "If you do not contemplate death in the morning, the morning is wasted. If you do not contemplate death in the afternoon, the afternoon is wasted. If you do not contemplate death in the evening, the evening is wasted." The four reminders remove the waste.

One of the best ways to prepare for death is to acknowledge that we really are going to die. We are falling in the dark and have no idea when we will hit the ground. Buddhist scholar Anne Klein says, "Life is a party on death row. Recognizing mortality means we are willing to see what is true. Seeing what is true is grounding. It brings us into the present."[23] We all know that we're going to die. But we don't know it in our guts. If we did, we would practice as if our hair was on fire.

Trungpa Rinpoche said that until we take death to heart, our spiritual practice is dilettantish. Author Sam Harris wrote, "While we try not to think about it, nearly the only thing we can be certain of in this life is that we will one day die and leave everything behind; and yet, paradoxically, it seems almost impossible to believe that this is so. Our felt sense of what is real seems not to include our own death. We doubt the one thing that is not open to any doubt at all."[24]

We see others dying all around us but somehow feel entitled to an exemption. In the Hindu epic the *Mahabharata*, the sage Yudisthira is asked, "Of all things in life, what is the most amazing?" Yudisthira answers, "That a man, seeing others die all around him, never thinks he will die." If we acknowledge death and use it as an advisor, however, it will prioritize our life, ignite our renunciation, and spur our meditation. The Buddha said, "Of all footprints, that of the elephant is the deepest and most supreme. Of all contemplations, that of impermanence is the deepest and most supreme." He who dies with the most toys still dies.

Bring these supreme reminders into your life. Realize that life is like a candle flame in the wind. Visualize friends and family and say, "Uncle Joe is going to die, my sister Sarah is going to die, my friend Bill is going to die, *I* am going to die." Put pictures of dead loved ones on your desk or shrine; put sticky notes with the word "death" or "I am going to die" inside drawers or cabinets to remind you; read an obituary every day; go to nursing homes, cemeteries, and funerals. The essence of spiritual practice is remembrance, whether it's remembering to come back to the present moment or recalling the truth of impermanence. Do whatever it takes to realize that time is running out and you really could die today. You are literally one breath away from death. Breathe out, don't breathe in, and you're dead.

One of the marks of an advanced student is that they finally realize that today could be the day. As Paul Simon sang, "I'll continue and continue to pretend that my life will never end..." We essentially spend our lives moving deck chairs around the Titanic. No matter how we position ourselves—how comfortable we try to get—it's all going down.

These teachings exhort us not to spend our lives, which most of us do literally and figuratively. Reinvest. Take the precious opportunity that has been given to you, and do not waste your life. The four thoughts that turn the mind turn it from reckless *spending* to wise *investing*. Invest in your future lives now.[25] On a personal note, this has been the greatest gift in my study and practice of the bardos. I'm thick-headed but I finally get it: I am going to die—and it could be today. My life has been completely restructured because I now believe it.

These reminders may seem like a morbid preoccupation with death, but only because of our extreme aversion to dying. For most of us, death is the final defeat. Historian Arnold Toynbee said, "Death is un-American." Jack LaLanne, the fitness and diet guru, once said, "I can't afford to die. It would wreck my image." We live in denial of death, and suffer in direct proportion to this denial when death occurs. The four reminders remind us of the uncompromising truth of reality and prepare us to face it.

Lama Zopa Rinpoche writes:

> The very last thing [the Buddha] left, his very last teaching— like a will that ordinary people leave that talks of worldly things, the most precious things to the ordinary person—the most important and beneficial thing that Shakyamuni Buddha could bequeath, the most important thing for us to realize and understand, is the truth and reality of impermanence . . . his entire teaching career ended with this. This one word, impermanence, captures the full range of samsaric suffering.[26]

The four reminders, joined with shamatha, instill a strength of mind that benefits both self and other. The Sakyong Mipham Rinpoche taught, "The strength of shamatha is that our mind is slow enough and stable enough to bring in the reality, to really see it. Then when someone we know is dying, we aren't so shaken up. We may be sad, in the sense of feeling compassion, but we have thoroughly incorporated the notion of death to the point that it has profoundly affected our life. That is known as strength of mind."[27] That stability naturally radiates to stabilize the mind of the dying person, which helps them when everything is being blown away.

Dying people are sometimes jealous of those still alive. "Why do I have to die when everyone else keeps on living? It's so unfair, why me?" At that point they need to remember that those left behind are not returning to a party that lasts till infinity. Those left behind are returning to a challenging life that is filled with the three kinds of suffering.[28] As you are dying remember that it's just a matter of time before everyone else joins you, just as you are about to join the billions of others who have already left this life for another one. Those left behind are a minority. No one is going to get out of this alive.

Doctrinal Preparation

One of the best preparations for the bardos is learning about them. Study the map and you will recognize the territory. Studying the bardos is like installing a psychic GPS. After death, you will know where you are and what you need to do.

Learning about the bardos establishes the proper view. This view allows you to see your way through the darkness of death and to eliminate fear. It also inspires you to do the meditation that prepares you for death, to go beyond understanding into direct experience. The confidence born from view and meditation then leads to the fruition of action. With a stable mind cultivated by view and meditation, we can benefit ourselves and others because now we know what to do. This trilogy of view, meditation, and action is a central teaching for how to progress along the spiritual path.

The Tibetan word for meditation is *gom*, which means "to become familiar with"—the central theme of this book. Meditation is about becoming familiar with every aspect of your mind. This is important because, as we have seen, the journey through the bardos is really a journey of the mind. It is a journey *through* the mind, through both its wisdom and confusion. Learning to face death is therefore learning how to face ourselves.

By becoming familiar with the bardos through study, we're becoming familiar with our mind. And by becoming familiar with our mind through meditation, we're becoming familiar with the bardos. Death is never the enemy. Ignorance and unfamiliarity are the only enemies. Practice and study defeat this enemy.

As we will see in the following pages, the confused aspects of our mind die during the bardo of dying, the wisdom aspects are revealed during the bardo of dharmata, and the confused aspects are reborn in the bardo of becoming. This is why people experience the bardos differently.[29] And this is why we should never let any map, no matter how sophisticated, constrict the experience of the territory.

When the mind is liberated from the body, it is seven to nine times clearer. This opaque statement in the bardo literature is clarified in Thrangu Rinpoche's comments below. It suggests that instructions heard now can be recalled after death. Thrangu Rinpoche says:

> Having heard these [bardo] instructions will have placed a certain habit or imprint in your mind and you will recall this imprint when you reach that phase of the bardo. For example, when you find yourself in the bardo of becoming, you will notice what is happening and you will think, "Oh, wait a second, I have heard about this; let's see, I'm supposed to do such and such when such and such happens." And that will obviously benefit you tremendously. . . . [Bardo instructions] are particularly helpful to you at that time when you are in the most danger and are undergoing the most stress and terror—in other words, when you need them the most.[30]

You may not feel that you'll be able to remember these instructions in the bardo and resign yourself to a difficult journey, but, Rinpoche continues,

> [since] you have no corporeal body, your mind is the most powerful thing in your experience; therefore, virtuous states of mind and states of meditative absorption and so on have much more power in the bardo than in our ordinary lives. . . . All of these types of meditation will have much more power and be much clearer in the bardo. . . .[31]

Fear is always associated with the unknown and the unfamiliar. Fear and ignorance are virtually synonymous. Through our study and practice, we remove the darkness of ignorance that surrounds death and transform fear into fearlessness. This is the job of Manjushri, the deity of wisdom. His wrathful manifestation is called Yamantaka, the "destroyer of Yama." Yama is the embodiment of death. So Yamantaka, uncompromising and almost wrathful wisdom, is how we can conquer death. In other words, we conquer and transform death by becoming familiar with it.

One of the reasons it's difficult to leave this world is because we're so familiar with it. It's all we know. Even though it's samsara, we feel snug and secure in its ways, and these ways are hard to abandon. Conversely, one of the reasons it's difficult to enter the next world is because it's so unfamiliar. We don't know it at all. Even though it presents great opportunities for enlightenment, we're afraid to step into the unknown. So too much familiarity with this world, and not enough with the next, is what makes this transition difficult. In other words, too much familiarity with our superficial confusion and not enough familiarity with our innate wisdom—both of which are revealed in the bardos—is the basis for a rough journey after death.

We will return to this important theme throughout the book because this lack of familiarity is what shoots us out of the bardo of dharmata and into the bardo of becoming—and therefore back into samsara. It's the basis of reincarnation. Do we choose wisdom, which is brilliant and unfamiliar, and wake up? Or confusion, which is cozy and familiar, and fall back asleep?

Learning about the bardos is also more than just learning about death. They are a condensation of the entire path. This means that a concordant experience of the bardos occurs in a microcosmic form every night when we "die" into sleep and are "reborn" the next morning; it also occurs between the birth and death of every thought. Studying the bardos helps us not only to have a good death but to lead a good life. This is another theme we will return to frequently.[32]

Tonglen

Tonglen ("sending and taking"), which is the practice of taking in the suffering of others and giving out the goodness within ourselves, is a strong preparation for death. It is especially powerful for a dying person to practice and for others to do when someone has died.[33] The rugged quality of this practice can match the toughness of death. The more I'm around death, the more I find myself taking refuge in tonglen.

The reason we suffer during life, or death, is because we are selfish. When we think small, every little irritation gets big. Conversely, when we think big, difficulties get small. Tonglen is about thinking and feeling big. To think big we should first reflect upon our good fortune. We have the precious dharma to guide us through the bardos, and we have the potential to transform death into enlightenment. We are incredibly fortunate to die held by the teachings of the Buddha, the awakened one who transcended death.

Now think about the millions who are dying without being held. Imagine all those who are dying alone, without physical or spiritual refuge, or under violent conditions. We can reduce our anguish by putting our death in perspective. Tonglen instills that perspective and brings greater meaning to our death.

If you take a teaspoon of salt and put it into a shot-glass of water, the water is powerfully affected. It gets super salty. If you take the same amount of salt and put it into Lake Michigan, it has virtually no effect. Tonglen transforms our mind from a shot-glass into Lake Michigan. On every level, suffering is the result of the mind's inability to accommodate its experience. Lama Zopa Rinpoche says:

> Try to die with this motivation. If you die with this bodhichitta thought, your death becomes a cause of your enlightenment and a cause for the enlightenment of all sentient beings. Live your life with this precious thought . . . . As you get closer to death, you should think, 'I'm experiencing death on behalf of all sentient beings.' Try to die with this thought. In this way you are dying for others. Dying with the thought of others is the best way to die.[34]

The Indian sage Shantideva said, "If you want to be miserable, think only of yourself. If you want to be happy [even in death], think only of others." Tonglen is therefore a way to practice the good heart of bodhichitta. When asked what practice he would do during death, Trungpa Rinpoche once replied, "Tonglen."

Reverse Meditations

Tonglen is part of a family of practices we could call "reverse meditations."[35] They are called "reverse" because with these practices we do things that are the opposite of what we usually associate with meditation. Reverse meditations expand our sense of meditation and prepare us for death. They are based on this tenet: if you can bring unwanted experience into the sanctuary of sanity provided by meditation, you can transform that obstacle into opportunity. This approach applies to life and especially to death. If you can bring death onto the path, you can flip it into enlightenment. The most unwanted experience transforms into the most coveted experience. Tonglen is a classic reverse meditation because it takes in the darkness of others and sends out our light. This is the reverse of how ego operates.[36]

Pain meditation is a reverse meditation that prepares us for the painful bardo of dying. In addition to the emotional pain of letting go, there is often physical pain associated with disease. To prepare for this pain, we voluntarily bring it into our experience now, on our terms.

Reverse meditations are done within the context of shamatha meditation. This provides the crucible for establishing a proper relationship to the unwanted experience. For the pain meditation, after doing shamatha for a few minutes you can bite your lip or tongue, or dig your fingernail into your thumb, and explore the sensation. Go into the pain. What is pain? What is it made of? What happens if I dissolve into it? Reverse meditations are not pleasant. But neither is death. Do them for short sessions, and remember that masochism is not the point.

While the pain may not disappear, the suffering does. Pain meditation helps us erase what Trungpa Rinpoche called "negative negativity," which is the resistance to the pain. Negative negativity is like being shot with two arrows. The first arrow hurts you physically. If you can stay with that pain and relate to it directly, it will still hurt, but not as much as when you bring in your story lines. The second arrow is the mental commentary that transforms simple pain into complex suffering.

By becoming one with the pain, there is no one to hurt. And the character of the pain changes.[37] This practice radically alters our relationship to discomfort. It reverses it. The next time you get a headache, turn that pain into meditation. Watch the pain transform before your eyes.

Reverse meditations require diligence. We would rather sit in tranquility than plunge into pain. But to establish a healthy relationship to unwanted experiences we have to spend time with them. It's always easier to do so on our own terms. We may think we'll be able to relate to pain or death just by having read about it, but that attitude is seldom realized when we actually hurt or die.

Dzogchen Ponlop Rinpoche says:

> It is very difficult to transform an experience of intense suffering if we have no basis for working with pain to begin with. Therefore it is initially necessary to work with minor pains and illness

and discover how we can bring these to the path. Then, as more severe sicknesses come to us, we are able to bring those to the path as well. Eventually, we become capable of bringing even the most debilitating conditions to the path.... if you become accustomed to looking at the experience of pain—if that looking is genuine and you can rest your mind in the pure sensation—then you will see a difference in how you experience the pain.... when a greater sickness strikes us, we will not be hit by it in the same way. It will not be such a problem or a shock. We can face even the pain and suffering of dying with greater confidence because we are facing familiar territory instead of the unknown. When the actual moment of death arrives, we will be able to look at that pain and transform it.[38]

Having done this pain meditation for years, I now relate very differently to the sting of an insect bite or a stubbed toe. Instead of my knee-jerk aversion to pain, it almost becomes spiritual. My throbbing toe reminds me to meditate, which alters the intensity of the pain. I'm beginning to bring pain onto my path.

Another reverse meditation is to *create as many thoughts as possible*. Instead of calming your mind down, whip it up. Again, start with shamatha, then make your mind as stormy as possible. Think of yesterday, think of tomorrow, visualize Paris, New York, or the pyramids. Do so as quickly as you can. Now is your chance to do what you always wanted to do on the meditation cushion—go hog wild mentally. This is particularly helpful for the karmic bardo of becoming, where the gales of karma re-arise and blow us into our next life. By becoming familiar with those winds now, we'll be able to sail in stormy seas later.

Notice that you can sit quietly in the center of this voluntary cyclone and not be moved by it. You're practicing how to hold your seat in the midst of mental chaos. Don't buy into the thoughts and emotions. Just watch the upheaval. This practice expands the sense of shamatha because even though your mind is howling, you're able to maintain inner peace. As the sage Sri Nisargadatta Maharaj said, "It is disinterestedness that liberates."

Do the meditation for a minute. Rest in shamatha, then do it again. Because reverse meditations are intense, short sessions prevent resentment. Don't underestimate the power of short meditations. Ponlop Rinpoche says, "[W]e usually view anything small as unimportant and not really worth doing. For example, if we only have five minutes to meditate, we tell ourselves, 'Oh, five minutes is nothing. It is not enough to change my life. I need to practice for at least an hour.'"[39] But with meditation, short is sweet. It's like running. You don't start with a marathon. You start with short runs and work your way up. Short sessions repeated frequently are just as effective, if not more so, as longer sessions done infrequently. And when it comes to mixing meditation and post-meditation, which is how to transform your life into meditation, short frequent sessions reign supreme.

Another meditation is to *place yourself in a loud and overly stimulating environment*, then work with staying centered. Flip on the television, crank up the stereo, turn on the alarm clock, and sit with the cacophony. Go to a loud and crazy place and meditate. If you have kids, this environment is part of your life. One of Tulku Urgyen Rinpoche's sons once complained to him about how hard it is to meditate in Kathmandu, Nepal, because of all the noise and distraction. Rinpoche said to him, "If you can't practice under these conditions, how will you ever practice in the bardo?"

As with all reverse meditations, find the silence in the noise, the stillness in the motion. Even if you never do these meditations, just knowing about them helps you reverse your relationship to unwanted experience. The next time you're in a crazy environment, like a subway station or Times Square, you might remember these instructions and transform the mayhem into meditation.[40]

I frequently travel to India, a land of intense chaos. Instead of getting irritated when the flies, heat, noise, beggars, and pollution assault me, I try to relax into the pandemonium. I reverse my usual defensive approach to these unpleasant situations and bring them onto my path. There are times when I just can't do it and run away. But even then, I remember the spirit of these strange meditations and try to convert my automatic aversion.

All the reverse meditations culminate in equanimity, which is the ability to relate to whatever arises without bias. At the highest stages of the path, one no longer has any preference for chaos or calm, samsara or nirvana. Everything is experienced evenly. Pleasant experiences are not cultivated; unpleasant ones are not shunned.

As we have seen, distraction is one of the biggest problems in life and death. Therefore one of the most important instructions is "do not be distracted." The reverse meditations are a formidable way to end distraction because they bring distraction onto the path. They show us how to reverse our relationship to distraction. Instead of feeling that our meditation is constantly being interrupted—by a thought, a noise, or even life itself—the reverse meditations bring these interruptions into our practice. They *become* our practice. Khenpo Tsültrim Gyamtso Rinpoche said that if you're in retreat and hear a noise that makes you angry, it's a sign that you're unable to bring distraction onto your path.

Since fear is common in the bardos, Khenpo Rinpoche recommends *watching horror movies* as a way to work with it. This is a potent reverse meditation for all the bardos, but especially for the bardo of becoming. Because we don't recognize the appearances of this bardo to be projections of our mind, the farther we go into it the more terrifying it becomes. The fear becomes so piercing that it can force us to grasp an unfortunate rebirth just to escape the intensity of our own mind.[41] Establishing a relationship to fear now helps us relate to it then and can prevent such a birth.

I find this reverse meditation really challenging. The films are wretched, violent, and extremely difficult to watch. I usually have to look away, or pause the movie, to bring any sense of meditation to it. My normal response is tremendous revulsion. But as contrived and almost silly as this practice appears, it does evoke a host of nasty feelings. It allows me to become familiar with the shadowy side of my being, a dark side that comes to light in the bardo of becoming. Horror movies give me the opportunity to befriend horrible feelings I would otherwise never encounter.

A key instruction, in life or death, is to join whatever we experience with meditation. But without actually practicing this it's hard to do. An unwanted experience arises, habitual patterns immediately kick in, and we run from the experience or relate to it poorly. The reverse meditations allow us to replace these bad habits with good ones. When difficult situations arise, wisdom kicks in instead of confusion.

Pure Land Practice

Several years ago I asked Thrangu Rinpoche, who has taught extensively on the bardos, this question: "If a Buddhist realized they only had a year left to live, what practice should they emphasize?" He replied, "Pure Land practice." His answer may surprise students of Tibetan Buddhism, where pure lands are rarely mentioned. Khenpo Karthar Rinpoche says that as death approaches, the main deity we should relate to is Amitabha, the principal Pure Land buddha. Pure Land practice is important because if you don't attain enlightenment in the bardos, the next best thing is to gain rebirth into a pure land.

There are a number of reasons for doing this. First, pure land rebirths, while not yet nirvana, are outside of samsara.[42] They're free from the aging, sickness, and death of samsaric existence. There is no overt suffering. Second, they are nonretrogressive. Once you're born into a pure land you'll never fall back to samsara, unless you do so voluntarily. Third, spiritual progress is rapid in a pure land. It's like being born into a country where everyone is a lama and everybody practices the dharma. The developmental center of gravity is so high that you have no choice but to evolve. Fourth, this spiritual progress allows you to develop powers of super-cognition. With these abilities, you're more effective in helping others. Going to a pure land is not getting out of your bodhisattva vow to benefit all beings—it is fulfilling it more rapidly. It's like going to graduate school instead of staying back in kindergarten. Fifth, birth into a pure land is your last rebirth before attaining enlightenment.[43]

The most famous pure land, and the one at the heart of the Pure Land tradition, is Sukhavati, the "land of bliss." Sukhavati is generally regarded as the only pure land where ordinary beings like ourselves can be reborn. Almost all the other pure lands require the attainment of the first *bhumi*, which is a lofty level of realization.[44]

The Tibetan tradition, whose approach to the pure lands differs from traditional Korean, Chinese, or Japanese Pure Land practice, is centered on a tenet that we will return to frequently: the mind leads all things. By cultivating pure states of mind in this life, that will lead us to a pure land after death. Kalu Rinpoche says:

> By the orientation given to our mind [in this life], once in the bardo, we become conscious that we are dead and we see Amitabha coming to welcome us. We will recognize him, and wish for rebirth in his pure land. This thought is enough to make us go there immediately.[45]

Four principal meditations cultivate the conditions necessary for rebirth in Sukhavati. The first is to contemplate the details of Buddha Amitabha, the Buddha who created this pure land for us, and of Sukhavati itself. This is done by studying the descriptions found in the *Longer Sukhavati Sutra*, or the progressive visualizations of the *Meditation Sutra*.[46] At the moment of death, mindscape becomes landscape.

Second, accumulate merit.[47] Even though the transfer of merit from Amitabha is a principal force in our rebirth in Sukhavati, we need our own merit. Third, develop the mind of enlightenment, or bodhichitta. Tulku Thondup says, "[Y]ou must vow or be determined to lead all mother-beings, without exception, to the Blissful Pure Land without any selfishness, and you must put that aspiration into practice through meditation and beneficial deeds."[48]

Fourth, dedicate the merit you have gathered for rebirth in Sukhavati, and make heartfelt aspirations to be reborn there. Ascertain that you are dedicating merit exactly as your forefathers did on their path to enlightenment. These dedications and aspirations are like a steering wheel that guides our merit toward the goal of rebirth in Sukhavati.

All four causes are based on faith in Amitabha and his pure land. This is the most important factor for entry into Sukhavati. We have to really believe in this pure land and in the power of Amitabha to help us at the moment of death. These four factors are encapsulated in the famous Sukhavati Aspiration Prayer by Karma Chagme Rinpoche. There are Amitabha meditations, and many other aspiration prayers, but this is the most widely practiced liturgy for Tibetan Buddhists.[49]

Tulku Nyima Rinpoche describes an Amitabha practice to do every night. As you lie down to sleep, visualize Amitabha on top of your head (see figure 1); recite his mantra OM AMIDEWA HRIH three times; dissolve the visualization of Amitabha into your heart; feel his bliss and light; then go to sleep with Amitabha tucked into your heart and mind.

Vajrayana students practice an esoteric form of Pure Land Buddhism with meditations on sacred outlook, or pure perception.[50] This is the "Pure Land of the Present Moment," as Thich Nhat Hanh refers to it, particularly the fourth moment we discussed earlier. Sacred outlook is an important preparation for the bardos because a key instruction, while in the bardo, is to see everything as perfectly pure. This shifts our relationship to whatever arises. It erases our tendency to poison experience with passion, aggression, or ignorance. These three root poisons are the spark plugs that drive the engine of samsara: I want it (passion); I don't want it (aggression); I couldn't

Figure 1. Amitabha Buddha. Courtesy of the author.

care less (ignorance). They define our existence. The three poisons transform an inherently pure world into the impure land of daily life.[51] In the bardo, this impure perception hurls us into an impure birth.

Because Vajrayana (esoteric) Buddhism emphasizes pure mind, it's easy to dismiss the exoteric schools and their emphasis on Pure Land. Many people dismiss the Pure Land tradition as easy or lazy Buddhism. They denigrate it as being for those who can't handle the rigors of "real" Buddhism. Some writers say the pure lands are for beginners. For others it sounds theistic: Amitabha sounds like God and Sukhavati sounds like heaven.

But the Buddha taught on Sukhavati, and some of the greatest masters in Tibetan Buddhism wrote extensively about it. They spurred their disciples to engage in the practices to get there.[52] Even though there is no Pure Land sect in Tibetan Buddhism, there is a strong Pure Land orientation.

It's also tempting to regard Sukhavati as merely symbolic. But Sukhavati is just as real, or unreal, as this earth.[53] It's a place, created by the merit of Amitabha, for people like us. We should take it seriously. For most of us, going to Sukhavati is the best thing we can do after we die.

Preparation for Sudden Death

We may have our vision of a perfect death, but life doesn't always cooperate. One out of ten people will die suddenly and unexpectedly. What should we do if we're about to die in an accident? The instruction is simple: bring your awareness to the top of your head, and recite the mantra OM MANI PADME HUM. Bringing awareness to the top of your head is a form of emergency *phowa* (discussed below on page 54). Reciting the mantra of Chenrezig, the bodhisattva of compassion, closes the doors to the six realms of samsara. It also invokes his blessing. If compassion has a sound, it is OM MANI PADME HUM.[54]

By bringing your awareness to the top of your head, you open the door to rebirth in the pure realms.[55] This can be done by visualizing your guru or a deity directly above you, or by merely turning your gaze upward. If you panic and can't remember what to do, then cry out to your teacher or a spiritual being for help. Instead of having "Oh shit!" on your mind when you're about to die, it's better to have your teacher or Amitabha on your mind and to be reborn in his pure land.

The way to practice for sudden death is to recite the mantra, or visualize the deity, whenever you receive sudden bad news or are somehow shocked.

Any experience that throws you into a feeling of groundlessness is an opportunity to practice for sudden death. It's like appending "Bless you!" after someone sneezes. For most people this polite habit is automatic, but it didn't happen automatically. You had to practice it.[56]

When your lover tells you he or she is leaving you, have the presence of mind to say to yourself, OM MANI PADME HUM. Or a friend just died, OM MANI PADME HUM. You just got fired, OM MANI PADME HUM. Small sudden deaths happen all the time and give us opportunities to practice for the big one.

I started practicing this whenever I read about a violent death in the paper or heard about it on the news. A suicide bomber blew up twenty people, OM MANI PADME HUM; a teenager was killed in a car accident, OM MANI PADME HUM; a tornado destroyed an entire town, OM MANI PADME HUM. My usual response had been to close down around such news. It was too painful. But this "bless you" mantra showed me how to keep my heart open, and to connect to the suffering of others. After a few weeks of mindful effort, this good habit took root. With this preliminary practice directed to others, I was then able to extend it to my own daily deaths.

If you're trained in phowa, then the instructions for sudden death may vary depending on your training. But the essential practice is simple, which is what we need in a time of crisis. Gauge your readiness for sudden death by looking at how you react to critical situations. When you wake up sweating from a nightmare, do you respond with practice or don't you? When a car cuts you off and almost sends you into the ditch, what happens to your mind? Use any heart-pounding situation both to assess your readiness, and to practice for, any heart-stopping accidents.[57]

Noble Truths

If you can let go and relax, the transitional process will occur naturally and you will glide through the bardos. This is the most important instruction. But some bardo teachings can have the opposite effect. For example, saying that the last thought before death has a big impact after death may stress you out—which is exactly what you don't want. "Will I be able to have good thoughts when I need them the most?!" "What will happen if I freak out at the moment of death?"

That the bardos are both a time of danger and a time of opportunity is a core teaching. To gloss over the danger in order to prevent anxiety doesn't honor the tradition. In Buddhism, ignorance is never bliss. The Buddhist path is about truth, as embodied in the Buddha's first sermon on the Four Noble Truths. They are called "noble" because it takes a noble character to recognize their uncompromising nature. If you look closely at reality, the Four Noble Truths simply describe it.[58] This is just the way it is.

The good news/bad news of the bardos is also just the way it is. The Buddha brought this truth to light and showed us how to transform peril into promise. This truth may instill some anxiety now, but this is healthy. It's what Lama Zopa calls "wholesome fear." This is why the four reminders are so important—they make us anxious in a good way. Trungpa Rinpoche writes:

> [I] am afraid it is really terrifying when we come to think of it [death]. It is terrible. You are going to be dropped very abruptly, and you're going to be suddenly without breath. That is quite shocking! . . . It is questionable whether you will have enough memories and imprints in your mind to return to a new situation where the Buddhist teachings are flourishing. The level of your confusion is so high that you will probably end up being a donkey. I don't want to freak you out, particularly, but that is the truth.[59]

Trungpa Rinpoche popularized the phrase, "first thought best thought." This refers to the freshness of whatever arises, before the "second thought" of concept barges in to put its spin on reality. In the bardo world, we emphasize "last thought best thought." This refers to how the last thought on your mind before you die can strongly influence your next life.[60] Sogyal Rinpoche says:

> Therefore our state of mind at death is all-important. If we die in a positive frame of mind, we can improve our next birth, despite our negative karma. And if we are upset and distressed, it may have a detrimental effect, even though we may have used our lives well. This means that *the last thought and emotion that we have before we die has an extremely powerful determining effect on our immediate future* [emphasis added]. Just as the mind of a mad person is usually entirely occupied by one obsession, which returns again and again, so at the moment of death our minds are

totally vulnerable and exposed to whatever thoughts then preoccupy us. That last thought or emotion we have can be magnified out of all proportion and flood our whole perception. This is why the masters stress that the quality of the atmosphere around us when we die is crucial. With our friends and relatives, we should do all we can to inspire positive emotions and sacred feelings, like love, compassion, and devotion . . .[61]

Milarepa is one of the most revered meditators in Buddhism. He is renowned for his perseverance and for having attained enlightenment in one life. How did he do it? What drove him so fiercely to enlightenment? It was his fear of death and his understanding of the laws of karma.

When Milarepa was young he killed thirty-five people. That's a serious karmic load that would guarantee a difficult time in the bardo and almost certain rebirth into a lower realm. When he realized the karmic implications of his actions, he practiced as if there was no tomorrow. After twelve years of legendary hardship, Milarepa purified his karma and attained liberation. We may not be murderers, but we have our own karma to purify and would do well to heed his words:

> In horror of death I took to the mountains—
> Again and again I meditated on the uncertainty of the hour of death,
> Capturing the fortress of the deathless unending nature of mind.
> Now all fear of death is over and done.[62]

It was Milarepa's fear of death that led him to conquer death. We should instill a similar level of wholesome anxiety. This distress eventually—and paradoxically—allowed him to relax at the moment of death. It transformed an otherwise horrific bardo experience into awakening. With Milarepa as our inspiration and guide, the uncompromising truths of Buddhism can speak for themselves. Let's not dilute them for Western consumption. Most of us don't like to hear about death or the jagged truths that accompany it. But like any final exam, a little stress now can spur us to prepare and help us relax at the time of the test.

Unless we take control over our own destiny, karma takes control. As a fundamental force in nature, karma is nonnegotiable. We may not like gravity or electromagnetism, but our likes and dislikes do not affect these forces. We can jump out of a window with every good intention to fly, but gravity is not influenced by our fantasies. In the same way, we can enter the bardos without preparation and hope for the best, but the force of karma is not swayed by blind expectation. Sogyal Rinpoche says:

> There are those who look on death with a naive, thoughtless cheerfulness, thinking that for some unknown reason death will work out all right for them, and that it is nothing to worry about. When I think of them, I am reminded of what one Tibetan master says: "People often make the mistake of being frivolous about death and think, 'Oh well, death happens to everybody. It's not a big deal, it's natural. I'll be fine.'" That's a nice theory until one is dying.[63]

Buddhism is an elegant but raw description of reality. It's our job, as practitioners of the truth, to align ourselves with reality—not our versions of it. Buddhist scholar B. Alan Wallace writes:

> [I]t is improbable that you will be able to marshal all of your future lifetimes like ducks in a row, where each one provides all of the circumstances necessary to continue on the path. That's extremely difficult, considering the hodgepodge of karma, mental afflictions, and habitual propensities accumulated in the past. If the texture of our lives up to now has been such a mishmash, it is difficult to imagine having uniformity in the future.[64]

Khenpo Karthar Rinpoche concurs:

> [I]t is quite wrong to assume that after death, a human being will be reborn as a human being again; for in beings with consciousness, karmic patterns abound, multiplying and increasing the variety of possible rebirths. We experience the existence of these karmic patterns throughout our life. As time passes, we are not always agitated, bored, or aggressive, nor are we continually joyful and stable. . . . We are continually colored by these changing karmic patterns. In the same way, our different births are determined by whichever karmic patterns, wholesome or unwholesome, predominate at the time of rebirth.[65]

In other words, what is found then is found now.

There is a reason for both peaceful and wrathful deities in Buddhism.

When the peaceful deities are unable to rouse us from our slumber, the wrathful ones are there to shock us into truth. The fact that there are more wrathful (fifty-two) than peaceful (forty-eight) deities in the bardo of dharmata should tell us something.

Waking up to truth is not always pleasant. But it's always real, and reality is the essence of Buddhism. So when countless masters tell us that the bardos are dangerous, we should use the anxiety delivered by such statements—as Milarepa did and as our practice of the four reminders attempts to do—to transform danger into opportunity.[66] Trungpa Rinpoche said:

> It seems, quite surprisingly, that for many people, particularly in the West, reading *The Tibetan Book of the Dead* for the first time is very exciting. Pondering this fact, I have come to the conclusion that the excitement comes from the fact that tremendous promises are being made. Fascination with the promises made in the *Book of the Dead* almost undermines death itself. We have been looking for so long for a way to undermine our irritations, including death itself. Rich people spend a lot of money on coffins, on makeup for the corpse, on good clothes to dress it up in. They pay for expensive funeral systems. They will try any way at all to undermine the embarrassment connected with death. That is why *The Tibetan Book of the Dead* is so popular and is considered to be so fantastic.
>
> A few decades ago when the idea of reincarnation became current for the first time, everybody was excited about it. That's another way of undermining death. "You're going to continue; you have your karmic debts to work out and your friends to come back to. Maybe you will come back as my child." Nobody stopped to consider that they might come back as a mosquito or a pet dog or cat.[67]

Whether it is the best of times or the worst of times—a tale of two experiences—is up to us.

Devotion

For Vajrayana students, devotion is the central ingredient on the path. It's also a key preparation for the bardos. Devotion, like love, is difficult to define. It's the feeling of heartbreaking trust and heartbreaking certainty in a spiritual master or divine being. Devotion is another word for a totally open heart. Sogyal Rinpoche says, "It is essential to know what real devotion is. It is not mindless adoration; it is not abdication of your responsibility to yourself, nor indiscriminately following of another's personality or whim. Real devotion is an unbroken receptivity to the truth. Real devotion is rooted in an awed and reverent gratitude, but one that is lucid, grounded, and intelligent."[68] If you have devotion, you're a Vajrayana student at heart, even though you may not have received formal introduction. If you've received entry into the vajra world but don't have devotion, you're a Vajrayana student in name only.

Devotion, without recourse to any other method, leads to enlightenment in this life—or in death. The Buddha himself taught, "It is only through devotion, and devotion alone, that you will realize the absolute truth." The master Asanga echoed this when he said that the truth can only be realized through devotion. Devotion opens your heart. It's a gesture of surrender and release that instills blessings. It's about dropping any form of resistance, dying to your defensive self-contraction. Anam Thubten says, "When our heart is completely taken over and seized by the force of devotion, then self does not have any power to maintain its composure. Ego just dies right there on the spot.... Self is gone the moment our heart is completely taken over by the spirit of devotion."[69]

Sogyal Rinpoche says that the three best things we can do when we die, in order, are (1) rest in the nature of your mind; (2) guru yoga; and (3) phowa. Resting in the nature of your mind is cultivated with the formless meditations of the *dharmakaya* (see below). Guru yoga nurtures devotion. And phowa is a practice discussed below.

Devotion matures into the realization of the nature of mind, so the first two methods are intimately connected. Guru yoga is the practice of mixing your mind with the guru's mind, which boosts you into their realization. It's like a temporary mind transplant. There are many accounts of people who remembered their guru while in the bardos and attained enlightenment. If you cry out from the bottom of your heart, it's a characteristic of enlightened beings to *instantly* respond. So if things are getting out of control, or you just don't know what to do, cry out for help.

We're starting to enter esoteric material. If a teaching doesn't resonate with you, then skip it. You don't need to master every practice or instruction to prepare for death. The point is to find a practice that you connect with and develop familiarity with that. Presenting all these meditations is designed to help you find that right practice and to offer the rich array of preparatory practices.

The Bardos and the Trikaya

The *trikaya*, or "three bodies," is a central doctrine that relates to the three stages of dying, death, and rebirth.[70] It describes how a Buddha manifests in three bodies, dimensions, or modes. A Buddha is one with the formless absolute (*dharmakaya*, "truth body"), yet manifests in relative form (*sambhogakaya*, "enjoyment body," and *nirmanakaya*, "emanation body") to benefit others. In other words, the dharmakaya is the essence of the mind, and the sambhogakaya and nirmanakaya are the display of the mind. The doctrine expanded to include the three modes of existence. These are three levels of reality, going from complete formlessness (the dharmakaya), to completely formed (the nirmanakaya), and everything in between (the sambhogakaya).

The doctrine of the three bodies describes reality in terms of decreasing levels of density, or materiality. The dharmakaya is less solid than the sambhogakaya, which is less solid than the nirmanakaya. Each preceding kaya, or "body," therefore, is in a sense more spiritual. Each kaya is also associated with one of the three bardos (see table 1). The study of the three bodies, and the meditations associated with them, help us organize an otherwise confounding set of experiences and to prepare for them.

Liberation at any kaya, in any bardo, is equivalent. One level is not better than another. Recognition at the end of the bardo of dying results in liberation at the level of the dharmakaya; recognition in the bardo of dharmata

Kaya	Manifestation	Opportunity for recognition
Dharmakaya	Formless	At end of bardo of dying
Sambhogakaya	Ethereal form	During bardo of dharmata
Nirmanakaya	Form	During bardo of becoming

Table 1. The three kayas and opportunities for liberation in the three bardos

results in liberation at the level of the sambhogakaya; and recognition in the bardo of becoming results in liberation at the level of the nirmanakaya.[71] As we go through this book, we'll explore the transition from one bardo (kaya) to another. We will learn what characterizes the end of one bardo (kaya) and the beginning of the next.

Buddhahood is defined as the full realization of the trikaya. This is because the trikaya is the essence of who we are, and that essence is awake, the buddha within. Death is an involuntary journey into who we really are, a plunge into the depths of our mind and therefore into our buddha nature. In other words, death is a tour into the trikaya. So if we study the trikaya in life, we will recognize our enlightened aspects as they are revealed at death. Recognition and liberation are simultaneous.

Dharmakaya and Formless Meditation

At the end of the bardo of dying, mind is stripped of all of its obscurations, of who and what we think we are. All form melts back into the formlessness from which it arose. The nature of mind, the dharmakaya (dharmata) or clear light mind, is then revealed. In other words, *death is the dharmakaya.*

If we can recognize the dharmakaya at death, we will attain enlightenment. This is the glorious occasion, in a famous phrase from the bardo literature, when the mother and child luminosities unite. The child luminosity, which is the level of our recognition of the dharmakaya cultivated during life, recognizes its mother, which is the dharmakaya from which everything arises and then dissolves. Enlightenment is the result of this mother and child reunion.

How long and how stable does your recognition of the dharmakaya have to be for a successful reunion? Tulku Urgyen Rinpoche says that if you can rest in the dharmakaya for the time it takes to wave a long Tibetan sleeve three times, you will attain liberation in the bardo. Other lamas say that the time is not set. Padmasambhava, who is often considered the reincarnation of the Buddha, offers these encouraging words:

> Why is it, you might wonder, that during the bardo state you can find stability by merely recognizing the nature of mind for a single instant? The answer is this: at present our mind is encased in a net, the net of the "wind of karma." And the "wind of karma" is encased itself in a net, the net of our physical body. The result is that we have no independence or freedom. But as soon as our

body has separated into mind and matter, in the gap [bardo] before it has been encased once again in the net of a future body, the mind, along with its magical display, has no concrete, material support. For as long as it lacks such a material basis, we are independent—and we can recognize. This power to attain stability by just recognizing the nature of mind is like a torch which in one instant can clear away the darkness of eons. So if we can recognize the nature of the mind [dharmakaya] in the bardo in the same way as we can now when it is introduced by the master, there is not the slightest doubt that we will attain enlightenment. This is why, from this very moment on, we must become familiar with the nature of mind through practice.[72]

This equation of death and the dharmakaya puts us in a double bind. On one hand, more than anything we (ego) want to attain enlightenment, the dharmakaya. On the other hand, more than anything we fear the dharmakaya, for it is death (egolessness). Until we realize that to be free we have to "die"—that enlightenment demands egolessness—we will have one foot on the spiritual path leading to enlightenment, and the other foot safely on the worldly path leading the other way.

Renunciation is when we finally realize the futility of the worldly path. We decisively place both feet heading in the same direction on the spiritual path. Until then it's an inner tug-of-war. One day we sustain hope that samsara will make us happy; the next day we realize that only the spiritual path leads to happiness.

The formless meditations prepare for liberation at the level of the dharmakaya. They give birth to the child luminosity and nurture our recognition so that the child grows up to recognize its mother at death. *Mahamudra*, *trekchö*, luminosity yoga, the completion phase of deity yoga, the emptiness of the *prajnaparamita* sutras, and *Madhyamaka* are some of the ways we become familiar with the dharmakaya during life.[73]

Sambhogakaya, Deity Yoga, and Thögal

Recognition in the bardo of dharmata, which is liberation at the level of the sambhogakaya, is brought about by becoming familiar with the sambhogakaya through *thögal* ("leaping over," or "direct crossing") practice, or the generation phase of deity yoga. In deity yoga, you visualize yourself as a deity and recite the deity's mantra, which is like downloading the deity into your body-mind matrix.[74] You are working with enlightened sound (mantra) and light (visualization)—the very first forms that arise out of the dharmakaya. In other words, the sambhogakaya.

The forty-nine day dark retreat, also called the bardo retreat of thögal, is among the most powerful and dangerous of all meditations.[75] It requires support in terms of food, basic necessities, and spiritual guidance. In this practice, you enter a room where light is gradually removed, resulting in total darkness. At a certain point, visions appear, as clear as day. These are the visions of the dharmata, the luminous shine of your own mind.

Over the remaining weeks the retreatant becomes familiar with these visions, which are the expressive power of the mind undiluted by daily distractions. We remove any fear of the "dark" by stabilizing the realization that whatever appears is just the display of our mind. And this mind is basically good. The fear of darkness that's removed is the fear of the unknown depth of our empty but luminous mind. We finally become familiar with the absolute ground of the mind.

Fear is removed because, as it says in the Upanishads, "Where there is other there is fear." The dark retreat removes any sense of "other." What are these visions that seem so real? Why do I see them when my eyes are open or closed? Where do they appear? Are they in the outer space of the world, the inner space of my mind, or somewhere in between? *Are they other than me?*

Without a solid basis in trekchö, or emptiness (dharmakaya), it's easy to take these visions to be real. Then instead of becoming enlightened we become insane. Instead of finding reality, we lose it. We don't know what's real anymore, and it's hard to separate inside from outside.

For the unprepared mind, this insanity is only natural. This is because from an enlightened perspective, taking things to be real even during the day is just as insane. When this bad habit of reification (taking things to be real) is extended into the dark retreat, or into the bardo, we flee from the display of our own mind (because we think this display truly exists), and into madness or into samsara—which are fundamentally equivalent. It's like running away from a nightmare, or in this case *into* one.

We run from the bardo of dharmata (reality), sprint through the bardo of becoming, and take false refuge in the samsaric sanctuary of physical birth and the bardo of this life. We can't stand reality (dharmata), so we find another place to stand. We bolt from a world of pure sound and light (the bardo of dharmata), transforming it into concrete and steel (the frozen bardo of this life), then wonder why the world is so hard.

As we take our first breath of life we are actually breathing a huge sigh of relief: finally, some solid ground upon which to stand. This is what drives the process of reincarnation.

A more workable version of thögal was introduced by Khenpo Gangshar, a teacher of Trungpa Rinpoche and Thrangu Rinpoche. It's a gentler way to become familiar with the luminosity of your mind. In this practice you close your eyes very tightly and clench your teeth. As strange as this seems, even stranger is what happens next. Khenpo Gangshar says:

> When you press your fingers on your ears or on your eyes, sounds naturally resound and colors and lights naturally manifest. Rest naturally for a long time and grow accustomed to the appearance of the utterly empty forms that don't exist anywhere—neither outside, inside, nor in between. Since, at the time of death, there is nothing other than this, you will recognize these sounds, colors, and lights as your self-display and be liberated, just like meeting a person you already know or a child leaping onto its mother's lap.[76]

It's not mandatory to press your fingers on your eyelids or to plug your ears. If you do, be careful not to hurt yourself. At first you only see darkness. But if you rest your mind within that blackness, eventually red, green, blue, or yellow "lights" of various shapes and sizes can arise. These appearances are the natural radiance of the dharmata—your own mind. Thrangu Rinpoche elaborates:

> When the eye faculty has stopped at death, the natural radiance of the dharma nature will occur, and if we have no experience of this, then we will wonder what these lights are. We will be terrified of these confused appearances. This is why we practice now .... These lights appear, but there is nothing about them that can be established as real .... When you do this, the empty lights of the dharma nature do not disappear, but your fear of them will diminish.[77]

You can do the same thing with the sound of the dharmata. Rest your mind in samadhi (as free from thoughts as possible), then clench your teeth. You may hear a background sound that has no discernable source. This can crescendo into the roar of the nature of mind. As it says in *The Tibetan Book of the Dead*, "The sound of dharmata roars like a thousand thunders." Rinpoche continues:

> This sound will also occur when we are in the bardo, and it is quite possible that we will be terrified of it when we hear it then. So we need listen to it now, so that it will not be so frightening when we hear it in the bardo. . . . When we just listen to it, our minds relaxed and not altering anything, the sound does not disappear, but there is no object to be afraid of nor any way the sound can harm you. The reason we need to get used to these appearances [of sound and light] is that the appearances we see at the time of death are no different from these. These lights and sounds will occur.[78]

This is why mantra (which works with primordial sound), visualization practice (which works with primordial light), and thögal (which works with both) are so powerful. These meditations play with the elemental forces of creation. We're playing with fire. So while these latter two meditations are something we can explore, full-blown thögal needs to be practiced under the supervision of a meditation master—or you risk getting burned.

If you don't do these esoteric practices, you can gain a concordant familiarity of the bardo of dharmata by studying tantric iconography. Look at *thangkas* (religious paintings) of deities, especially the peaceful and wrathful deities of this bardo[79] (see figure 2). There are also lama dances that display the deities, accompanied with shrieking whistles and screeching sounds. It's recommended that the elderly pay particular attention to these dances, for they are a way to prepare for what lies ahead.

Because we're unfamiliar with our mind at these subtle levels, for most people the bardo of dharmata flashes by completely unrecognized. But with the familiarity cultivated by these practices, we will recognize these dimensions when they are revealed after death and attain enlightenment.

Nirmanakaya, Illusory Form, and Dream Yoga

The movement from the sambhogakaya to the fully embodied nirmanakaya is echoed in the Christian tradition when it's said: "In the beginning was the word [sambhogakaya], and the word was made flesh [nirmanakaya]."

Recognition in the bardo of becoming, which is liberation at the level of

Figure 2. The Peaceful and Wrathful Deities. Courtesy of the author.

the nirmanakaya, is facilitated by dream yoga, illusory form practice, contemplating the absolute bodhichitta slogans in *lojong* (mind training), and the study of emptiness. This is the bardo where we will spend most of our time. For many people it constitutes their entire bardo experience.[80]

Khenpo Karthar Rinpoche says, "Dream yoga exists largely because it is the best preparation for this phase of the bardo."[81] Khenpo Tsültrim Gyamtso Rinpoche taught:

> The bardo is called a treacherous passage because it is a fearsome experience fraught with difficulty. It is a great advantage to purify one's perception of the bardo beforehand through the practice of dream yoga. Then it will be easy to get through it when the time comes. If you do not make preparations, the bardo will be extremely difficult to traverse when you are in the throes of it.[82]

Padmasambhava, who wrote *The Tibetan Book of the Dead*, and Karma Lingpa, the master who rediscovered it, said that if we can become lucid in our dreams seven times, we'll be able to become lucid in the bardo of becoming. Lucid dreaming instructions are available in books; in addition, retreats are frequently offered that teach dream yoga.[83]

In order to wake up and recognize that we're in the bardo of becoming, it helps to learn how to wake up while we're dreaming and recognize our dreams. And in order to wake up in our dreams, it helps to learn how to wake up during the day. In other words, we have to change the way we relate to appearances. This is the function of illusory form practice. Illusory form, dream yoga, and bardo yoga are a progression of practices that build on each other.

Bardo yoga is a contemplation practice. It's what we're doing here as we study the bardos. In some classifications, all three practices are subsumed under the category of illusory form. Dream yoga and illusory form are reciprocating practices. They're essentially the same meditation applied to two different states of consciousness. Practicing one therefore helps us in our practice of the other. Illusory form helps us recognize dreams, dream yoga helps us work with illusory form—and both prepare us for death. Khenpo Karthar Rinpoche says, "To prepare for the bardo, you need to practice dream yoga, and to practice dream yoga, you need to practice illusory form."[84]

In its traditional presentation, illusory form yoga is one of the Six Yogas of Naropa, an advanced collection of meditations. But it can also be practiced by studying emptiness and the absolute bodhichitta slogans. The idea is simple: if you can remain lucid during the day, you will become lucid in your dreams, and then lucid in the bardo. Being lucid during the day means being mindful and, consequently, seeing everything as an illusion (which is the way things really are). Khenpo Tsültrim Gyamtso Rinpoche summarizes illusory form practice in this way:

> Look nakedly at these forms that are like rainbows, appearance-
>   emptiness;
> Listen intently to these sounds that are like echoes, sound
>   and emptiness;
> Look straight at the essence of mind, clarity-emptiness
>   inexpressible
> And fixation-free: at ease in your own nature, let go and relax.[85]

Deity yoga also applies in the bardo of becoming. If you can visualize yourself as a deity, or your future parents as deities when you see them at the end of this bardo, that pure perception will transfer your consciousness to a pure land. Pure perception, or sacred outlook, is a central aspect of deity yoga and a step beyond illusory form practice. Sacred outlook involves not only seeing everything as illusion but as a perfectly pure illusion. In the bardo, this pure perception transforms your impure projections into purity, cuts your negative reactions to whatever arises, and allows you to relate to everything with equanimity.

In order to apply the remedies appropriate to any bardo, we first have to realize we are in them. Without preparation this is unlikely. Most people go unconscious at the end of the bardo of dying, miss the bardo of dharmata, and even miss recognizing the bardo of becoming. They end up in their next life, thrown into it by the winds of karma. And so the cycle of samsara continues—until we wake up to the process.

To glimpse how conscious you'll be during the bardos, look at how conscious you are during deep dreamless sleep and during dreams. Every night you cycle through the kayas and therefore get a glimpse of the bardos. Every night is a mini-death, and every morning is a mini-rebirth. As we have seen, going to sleep is similar to dying, deep dreamless sleep is similar to the bardo of dharmata, and dreams are similar to the bardo of becoming. This isn't meant to discourage us in the event we don't have recognition during the night but to encourage the practice that develops that recognition.

Mind Leads All Things

The important point in the bardos is that the mind leads all things. Mind literally becomes your reality. There's nothing else. The closest experience is our dreams, which is why dream yoga is so helpful for death. By realizing that mind becomes reality, we prepare for the bardos by becoming familiar with mind's wilderness now—a central theme of this book. Sooner or later we have to face it. Sogyal Rinpoche says, "The still revolutionary insight of Buddhism is that *life and death are in the mind, and nowhere else*. Mind is revealed as the universal basis of experience—the creator of happiness and the creator of suffering, the creator of what we call life and what we call death."[86]

Our relationship to our mind at death is the Buddhist version of "judgment day." But in Buddhism there's no one to judge us. We're judged solely by the level of our familiarity with our mind. Are you prepared to meet your maker? *Are you prepared to face your mind when you die?*

This is why the bardos are a very charged time. One poorly timed bad thought, and our attachment to it, can drag us into the lower realms. One properly timed good thought, and our cultivation of it, can lift us into the higher realms, or even a pure land. This premise forms the basis for the entire Pure Land tradition. Sakyong Mipham Rinpoche writes: "[I]t is said that every thought that occurs in the mind, especially if it is watered with intention, is planting a seed for an entire lifetime. If I am sitting here feeling upset . . . then according to Buddhist tradition I am planting the seed of a rebirth into that realm of irritation. I will be unfolding that thought for who-knows-how-long."[87]

The six realms of samsara are divided into twenty-seven possible states of existence. Each state of existence is entered by spending time with that respective state of mind now. This cultivates the karma of that state.[88] For example, if we spend lots of time being angry, we're becoming familiar with the hell realm whether we know it or not. We are paving our way into hell.

By nurturing higher states of mind, and abstaining from lower states, we are cultivating our eventual rebirth. This is how to prepare for rebirth. Look at your mind. Notice the psychological realms that you inhabit, and you will get a preview of your next life.

Phowa

Phowa, or "transference of consciousness," is perhaps the most famous of the esoteric practices. It's principally a Vajrayana method, but there are sutra forms of phowa taught for the general public.[89]

In the bardos, our consciousness habitually transfers into another form whether we like it or not. Phowa is a voluntary and directed form of transference. Without phowa, consciousness will be transferred by the uncontrollable winds of karma, which may result in an unfortunate rebirth. Once again, if we don't take control, karma does. Kalu Rinpoche says:

> The verb *powa* in Tibetan carries the idea of leaving one place for another. For example, it is used to mean *moving* . . . it is related to a technique used at the moment of death, which allows one to leave the six realms that compose samsara and go to a land of pure manifestation as the Land of Bliss. The person knowing how to apply this meditation can go where he or she wants by directing his or her thought at the right moment to one of the pure lands.[90]

After we die, consciousness leaves the body from one of nine exits.[91] Where it leaves is not the principal karmic cause for where we will take rebirth, but it is a powerful contributing condition. This exit is something we can control.[92] We want to direct our consciousness out the top of the head, at a point eight finger-widths behind a normal hairline. This point is called the *brahmarandhra* (the exit of Brahma), which lies at the top of the central channel of our inner subtle body.[93] If consciousness transfers through this exit, it will be directed toward rebirth into a pure land. Even if we don't make it to a pure land, we're "shooting for the top." Falling short could mean we take rebirth in a human realm, which is the next best thing.

The practice consists of opening the central channel through a series of visualizations and breath control. When the central channel has been cleared, signs occur that indicate the practice has been accomplished.[94] At the time of death, practice turns into performance, and you eject your consciousness through the cleared pathway.[95] Tuning up the practice of phowa every year, even if signs were initially visible, helps keep the central channel open. If someone is doing phowa for you (see Iron Hook of Compassion in chapter 6), you can help them with these instructions from Anyen Rinpoche: "At the time of death, your consciousness will be very heavy, so even the simple effort of turning your eyes upward will make it lighter and easier for someone to help lift it out of you."[96]

The success of phowa depends mostly on the weight of our unwholesome mental accumulations (negative karma). They drag us down in life and especially in death. To facilitate transference, cut your worldly attachments. For example, if you know you're dying, give everything away. In a sense, as we age we're all dying, even if we don't have a terminal disease. So lighten your load now. Giving, at any level, is a preparation for phowa. Look at the way many spiritual masters live. Their possessions amount to nothing, and so do the ties that bind them. In Tibetan, the word for "body" is *lu*, which is sometimes translated as "something you leave behind," like baggage.

The logic is simple: lighten the load on your mind so you can easily move it. Drop any excess baggage. In addition to giving your physical possessions away, as death approaches you can make mental offerings with the intent to benefit others. Imagine giving things away, or emphasize the sending part of tonglen. For Vajrayana students, this is the essence of the mandala offering, which represents offering the universe. The problem after death is a weight problem. The spiritual path is the diet. Now is not the time to latch on to things and thoughts, creating a burden for your mind. Now is the time to let go and travel light.

Sakyong Mipham Rinpoche empowers the practice of bodhichitta in this regard: "Bodhichitta is our lightest mind. It's light because it lacks the reference point of self." A selfish mind is our heaviest mind, the anchor that holds us back in life or death. A selfless mind is light as a feather and easily moves forward. This is why the Dalai Lama says, "At the moment of death, I will meditate on bodhichitta. It will help me continue on my way to enlightenment." *Enlightenment* is such a beautiful word, with many implications. Here it implies the need to lighten up.

As we will discuss later, phowa is also one of the best practices for the post-death bardos. To convey its power and importance, consider these statements: from Buddha Vajradhara, the primordial Buddha:

> You might have killed a brahmin every day,
> Or committed the five acts with immediate retribution,
> But once you encounter these instructions,
> You will, beyond any doubt, be liberated.[97]

Tilopa, the father of the Kagyu lineage: "Phowa is the only method in the dharma where a being can be liberated without profound meditation experience." Padmasambhava, the tantric Buddha, said:

Everyone knows about Buddhahood through meditation,
but I know a path without meditation [phowa]."[98]

Naropa, supreme scholar-practitioner, said:

The nine openings open on samsara,
But one opening opens up to Mahamudra [enlightenment].
Close the nine [sic] openings and open up the one;
Do not doubt that it leads to liberation."[99]

Milarepa said:

These instructions which blend, transfer, and link,
Are the essential guide to overcoming the intermediate state.
Is there anyone with such a path?
How happy the person whose life-energy enters the central
    channel—
How wonderful! He arrives in absolute space![100]

Patrul Rinpoche said:

Unlike the other practices . . . these instructions on the profound
path of transference do not require a long training period. Signs
of success will definitely come after one week. That is why the
method is called 'the teaching that brings Buddhahood without
any meditation,' and that is why everyone should take this unsur-
passable shortcut as their daily practice.[101]

And finally, Lama Yeshe says:

[W]e call transference of consciousness a super method. Even
a person who has done incredibly negative things . . . can say
goodbye to all his negativity if he uses this method perfectly at
the time of death and dies with a clean clear mind. Since death

really is a kind of final destination, we have to make sure we're clean clear at that time. If we can, that's our insurance for a perfect next life.[102]

Shitro and Vajrasattva Practice

For serious students, the *shitro* (the Tibetan *shi* means "peaceful"; *tro* means "wrathful") practice is important for the bardo of dharmata. It prepares us to recognize the peaceful and wrathful deities.[103] If we become familiar with the deities now, recognition and liberation can be attained then.

In this practice, we imagine our body as the mandala of these deities. The peaceful deities are visualized in our heart, and the wrathful ones in our head. Shitro practice requires an empowerment and specific instructions. Thrangu Rinpoche says, "When the wrathful deities appear, someone who has no experience of meditation and who is unfamiliar with the appearances of these deities will be terrified and will suffer tremendously. So, meditation on the wrathful deities, in particular, during one's life is recommended."[104]

The shitro deities are also associated with the practice of Vajrasattva. The hundred-syllable Vajrasattva mantra represents the hundred seed syllables of the peaceful and wrathful deities. By reciting the mantra, we are establishing a relationship to these energies within our body. When the deities that represent these energies are released in the bardo of dharmata, we will recognize them. By reciting the Vajrasattva mantra, the seed syllables of each deity within us reverberates. The wisdom channels then open, and the deities come to life to perform their transformative magic. The Tibetan scholar Francesca Fremantle says of the bardos in general:

> Recognition is the keynote of this whole teaching, but we cannot recognize what we have never met. So its message to us during this life is to get to know all these manifestations of mind while there is still time. All meditation is about getting to know the mind: first our individual minds, and then the essence of mind itself. There is no bardo outside the mind, no gods or demons outside the mind, no existence or awakening outside the mind. If we learn to know our mind during this life, we shall understand that the same mind continues after death, and that whatever occurs after death also happens here and now.[105]

Vajrasattva, as a deity yoga, is a generation stage meditation. Deity yoga, as we have seen, is a Vajrayana method that helps with recognition during the bardo of dharmata, and with transformation during the bardo of becoming. In generation stage meditation, you visualize (generate) yourself in an enlightened form. Instead of unconsciously (karmically) becoming a form of confusion, a sentient being, you consciously become a form of wisdom, a deity. This is how generation stage meditation purifies birth.

Vajrasattva is also a principal purification practice. The biggest problems we encounter in life and death are the repercussions of our negative karma, which takes on overwhelming force in the bardos. Any purification practice that erases or softens these negative mind states will therefore benefit us after death.[106]

Seeing everything as emptiness—the way things really are—is the ultimate practice of purification.[107] It's also our principal defense after death. As it says in *The Tibetan Book of the Dead*, "Emptiness cannot harm emptiness." When the terrifying forms of our negative karma attack us in the bardo, seeing them as empty melts them on the spot. It's like recognizing a dream to be a dream.

Because we don't recognize emptiness, our body seems so solid and real. We feel that "I" exists, and therefore that "other" also exists. You can't have self without other. This dualistic relationship means that others can now hurt us. This is the basis of all fear, which is the fundamental emotion of samsara, and the heartbeat of the ego. Remember, where there is other, there is fear.

In the bardos we literally become no-body. Our physical form dies and a mental body continues. How can anything harm a mental body? But because habitual patterns continue, we still believe we are somebody. So we experience fear—just like in a dream. There's no-body to hurt in a dream, yet we still have nightmares. To erase this fear we have to erase the sense of self and wake up to the fact that we do not inherently exist. All the purification practices, the spiritual path itself, are designed to instill such realization.[108]

Working with Passion

The bardo teachings recommend periods of celibacy, or relating with sexual energy, as a way to prepare for the bardo of becoming. This is because at the end of the bardo of becoming, we will witness our future parents in sexual union. Our own habitual desire will be ignited and we'll long to get in on the act—which gets us into samsara. If we can hold that passion and transform it into compassion, we can block the womb door, and therefore our entry into samsara. The other remedy, which we will discuss in chapter 5, is to view our parents as deities in union. Thrangu Rinpoche says:

> What propels you into the womb—into any kind of womb— is the desire for sexual intercourse. And if you come under the power of that, so that you just cannot control yourself, then you would not have the time to look at what kind of parents you were getting involved with and you would just be overpowered by it and find yourself in the womb. If you are not overpowered by sexual desire, then your mind will become stable and the whole thing will slow down somewhat so that you can examine the situation that you are moving toward.[109]

We can also watch erotic movies, and work with the energy of desire that way. Working with passion means not indulging it. The energy arises, and we try to relate *to* it instead of *from* it. Explore the passion. What is it made of? Discover its emptiness, which purifies the passion. If we can control these energies now, we'll be able to control them in the bardo. Like the reverse meditations, the point is to establish a healthy relationship to passion—on our terms.

Insurance Dharma

Even for someone well versed, this rich array of practices can be intimidating. Which one do we emphasize? How many should we do? How well do we have to do it? As death approaches, rely on the practice with which you are most familiar. It's like staying with an old friend. Take refuge in your favorite meditation, or recite your favorite mantra. Stability, relaxation, and peace of mind are all you really need. From an absolute perspective, remember this Taoist adage: by doing nothing, nothing is left undone.

But doing nothing is often the hardest thing to do. These practices give us something to hold on to at a time when everything is slipping away. The Third Dodrupchen Rinpoche says:

> At the actual time of death, it might be very hard to gather any mental ability to start a meditation. So you must choose a

meditation in advance and marry your mind with it, as much as you can . . . think again and again, "At the time of death, I will not let myself be involved with any negative thoughts." In order to achieve meditative clarity and peace in your mind, it is important to meditate again and again, well before the arrival of death. Then, when the time of death arrives, you will be able to die with the right mental qualities.[110]

We want to be protected from the pollution of the confused mind when we die. The meditations listed above provide that protection. Mantras, literally "mind protectors," also provide this armor. The mantras discussed earlier, OM MANI PADME HUM and OM AMIDEWA HRIH, are two of the best. Another form of protection is to listen to your favorite teaching as you die. This doesn't give negative thoughts a chance to arise, and connects you to your guru. As Sogyal Rinpoche says, "The teachings are louder than your thoughts." Allow your mind to be captured by wisdom, not confusion.[111]

Phowa, Pure Land, and the bardo teachings are insurance dharma. I am an insurance salesman. If your main practice is stable, you don't need this insurance. Many masters rarely teach these adjunct methods because proficiency in the main practices naturally extends into the bardos. The main practices vary according to your teacher or lineage, but they are usually shamatha, vipashyana, and bodhichitta. For Tibetan Buddhists, deity yoga, guru yoga, and mahamudra or *dzogchen* are emphasized. Dzogchen ("great perfection"), like mahamudra, is one of the highest teachings in Tibetan Buddhism. It describes the enlightened mind and how to realize it.

But phowa, Pure Land, and the bardo teachings are there to catch us if we fall. They're in the tradition for a reason and have been taught by countless masters for centuries. If everything else fails in the bardo, it's nice to know we have these emergency teachings in our pocket.

Part 1 of this book is summarized by the mystic Abraham a Sancta Clara: "If you die before you die, then when you die you will not die." If you can "die," or let go of your ego now, then when you physically die you will not die—because you're already "dead." You've let go to the point that you discover the formless dharmakaya (dharmata) during life. Anam Thubten Rinpoche says, "After death [of ego] you become fully alive. If you want to live fully, you first have to die. Only a dead man has nothing to lose and nothing to gain."[112] Rinpoche is not talking about the bardos here, but his words apply directly to them. I have inserted some commentary to connect his words to the bardos:

> People always ask me what it means to be a Buddhist. My reply is, "It means being nobody" [resting in the bardo of dharmata, our egoless true nature]. The true spiritual path is not about becoming. It is about *not* becoming. [It's not about endless rebirth via the bardo of becoming, it's about staying with the deathless dharmata.] When we let go of this futile effort to be or become somebody, freedom and enlightenment take care of themselves. [We remain in the dharmata, as no-body, and don't fall into the bardo of becoming somebody.] We see that we are inherently divine already [the truth of our dharmata nature] and we are enchanted to see how effortlessly liberation unfolds [we only have to let go, and die into our true nature—we only have to relax]. . . . One has to allow this illusory self to die again and again. This death is deeper than physical death. This death allows all of our anguish to dissolve forever. It is not the end of something. It is the beginning of a life where the flower of love and intelligence blossoms.[113]

Become familiar with your deathless nature now, and you will recognize it at death. You will become egoless before you're forced to do so, and therefore the child luminosity will easily recognize its mother.

Dharma Wills and the Dharma Box

Finally, Anyen Rinpoche offers good advice on dharma wills, entrusted dharma friends, and the dharma box.[114] These are practical measures that will ensure that you, and your dharmic caregivers, implement the practices and teachings that you want when you die. Briefly, entrusted dharma friends are those who carry out your dharma will, which they will find in your dharma box.

Entrusted dharma friends are spiritual friends who agree to help each other die, according to the directives left in their dharma wills. These spiritual friends create a pact with each other. They share their dharma wills, and their visions for how they want to die. Then they implement those wishes. It's good to meet every year to update your wishes and to share new insights or teachings around death. If an entrusted friend gets seriously ill, the group gathers to develop a strategy of spiritual care.

Choose your entrusted dharma friends with this in mind: who do you want at your side when you die? Who do you trust to manage your death, and therefore even the seeding of your next life? Who do you want to take control when you no longer can?

The dharma will is an informal document that tells our dharma friends what we want them to do during and after our death. It designates our entrusted friends, provides contact information for our teachers so they can be notified of our condition, lists the information for the monasteries (and how to contact them) if we want specific ceremonies performed for us, when to conduct post-death rituals, etc. Even though the dharma will is more informal than a legal will, there could be areas where they overlap. You may want to check with an attorney to see if what you're requesting can actually be carried out.[115]

Visit funeral homes now to discuss any special requests, then leave the name of the funeral home in your dharma will. If you die in a hospital, but want time for your family to be with your body at your home, leave this request in your dharma will. Anyen Rinpoche says, "If we do not actually write these documents in a timely manner and give them to our family and entrusted Dharma friends, and place extra copies in our dharma box, we risk losing precious opportunities for liberation when we die."[116] After you write your dharma will, review and amend it annually. Do I see things differently this year? What's important to me now? This annual review also helps you evaluate your spiritual progress and reminds you of impermanence.

The dharma box is a box that contains everything our spiritual friends need to know, and to have, to help us die. Visualize your ideal death. Then write down what others need to know to make it happen. Who do you want with you, what do you want around you, what teachings do you want read to you? Be mindful not to overwhelm your entrusted friends with unreasonable requests. This is why it's important to discuss your dharma wills with each other. Is this something that others can actually implement? How would you feel if they asked *you* to do this?

The box would include copies of your legal documents, ritual items, liturgies you want read (including several copies of these liturgies if you want others to read them together), and instructions for family and friends. Inform your family, or other "nonspiritual" friends who may be involved with your death, about this box and the instructions it contains. Otherwise it could be awkward if your spiritual friends arrive to carry out your directives and inadvertently push other loved ones aside. Let your family know that it's your heartfelt wish to have your spiritual friends help you with your death. It's your present job to ease the future job of your entrusted friends. Your spiritual friends should then do everything possible to include outsiders. They should explain the practices and rituals, and welcome outside family to participate.

In addition to formal advance directives, it's important to have discussions with family members about your wishes for end-of-life care. Inform non-Buddhist family and friends of your need for a calm and peaceful environment. Let them know that if they're too outwardly emotional they may be asked to leave. Explain why. These uneasy discussions can prevent really uncomfortable situations at the time of your death. Appendix 1 offers further suggestions for what to place in the dharma box. Make sure family and friends know where it can be found.

Creating your dharma will, placing your ritual items, sacred texts, and wishes in a dharma box, and having trusted spiritual friends to put it all into effect helps everyone to relax—the key instruction for a good death. Imagine your peace of mind knowing that everything possible is being done for you, by people you trust, and at a time when you need it the most.

Final Advice

We end this first section with the main verses from *The Tibetan Book of the Dead*, and summary advice for what to do before death. Since the bardo of this life, which is where preparation for the death bardos occurs, includes the bardos of dream and meditation, there are three central instructions from *The Tibetan Book of the Dead*:[117]

> Now when the bardo of birth is dawning upon me,
> I will abandon laziness for which life has no time,
> enter the undistracted path of study, reflection, and meditation,
> making projections and mind the path, and realize the three kayas;
> now that I have once attained a human body,
> there is no time on the path for the mind to wander.
>
> Now when the bardo of dreams is dawning upon me,
> I will abandon the corpse-like sleep of careless ignorance,

and let my thoughts enter their natural state without distraction;
controlling and transforming dreams in luminosity,
I will not sleep like any animal
but unify completely sleep and practice.

Now when the bardo of samadhi-meditation dawns upon me,
I will abandon the crowd of distractions and confusions,
and rest in the boundless state without grasping or disturbance;
firm in the two practices: visualization and complete [generation and
    completion],
at this time of meditation, one-pointed, free from activity,
I will not fall into the power of confused emotions.[118]

The Buddha taught eighty-four thousand teachings, which can be condensed into the following three lines. Since the dharma altogether is the best preparation for death, this is a good summary:

Do as many good actions as you can.
Avoid as many bad actions as you can.
Tame your mind.

Sogyal Rinpoche summarizes his advice: "At the moment of death, there are two things that count: Whatever we have done in our lives, and what state of mind we are in at that moment.... Be free of attachment and aversion. Keep your mind pure. And unite your mind with the Buddha."

My own heart-advice is to practice the good heart, which creates good karma. Practice shamatha to stabilize your mind. Let go.

2. What You Can Do for Others Before They Die

The vanguard of death is uncertainty and complete bewilderment.
It would be much healthier and more helpful to relate directly
to this possibility, rather than just ignoring it.
—Chögyam Trungpa

Practice dying.
—Plato

ONE JOB of the spiritual community is to keep fellow practitioners on the path. It's the unwritten contract among members of the sangha. But overt reminders are usually too obtrusive. If you're a teacher, offering talks about impermanence and karma can remind people that death really does come without warning, that absolutely everyone will die, and that karma follows you wherever you go. Sooner or later a student of Buddhism will wake up to the truth of impermanence. How much we remind them of that is a delicate issue.

If someone is receptive, sharing a book about karma or the bardos can rouse them from their slumber. Teachings on death-related topics are frequently offered at spiritual centers. Inform your friends about those programs. Tell them that you just wrote your will, or advance directives. They may follow your example. Talk to them about dharma wills, the dharma box, and entrusted dharma friends. We can only plant seeds and see if they germinate.

If the person isn't a Buddhist, discussing the importance of preparation is difficult. How would you feel if a well-intentioned friend from another tradition tried to remind you of the reality of death?

Yet there are gentle ways to remind others. Exploring the hard questions pertaining to the end of life may ignite their interest. Ask them if they've ever thought about what happens after death, or if they believe in reincarnation. This could unearth issues they have considered but were hesitant to express. It might plant ideas for reflection. I tried doing this with my father in casual conversation, but it didn't work. He just didn't want to go there. In those instances we have to let it go. But I have tried it with others when it did work. They asked for a book or about other ways to learn about death.

People are often influenced the most by the way other people live their lives. The maxim that actions speak louder than words remains a good one. Set a good example by the way you prepare, tell them about your preparation if it seems appropriate, and leave it at that.

On a spiritual level, we have touched on the power of merit, which we will return to in detail later. A proper dedication of merit benefits others discreetly. Merit has particular force after someone has died, but it also benefits others while they're still alive. Perhaps the best way to help others before they die is to love them unconditionally. Accept them for who they are. Help them live their lives to the fullest. And unless there is an invitation, keep your views about death to yourself.

3. What to Do for Yourself As You Die

Death is not extinguishing the light, it is only putting out
the lamp because dawn has come.
—Rabindranath Tagore

When the last hour is at hand, you will stand at a crossroad.
If you have prepared in advance, you will be ready to move on
with great ease and confidence, like an eagle
soaring into the sky.
—Tulku Thondup Rinpoche

IF YOU ARE prepared, when death arrives simply relax. Have confidence in your preparation, and that your good karma will take care of you. Remember that death is a natural part of life and that you're not the only one dying. Billions of people have died throughout history, vastly more than are currently alive. Life is but a tiny speck floating on an ocean of death.

Demographer Carl Haub, using 50,000 B.C.E. as his starting point, calculated that including the seven billion people now alive, around 108 billion people have walked on this planet. That means over 100 billion people have already died. Accounts vary, but between 156,000 and 250,000 people die each day. This doesn't include the untold numbers of animals, insects, and unseen forms of life. About 383,000 people are born each day (140 million per year). In addition to these numbers, there are countless beings transmigrating through the twenty-seven states of samsaric existence.[1]

As we approach death, we are about to experience what countless beings have already experienced. Not only that, *we* have already experienced death countless times. Remind yourself, "I'm not the only one traveling this road. All beings of the past have died, all those alive will die, and all who come in the future will die. No one escapes death." The play of birth and death is taking place at a scale we can't even imagine. Now it's our turn to enter this play once again.

There are three levels of practitioner for the bardos. Each one is based on proper vision and perspective. Those of the highest level look forward to death, because they realize it is the greatest opportunity for awakening. They know they're heading for enlightenment. Those of the middling level have no fear, because they understand the process. Those of the lowest level have no regrets, because they've lived a good life and done their best to prepare. If we elevate and improve our vision, we can enter any of these levels and die with ease. Open your mind. Accept death as nature's way of recycling spirit into infinite new forms.

LETTING GO

The painful bardo of dying is painful because it hurts to let go. But now is the time when we have to. Letting go is just a euphemism for death, and releasing our grip is what transforms the painful bardo of dying into simply the bardo of dying. To be like an eagle soaring into the sky, we have to cut the fetters of everything that holds us down. Sogyal Rinpoche says:

> Slowly it dawns on us that all the heartache we have been through from grasping at the ungraspable was, in the deepest sense, unnecessary. At the beginning this too may be painful to accept, because it seems so unfamiliar. But as we reflect, slowly our hearts and minds go through a gradual transformation. Letting go begins to feel more natural, and becomes easier and easier. It may take a long time for the extent of our foolishness to sink in, but the more we reflect, the more we develop the view of letting go. It is then that a complete shift takes place in our way of looking at everything.[2]

In many ways, the entire spiritual path is about letting go. It's death in slow motion. So if we travel our path genuinely, death is but a graceful exit from a path well traveled. We can choose to let go now and die before we die, easing our transition. Or we can wait and be forced to let go during death, which often results in a bumpy ride.[3] As Rinpoche says, letting go is initially unfamiliar to us, which is why it hurts. But meditation is about "becoming familiar with" letting go and therefore eases all the transitions in life—and death.

The Sixteenth Karmapa, an enlightened being, said that "nothing happens" at death. This was a cryptic statement, left open for interpretation. One view would be that for someone who has completely let go during life, nothing happens at death because there's nothing left to release. Bardos only exist in samsara, which is defined by grasping and attachment. For someone like the Karmapa there is no bardo.

Even though you may have practiced well, don't turn your death into a performance. And don't compare. Feeling that your death has to measure up to someone else's is the surest way to have a rugged death. While you might sustain the inspiration of the Karmapa, don't expect to die like him. Die like yourself.

Be genuine, simple, and ordinary. Like death itself. If we don't interfere, dying is easy. It's the one thing in life we don't have to do. And no matter how much we have studied the bardos, the experience is always fresh. Our experience is far richer than the best map, so don't let it cramp your journey, and don't expect to die in a prescribed way. Sogyal Rinpoche says, "Expectation is premeditated disappointment."

Remember that we are composed of three bodies: the gross physical body, the subtle body, and the very subtle body. The gross body of flesh and blood is what dies during the outer dissolution. The subtle body, which is made up of the channels (*nadi*), winds (*prana*), drops (*bindu*), and chakras, is what dissolves in the inner dissolution. And the very subtle body, which is composed of very subtle prana and mind, is what's revealed at the end of the inner dissolution, which is the point of death. *This very subtle body does not die.*[4]

The very subtle body sheds the two outer bodies and continues merrily along its way to infinity. In the next life, which begins in the cosmic dressing room of the bardo of becoming, this very subtle body will temporarily cover itself yet again with a new subtle and gross body, only to strip it all off when that next life ends.[5] Lama Yeshe says, "Understanding the subtle body and the very subtle body helps us to recognize that we have other bodies within us in addition to our physical body—so we don't have to worry too much when our gross body is degenerating or being uncooperative."[6]

Even during life, if we only relate to our gross body we're going to get into trouble. This body is the basis of our egoic urges. If our focus stays on this superficial level we will lead a superficial life. This outer body, with its externally oriented senses, is always directed out and away from who we truly are. It points us in the wrong direction. The inner yogas, which work with the subtle body, allow us to become familiar with our two inner bodies and therefore with our immortality. They point us in the right direction.[7]

We avoid the core of our body like we avoid the core of reality. The inner yogas direct us to reality. They access and exercise our two inner bodies, weakening our exclusive identification with outer form and strengthening our identification with the formless. They allow us to touch our deathless nature.

This is the guiding view, and all we have to do to die well. We can strengthen this view by understanding the eight phases of the outer and inner dissolutions and their accompanying signs. These signs arise as physical and mental functions cease, signaling the advancement of death. It's like learning about Notre Dame before visiting it. Having studied, we can better appreciate the nuances of the experience.

DISSOLUTION AND SIGNS

The eight stages of the bardo of dying, and the complexities of the bardo of dharmata, are described in many books.[8] I will highlight the salient features of these stages in terms of what the dying person, and their caretakers, should know. With this concentrated overview we are plunging into the depths of the bardos. The teachings are as brilliant, and subtle, as the experiences themselves. Many of us will not recognize the bardos when we enter them, and in the same way, a first exposure at the doctrinal level can be bewildering. What on earth are they talking about?

It's not like anything on earth. So we need to be patient as we explore a brand new world—the inner world of our own mind. The Dalai Lama says, "In the mind that is untrained in meditative practice, this sequence of the mind becoming more subtle will frequently not be evident. There are eight stages in this process of going into sleep [and dying]. For a mind that is very finely disciplined in meditation each of those stages will become evident experientially."[9]

When I started teaching on the bardos, I noticed a curious thing. People would sit patiently as I described the material we have presented so far in this book. But when I got deeper into the bardo of dying, and then into the bardo of dharmata, people started to squirm. The minute the class was over, many of them darted toward the exit. I felt a sense of "get me out of here!" It struck me that this was a metaphor. After death, the intensity of the bardo of dharmata will spur us toward the exit of the bardo of becoming. "Get me out of here!" is the impetus that will propel us into our next life.

People tend to skip over this material the same way they'll skip over these bardos when they experience them. But taking the time to become familiar with these bardos now allows us to recognize them later, increasing our chances for enlightenment. Recognition and liberation are simultaneous—but you won't recognize something you've never met. Work with these baffling teachings now so you won't be baffled later. The teachings are unequivocal: relate to it now or be forced to relate to it when you die.

The painful bardo of dying begins with the outer dissolution, which is the five stages of the death of the body. This is followed by the inner dissolution, which is the three stages of the death of consciousness. Each stage is accompanied with signs that can help the dying person and those around them. The signs help us recognize where we are and where we are going. When someone stops eating, for example, that can be a sign that the fire element is dissolving and death is imminent. The fire element is involved in digestion, the "burning up" of food. If a seriously ill loved one stops eating, it's time to go see them if we want to be there before they die.

Not everyone will experience all eight stages clearly, or in the following order. Thinking that death will unfold in such a systematic and predictable fashion can hinder our experience instead of enhancing it. These stages are orienting generalizations, not immutable and definitive steps.

But I have found them remarkably helpful in understanding what's happening to the dying person. I often ask hospice doctors and nurses how much time they think a person has, and compare that to my own intuition based on the five outer stages. The guidance provided by the five stages is usually more accurate than professional predictions. When my father stopped eating and drinking, I could see the dissolution of the fire and water elements. When he entered a period of labored breathing, followed by a rapid decrease in respiration, I knew he was losing the wind element and death was near. Because of these signs I was able to be there when he took his last breath.

The outer signs are visible to caretakers. They relate to experiences of the body. Inner signs are visible to the dying person, and sometimes to caretakers. They relate to experiences of the mind, or cognitive function. Secret signs are only visible to practitioners.[10] They are meditation signs, and correlate to the experiences of luminosity, as explained below. The outer and inner signs convey the loss of connection between body and mind as well as our severance from the outside world. They signal the end of who we think we are. The secret signs indicate our approach to our ultimate nature (luminosity). They signal our proximity to who we really are.

The five stages of the outer dissolution are the elements of the body melting from gross into subtle: earth into water into fire into wind into consciousness. In Sanskrit, it's considered impolite to say someone has died. It's more considerate to say *pancatvam gatah*: "they have returned to fiveness"—to the five elements.

The three stages of the inner dissolution involve consciousness melting into "space." This isn't outer space, but the infinite space of the awakened mind (dharmakaya-luminosity) that's revealed at the end of the inner dissolution.

The outer signs of the bardo of dying begin as we age. If we're sensitive to it, aging prepares us for death. Growing old and falling apart is nature's way of teaching us how to release our obsession with form. It's humiliating. Old age, sickness, and death are the ultimate insults to your ego, but the best compliments to your spirit.

Even before we enter the actual stages of dying, our body, and even our mind, starts to let go as we age. We lose our hair, our teeth, our vision, hearing, mobility, flexibility, endurance, memory, and countless other physical and mental aspects of our form. We lose control, productivity, independence, security, dreams for the future, and even meaning. Aging is a preliminary practice (*ngöndro*) for the letting go that is forced upon us at death. The spiritual teacher Eckhart Tolle writes:

> The return movement in a person's life, the weakening or dissolution of form, whether through old age, illness, disability, loss, or some kind of personal tragedy, carries great potential for spiritual awakening—the dis-identification of consciousness from form. . . . Since death is only an abstract concept to them, most people are totally unprepared for the dissolution of form that awaits them. When it approaches, there is shock, incomprehension, despair, and great fear. . . . [But] what is lost on the level of form is gained on the level of essence . . . . [If related to properly,] old age or approaching death becomes what it is meant to be: an opening into the realm of spirit.[11]

Each stage of the outer dissolution is associated with the disintegration of one of the *skandhas*.[12] By learning about the skandhas we can understand what to expect as they dissolve. Each of the five skandhas corresponds to one of the five wisdoms, so we can also learn about what lies ahead by studying the five wisdoms.[13] Each of the eight stages of the outer and inner dissolution is associated with the eight consciousnesses of the Yogachara tradition. Many teachers say this correspondence is exact. The outer dissolution corresponds to the dissolution of the first five consciousnesses, and the inner dissolution corresponds to the evaporation of the sixth, seventh, and eighth consciousnesses. Other teachers say it's not this crisp.[14]

Finally, each dissolution is associated with the dissipation of a chakra and inner wind. Once again, learning about the functions of these consciousnesses, chakras, and winds can help us understand the sequence of experiences.[15] Anyen Rinpoche says:

> When we talk about the dissolution of the elements during the dying process, we are talking about the dissolution of each element's impure aspect, which leaves its pure wisdom aspect behind. Thus, when an element dissolves, we have an enhanced capacity to abide in or experience the nature of mind. This is due to the increased pure energy, or "wisdom wind" in the central channel as each element is purified.[16]

In other words, as the impure aspect of each element dissolves, the pure wisdom aspect enters the central channel. This affords a heightened opportunity to realize the nature of mind.

While it's helpful to understand each of these doctrines, we will limit our focus to the outer, inner, and secret signs associated with each of the eight stages. This keeps it more practical. We're trying to install that bardo GPS to help us understand what's happening.

OUTER DISSOLUTION

The pattern of the outer dissolution is as follows:

1. Earth element dissolves into water

- ▸ Outer signs: The body loses strength; one feels drained of energy; the complexion fades and pallor sets in; the cheeks sink; stains appear on the teeth; it's harder to open the eyes. The person may seem physically smaller; he or she can't get up or hold anything, can't support the head, and has difficulty moving. The dissolving element often spikes, or is exaggerated, before it fades. When the earth element spikes, one feels depressed, overwhelmed with heaviness, or a sense of crushing weight on the chest. Aging, especially old age, suggests the beginning of this dissolution. The sense of sight degenerates at this first stage.

▸ Inner signs: The mind feels heavy and listless; perception dims; things become unclear, as if there's not enough light in the room. As a sign of the skandha of form dissolving, the mind is agitated and delirious, then sinks into drowsiness. Things are unclear and dull, and everything becomes unstable. We lose our sense of ground and feel as if our world is being swept away. As a sign of mirror-like wisdom dissolving (our partial experience of this wisdom), we no longer hold things clearly in mind and lose visual and mental clarity. Some lamas say everything becomes yellowish, the "color" of earth.[17]

▸ Secret signs: A shimmering mirage appears, which is the image of earth melting into water.

2. Water dissolves into fire

▸ Outer signs: We lose control of bodily fluids. Our nose runs, we dribble and drool, we become incontinent. There's a discharge from the eyes; we can't move our tongue. The lips are drawn and bloodless; nostrils cave in; we tremble and twitch. As "water" spikes before it dissolves, we first feel saturated with water, as if carried away by a flood. Then our mouth, tongue, and nose dry out. We feel thirsty; blood and lymph circulation slows. The sense of sound degenerates.

▸ Inner signs: Mind is more unclear, vague, and foggy. We become emotionally touchy, or easily provoked. Signs of the skandha of feeling dissolving: the mind is hazy, frustrated, confused, and fearful. Sensations are dulled. Sign of wisdom of equanimity dissolving: we lose our sense of emotional balance, become nervous, irritable. Some say everything becomes whitish, the "color" of water.

▸ Secret signs: We see smoke swirling around us, or feel we're in a smoke-filled room, which is an image of water being poured onto fire. Everything is cloudy and steamy.

3. Fire dissolves into wind

- ▸ Outer signs: We get hot, feverish, then cold. Our mouth and nose dry up. Our breath is cooler. We can no longer drink or digest anything. We stop eating. The environment is burning, then our limbs grow cold. Our sense of smell degenerates.

  Some say that if heat dissipates from the lower parts of the body first, that can signal impending rebirth into a higher realm. If the heat dissipates from the upper parts first, that can signal rebirth into a lower realm.

- ▸ Inner signs: Mind alternates between clear and unclear. Sign of the skandha of perception dissolving: we lose our ability to identify and define information received from the senses; we can't recognize family and friends, can't remember names. Sign of discriminating wisdom dissolving: it's hard to distinguish people and things around us. Everything is reddish.

- ▸ Secret signs: The smokey appearance of the last stage gets sharper; then sparks or fireflies appear, which are images of wind blowing into fire.

4. Wind dissolves into consciousness

- ▸ Outer signs: Breathing is harder. Inhalation is short and rough; exhalation is long and sighing. Rasping and panting occurs, the "death rattle."[18] Eyes roll up. Sense of taste degenerates.

- ▸ Inner signs: The sensation is one of floating or of being blown about by strong wind. The experience is of being extremely confused, bewildered, and unseated. Kalu Rinpoche writes, "The internal experience of the dying person is of a great wind sweeping away the whole world . . . an incredible maelstrom of wind, consuming the entire universe."[19] One is unaware of the outside world. A variety of hallucinations can occur, which are just thoughts becoming more vivid and intense. If we led a good life, we tend to see good visions at this point. We may see angels, deities, or teachers. If we led a bad life we might see bad visions.[20] Sign of the skandha of formations dissolving: we lose all motivation and sense of purpose. Sign of all-accomplishing wisdom dissolving: we're no longer able to perform actions. Some say everything is greenish.

- ▸ Secret signs: A butter lamp or torch appears. The point is to attend to and rest in these secret signs.

5. Consciousness dissolves into space

While the first four dissolutions occur at the level of the gross body, the fifth dissolution occurs at the level of the subtle body. This stage is the most ambiguous, almost like a mini-bardo between the outer and inner stages.

- ▸ Outer signs: The body becomes motionless. We're gasping for breath, and respiration ceases with one final exhalation. The sense of touch degenerates.
- ▸ Inner signs: Continuity of signs from the last dissolution, and the skandha of (gross) consciousness dissolves. The complete dissolution of consciousness occurs in the inner dissolution.
- ▸ Secret signs: The appearance of a butter lamp or torch continues from stage four.

See table 2 for a summary of the outer dissolution.

WHAT IS HAPPENING?

At the end of the outer dissolution the gross body is dead and the outer respiration ceases. During the inner dissolution the subtle body will die and the inner respiration ceases. In terms of the outer dissolution, there is another pattern that can further orient this process: our senses, and our experiences, are becoming increasingly nondual.

The senses dissolve from the top down. First the eyes, then the ears, nose, tongue, and finally touch.[21] We're descending into the heart of the body and then into the heart of the mind. We're going from the most dualistic to the least dualistic. In other words, the eyes perceive the farthest, they're the most "dualistic" sense. Sound is less dualistic (we can't hear as far as we can see), smell even less, taste and touch even less. Touch is not quite nondual since we're still touching an "other," but it's the most nondualistic sense. Perhaps this is why we crave to be touched so much.

When we die we're heading into nonduality, or luminosity. This enlightenment fully occurs at the end of the inner dissolution, when consciousness (duality) dissolves into wisdom (nonduality). That this occurs in the heart center, which is the center of our body, mirrors the centering that also takes place in our mind. We are returning to the center of the mandala.

With this eightfold dissolution we're being forced to relate to our mind, simply because there's nothing else to relate to. Everything else is gone. The outer world, and all sensory distractions, are gone. The only thing left is our internal experience. In other words, we are being forced to meditate.

	STAGE 1	STAGE 2	STAGE 3	STAGE 4	STAGE 5
element	earth to water	water to fire	fire to wind	wind to consciousness	consciousness to space
chakra	navel chakra	heart chakra	throat chakra	secret chakra	crown chakra
wind	equal wind	life wind	descending wind	ascending wind	pervading wind
sense	sight	hearing	smell	taste	touch
skandha	form	feeling	perception	formations	consciousness
outer sign	body loses strength	control of fluids is lost	hot, then cold	short inhalation; long exhalation	respiration ceases
inner sign	heaviness	hazy, foggy	loss of recognition	floating, hallucinations	continues from stage 4
secret sign	shimmering mirage	smoke	fireflies, sparks	butter lamp	continues from stage 4

Table 2. Stages of the outer dissolution and their correspondences

Meditation is about establishing a proper relationship to mind, and death forces this relationship by the process of progressive exclusion. External sight is excluded, then sound, then smell, then taste, and finally touch. This is why meditation is a complete preparation for death. Lama Yeshe says, "Meditation cuts the gross, busy mind and allows the subtle consciousness to function. In that way it performs a similar function to that of death."[22]

This is also why deep meditation can get frightening, because our normal sense of self is dying. Lama Yeshe continues,

> Some people experience loss of identity in meditation and get scared. That's good. You should be scared. Why are you afraid? Why are you afraid of losing something? What you're losing is your self-existent or concrete preconception of yourself; that's what's shaken. It's your projection of yourself that shakes, not your nonduality. Your own true nature isn't shaken. . . . When we're dying, everything internal and external deteriorates and disappears, so we get very scared because we're losing our normal security.[23]

With the proper view, we realize that what we're losing on the relative level is offset by what we're gaining on the absolute level. As our false sense of self evaporates, it is replaced by our authentic and immortal sense of "Self."

The end of the outer dissolution is the time to do phowa, just before we stop breathing. However, some masters say we can start phowa at any stage of the outer dissolution. This is another reason why it's helpful to become familiar with these stages and their signs.[24]

INNER DISSOLUTION

As we progress deeper into the bardo of dying, we are advancing toward more profound and subtle aspects of mind. The teachings, and the experiences, are therefore more challenging for the confused and dualistic mind. The inner dissolution of the bardo of dying, and then the bardo of dharmata, are the most difficult topics of our journey simply because they are the most nondualistic. Most of us are very familiar with confusion because we practice it all the time. Few of us are familiar with wisdom. Hence the challenge.

By the end of the outer dissolution, the body is dead. Now consciousness will die in three stages as it evaporates into space during the inner dissolution.[25] There's a difference between consciousness and wisdom. Consciousness has a negative connotation in that it's always dualistic. We're always conscious of something "out there." Consciousness is associated with duality and samsara.

Wisdom, on the other hand, is nondualistic. It is associated with nirvana. During the inner dissolution, consciousness dissolves into wisdom, duality melts back into nonduality. Our subtle form dissolves into formless space. We are coming home to the natural state.

The outer and inner dissolutions are fundamentally eight stages of relaxation. Ego is relaxing back into the dharmakaya. Another way to view this is as eight stages of letting go, or loss. If related to properly, this loss is actually gain. We gain liberation. When everything is fully released, freedom is finally attained.[26] Freedom is just another word for nothing left to lose, as Janis Joplin put it.

During the inner dissolution there are no longer any outer signs. This is why from a clinical perspective you are dead at the end of the outer dissolution. But there are inner and secret signs. The inner dissolution takes about twenty minutes, or "the time it takes to eat a meal." Because there are no external distractions, our inner world is dramatically heightened. In other words, with the disappearance of the outer world, mind becomes reality, just like in a dream.

The experiences that now arise are the result of the dissolution of the subtle body. As discussed earlier, this body is made up of channels (nadis), the winds (prana) that move through them, and the mind pearls (bindus) that ride the winds. During the inner dissolution, all the winds that kept the body alive will merge into the central channel. Then the bindus that reside at the top and bottom of the central channel (that "trap" the life-force wind and keep us alive) will collapse into the heart center. When the white bindu that drops from the top of the central channel meets the red bindu that ascends from the bottom, that is final death.[27]

It's not only the body that breathes. The inner respiration is the breath of the mind. This breath is the subtle movement of the winds of the mind that move it out toward its objects. If that wind is coarse, it moves the mind roughly toward its objects and we experience this as aggression (which ends at stage six; see the list below). If that wind is less forceful, it moves the mind more gently toward its objects and we experience this as passion (which ends at stage seven). And if the wind is very subtle, it moves the mind ever so slightly toward its objects and we experience this as ignorance (which ends at stage eight).

Most of us don't experience this very subtle movement of mind, let alone experience it as ignorance. This is one reason why it *is* ignorance. We're not aware that we're not aware. This very subtle wind is the fundamental breath of duality that blows life into confusion, or confusion into life. It's the primordial puff of ignorance that inflates into passion and aggression. Like a hot air balloon, this subtle wind lifts us out of the nature of mind (nirvana) and into samsara.[28]

During life, the breath of the mind is connected to the breath of the body. When you're angry, notice how your breath is rough. When you're passionate, notice how you pant. And when you rest your mind without thought, notice how breathing virtually stops. Most of us don't experience these subtle movements of the mind as "winds." We simply experience the thoughts and emotions that ride on these winds. We're unaware of the subtle basis of thought, and therefore of samsara. This isn't the conventional ignorance of not knowing about a topic. This is the primordial ignorance (*marigpa*, "no awareness") that is the ground of samsara.[29] Ignorance here means taking things to be real. From this imperceptible breeze of the mind arise the swells of passion and the tornadoes of aggression. Once we take something to be real, we then suck it in or blow it away.

This very subtle wind of ignorance blows across the surface of the mind, which can be likened to a mirror-like surface of water, and creates waves that then forget they are made out of water. In other words, this is the birth of duality.[30] At first, this primordial puff creates a mere ripple, a subtle sense of self and other. But if this puff isn't recognized and released, it picks up strength and the waves get bigger, more real, more "other." Instead of settling back down into the ocean from which it arose, the ripple starts to roar.[31]

When the winds collapse during the inner dissolution, so do the waves. Big waves (aggression) settle into medium waves (passion) which settle into the ripple (ignorance). When the subtle wind ceases at the end of the inner dissolution, the ripple (duality, consciousness, alaya vijnana, marigpa) relaxes back into the mirror-like ocean (nonduality, wisdom, alaya jnana, rigpa-dharmakaya), and the last vestige of samsara settles back into nirvana.

At the end of the outer dissolution, the body fully exhales. At the end of the inner dissolution, consciousness exhales. With a primordial sigh of relief and release, we return to our enlightened state, dissolving back into the ocean of enlightened mind from which we arose.

The three stages of the inner dissolution are as follows:

6. White appearance

"White" is the expression of the perfectly pure radiance of consciousness, and "appearance" is the radiance that naturally appears. The prana below the white bindu at the top of the head in the central channel collapses, and therefore the white bindu descends to the heart.

- ▶ Inner sign: Like a pure sky filled with moonlight, everything appears white.[32]
- ▶ Secret signs: Thirty-three thought states resulting from anger cease. Anger dissolves into the experience of clarity.[33]

7. Red increase

The prana above the red bindu at the bottom of the central channel collapses, and the red bindu ascends into the heart.

- ▶ Inner sign: Like a sun shining in a pure sky, everything appears red.
- ▶ Secret sign: Forty thought states resulting from passion cease. Passion dissolves into the experience of bliss.

8. Black attainment

The white and red bindus meet at the heart, "cupping" the indestructible bindu residing at the heart. Consciousness is squeezed out and wisdom is revealed.[34]

- ▶ Inner sign: Like an empty sky shrouded in darkness, we "black out" into unconsciousness. The experience is of being overwhelmed with blackness or falling into dense darkness.
- ▶ Secret sign: Seven thought states resulting from ignorance cease. Ignorance dissolves into the experience of nonthought.[35]

The whiteness, redness, and blackness that's experienced is the luminosity of the mind glimpsed through filters tinged by the colors of the three root poisons, which are now being uprooted. At the end of this inner dissolution, all the winds that have moved us through life have been exhausted. We have literally run out of breath. We have reached the end of the bardo of dying. Depending on how familiar we are with the nature of mind, the dharmakaya that awaits us at this point, we either light up and attain nirvana, or black out and slip back into samsara.

This is the point of death. It's a concentrated moment, a space from which everything arises, and to which everything returns. It is simultaneously nothing (emptiness) and everything (luminosity). It is both the black hole and the big bang of manifest reality, the cradle and the grave of the cosmos. Because everything is packed into this point, the teachings here are also dense. And because it's so brilliant, unless we're prepared for this light of the mind, it is blinding. Instead of waking up, the intensity of the light stuns us back into sleep.

Once again, death is the dharmakaya.[36] As the Persian poet Rumi puts it, "Death is our wedding with eternity." The following sections are for those who can recognize it to some degree and who will therefore experience the two phases of the luminous bardo of dharmata. They describe the yogi's honeymoon.

TUKDAM

Because of our lack of familiarity with these subtle aspects of mind (the dharmakaya and sambhogakaya), most people go unconscious at the end of the inner dissolution. They miss the bardo of dharmata, and regain consciousness in the bardo of becoming. We will return to these last two bardos later. A practitioner with some familiarity with the dharmakaya, however, enters meditative absorption. This is called *tukdam* (an honorific term for meditative practice), and it indicates some level of enlightenment.[37]

Tukdam signals the union of the mother and child luminosities that we discussed earlier. If we recognize our primordial mother, we will dissolve into her embrace and attain enlightenment. If we don't have recognition, or the recognition is partial, we will unwittingly leap out of her lap and begin the paradoxical search for her outside. This constitutes the leap from the bardo of dharmata into the bardo of becoming—and our next life. This metaphor becomes a literal description of our entry into samsara as we physically "leap" out of our mother's lap during birth.

That we return to this primordial mother at death, and leave her at birth, is expressed by the poet Rabindranath Tagore:

> I am death, your mother,
> From me you will get new birth.[38]

As caretakers, it's important to be aware of the signs of tukdam. If they manifest, we need to know what to do. The mind of someone in tukdam is resting in meditation at the heart. The mind is still in the body, and this presence is noticeable. The person doesn't look dead but appears to be asleep. There's warmth around the heart, the body doesn't start to smell, and rigor mortis doesn't set in. If you pinch the skin it returns to normal. If you pinch the skin of someone whose life force has left the body, it tends to stay where you pinch it and not move back.[39]

To avoid disrupting the samadhi of someone in tukdam—to avoid disrupting their best chance for attaining enlightenment—the classical instruction is not to disturb the body for at least three days. Depending on the instructions left by that person, we need to be sensitive to these signs of tukdam. It happens more than we think. We will return to this topic when we discuss organ donation and whether or not that disrupts tukdam (see page 261 on organ donation).

The amount of time someone spends in tukdam, and therefore in the bardo of dharmata, is measured in meditation days. The bardo of becoming, and the forty-nine days taught in *The Tibetan Book of the Dead*, are normal solar days.[40] A meditation day is five times the length of time you can rest your mind now without distraction. If you can rest for five minutes, a meditation day lasts twenty-five minutes.[41]

At a certain point, intentionally or through the reactivation of the winds of karma, consciousness leaves the body out of one of nine portals. The red bindu continues its ascent and can sometimes be seen as blood coming out of the nose or mouth. The white bindu continues its descent, and can sometimes be seen as a white discharge from the urethra. This separation of the red and white bindus releases the indestructible bindu at the heart, where consciousness is held. The winds of karma reignite, and we are blown off into the bardo of becoming.[42] Stiffening of the body, odor, coolness around the heart, inflexibility of the skin, and the fact that the person just looks dead are other signs that death is complete and that consciousness has left the body.

THE PEACEFUL AND WRATHFUL VISIONS

The bardo of dharmata can be placed in the section for what to do during death, or what to do after death. It is the "point" of death and fits into either category (see figure 3). *The Tibetan Book of the Dead* is the seminal instruction text for what to do during this bardo.[43] The instructions are thorough and will be summarized in chapter 5. Two central instructions, as mentioned earlier, condense the main points: rest your mind on whatever arises (shamatha); and recognize whatever arises to be the radiance of your own mind (vipashyana). Sogyal Rinpoche says:

> The Dzogchen Tantras, the ancient teachings from which the bardo instructions come, speak of a mythical bird, the *garuda*, which is born fully grown. This image symbolizes our primordial nature, which is already completely perfect. The garuda chick has all its wing feathers fully developed inside the egg, but it cannot fly before it hatches. Only at the moment when the shell cracks open can it burst out and soar up into the sky. Similarly, the masters tell us, the qualities of buddhahood are veiled by the body, and as soon as the body is discarded, they will be radiantly displayed.[44]

The bardo of dharmata is where the hundred peaceful and wrathful deities arise. They are part of this radiant display, so don't be afraid of them. The visions are your wisdom mind manifesting in its most primordial expression. The deities are the purified aspects of your mind, the first forms of the sambhogakaya. If you can recognize them as such, you will be liberated. So train in that recognition now.

As mentioned earlier, people often wonder who will perceive these deities. Only practitioners who are familiar with the Tibetan pantheon of deities will recognize them as described in *The Tibetan Book of the Dead*. Those with no familiarity may only see glimmerings of light. This, again, is not physical light, but the light of the mind. The appearances are unique to your own state of mind. Any manifestation of form, or color, is not important. What's important is to recognize those expressions as the play of your mind and to allow them to self-liberate in that recognition. It's more important to understand how these appearances arise, and the opportunities they present for liberation, than to get hung up on the forms they take. The Dalai Lama says:

> The whole presentation of deities within mandalas comes from India, and it thus draws upon Indian culture. It's very likely that a person from another culture would have different experiences. ... if you want to say what the actual nature of the Sambhogakaya is, you have to say it is a form endowed with the greatest possible

adornments, beauty, and perfections. . . . as soon as that statement is made within a specific culture, then of course people look around them and try to imagine what this perfect body might look like; and they might think of the adornments of a king and so forth.[45]

His Holiness continues, and connects the deities to the sambhogakaya, which is the main point:

> Moreover, the Sambhogakaya is a Rupakaya, a form body, and the very purpose of the Buddha manifesting a form body is for the sake of others. This being the case, the appearance assumed would be something appropriate for others, since it's intended for their service. It's not the case that there is some kind of intrinsic autonomous form of this Sambhogakaya totally independent from those whom the Sambhogakaya is designed to help. . . . The very detailed descriptions of the visions of wrathful and peaceful deities that the person in the intermediate state experiences are very specific descriptions for practitioners following a particular Nyingma practice. Therefore, it is not the case that all Tibetans even will necessarily experience the same pattern of visions in the intermediate state.[46]

THE HOURGLASS

A diagram in the shape of an hourglass summarizes our journey through the bardos (see figure 3). The top half represents the bardo of dying, the center point represents death and the bardo of dharmata, and the bottom half represents the bardo of becoming. The two lines that funnel into the point, and then spread out beneath it, represent the decrease and increase of duality respectively.

Above the point is the eight-stage dissolution, going from the most dualistic at the top into nonduality at the point. Below the point the eight stages manifest in an inverse fashion, going from nonduality at the point to complete duality at the bottom. In other words, out of the dharmakaya-emptiness of the point arises the stage of black attainment, and the seven basic instincts of ignorance. From that arises red increase and the forty thought states of passion. From that arises white appearance and the thirty-three thought states of aggression. And from that arises the remaining five stages of the outer dissolution, now appearing in reverse, from subtle to gross.

In other words, the *subtle* form of the elements arise in reverse order: from space arises the energy of wind; from that, fire; from that, water; and from that, earth.[47] But instead of manifesting a physical body composed of the five gross elements (which doesn't happen until conception and the beginning of the next life), a mental body is generated. This is what travels

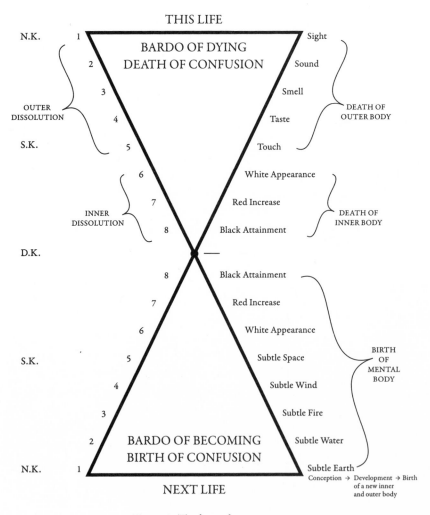

Figure 3. The hourglass

through the bardo of becoming.[48] In terms of the eight consciousnesses, it's stages one to eight going into the point and stages eight to one coming out, in mirror image.[49]

The two lines, which also represent self and other, are widest apart (most dualistic) when we start to die at the "rim" of the bardo of dying. They come together at the point, the final moment of death, when self and other merge into nondual bliss.[50] As we descend into the point we're also running out of time and space, since these are both dualistic constructs. Everything material is falling apart, but everything spiritual is coming together. Duality disintegrates while nonduality integrates. Death is bad news for matter but great news for spirit. If you're spiritually minded, you really do have something to look forward to.

If we extend the two lines past the rim of the bardo of dying, the space they enclose represents the bardo of this life. This shows us that whether we acknowledge it or not, we're always running out of time. As you read these words, the grains of time are slipping through this cosmic hourglass.[51]

The two lines also represent the extended arms of Yama, the Lord of Death, who holds the Wheel of Life (see figure 4). You will find this Wheel of Life at the entrance to most monasteries, placed there to remind us that life is always held by death. Because we're alive, Yama's grip is temporarily relaxed. We don't feel his squeeze. But as we age, get sick, and die, his vise-grip increases into a suffocating crush. Yama's muscular arms contract into the point of death, squeezing any remaining life out of us.[52]

This image also helps us understand that what we experience with our mind during death is exactly what we have put into it during life. The mind is like a sponge. It absorbs the contents of its environment. As we die, the contents of this sponge are squeezed out and become our entire experience. This is why we want to soak our minds with bodhichitta and create as much merit as possible. Our karma, once again, will take care of us as it is expressed out of us. This same process occurs in life. If you want to know the real character of someone, their inner contents, see what comes out of them when they're in a squeeze.

To mix metaphors and introduce some gallows humor: the upper aspect of the hourglass is more graphically depicted as a chipper, one of those roadside machines that grinds up branches into sawdust. The bardo of dying is a chipper for anything material. Any *thing* constituted of form cannot pass through the infinitely narrow confines that is the bardo of dharmata, the

Figure 4. The Wheel of Life. Courtesy of the author.

nondual point of reality. Just like a black hole, not even space or time can fit through this singularity. This is why the bardo of dharmata is beyond space and time. Nothing in this manifest world goes through to the "other side."

In the upper reaches of the chipper, the gross outer body is ground up (outer dissolution). In the inner reaches, the subtle body turns into dust (inner dissolution). Any form—physical (body) or mental (consciousness)—is chewed up and left behind. It's only the extremely subtle and indestructible body, where body at this level is made of prana, that fits through the nondual point. This indestructible "body" is formless awareness, your innermost nature. Because it is formless it can go through. It doesn't die. Fremantle writes:

> The indestructible bindu [body] is eternal and unchanging. It continues from life to life, without beginning and without end. It is the basic nature of mind and the essence of life, a continuity of luminous awareness. It is bodhichitta, the awakened heart-mind, and it is tathagatagarbha, the intrinsic buddha-nature, which we all possess but of which we are unaware. . . . This is the realization of the dharmakaya, the ultimate source of life and of all appearances. From that state, one can then take on a body of form, arising with the body of a deity in the sambhogakaya or with a physical body in the nirmanakaya.[53]

In other words, naked awareness (dharmakaya) is clothed with fresh underwear (sambhogakaya) and fashionable outerwear (nirmanakaya) as it takes birth into a new form. It may seem fresh and fashionable, but it's simply a new form of old habits. It's the same old story of birth, old age, sickness, and death. "Our" dharmakaya, the child luminosity, fits through the point because it *is* the point, like water poured into water. Luminous emptiness, our empty yet pregnant essence, is the only "thing" that slips through to the other side.[54]

We will discuss the bottom half of the hourglass later, when time, space, and all of manifest reality returns in the bardo of becoming.

CONCLUSION

Here are the main verses, and summary instruction, for the bardo of dying and the bardo of dharmata, taken from *The Tibetan Book of the Dead*:

> Now when the bardo of the moment before death dawns upon me,
> I will abandon all grasping, yearning and attachment,
> enter undistracted into clear awareness of the teaching,
> and eject my consciousness into the space of unborn mind;
> as I leave this compound body of flesh and blood
> I will know it to be a transitory illusion.

Now when the bardo of dharmata dawns upon me,
I will abandon all thoughts of fear and terror,
I will recognize whatever appears as my projection
and know it to be a vision of the bardo;
now that I have reached this critical point,
I will not fear the peaceful and wrathful ones, my own projections.[55]

Final pith instruction for what to do during death: release everything that will hold you back. Look forward, let go—and relax.

4. What to Do for Others As They Die

At the moment of their greatest vulnerability, people in our world are
abandoned and left almost totally without support or insight. This is
a tragic and humiliating state of affairs, which must change.
—Sogyal Rinpoche

The View

WHEN SOMEONE is dying, there is much that we, as close family or
friends, can do to help spiritually. Even though taking care of them
physically may be part of our job, our main concern is taking care of the
mind, both theirs and ours. This first of all means taking care of our own
mind, because states of mind are easily transmitted, and the attitudes of
caregivers can significantly help or hinder a dying person. The essence of the
following instruction is to help everyone, especially the dying person, relax.
We want the dying person to depart in a positive state of mind filled with
love.[1]

This isn't easy, because death is a squeeze. Sogyal Rinpoche says that
death is a mirror in which the whole of life is reflected. I would add the
words: *and magnified.* The good, the bad, and the ugly all squirt out of the
dying person, family, and friends. Family dynamics, which often means family
neurosis, is heightened and exposed. Love, compassion, regret, anger,
resentment, stress, greed, envy . . . virtually every human emotion is brought
out and blown up.

In caring for my terminally ill parents, I was sometimes startled by what I
said and did. My mother died of Alzheimer's, which can be brutal for caretakers, and my father died from esophageal cancer, which required multiple
hospital visits and challenging home care.[2] I expressed moments of genuine

selflessness mixed in with times of real selfishness. In retrospect it was like a test. It showed me how far I had progressed on my path—and how far I had yet to go. I didn't always like what I saw in this mirror of death. But I saw it and learned. You can study, practice, and read about death all you want, but until it is in your face it's difficult to know how you will respond. This is why it's good to be around death. It helps you to both assess and prepare.

So acknowledge the crunch, and that you are human. Be patient with what you see reflected in yourself and others. Be kind to yourself, to those around you, and realize that everybody is doing their best.

Don't get hung up on helping.[3] As caregivers, we may receive a subtle self-directed pat on the back from serving others. Always check your motivation. Don't come in with an agenda to conduct a good death or to impose your version of one. This is not your death. Let the dying person die in their own unique way and support them in that. If they want to resist death, or deny that they are dying, we should support them, even though that view may be difficult for us. There's no need to encourage such a view, but it's not our place to challenge it. Dying people want comfort, not confrontation.

For caregivers, be careful not to "should" on the dying person or yourself. Do not feel that things *should* go a particular way, or that you *should* be feeling a certain emotion. Bring the confidence born from preparation, then let the situation, and the dying person, guide you. In this delicate dance the dying person leads. Your job is to be aware of their needs, not to impose your own. Do not force them into your version of a good death. I once saw a cartoon of a man lying on his death bed, looking concerned. A few people were standing around the bed, and the caption above the worried man said, "How's my dying?"

Joan Halifax, who has worked with the dying for over thirty years, writes:

> The concept of a good death can put unbearable pressure on dying people and caregivers, and can take us away from death's mystery and the richness of not knowing. Our expectations of how someone should die can give rise to subtle or direct coerciveness. No one wants to be judged for how well she dies! "Death with dignity" is another concept that can become an obstacle to what is really happening. Dying can be very undignified. Often, it's not dignified at all, with soiled bedclothes and sheets, bodily fluids and flailing, nudity and strange sexuality, confusion and rough language . . . good death, death with dignity—can be

unfortunate fabrications that we use to try to protect ourselves against the sometimes raw and wondrous truth of dying.[4]

Frank Ostaseski, the founding director of the first Buddhist hospice in America, says, "Everybody who is dying has a story about how one dies, and that story shapes the way they die. It helps to discover more about the story someone is holding and to work with it, rather than to try to change it or impose some other story."[5] Approach the dying person not with answers but with openness. Don't feel like you need to get it all right. As Ostaseski says, the process is characterized much more by mystery than mastery.

If you're close to the person, it can feel like part of you is also dying. Be aware of your place in the death and your sense of empathetic merging. Balance this with a healthy separation from the dying person and the events that surround them. You have to take care of yourself in order to take care of them.

The most helpful person is one who is comfortable with death, with groundlessness, and with not knowing. Like a strong rider on a frisky horse, this is someone who can ride on top of whatever's happening without being thrown by it and without trying to fix it. Expect the unexpected. Learn to appreciate silence and uncertainty. This is where your practice of bodhichitta, which helps you keep an open heart, and shamatha, which helps you keep a steady mind, places you in good stead.

Death is unsettling because it is foreign. This is what's meant by groundlessness. Trungpa Rinpoche said that groundlessness means that ground is unknown to you. You just don't know what's going on, but you're okay with that. It's your stability in the midst of such instability that brings the most benefit. Steadiness naturally attracts and soothes others—especially when they're losing it. They will take refuge in your presence and peace of mind.

Some people want a great deal of support from their spiritual community while they die. Others want a more retreat-like approach. Complicated helping strategies and micro-managing everything can overwhelm the dying person and their caregivers. Keep it genuine and simple. And work from your heart.

While there is much that we can do, the "know-it-all" does more harm than good. Our task is to support, love, and release the dying person. Don't get too invested in guiding them. Let them guide you.[6] Be wary of talking traps, the things we might say out of anxiety, or to break the silence. Avoid clichés like "I know how you must be feeling." If you're not sure what to say, say that—or don't say anything. Be quiet and listen. Don't be afraid of space.

Be sensitive to the needs and wants of the departing person. Never impose your own. As Kahlil Gibran said, "All can hear, but only the sensitive can understand." We often want things to go a certain way and don't realize how we influence events to that effect. Don't be religious, dogmatic, or too spiritual. You are there in someone's greatest hour as a caretaker and honored guest. Remind yourself that it's a privilege to be with this person during this once-in-a-lifetime transition.

Even though death is serious, there's no need to lose your sense of humor. On an absolute level death is a big joke—there's no such thing as death. The yogi Gotsangpa sang:

> When it's time to leave this body, this illusionary tangle,
> Don't cause yourself anxiety and grief;
> The thing that you should train in and clear up for yourself
> There's no such thing as dying to be done
> It's just clear light, the mother, and child clear light uniting,
> When mind forsakes the body, sheer delight![7]

Events surrounding death can be truly funny. There's no need to be overly somber. But don't bring a forced sense of humor, or artificially try to enlighten the atmosphere. Just touch deeply into your heart, be yourself, and err on the side of silence.

We are there to hold the dying one, to provide a loving container that allows them to relax, and to encourage them not to be afraid. The key to what generates the best container is often provided by the dying person themselves. There are two helpful things to practice in this situation: sacred listening and unconditional presence.

SACRED LISTENING

Sacred listening means to listen not just with your ears but with your heart. You won't hear what needs to be heard if you're speedy or overly emotional. Slow down, pause before you enter the room, and collect yourself. Check your motivation for being there. Don't be afraid to pause while in the room, or to step out if you need to get it together. You can't offer the healing power of space until you give yourself some space. Joan Halifax says:

Listening means that we have stabilized our minds so completely that the person who is speaking can actually hear themselves through our stillness. It is a quality of radiant listening, of luminous listening, of vibrant listening, but it is very still. It is listening with attention, with openheartedness, without prejudice. The quality of attention that we are invited to bring is as if the person who is speaking will not live another day, as if they were saying their last words. We listen with our whole being.[8]

The Roman Stoic philosopher Seneca said, "Behold me in my nakedness, my wounds, my pain, my tongue which cannot express my sorrow, my terror, my abandonment. Listen to me for a day—an hour!—a moment!—lest I expire in my terrible wilderness, my lonely silence! O God, is there no one to listen?"

Be prepared to hear the same old stories from elderly relatives. For whatever reason, this satisfies a need for them. Be ready for outbursts of anger or frustration, sometimes directed at you. Don't take it personally. Anyone under severe stress needs to release the tension. Meet them emotionally and spiritually where they are, not where you want them to be. Be sensitive to the possibility that you may not be needed or even wanted. And watch for signs of fatigue, things like lack of concentration, restlessness, drowsiness, and labored breathing. If those occur, it's time for you to leave or to let your loved one doze off.

Sacred listening is an exercise in empathy. It's the ability to think and *feel* yourself into the inner life of another person. Put yourself in their shoes, crawl into their skin. Get out of yourself and into them. An empathic (not reactive) response validates the person's feelings, and invites them to open up and express themselves. It helps them relax. Guidelines for sacred listening and empathic response include the following:

- ► Don't interrupt the speaker and don't rush them.
- ► Be aware of yourself, your personal issues and fears, as you enter their space and as you converse.
- ► If you don't understand something, ask for clarification. Show your concern by asking considerate questions.
- ► Realize you can't fix the situation. Accept it.
- ► Refrain from advising or contradicting.
- ► Display empathy, not pity.
- ► Keep on subject until the person has finished expressing themselves.

- ▸ Be aware of when you feel the urge to be cheerful or want to falsely reassure them.
- ▸ Never prolong a conversation where you are doing most of the talking. Be sensitive to your own anxiety and urge to fill space.
- ▸ Relate to the person, not the illness.

Let the dying person talk about issues of their choice. Acknowledge them with a nod, a gentle squeeze of their hand, or reflect back what you just heard. People who are dying want to be heard, not taught. Sogyal Rinpoche says:

> I have been amazed again and again by how, if you just let people talk, giving them your complete and compassionate attention, they will say things of a surprising spiritual depth, even when they think they don't have any spiritual beliefs. Everyone has their own life wisdom, and when you let a person talk you allow this life wisdom to emerge. I have often been very moved by how you can help people *to help themselves* by helping them to discover their own truth, a truth whose richness, sweetness, and profundity they may never have suspected. The sources of healing and awareness are deep within each of us, and your task is never under any circumstances to impose your beliefs but to enable them to find these within themselves.[9]

Here are some tips for what to say and what not to say to someone who is facing death:

- ▸ What not to say: "Hang in there, you're strong, you can make it." "Fight it! Don't let it get you!" "What does the doctor know? You may live for years." "Don't give up, we need you." "Everything will be fine."
- ▸ What is helpful to say: "I'm here for you." "How can I help you?" "How do you feel?" "Would you like to talk about anything in particular?" "It must be so hard for you." "I'm so proud to be your friend, brother, child." "I love you."

HOPES AND FEARS OF THE DYING

Effective communication can be enhanced by having some understanding of what the dying person may be going through. Some of the unspoken hopes of the dying include the following:

- that we will pass with dignity, surrounded by loved ones
- that we will get better and be productive again
- that tomorrow will be a better day, next week a better week
- that our dying will not be prolonged or painful
- that we will not be a burden
- that our families will be able to go on without us—that everything is taken care of
- that we are having a good dharmic death
- that we will reunite with our guru or go to a higher rebirth

Fears around dying include the following concerns:
- fear of annihilation
- fear of not being a good dharma student, of not having a good death
- fear of being unprepared and slipping into the lower realms
- fear of karma, of what the next life might be
- fear of abandonment or isolation
- fear of the process of dying, which includes fears that it will be painful, that we will lose our dignity and independence, that we will become a burden
- fear of the unknown
- fear of leaving everything behind—of letting go

HOLDING ENVIRONMENTS

Dzogchen Ponlop Rinpoche says that the best thing we can do for the dying is to create a proper environment. The pediatrician and child psychiatrist Donald Winnicott wrote about "holding environments"—how a proper environment is critical for healthy growth and development. As with the beginning of life, so with its end. If a proper holding environment is established around death, a good death will naturally take place within it. The caregiver's job, as a midwife into the bardos, is to create the space that allows the dying person to relax and release.[10] The Buddha's teaching, the dharma, is expressly for this purpose. It offers the ultimate holding environment. *Dharma* is derived from the Sanskrit root *dhr*, which means "support, carrying, holding."

If someone is held properly—physically or spiritually—they will surrender to that loving embrace. Think about how good you feel when you get a nice warm hug. That's the feeling you want to create. Holding environments are really hugging environments.

I have been with dying people who ask that their bed be moved into the center of the room, so their loved ones can sit all around them. At the request of the dying person, I have seen family members, caretakers, and even pets crawl into bed with the dying person so they can better hold them.[11] As with meditation, the maxim "not too tight, not too loose," is the key. If we hold them too tight, that amounts to grasping and will hinder their transition. If we hold them too loosely, or not at all, that can make them feel abandoned.

We always bring an environment with us, a space or mood that represents our state of mind. If we're anxious and uptight, the dying person tunes into that. If we're open, spacious, and relaxed, they will tune into that. Many hospice workers comment that as the dying person nears death, their mind becomes less contained by their body. They're more aware of the atmosphere. It's almost as if their mind is spilling into the room. The greatest gift we can therefore bring to a dying person is our unconditional presence, an attendance that fills the atmosphere with stability and love. Khenpo Karthar Rinpoche says, "[E]ven if the person has lived a very unwholesome life, if you have been able to positively affect that person's final state of mind, a beneficial rebirth may occur. That is one of the highest benefits you could have effected in the life of another person."[12]

Unconditional presence means unconditional acceptance. This is the best holding environment. If the death is rough, we accept and work with that. If it's easy, we accept that. We don't judge, impose, expect, or desire anything. This atmosphere of acceptance is contagious, and will help the dying person slide into a similar state of ease. Psychologist Marie de Hennezel writes: "Creating this atmosphere of warmth and calm around a sick person who is in torment is unquestionably the most beneficial thing one can do for him or her."[13] She relates that for one nurse who was able to do this consistently, the patients on her shift always required fewer tranquilizers.

Unconditional presence is a state developed by meditation, and it propagates the space of meditation. Therefore one of the best things to do for the dying is to practice with them. If the person isn't a meditator, ask them first if it's okay to sit quietly with them, or just do it unobtrusively. Never force anything. An excessively "spiritual" atmosphere can have the opposite effect and unsettle the dying person.

Because their heart-mind is spilling into space, we can mix our heart-mind with theirs and actually practice for them. Christine Longaker writes:

At the time of death, our spiritual practice can affect the person's mind and heart in an extraordinary way. When we are resting in the vivid presence of the true nature of mind, or invoking the radiant, loving presence of a buddha or Divine Being, we are literally creating a sacred environment for him to die within. Our devoted spiritual practice may become his actual experience at the moment of death. It will make a strong imprint on his mind— and this last imprint is what he will wake up to after death.[14]

The dying person tunes into all kinds of unconscious messages, so honesty—particularly honesty with ourselves—is crucial. Now is the time for heart-to-heart communication. But don't be too forward: even though the raw nature of death invites truth, this doesn't mean we have to express every thought. Unloading on the dying person only serves ourselves. Sacred listening helps us decide what needs to be said.

If your loved one is open for guidance, it's important not to give too many instructions and that they not be too profound. This can overwhelm a person when their energy is low. Share something pithy and heartfelt, an inspiring message they can take with them. Gently repeat the instruction. Keep it simple. Trungpa Rinpoche said:

> It seems that actually relating with the dying person is very important, to provide the whole ground of dying. Death is no longer a myth at that point. It is actually happening: "You are dying. We are watching your dying. But we are your friends, therefore we watch your dying. We believe in your rugged quality of leaving your body and turning into a corpse. That is beautiful. That's the finest and best example of friendship that you could demonstrate to us: that you know you are dying and we know that you are going to die. That's really beautiful. We are really meeting together properly and beautifully, exactly at the point. It is fantastic communication." That in itself is such a beautiful and rich quality of communication that it really presents a tremendous further inspiration, as far as the dying person is concerned.[15]

One central ingredient in a good holding environment is the reliability of it. Dying people are dealing with unpredictability and groundlessness, so it's important for them to know they can count on someone, or something. Never offer more than you can deliver. Their body and mind—life itself—is already letting them down. Don't let them down further by not showing up when you said you would, or not keeping a promise. The bedridden have few distractions. Every outside contact becomes disproportionately important. Your visit might be an insignificant part of your week, but it may be the one event the person was eagerly awaiting. Be firm in your commitments.

CREATING THE ENVIRONMENT

With this guiding view, there are many things we can do to create a good holding environment. The dying person can help by planning this environment in advance and leaving instructions in a dharma box. In addition to the "Farewell Checklist" in appendix 1, here are some suggestions: set up a shrine in the room. Put up photographs of their teachers. Burn incense, play recordings of their favorite talks or chants. Play uplifting music.[16] Namkha Drimed Rinpoche says that it's important to have a statue of Guru Rinpoche in the room. Bring flowers, beautiful art, or whatever the dying person feels will enrich their space. The idea is to generate an uplifted atmosphere. Create a space that elevates the mind of the dying person or anyone who walks into the room.

People often want to come by and lend support or say goodbye. While this is a wonderful offering, caretakers should be sensitive to how this can drain the dying person. Dying means that the life force is being exhausted, which implies that energy is low. The need for sleep increases. Don't be shy to tell people that visits may not be possible.

When the dying person stops communicating, or is slipping in and out of consciousness, it could be time to curb or end the visitations. Limit the space to caretakers and loved ones. They may be dealing with perplexing experiences as the outer world disappears and their inner world takes over. Now is the time to let them go into that inner world. Tugging them out may confuse them, so honor their silence with your own. To let them rest in peace we have to let them go in peace.

When death is imminent, overly emotional people should settle themselves or leave. Strong emotions, while understandable, can disturb the dying person and adversely affect their transition. Because of the law of proximate karma, the last thing on a person's mind before death often becomes the first thing on their mind after death.

The wailing and weeping of loved ones can make the dying person grasp on to life and prolong unnecessary suffering. They often hold on for the sake of those around them. How would you feel if you knew you had to go but your loved ones were holding on to you and begging you to stay? This grasping mentality favors rebirth as a hungry ghost, which is an unfortunate rebirth. More helpful is to try to lift the dying person into higher states of mind and send them on their way.

LOOKING FORWARD

If the dying person is receptive, remind them that their nature is completely pure and good, and that they are about to experience that purity and goodness. Tell them that their innate brilliance and perfection are about to shine forth. This gives them something beautiful to look forward to. For a strong practitioner, death and rebirth are like going to sleep and waking up to a new day. Go to "sleep" satisfied with your life, and realize you have something to look forward to tomorrow.

One of the best things we can therefore do to benefit the dying person is to help them look forward. Tsoknyi Rinpoche says, "Tell them that the relative is dying, the ultimate is not dying. Give them hope that they can recognize the ultimate, the nature of their mind, the mind that is unchanging and undying. You have to give a little promotion on the deathless side." This is why it's so important to understand what happens after death.

So much suffering occurs because everyone is looking back. While it is healthy, up to a point, to reminisce over a life well lived and to celebrate one's accomplishments, it's more important to let go of that life and look forward. Death forces the issue and demands release. The sooner we get this lesson the easier the journey will be.

If we remain anchored in the past—even during life—we will suffer unnecessarily. Depression is nearly synonymous with having nothing to look forward to, and a great deal of psychopathology is born from our inability to let go. If we view death as total annihilation, with nothing whatsoever to look forward to, we may suffer in direct proportion to the strength of that view—which is actually no view at all. *That* is depressing.

Death is transformed when we replace that dark view with one based on light. This is why the greatest practitioners, like Gotsangpa, look forward to death with sheer delight. The greatest opportunity for enlightenment is about to unfold. If that doesn't excite you, nothing will.

So if the dying person is open to it, remind him or her of this view by pointing out that the greatest practitioners look forward to death. It's never too late to be inspired. Sogyal Rinpoche says, "Even if we have accumulated a lot of negative karma, if we are able to make a real change of heart at the moment of death, it can decisively influence our future, and transform our karma, for the moment of death is an exceptionally powerful opportunity to purify karma." Remind the departing one that they are about to merge their mind with the wisdom mind of their master, and that the compassionate buddhas are waiting to lead them to a pure land. Remind them that the truest aspect of their being, the very subtle inner body, does not die. Replace fear with hope.[17]

People often grow a great deal when they are faced with their own mortality. Never underestimate someone's capacity for progress. Many hospice workers and spiritual caretakers say that the changes are sometimes phenomenal. With the proper view, it's easy to become inspired about death. Not in a suicidal way, but in realizing the incredible opportunity that lies ahead. The end of life is the culmination of life, its crowning moment. So elevate your view and look forward to the coronation.

ADVICE FROM SOGYAL RINPOCHE

Sogyal Rinpoche's book *The Tibetan Book of Living and Dying* is a modern masterpiece. Every serious student should own this text. In part 2, "Dying," it offers some of the best advice ever written. In multiple readings of this seminal book, I have realized that in terms of helping others to die, there's simply no better way to say it. The following section is a collection of excerpts summarizing Rinpoche's teaching on how to help others die. I have inserted my own commentary between his extensive quotations to elaborate some of the important points. Unless noted otherwise, every quote in this section is from Sogyal Rinpoche.

> The most essential thing in life is to establish an unafraid, heartfelt communication with others, and it is never more important than with a dying person ... Often the dying person feels reserved and insecure, and is not sure of your intentions when you first visit. So don't feel anything extraordinary is supposed to happen, just be natural and relaxed, be yourself. Often dying people do

not say what they want or mean, and the people close to them do not know what to say or do. It's hard to find out what they might be trying to say, or even what they might be hiding. Sometimes not even they know. So the first essential thing is to relax any tension in the atmosphere in whatever way comes most easily and naturally.[18]

Don't try to impress anyone with your wisdom and compassion. Be yourself. That is wisdom and compassion. Try to imagine what the dying one must be going through. Rinpoche continues:

Once trust and confidence have been established . . . allow the dying person to bring up the things he or she really wants to talk about. Encourage the person warmly to feel as free as possible to express thoughts, fears, and emotions about dying and death. This honest and unshrinking baring of emotion is central to any possible transformation—of coming to terms with life or dying a good death—and you must allow the person complete freedom, and give your full permission to say whatever he or she wants.[19]

Don't interrupt, deny, or negate what the dying person has to say. Give them the space they need. The dying are in the most vulnerable time of their lives. They're often confused and overwhelmed, so be sensitive and open. Practice sacred listening, and allow them to feel your unconditional presence.

[Y]ou will need all your skill and resources of sensitivity, and warmth, and loving compassion to enable them to reveal themselves. . . . sit there with your dying friend or relative as if you had nothing more important or enjoyable to do.
. . . [A]s in all grave situations of life, two things are most useful: a common-sense approach and a sense of humor. Humor has a marvelous way of lightening the atmosphere, helping to put the process of dying in its true and universal perspective, and breaking the over-seriousness and intensity of the situation.[20]
. . . [I]t is essential not to take anything too personally. When you least expect it, dying people can make you the target of all

their anger and blame. As Elisabeth Kübler-Ross says, anger and blame can 'be displaced in all directions, and projected onto the environment at times almost at random.'[21]

They are losing everything—their home, relationships, body, even their mind. Who wouldn't feel sad, panicky, or angry? They may feel that no one wants to comprehend their innermost needs, so look past the momentary upheavals and look into their basic goodness. Let that goodness guide you. That is actually a buddha that is dying. As Joan Halifax says, "We don't help Buddhists die. We help Buddhas die." Don't forget their buddha nature, and avoid getting tripped up by the momentary outbursts.

Sometimes you may be tempted to preach to the dying, or to give them your own spiritual formula. Avoid this temptation absolutely . . . . No one wishes to be "rescued" with someone else's beliefs. Remember your task is not to convert anyone to anything, but to help the person in front of you get in touch with his or her own strength, confidence, faith, and spirituality, whatever that might be. Of course, if the person is really open to spiritual matters, and really wants to know what you think about them, don't hold back either.

Do not expect too much from yourself, or expect your help to produce miraculous results in the dying person or "save" them. . . . People will die as they have lived, as themselves. . . . Also don't be distressed if your help seems to be having very little effect and the dying person does not respond. We cannot know the deeper effects of our care.

A dying person most needs to be shown as unconditional a love as possible, released from all expectations. Don't think you have to be an expert in any way. Be natural, be yourself, be a true friend, and the dying person will be reassured that you are really with them, communicating with them simply and as an equal, as one human being to another.

. . . Imagine that you are on that bed before you, facing your death. Imagine that you are there in pain and alone. Then really ask yourself: What would you most need? What would you most like? What would you really wish from the friend in front of you?

... [Y]ou would find that what the dying person wants is what *you* would most want: to be really loved and accepted.[22]

People who are sick often long to be touched, to feel human. No one wants to be seen as a bag of disease. Remember the importance of physical holding environments.

> A great deal of consolation can be given ... simply by touching their hands, looking into their eyes, gently massaging them or holding them in your arms, or breathing in the same rhythm gently with them. The body has its own language of love; use it fearlessly, and you will find you bring to the dying comfort and consolation.[23]
>
> ... [R]eassure that person that whatever he or she may be feeling, whatever his or her frustration and anger, it is normal. Dying will bring out many repressed emotions: sadness or numbness or guilt, or even jealousy of those who are still well.[24]

Allow these waves of strong feelings to wash over you, and your stability will invite their own.

> Don't try to be too wise; don't always try to search for something profound to say. You don't have to *do* or say anything to make things better. Just be there as fully as you can. And if you are feeling a lot of anxiety and fear, and don't know what to do, admit that openly to the dying person and ask his or her help. This honesty will bring you and the dying person closer together, and help in opening up a freer communication. Sometimes the dying know far better than we how they can be helped, and we need to know how to draw on their wisdom and let them give to us what they know.[25]

Telling the Truth

When people are dying they should be told so, "as quietly, as kindly, as sensitively, and as skillfully as possible."[26] Most of the time they know anyway, as Elisabeth Kübler-Ross says, "They sense it by the changed attention, by the new and different approach that people take to them, by the lowering of voices or avoidance of sounds, by the tearful face of a relative or ominous, unsmiling member of the family who cannot hide his true feelings."[27] They seem to know instinctively, and often count on us to confirm their intuitions. Kübler-Ross also says that people often have an inner alert system that warns them of their own death.

They need to prepare, to say goodbye, and to deal with practical issues. Rinpoche says, "I believe dying to be a great opportunity for people to come to terms with their whole lives . . . we are really giving them the chance to prepare, and to find their own powers of strength, and the meaning of their lives."[28] We think we're protecting the person who is dying by not telling them, but we're probably trying to protect ourselves. For many people, death is almost an embarrassment, a failure, the ultimate defeat. But it's more accurately a time of truth, a time to face reality. Codependent denial does not honor reality. Don't underestimate the dying person's capacity to face things squarely. There is power in acknowledging reality. Nothing cuts through ego's games, and hurls you more directly into reality, than death.

Fears about Dying

Being around dying people will almost force you to establish a relationship with your own fears about death. If you really want to help someone who is dying, especially with their fear of death, you have to relate to your own trepidations. By becoming familiar with your own fears, and developing fearlessness, you will naturally convey that fearlessness to the dying person. Sogyal Rinpoche says, "Sometimes I think there could be no more effective way of speeding up our growth as human beings than working with the dying."[29] Your fearlessness is contagious. It can provide exactly what the dying person and those around you need—the confidence to relax and let go.

Imagine the anxiety and fear that may be screaming through the dying person: fear of pain, suffering, indignity, dependence, meaninglessness, separation, the unknown, of losing control, of being forgotten. We leave this world alone, and fear heightens the sense of isolation. "But when someone keeps company with you and talks of his or her own fears, then you realize fear is universal and the edge, the personal pain, is taken off it. Your fears are brought back to the human and universal context. Then you are able to understand, be more compassionate, and deal with your own fears in a much more positive and inspiring way."[30]

Our lives are lived with the unconscious motivation to avoid fear. It's the primordial emotion of samsara, that from which all other samsaric emotions arise. Now, at last, we have the opportunity to face it directly, befriend it, and transform it.[31]

Unfinished Business

Many dying people suffer from a sense of unfinished business. This is partly why the bardo of letting go is painful. Sometimes this feeling comes from unfinished practical matters as mundane as the roof needing to be fixed. But most unfinished business is emotional, the dissonance of unresolved relationships. "Usually unfinished business is the result of blocked communication; when we have been wounded, we often become very defensive, always arguing from a position of being right and blindly refusing to see the other person's point of view."[32]

Most of us would rather be right than intimate. But death invites intimacy and the truth that is borne from it. We should strive for intimacy and truth, first with ourselves and then with others. This is one of the great gifts of death and of a life spent preparing for it. So try to resolve unfinished business before you no longer have the chance to do so. It can ease the burden on your mind and help you glide through the bardos.

Giving Hope and Finding Forgiveness

I would like to single out two points in giving spiritual help to the dying: giving hope, and finding forgiveness. Always when you are with a dying person, dwell on what they have accomplished and done well. Help them to feel as constructive and as happy as possible about their lives. Concentrate on their virtues and not their failings. People who are dying are frequently extremely vulnerable to guilt, regret, and depression; allow the person to express these freely, listen to the person and acknowledge what he or she says. At the same time, where appropriate, be sure to remind the person of his or her buddha nature [basic goodness], and encourage the person to try to rest in the nature of mind through the practice of meditation. Especially remind the person that pain and suffering are not all that he or she is. Find the most skillful and sensitive way possible to inspire the person and give him or her hope. So rather than dwelling on his or her mistakes, the person can die in a more peaceful frame of mind.[33]

Giving, in its many forms, is one of the best environments to create around death. Create a sense of service to the dying. Give to them. Help the dying person, and loved ones, to give in to the natural process of transition. And help the dying person and loved ones to forgive. Encourage the dying person to release their grudges and to erase any lingering resentment. They might be able to contact the person where hard feelings remain, or to write a message that helps them forgive. Forgiveness is about letting go. It's the way to live and die with grace.

It's never too late to forgive and to benefit from this form of release. "The moment of death has a grandeur, solemnity, and finality that can make people reexamine all their attitudes, and be more open and ready to forgive, when before they could not bear to. Even at the very end of a life, the mistakes of a life can be undone."[34]

Saying Goodbye

We can help the dying person let go by letting go of the dying person ourselves. We can still be there for them, caring deeply, loving profoundly, and do it all without attachment. Khenpo Tsültrim Gyamtso Rinpoche always emphasizes love without attachment. That is clean love. "Without attachment" does not mean apathetic detachment. We still want to be present and respond appropriately, but without sticking to everything.

Christine Longaker says that for someone to let go and die peacefully, he or she needs to hear two things from loved ones. First, the loved ones must give the dying person permission to die. Second, the loved ones must reassure the dying person that they will be okay when he or she dies. In order to give loved ones time to accept their loss, a dying person often hangs on despite being in great pain. The gift of presence may be all a dying person still feels he or she can offer, and the physical pain may be secondary to the desire to give. Let the dying person know you appreciate the offering—their very life—but that now is the time to let go of that life. Say your goodbyes and offer your final gift of love. That can achieve the closure that facilitates the final release.

When I flew back to see my mother for the last time, I had a feeling she was waiting for me. During this precious weekend I told her that while I would miss her, I would be fine and that it was time for her to let go. I told her she had lived a long and wonderful life, accomplished so much good, and brought a happy family into the world. She was unable to speak, but I could tell from her eyes that she heard me. A few hours after I left she peacefully died.

My father had a special relationship with his ten-year-old granddaughter, Taylor. They were so close that she had a hard time seeing him in his final weeks. She couldn't bear to see him suffer. A few days before he passed, one of the few words my father could still whisper was "Taylor, Taylor." She finally mustered the strength to see him, at a time when he appeared unresponsive. She told him it was hard for her to see him like this, that she would miss him, but that she would be okay. My father turned his head slightly toward her, and she kissed him on the forehead. Taylor left the room, and within three minutes my father was dead. This is what he had been waiting for. His beloved granddaughter gave him the permission he needed to finally let go.

Sogyal Rinpoche offers these beautiful words: "I am here with you and I love you. You are dying, and that is completely natural; it happens to everyone. I wish you could stay here with me, but I don't want you to suffer any more. The time we have had together has been enough, and I shall always cherish it. Please now don't hold on to life any longer. Let go. I give you my full and heartfelt permission to die. You are not alone, now or ever. You have all my love."[35]

Family and friends may be at different levels of acceptance around the death of a loved one, and therefore at different stages of letting go. Letting go is not a sign of insufficient love. It's a sign of mature love, love that puts the needs of the dying before your own. If you're having a hard time, ask the professionals for help. Hospice workers and grief counselors are trained in helping the family deal with letting go.

Toward a Peaceful Death

It's good to die in familiar surroundings, where it's easier to relax. There is so much unfamiliar experience already happening that any level of familiarity, physical or otherwise, can help. But even if someone dies in a hospital, we can still do a great deal to create a good holding environment. Eighty percent of Americans die in a nursing home or hospital. Dying in a hospital, or anywhere outside the home, does not imply a second-rate death. The important point is the dying person's state of mind, not the physical state.

> When a person is very close to death, I suggest that you request that the hospital staff do not disturb him or her so often, and that they stop taking tests. . . . [B]eing in an intensive care unit will make a peaceful death very difficult, and hardly allow for spiritual practice at the moment of death. . . . [Y]ou should arrange with the doctor to be told when there is no possibility of the person recovering, and then request to have them moved to a private room . . . . Make sure the staff knows and respects the dying person's wishes, especially if he or she does not wish to be resuscitated . . . . Try and make certain also that while the person is actually in the final stages of dying, all injections and all invasive procedures of any kind are discontinued. These can cause anger, irritation, and pain . . .[36]

Even though many people seem to die in a state of unconsciousness, they are often aware of what's happening. I have seen the tiniest eye movements from people on the edge of death, clearly responding to comments in the room. Even though the sense of hearing mostly dissolves in the early stages of the outer dissolution, we should sustain loving thoughts and be mindful of our speech in the presence of the dying.

By the Bedside of the Dying

Encourage the dying person to take refuge in whatever spiritual practice he or she is comfortable with, and practice with them. The atmosphere of dying—before, during, and after death—can be transformed through meditation. Sogyal Rinpoche emphasizes Essential Phowa to benefit others.[37] In this practice, you imagine a spiritual presence, like the Buddha, above the head of the dying person. Then imagine rays of sacred light pouring down onto the dying person, purifying them. Finally, imagine that the dying person dissolves into light and merges into the spiritual presence. Rinpoche says, "If a person is going to be healed, it will assist that healing; if a person is dying, it will help them and heal their spirit in death; and if the person has died, it will continue to purify them."[38] He writes:

[W]hen you don't know what to do, when you feel hardly able to do anything to help, then pray and meditate, invoke the Buddha or any other figure whose sacred power you believe in. When I'm faced with someone going through terrible suffering, I call down with fervor the help of all the buddhas and enlightened beings, with my heart completely open to the person dying in front of me, and compassion for their pain filling my being. I invoke as intensely as possible the presence of my masters, the buddhas, of those enlightened beings with whom I have a particular connection. Summoning all my powers of devotion and faith, I see them in glory above the dying person, gazing down at them with love, and pouring down light and blessing on them, purifying them of all their past karma and present agony. And as I do this, I keep praying that the person in front of me should be spared further suffering, and find peace and liberation.[39]

Dedicating Our Death

One of the best ways to remove the suffering of death is to put it in perspective. If someone is asking for help as they die, have them imagine all the other people who are dying today. Remind them of the vast scale of the universe, and the endless play of life and death. Acknowledge their pain and help them find meaning in it. Rinpoche suggests saying,

Imagine now all the others in the world who are in a pain like yours, or even greater. Fill your heart with compassion for them. And pray to whomever you believe in and ask that your suffering should help alleviate theirs. Again and again dedicate your pain to the alleviation of their pain. And you will quickly discover in yourself a new source of strength, a compassion you'll hardly be able now to imagine, and a certainty, beyond any shadow of a doubt, that your suffering is not only not being wasted, but has now a marvelous meaning.[40]

This is a form of tonglen. We then breathe out all the goodness, wisdom, and natural wealth within us, sending it to those in pain.

From a spiritual point of view, the world is not made of matter, and we are not separate from other beings. The world is made of heart-mind-spirit. When we touch deeply into our own heart-mind-spirit, we connect to this matrix of reality and can affect the world. Tonglen may use the medium of imagination, but that imagination has power.[41]

By dedicating our suffering and death, we infuse this hardship with meaning. Sogyal Rinpoche says:

> We have before us the noble and exalting examples of the supreme masters of compassion, who, it is said, live and die in the practice of Tonglen, taking on the pain of all sentient beings while they breathe in, and pouring out healing to the whole world when they breathe out, all their lives long, and right up until their very last breath. So boundless and powerful is their compassion, the teachings say, that at the moment of their death, it carries them immediately to rebirth in a buddha realm.[42]

Dedicating our death predisposes our rebirth into a pure land, because it purifies our mind of the self-centeredness that leads to the lower realms. If the dying person also holds the view that death is an opportunity to purify karma, and that the suffering of death is that of purification, they bring further meaning to the hardship of death. These views transform the near-sighted attitudes that often generate a difficult death. They help us raise our gaze.

Letting Go of Attachment

If you are close to the dying person, encourage them to work through their attachment and grief before the moment of death.[43] Rinpoche advises: "Cry together, express your love, and say goodbye, but try to finish with this process before the actual moment of death arrives."[44] Otherwise their attachment generates unnecessary suffering, and adversely affects the mind at the moment of death. "All my masters would give this as their advice, for this is the essence of what is needed as you come to die: 'Be free of attachment and aversion. Keep your mind pure. And unite your mind with the Buddha.'"[45] This advice also applies to you, or any other caregiver. Gently cut the strings of attachment before the moment of death.

The Grace of Prayer at the Moment of Death

> Make a one-pointed and concentrated wish that you will be reborn either in a pure realm or as a human being, but in order to protect, nurture, and help others. To die with such love and such tender compassion in your heart until your last breath is said in the Tibetan tradition to be another form of phowa, and it will ensure that you will at least attain another precious human body. To create the most positive possible imprint on the mindstream before death is essential.[46]

The practice of devotion is another way to generate positive states of mind at death. Imagine that you are about to merge your mind into the wisdom mind of the Buddha, or your guru. Remember the face of your teacher as you die. "When your consciousness awakens again after death, this imprint of the master's presence will awaken with you, and you will be liberated."[47]

The Atmosphere for Dying

It's ideal if a spiritual master can be at the side of someone as they die, but it's rare. Don't feel that your death, or that of a loved one, is imperfect if a master is not present. The spiritual community steps in to fulfill that role. Rinpoche says, "The loving and unflagging presence of the master or spiritual friends, the encouragement of the teachings, and the strength of their own practice, all combine together to create and sustain this inspiration, as precious in the last weeks and days almost as breath itself."[48]

> If the time comes when you cannot practice actively any more, the only really important thing for you to do is to relax, as deeply as possible, in the confidence of the View, and rest in the nature of mind. It does not matter whether your body or your brain are still functioning: the nature of your mind is always there, sky-like, radiant, blissful, limitless and unchanging.... Trust in the nature of your mind, trust it deeply, and relax completely. There is nothing new you need to learn or acquire or understand; just allow what you have already been given to blossom in you and open at greater and greater depths.... The simplicity of total

trust is one of the most powerful forces in the world. . . . Don't worry about anything. Even if you find your attention wandering, there is no particular 'thing' you have to hold on to. Just let go, and drift in the awareness of the blessing. Don't let small, niggling, questions distract you, like 'Is this Rigpa [dharmakaya]? Is it not?' . . . Remember, your Rigpa is always there, always in the nature of your mind."[49]

Your mind will dissolve into the wisdom mind, like water poured into water. Let the spirit of love pervade the atmosphere. Whatever thought or feeling you die with is usually the one that will return to you when you reawaken in the bardos. Give yourself a nice welcoming gift. Greet yourself on "the other side" with a positive state of mind.

"Everything I have been saying up until now about caring for the dying could perhaps be summed up in two words: love and compassion." Rinpoche then delivers this important point: "Compassion is not true compassion unless it is active."[50] There is a difference between *idealistic* and *realistic* compassion. Idealistic compassion is the desire to help all sentient beings. It's a noble aspiration. But if we get stuck in aspiration alone it doesn't help.

Realistic compassion is helping people in your life—right here and now. It's active compassion. It's easier to save everyone in your mind than to actually care for a single person with your hands. The dream of saving all sentient beings can ironically disconnect you from the one right next to you. Author Jonathan Franzen says, "Trying to love all of humanity may be a worthy endeavor, but, in a funny way, it keeps the focus on the self, on the self's own moral or spiritual well-being. Whereas, to love a specific person, and to identify with his or her struggles and joys as if they were your own, you have to surrender some of your self."[51]

One of the best ways to activate that compassion, especially when you don't know what to do for someone in pain, is to exchange yourself with them. Imagine what you would be going through if you were suffering from their condition. What would you want from those around you? By getting out of yourself and into others, action naturally unfolds because you're now helping others as if you were helping yourself. That's the real meaning of compassion: to suffer (*passion*) with (*com*).

These are the summary instructions for how to help someone who is dying, from one of the leading masters whose words have inspired millions.

ESOTERIC PRACTICES

Some of the contents of the bardo package (discussed in appendix 1) can now be applied: the sacred pills can be placed under the lip, and the sacred sand on top of the brahmarandhra. You can write the Vajra Guru mantra, OM AH HUM VAJRA GURU PADMA SIDDHI HUM, fold it into an amulet, and place it at the heart. Guru Rinpoche himself said, "When you die, if this amulet is burned with your corpse, rainbows will be seen and your consciousness will be transferred to the realms of supreme bliss."[52] Don't do this too early. It might unsettle the dying person if they feel that caretakers already view them as dead. Unless they requested otherwise, do these things when they're semi-comatose, or near death.

Caregivers and loved ones should gather around the upper part of the dying person, not at the feet. This is because the attention of the dying person will naturally focus wherever there's activity. According to the laws of phowa, we don't want their mind to gather and eventually exit from lower portals, and therefore into lower realms. When death is imminent, avoid touching lower parts of the body. Gently caress the top of the head. You can even tug on the hair at the brahmarandhra, or tap the head at that point. This draws the mind up and invites consciousness to exit there. The idea is to block off all possible exits into the lower realms, and to keep consciousness on track for the higher realms.

Final pith instruction for what to do to help others during death: create a peaceful space, hold whatever happens with love. Give them something to look forward to. Let them go.

5. What to Do for Yourself After You Die

I'm now going to say something that may surprise you. *Death can be very inspiring.* . . . Sometimes I see that the dying person also feels this atmosphere of deep inspiration, and is grateful to have provided the opportunity for our reaching, together, a moment of real and transformative rapture.
—SOGYAL RINPOCHE

THE VIEW

IF YOU ARE well trained, your first after-death experience will be the luminous bardo of dharmata. If you're unfamiliar with the subtle states of mind revealed in this bardo, it will flash by in an instant or be completely missed. Those who have practiced the meditations that facilitate recognition will reap the rewards and attain liberation at the level of the dharmakaya or sambhogakaya.

Without this preparation, most of us will wake up in the karmic bardo of becoming. For nearly everyone, the first experience after regaining consciousness is a sense of being in their own body. Even though the mind is without a body at this point, the habit (karma) of being embodied is so strong that it continues. You feel like your old self, but you don't know you are dead.

Since this bardo is ruled by the winds of karma, the experiences are particularly fickle. These "winds" are not literal winds, of course, but a metaphor for how we are blown around by the power of karma. Because we have a mental body in this bardo, we're tossed around like a leaf in an autumn windstorm. In the previous bardos there's at least a theoretical order. In the bardo of dying, there are the eight stages of the outer and inner dissolution.

In the bardo of dharmata, we have the two phases, and the march of the hundred peaceful and wrathful deities over twelve meditation days. In the bardo of becoming there is no such order.

The bardo texts present a somewhat standard set of experiences: hanging around people and places from your last life; waking up to the shocking fact that you're dead; coming upon three precipices; coming before Yama, the Lord of Death; seeing the lights of the realms of samsara; seeing your eventual parents in union; etc. But the timing is not definite. All sorts of things can happen at any time. The only framing is the recapitulation of the dying experience that occurs every seven days. This is discussed below.

We spend an average of forty-nine days in this bardo, though the time is not fixed. Because of all the "wind" in this bardo, nothing is fixed. This bardo can flash by in an instant, or we can get stuck in it for years. But on average, the first half of these forty-nine days is associated with the life that has just ended, while the second half is associated with the next one. About halfway through this bardo, there is a shift in experience: there is a growing dislike for the body of the previous life and a desire to get away from it.

To make things even more confusing, the world of this after-death bardo sometimes overlaps with our own. Especially during the first half, bardo beings will hover over their own physical bodies and visit family and friends. They tend to come by at meal times, fuss over our activities, and not even know they're dead.[1] As we will see, they're also clairvoyant. This is why we can call them into our mind space and help them.

One marker of experience is that situations get increasingly chaotic as one progresses through this bardo. The winds of karma pick up strength the further we go; recognition becomes increasingly difficult because of a developing panic; and unless you know what's going on and can direct these winds into a fortunate realm of existence, you will be tossed uncontrollably into your next life.[2] Kalu Rinpoche writes, "It is an entirely automatic or blind result of our previous actions or karma, and nothing that occurs here is a conscious decision on the part of the being; we are simply buffeted around by the force of karma."[3]

Once we leave the bardo of dharmata, the display of wisdom is over and confusion returns with a vengeance.[4] In the luminous bardo of dharmata all heaven breaks loose. There's so much wisdom that we're overwhelmed. In the karmic bardo of becoming all hell breaks loose. There's so much confusion that we're overwhelmed. In the bardos, the thermonuclear power of the mind—both its wisdom and confusion—is unleashed. This is why we want to become familiar with our wisdom and confusion now, while it's still contained and restrained by the body.

This is what the path is designed to do. In general terms, the first half of the spiritual path is about becoming familiar with our confusion—with who we are *not*. Starting with the gross form of our body, then the more subtle forms of our mind, we progressively dis-identify from who we think we are. The path reveals that I'm not my body, and I'm not my thoughts and emotions. If something is *mine* it can't be *me*. My body, my thoughts, and my emotions are something I possess. I am something more subtle than even the most subtle of forms. In a sense we're backing our way into enlightenment. We're discovering who we truly are, through the process of progressive dis-identification. We are first identifying, and then dying to, our false sense of self. This is what the Hindus refer to as *neti neti*—not this, not that—or the *via negativa*.

The second half of the path is about becoming familiar with our wisdom—with who we truly are. At a certain point, which is called the *path of seeing*, we finally see who we really are.[5] This is a pivotal moment, a major "before and after" experience. The obscuring clouds have thinned out on the first half of the path to the point that the sun finally breaks through. This sun is formless awareness, your true nature. And this sun never sets. It's the indestructible very subtle body, the luminous-emptiness dharmakaya that is your essential being, and it does not die. Unlike the mortal forms that are gradually shed on the first half of the path, or rapidly shed during the bardo of dying, this formless awareness—precisely because it is formless—is immortal.

The second half of the path, called the *path of meditation*, or the path of familiarity, is about becoming familiar with your true nature. This is what the Chandogya Upanishad refers to as *tat tvam asi*—thou art that—or the *via positiva*. Once you have positively identified yourself, you now work to stabilize, and become increasingly familiar with, this newfound identity.[6] By allowing you to see who you are not (confusion), and then pointing out who you really are (wisdom), meditation prepares you for every phase of death. These teachings bring new meaning to the ancient Greek aphorism, "Know thyself." Sogyal Rinpoche says:

> Why do we live in such terror of death? Perhaps the deepest reason why we are afraid of death is that we do not know who we are. We believe in a personal, unique, and separate identity; but if

we dare to examine it, we find that this identity depends entirely on an endless collection of things to prop it up: our name, our "biography," our partners, family, home, job, friends, credit cards . . . It is on their fragile and transient support that we rely for our security. So when they are all taken away, will we have any idea of who we really are? We live under an assumed identity, in a neurotic fairy-tale world with no more reality than the Mock Turtle in *Alice in Wonderland*. Hypnotized by the thrill of building, we have raised the houses of our lives on sand. This world can seem marvelously convincing until death collapses the illusion and evicts us from our hiding place. And what will happen to us then if we have no clue of any deeper reality?[7]

A principal feature of the bardo of becoming is that radiance is perverted into projection. In other words, the luminous shine of the awakened mind that radiates in the bardo of dharmata is now filtered, colored, and flipped upside down by the lens of the three poisons.[8] As depicted in our hourglass diagram (see figure 3), this happens rapidly in the first three phases of the bardo of becoming. It's the mirror image, or reverse, of what happened in the last three phases of the bardo of dying. Black attainment (ignorance), red increase (passion), and white appearance (aggression) act as a tri-colored lens to transform the luminosity of the mind into projection. Instead of shining out with nondual clarity, wisdom is twisted into dualistic confusion. This projective prowess of the confused mind is a central theme in this bardo.

The power of thought and habit becomes the overwhelming issue in this bardo. Thought becomes reality—just as in a dream. But unlike ordinary dreaming, we can't wake up and take refuge in a solid body. We're stuck having to face our own confused mind, which is why this bardo gets horrific. On one level, you can't distract yourself in the bardo. Distraction means you're distracted from something, some stable referent (a body). In the bardo there are no such referents. There's no hitching post. Distraction itself becomes your reality. So if you haven't learned how to control your distracting thoughts and emotions while they're still encased and therefore restrained by the body, when that body drops away and thoughts are set free, things get out of control.[9] The untrained mind runs wild. Thrangu Rinpoche says:

The mind of the being in the bardo of becoming has a very hard time coming to rest at all. Therefore, the hallucinations are extremely intense, and there are very many of them. The mind is so bewildered by all of this that it cannot control its thoughts of good and bad. Therefore, the most important preparation for this state is to develop stability of mind through the practice of shamatha. To the degree that you can control your mind now, you will be able to control it in the bardo, and to the same degree you will be better able to withstand the onslaught of your own thoughts.[10]

The bardo of becoming is a cosmic Pandora's box. The urge to escape from the contents of this box, the bardo itself, is nothing more than the urge to run away from the contents of our own mind (our karma). This is what forces us to take refuge in a new solid body. We want to get away from ourselves.[11] In this regard, it is like a dream. We eventually do take refuge in a new form, and wake up into our next life.

Finally, without the anchor of the body, things happen so quickly and intensely that we will be hanging on for dear life, a colloquialism that becomes literal. This is why we want to exit the bardos altogether during the bardo of dharmata, or as early as possible in the bardo of becoming. Otherwise the dreamlike nature of the bardos turns into a nightmare.

FIRST STEP

The first and most important thing to do after death is to recognize that you are dead. This isn't easy; many people will not recognize it. Without preparation, most of us will black out at the end of the inner dissolution. The next thing we know is that we've been reborn. Most of us aren't aware of our past lives, how we died in the last one, and how we took rebirth into this one. Similarly, the journey into our next incarnation happens without awareness.

To get a feel for this, look at what you're able to recognize every night. Most of us don't recognize the final stages of falling asleep (a concordant experience of dying), or deep dreamless sleep (lucid sleeping, a concordant experience of the bardo of dharmata). And most of us don't wake up in our dreams (lucid dreaming, a concordant experience of the bardo of becoming). We just go blank, partly remember some dreams, and wake up the next morning unaware of what happened during the past eight hours. We die to today and take rebirth into tomorrow, unconscious of what happened in between. A Tibetan saying asserts: "Based on my experience last night, I can infer I am going to have a hard time in the bardos tomorrow." Kalu Rinpoche says:

> After death, during the period called the bardo of becoming, a multitude of phenomena appear that, while being productions of the mind only, are not recognized as such. The deceased person does not know in fact that he or she is in the bardo, and passes through all kinds of pleasant and unpleasant experiences. Even if the person understands that he or she is dead, this discovery plunges him or her into such anguish and fear that the person falls again into a state of unconsciousness. The person who has practiced the instructions contained in the dharma of the bardo immediately recognizes being in the bardo and from then on applies the methods allowing him or her to be completely liberated. Even if this person cannot apply the methods, the capacity is present to freely move in the bardo and to go to the Land of Bliss or to another pure land. Instructions of the bardo open up many possibilities.[12]

So before we can apply any remedy to the bardos, we have to first recognize we're in them. Otherwise we spin helplessly from life to life. The practices for this recognition have been discussed. Others can help us recognize that we're dead and remind us of what to do. This is the purpose of guidebooks such as *The Tibetan Book of the Dead.*

If we can wake up to the fact that we're in the bardos, that recognition creates a hitching post. Awareness itself provides a new formless reference point. It allows us to observe the display of our mind instead of being swept away by it. We can now dispassionately witness the mind, the way we watch a movie, or take control and direct the action. Either way our recognition sets us free.

Both options can be experienced in dreams. "Witnessing dreams" are when you wake up in your dreams but elect not to engage in them. You are lucid but you prefer just to watch. Waking up in the dream, and taking active control, is the more classic lucid dream. But lucidity, the recognition that you're dreaming, is common to both. And so is the freedom from the contents of the dream—the contents of your own mind. The dream no longer has power over you. Similarly, if you can recognize that you're in the bardos, that recognition liberates.

AFTER REMEMBERING

Waking up to the fact that you're dead is half the remedy. The next thing is not to be distracted from that recognition, or from any meditation you may engage. *The Tibetan Book of the Dead* says:

> Do not be distracted. This is the dividing-line where buddhas and sentient beings are separated. It is said of this moment: In an instant, they are separated, in an instant, complete enlightenment.[13]

After you wake up in the bardo, steady your mind. This is difficult because we have a shifty mental body that darts around at the speed of thought. If you think of Paris, or New York, or your home, you're instantly there. This is why Thrangu Rinpoche says, "The basic preparation for this bardo consists of cultivating now, while you are still alive, the ability to rest your mind at will and, within that state of tranquil mind the ability to make choices mindfully. This needs to be cultivated during one's life and if it is cultivated, it will be of great benefit during the bardo of becoming."[14] With a measure of stability, we can apply our meditations and attain liberation. This is why shamatha is such a powerful preparation for death.

There is risk and reward in having a mental body. A mental body means it is easily directed.[15] But it also means it is easily distracted, and it easily forgets. Because of its light weight (it's as light as a thought), this body is easily tossed around by karmic winds. This means that not only is it difficult to recognize you're dead, it's also easy to forget once you do recognize. Again, look at your dreams. How stable is your mind in a dream? Even if you recognize it, how long can you remember to stay lucid? This is one reason *The Tibetan Book of the Dead* is meant to be read continuously for forty-nine days. We don't know where the dead person is on their journey. Even if they hear the reading, they tend to forget. For forty-nine days we remind them. It's as if we are practicing mindfulness for them.

There are signs to look for to verify that you are dead: (1) you cast no shadow; (2) you look into a mirror, or other reflecting surface, and see no reflection; (3) you walk on sand or snow and leave no footprints; (4) your body makes no sound; (5) people don't respond to you; (6) you can move unimpeded through matter; (7) you manifest miraculous power, such as the ability to fly, read minds, or travel very quickly; (8) you cannot see the sun or moon.[16] These are also some of the same indicators that help you recognize that you're in a dream. So to practice recognizing that you're dreaming or dead, look for these signs now. Create the habit of checking for these signs, and that habit will carry over into dream and death. Remind yourself to look for your shadow, or to check for a reflection. This practice also helps you flash on impermanence. Am I dead, dreaming, or alive and awake right now? How do you know for sure?

Once you realize you are dead, the impact can be stunning. *The Tibetan Book of the Dead* says, "[Y]ou will see your home and family as though you were meeting them in a dream, but although you speak to them you will get no reply; and you will see your relatives and friends weeping, so you will think, 'I am dead, what shall I do?' and you will feel intense pain like the pain of a fish rolling in hot sand."[17] Dzigar Kongtrul Rinpoche says, "Bardo beings often don't know they are dead. They will test themselves, by jumping into a fire to see if they get burned, or jumping off a cliff to see if they get hurt. When they are not burned, and not hurt, they suddenly realize they are dead, and this comes as a great shock."[18]

Even though experiences in the bardo are dictated by the projections of your own mind, you may encounter other bardo beings having similar experiences. You are all reaping the effects of similar karma. *The Tibetan Book of the Dead* says, "[T]hose who are going to be born with the same nature will see one another in the bardo state, so those who are going to be born as gods see each other. In the same way, whichever of the six realms they are going to be born in, those of the same nature will see each other."[19] Your experience while alive is also dictated by the projections of your mind, but you still share many of these experiences with others.[20]

Once you realize you're dead, then apply the instructions you've been given during life. Recognize that whatever appears is a projection of your own mind, just as it is in a dream. If you do generation stage practice, or are proficient in dream yoga, then transform your bardo body into the body of your chosen deity. For Vajrayana practitioners, generation stage practice is the primary method for transforming the bardo of becoming. This is because generation stage meditation is designed to purify birth, whether it's the birth of a thought or the birth of an entire life. At this stage in the bardo of *becoming*, or generation, you are about to generate an entire life. Generation stage practice shows you how to generate the best possible life.

If you're not a Vajrayana practitioner, or are unable to apply your generation stage practice, then direct your mind toward a pure land (more on this below). For most of us, this is the best thing we can do in the bardo. Tulku Thondup Rinpoche offers the following advice:

> ► Realize that you are at the most crucial juncture of your life. For the sake of your future, you cannot waste a moment. This is your greatest opportunity to advance.

> ► Remember and feel happy about whatever spiritual path you have pursued in your lifetime. That will be the great source of peace, joy, and strength for you.

> ► Remember any one of the following three practices, according to your ability and experience. Then try to stay with that practice without distraction.[21]

Here is a summary of these three practices:

First, perceive everything in the bardo as sacred, and realize it's all the play of your mind. Cultivate devotion to the buddhas, your gurus, and your meditation. Don't grasp or struggle. Open to whatever arises, and become one with it. Relax into the innate purity and goodness of whatever you see.

Second, calm and stabilize your mind. Remember any form of spiritual support, be it a teacher, a divine presence, or a positive experience. Keep your mind on this support without distraction. Rely on the confidence you have developed with your meditations. Sakyong Mipham Rinpoche says that confidence actually *becomes* your body in the bardo, a body you have strengthened with the exercise of meditation. Remember that everything is exaggerated in the bardo. This means that hesitation, the opposite of confidence, can flap you around like a flag in the wind.

Feel compassion for other beings you may encounter, and recite any prayers or mantras you remember. Help those you encounter in the bardo. Activate the force of your positive karma, and sustain positive states of mind. A single constructive thought, like thinking of Buddha Amitabha and Sukhavati, can project you into his pure land.

Third, don't be angry or afraid. See everything as illusory, like a dream. Avoid negative states of mind, for a single negative thought can project you into a lower realm. Pray to whatever divine presence you have a connection with, and ask for blessings and guidance. Keep your mind open, positive, stable, and peaceful. Don't be swayed by anything—hold your seat. Relate to everything with equanimity.

Now we can see why the preparatory practices, like those outlined in chapter 1, are so important. The momentum of these practices will automatically kick in during this bardo and take care of us. By practicing now we are using the power of karma, or habit, in a constructive way.

We spend so much effort investing in our future. We invest in IRAs, 401(k)s, pension plans, and retirement portfolios. Spiritual advisors exhort us to invest in our much more important bardo retirement plan. That's our real future. Don't worry so much about social security. Finance your karmic security. Invest in your future lives now. Investing so much in this life is like checking into a hotel for a few days and redecorating the room. What's the point? B. Alan Wallace says, "In light of death, our mundane desires are seen for what they are. If our desires for wealth, luxury, good food, praise, reputation, affection, and acceptance by other people and so forth are worth nothing in the face of death, then that is precisely their ultimate value."[22] And Sogyal Rinpoche adds, "Why, if we are as pragmatic as we claim, don't we begin to ask ourselves seriously: Where does our *real* future lie? After all, very few of us live longer than a hundred years. And after that there stretches the whole of eternity, unaccounted for . . . ."[23]

Because the mind is no longer restricted by the body, it's sharper and more powerful.[24] This means that both positive and negative experiences are heightened. But without a body, the mind is flighty. It's therefore harder to initiate new states of mind or to cultivate new habits. We need to rely on the good habits we bring with us. Tulku Thondup Rinpoche summarizes:

> In this life, our mind is relatively stable because it is anchored in this gross and earthly physical structure. This makes it easier to gain spiritual views and habits through meditation. But it is also harder to make big changes or improvements, precisely because the mind is trapped and programmed in the system of our rigid, earthly body. In the transitional journey of the bardo, however, the mind is rapidly changing without any structural restriction. It is therefore easier to change or improve our future journey. But it is also much harder to find a path and focus on it, since there is no anchoring faculty of a physical body. Our bodiless mind lives on with its past habits and floats rapidly without break at high speed toward its future destiny.[25]

OTHER PRACTICES

Many masters proclaim that the best practice to do in the bardo of becoming, and the best preparation for it, is to recite the mantra OM MANI PADME HUM, which blocks the doors to the six realms of samsara. The other mantra to recite is that of Amitabha, OM AMIDEWA HRIH, which opens the door to rebirth into Sukhavati.[26]

Keep your gaze up in this bardo, which predisposes you toward rebirth into a higher realm (remember that keeping your gaze up, literally looking up, facilitates phowa). Conversely, avoid looking down, which directs you to a lower realm (most animals are always looking down). Looking straight ahead directs you toward the human realm.

Think about what is happening. Don't make impulsive moves that can land you in karmically irreversible situations. Because you're becoming more desperate for a place of refuge, some body you can identify with, it gets more difficult to control yourself the further you progress into this bardo. Panic leads to bad choices. A general rule is to slow down. Don't let the winds throw you around. Take control over what's happening by taking control of your mind.

In the bardo of becoming we're like molten iron. With proper guidance, we can pour our formless awareness into any form and *become* anything we want. But once we decide to take on a form, or our karma decides for us, the molten iron cools and solidifies into our next life. At that point we're stuck. We're a karmic stiff once again. Now we have to wait until that form melts during our next death before we can become anything else.

If everything fails, Chökyi Nyima Rinpoche instructs us to cry out to our teacher, which is a natural thing to do:

> I have no power to choose, so please bestow your blessings that I may be born in a situation where I can connect with the teachings, receive the oral instructions, and quickly progress along the paths and stages toward enlightenment. Please make sure that I am not born as an ordinary person [without access to teachings], let me attain a precious human body.[27]

ADVICE FROM *THE TIBETAN BOOK OF THE DEAD*

Half of *The Tibetan Book of the Dead* is devoted to guidance for the bardo of becoming. Since the advice from other books is often taken from this central source, here are the primary "what to do" and "what not to do" instructions from this text. The instructions are summarized in the main verse for this bardo:

> Now when the bardo of becoming dawns upon me,
> I will concentrate my mind one-pointedly,
> and strive to prolong the results of good karma,
> close the womb-entrance and think of resistance;
> this is the time when perseverance and pure thought are needed,
> abandon jealousy, and meditate on the guru with his consort.[28]

The condensed instructions from the entire *Tibetan Book of the Dead:*

- ► Visualize your yidam or guru above your head and supplicate with intense devotion.[29]
- ► Cut off yearning for a body and rest in nonaction, undistracted.
- ► Supplicate the three jewels.
- ► Do not lie in front of Yama.[30]
- ► Do not be afraid.
- ► Meditate on mahamudra. If you can't, look closely at the nature of what makes you afraid.
- ► Remember your secret name (if you have one).[31]
- ► Do not create any feeling of passion or aggression.
- ► Give up attachments and yearning for your possessions—offer them to the three jewels.
- ► Look upon everything with pure thoughts, i.e., don't let any *kleshas* (conflicting emotions) arise.
- ► Whatever you concentrate on will come about, so do not think of evil actions, but remember the dharma, the teachings, the transmissions.
- ► Now you must concentrate your mind one-pointedly without distraction; one-pointed concentration is the most important thing.
- ► Strive to prolong the results of good karma. This is very important. Do not forget, do not be distracted. Now is the time which is the dividing-line between going up and going down.
- ► If you have no practice, feel devotion and have pure thoughts.
- ► Whatever light shines, meditate on that as the Lord of Great Compassion (Chenrezig). "This is the most profound essential point, it is extremely important and prevents birth."

▸ *Do not be distracted:* "Now is the time when by slipping into laziness even for a moment you will suffer forever; now is the time when by concentrating one-pointedly you will be happy forever."

▸ Do not enter between the couples making love. Meditate on them as the guru and consort; mentally prostrate and make offerings to them and ask for teachings.

▸ See everything as unreal and illusory:

> [I] believed the nonexistent to exist, the untrue to be true, the illusion to be real; therefore I have wandered in samsara for so long. And if I do not realize that they are illusions, I shall still wander in samsara for a long time and certainly fall into the muddy swamp of suffering. Now they are all like dreams, like illusions, like echoes, like cities of *gandharvas* [celestial musicians], like mirages, like images, like optical illusions, like the moon in water; they are not real, even for a moment. . . . By concentrating one-pointedly on this conviction, belief in their reality is destroyed, and when one is inwardly convinced in such a way, belief in a self is counteracted. If you understand unreality like this from the bottom of your heart, the womb-entrance will certainly be closed.[32]

Once again, don't feel that you have to do everything on this list. These are options we can draw upon in the bardos, any one of which has the power to liberate us.

Blocking

The final two instructions for this bardo, the last resort before taking birth, is blocking the entrance to an unfortunate birth and choosing a fortunate one. These are the instructions on how to take *conscious* birth. This isn't easy, because the wind is picking up. Thrangu Rinpoche says:

> What is going on at this point is that, through the force of very powerful karma, you are being impelled or propelled into a state of such agitation that you will be extremely tempted to take rebirth in the first place of birth you perceive. If you just go along with the flow or impulse of your karma, then you are apt to take birth mistakenly in extremely unfortunate circumstances. But if

you can hold back with mindfulness and alertness and be very careful, then you can choose a fortunate rebirth. At this point you have become extremely agitated and if you give in to the agitation and the panic, then you will have no control whatsoever over your subsequent birth. Therefore, you have to be very careful here.[33]

The Tibetan Book of the Dead offers five ways to block the entrance into a womb. These instructions deliver the same message in five different ways: do not fall under the influence of passion or aggression, and do not make a bad decision. Francesca Fremantle says, "Closing the womb door really means cutting off the mental conditions required for entering a womb by transforming our perception and attitude toward it."[34]

By blocking the doors to samsara we may find ourselves in nirvana. The central instruction in blocking the womb door to samsara is to accept whatever arises with equanimity. That opens the door to nirvana. That *is* nirvana.

The five instructions are, first, when you see your future parents in sexual union, do not enter between them. Meditate on them as being your spiritual teacher in union with his or her spiritual spouse. Be devoted to them and request teachings.

Second, if that doesn't work, and you find yourself being drawn nearer to them, meditate on your future parents as your meditation deity. If you don't have one, then see them as Chenrezig in union with his consort. This is also why it's helpful to work with the energy of passion ahead of time. This allows us to relate *to* the passion instead of *from* it.

Third, if that doesn't work and you are still being drawn in, now is the time to "turn away from passion and aggression." This is when *The Tibetan Book of the Dead* says that if you are going to be reborn as a male you will be attracted to your mother and have aversion toward your father. Conversely, if you are going to be reborn as a female you will feel passion toward your father and aggression toward your mother.[35] Don't act on this attraction or aversion.

Fourth, if you still find yourself being drawn in, see your parents as the illusory forms they really are. This will stop you from entering between them. How can you harbor passion or aggression for an illusion? "By knowing from the depths of your heart that all these [phenomena] are unreal, the womb entrance will certainly be obstructed."[36] Sogyal Rinpoche says, "Ultimately it is the mind's urge to inhabit a particular realm that impels us toward reincarnation, and its tendency to solidify and to grasp that finds its ultimate expression in physical rebirth."[37]

Fifth, if that doesn't work and you're still being sucked in, the final instruction is to rest in the nature of mind. Ponlop Rinpoche says, "Essentially, the entrance into another samsaric birth is stopped when we can connect with the true nature of mind and the empty, luminous nature of appearances."[38]

We can use these instructions now to prevent rebirth in unfortunate emotional states. This practice also prepares us for this stage of the bardo. For example, if you're in a situation and feel anger building up, don't give in to the urge to take rebirth in that hellish state of mind. Practice equanimity. Slow down, observe what's happening, and say to yourself, "I don't want to go there. I don't need to be reborn into a state of anger." This is what it means when *The Tibetan Book of the Dead* says, "Close the womb-entrance and think of resistance; this is the time when perseverance and pure thought are needed."[39]

Control your mind now, and block the womb door to anger by staying centered. This is exercised in sitting meditation. When we sit and label our thoughts "thinking," we're saying, "I don't want to go there." We're blocking the womb entrance to habitual pattern, to discursive thought and fantasy, and choosing to stay in the moment. We're stopping the flow of our mind from cutting deeper habitual grooves. The itch to act out in lust or anger is the same itch that eventually traps us into an entire life. Tenga Rinpoche said, "Bodhisattvas control their thoughts and therefore control their rebirths."

There are two principal blocking mantras. These are six-syllable mantras that close the door to the six realms: OM MANI PADME HUM, which we have already discussed, and A A HA SHA SA MA. The second mantra comes from the dzogchen tantras and is associated with *The Tibetan Book of the Dead*. Each syllable of the first mantra is associated with purifying one of the six principal negative emotions: passion, aggression, ignorance, jealousy, pride, and greed. This is a mantra of equanimity. By purifying these six states of mind we block rebirth into their corresponding six states of samsaric existence. As *The Tibetan Book of the Dead* says, "When the sound of dharmata roars like a thousand thunders, may it all become the sound of the six syllables [OM MANI PADME HUM]." May it roar with the thunder of equanimity.

In the bardo of becoming, there is a point where we will come upon three deep chasms. Unless we practice equanimity, we will fall into them. *The Tibetan Book of the Dead* says, "[Y]ou will be cut off by three precipices in front of you, white, red and black, deep and dreadful, and you will be on the point of falling down them. 'O [child] of noble family, they are not really precipices, they are aggression, passion, and ignorance.'"[40] We are meeting the three deepest grooves we have cut during life. The tendency to slip into them yet again, and therefore back into samsara, is overwhelming.

Habits cut grooves into the landscape of our lives, and then "force" us to fall into repetitive forms of behavior. In the bardos, we reap the results of all our digging. Every time we react with passion, aggression, or ignorance, we're digging ourselves into deeper and deeper ruts. No wonder it's so hard to climb out of samsara. Passion is present if you want something to keep happening; aversion is present if you want something to stop happening; and ignorance is present if you're not in touch with what's happening. This unholy trinity describes how we relate to virtually every moment—and therefore how we generate virtually every life.

Bright and Soft Lights

As we progress into the bardo of becoming, chasms are replaced by lights. Both images represent the power of habit, or karma, to seduce us. About halfway into the bardo of becoming, six soft and dull lights will appear. These are the soft lights of samsara that signal the approach of our rebirth into one of the six realms. They are more seductive than the bright lights of nirvana that we faced in the bardo of dharmata.

The softer the light the greater the seduction. And the softer the light the lower the realm associated with that light. In other words, the smoky light of the hell realm is softer and more seductive then the white light of the god realm. The light of the realm into which you will be reborn will shine the most for you, and you will be drawn toward it. In Shambhala Buddhism, the bright lights are the rays of the Great Eastern Sun, and the soft lights are the hazy rays of the setting sun. More people are seduced into watching muted sunsets than they are the glaring sunrise, so the softer lights invite us in.

In life, the bright lights symbolize the sometimes harsh truth of reality. Reality is often hard to accept. It's too bright. Instead of facing situations directly, we tend to look away into the softer lights of habitual pattern, comfort, and deception. Our preference for comfort over truth then seduces us into a particular, and often lower realm, response. This draws us into rebirth into a lower state of consciousness. Whenever we tell a white lie, we're feeling the seduction of the soft lights. By staying with the energy of a situation or emotion, which means not acting it out or suppressing it, we're practicing how to stay with the bright light. If we lose it emotionally, that's straying into the soft lights and taking birth in unfortunate emotional realms.

In the bardos, a dull white light represents the realm of the gods; dull red light represents the realm of the jealous gods; dull blue light the human realm; dull green light the animal realm; dull yellow light the hungry ghosts; and dull smoky light the realm of hell. Your bardo body may begin to take on the color of the realm into which you will be reborn. Even at this point, it's possible for these lights to appear as the five wisdom lights. A basic tenet of the Vajrayana is that wisdom can be found anywhere and any time. If we can tap into the *essence* of whatever arises, and not get swept up in the *display*, we free ourselves from the display. That's how to find wisdom in confusion, and instant liberation.

Because of our habitual tendency of taking things to be solid, it's difficult to realize that the six realms are essentially psychological states. These realms are not created by a supreme being. They are created by the individual and collective karma of the beings that inhabit that realm. We are the creator of these states as well as their experiencer—just as in a dream.

What is even harder to realize is that this process of projection and reification is taking place right now. We are currently in the human realm, a state of mind that has been frozen into a state of reality. As in life, so in death. Psychology leads to ontology.[41]

A key instruction for blocking the entrance into a womb is to view whatever light arises as being the deity Chenrezig. "This is the most profound crucial point. It is extremely important, because [this oral instruction] obstructs birth."[42] An alternative is to see the light as your meditation deity (yidam). The idea is to generate pure perception and transform the dull lights (samsara) into nirvana. Your mind is about to become your physical reality. If you can maintain pure perception, you will be reborn into a pure land. If you can't, your impure (reactive) mind will naturally lead into an impure realm. *The Tibetan Book of the Dead* emphasizes that this is when perseverance and purity of perception are critical.

Choosing

Look forward in the bardo. Never look back. This, again, is why it's so helpful to know what you can look forward to. In the Bible, when Lot's wife didn't follow the instructions and looked back, she turned into a pillar of salt. We may not turn into a pillar of salt in the bardo, but if we keep looking back we will probably turn into something we don't want.

The dull lights represent looking back—to the old, comfortable, and familiar. The bright lights represent looking forward—to the new, possibly uncomfortable, and unfamiliar. Tulku Thondup advises: "While you are wandering in the bardo, you must not think about your loved ones and your possessions back home, as these thoughts will only divert you away from your right path. You must focus your mind on your chosen birthplace."[43]

The bright lights also represent pure appearance in the bardos. This is what to choose. Thrangu Rinpoche:

> The brilliant light paths are the paths to the pure realms and the dull but familiar light paths are the paths back into samsara. The way you prepare yourself for this—and this is extremely important—is to lessen your attachment to the familiar world of impure appearances, which will be experienced as the dull light paths in the bardo, and to increase your familiarity and enthusiasm for pure appearances in general and yidam deities in particular, which will be experienced as brilliant light paths in the bardo.[44]

The instructions of blocking and choosing are the last chance to block our habitual urge to grasp. In this case the grasping is after existence itself. If we're forced to take form, due to the power of habit, at least we can choose the best possible form into which we pour our awareness.

Blocking the womb door is about what to reject. Choosing the womb door is about what to accept. We can't stay in the bardos forever. Eventually our karma will force us to take rebirth. The last thing we can do is choose the best rebirth, which in order of desirability would be: (1) into a pure land, (2) into the human realm, and (3) into the god realm.[45]

Rebirth into the pure land of Sukhavati is through the methods introduced earlier. Late in the bardo, the most important thing is to concentrate intensely on Amitabha. Maintain a deep longing to go to Sukhavati, and recite the mantra OM AMIDEWA HRIH. Francesca Fremantle says, "As soon as we think of our chosen pure land with complete faith, we shall instantly find ourselves there."[46]

If this doesn't work and we're still wandering in the bardos, we will perceive a variety of different scenarios. *The Tibetan Book of the Dead* says, "O [child] of noble family, now the signs and characteristics of the continent where you are going to be born will appear, so recognize them. Examine where you are going to be born and choose the continent."[47] These mindscapes will soon transform into landscapes—unless we catch on to what's happening and take appropriate action.

The Tibetan Book of the Dead describes the features of the six realms in detail. This helps us learn what to accept and what to reject.[48] To keep it simple and to avoid confusion, I will only describe where we should go—in other words, what to accept. When the karmic winds are howling, we need to keep things clear and easy.[49]

To take rebirth as a human, go toward visions of "grand and delightful mansions," or "luxurious beautiful dwellings."[50] Tsele Natsok Rangdrol says, "one will attain a precious human body if one has the experience of arriving in a mansion or city or among many people."[51] Tulku Thondup says, "When headed for the human realm we may perceive ourselves to be in the midst of many people. Or instead we might feel that we are approaching a lake with swans, horses, or cows, or entering a house, city, or crowd.... Aimlessly chattering people or houses that are ordinary, precious, or pleasant are [also] signs of a precious human birth."[52] And Ponlop Rinpoche says:

> If you seem to be entering a mist or you see a city with nice houses, that indicates rebirth in the southern continent [where you want to go]. The mist is said to indicate simply a human rebirth, while a city with nice houses indicates a "precious human birth," one that will provide the opportunity to practice the dharma. Then you will see a man and woman engaged in sexual intercourse. If you continue to follow this course, you will enter the womb of the female and this couple will become your parents.[53]

If you don't do that, then if you are to be reborn as a god, you will find yourself going toward "delightful celestial palaces, many-storied and composed of diverse jewels," or "beautiful many-storied temples made of various jewels."[54] Even more fundamental than these visions are the lights that are the foundation for them. Choose the blue light to be born in a human realm; choose the white light for the god realm. *The Tibetan Book of the Dead* offers haunting images about why it's important to know where to go in the bardo, and the intensity that builds the further you go into it:

O Child of Buddha Nature, although you do not wish to move forward, you are powerless not to do so. The avenging forces, who are the executors of the unfailing laws of cause and effect, will be pursuing you.[55] You will have no choice but to move forward. Before you, the avengers and executors will be leading the way. The experience will arise of trying to flee from these forces, of trying to flee from the darkness, from the most violent windstorms, from the [thunderous] tumult, the snow, the rain, the hail and the turbulent blizzards which swirl around you. [Frightened], you will set off to seek a refuge and you will find protection inside an enclosed space . . . or in rock-shelters, or holes in the ground, or amongst trees, or within the bud of a lotus flower. Hiding here, you will be very hesitant to come out, and you will think: 'I should not leave here now.' You will be very reluctant to be separated from this protected place and you will become utterly attached to it. Then, because you are so very hesitant to go outside, where you would be confronted by the fears and terrors of the intermediate state, you will, because of this fear and awe, continue to hide away. Thus, you will assume a body, however utterly bad that may be, and you will, [in time], come to experience all manner of sufferings.[56]

Remember your meditation deity. See the deity in a large and threatening form that "pulverizes every form of obstructing force." Protection from pursuing karma gives you the time you need to choose the proper womb.[57] It provides refuge from the overwhelming fear. You can safely pause, reflect on what's happening, and take appropriate action. Instead of being reactive and making bad choices based on fear, be proactive and make good ones based on wisdom. Your next life depends on it.

There are final warnings about making mistakes: don't mistake a good womb that's actually bad; don't mistake a bad womb that's actually good. The remedy is to remember the illusory nature of whatever appears. *The Tibetan Book of the Dead* says, "The essential point of the profound and genuine [instructions] is that you enter the womb in a state of great equanimity, utterly free from [the dichotomies of] good and bad, acceptance and rejection, or attachment or aversion."[58] It's the combination of the conflicting emotions of passion and aggression that finally propels you into the womb. Our lack of equanimity gives birth to samsara, moment-to-moment or life-to-life.

As you make the final approach into the womb, focus your motivation on taking birth for the benefit of others. Consecrate the womb by seeing it as a celestial palace of deities. Fill your heart with devotion.[59] This prevents you from entering the next life with a negative state of mind. The point is to give shape to wisdom, not to confusion. Khenpo Karthar summarizes:

> [T]hrough the force of love and compassion, and through the force of your aspirations for appropriate rebirth, you are able to stop inferior or inappropriate birth and choose a birth through which you can continue the path and be of benefit to others. . . . You can choose your family, as well as your gender, race, country, social circumstances, and so on—whatever you want and decide is going to be the best. . . . The point here is that you have gained the power of choice, and in order to employ this effectively you need to apply the faculties of mindfulness and alertness.[60]

You have gained the power of choice because of your preparation. Just as with blocking, practice choosing the best womb door now. Pause before you speak or act, and say to yourself, "If I react with aggression, this will create a hellish state of mind. If I respond with equanimity, this will generate a pure state of mind." Practice conscious reincarnation now. Remember that bodhisattvas control their thoughts and reactions, and that's how they control their rebirths.

"Insomnia yoga" is a good equanimity practice. This isn't the same as dream yoga, but it's a way to use sleeplessness as a preparation for death. When you wake up and can't go back to sleep, transform your sleeplessness into meditation. Witness your speedy mind without getting sucked into it. This is similar to the reverse meditation of generating as many thoughts as possible. Notice the temptation to flesh out some thoughts and images, but don't go there. Let whatever arises melt into space, like a campfire spark dissolving into the night sky.

All these instructions aren't meant to overwhelm us now or in the bardo. As Francesca Fremantle says, the bardo teachings are

> pointing out the multitude of possibilities continually present all around us as potential gateways to awakening. In life, just as in the after-death state, not all opportunities are available to everybody, and we are not always able to respond to them. . . . the point

of giving all [these details] is to make sense of the bewildering experience the dead person goes through, to provide some kind of map for this journey into unknown territory, where we are driven by karma toward the ripening of the seeds we have sown.[61]

Tulku Thondup offers this summary advice:

- ► Don't forget that you are in the bardo, the transitional passage.
- ► Remember to walk keeping your head pointing upward.
- ► Pray by continuously saying the names of the buddhas. Take refuge in them.
- ► Take refuge in the Three Jewels—the Buddha, the Dharma, and the Sangha.
- ► Pray to the Compassionate Ones, such as the Buddha of Infinite Light [Amitabha] and your own spiritual masters.
- ► Let go of attachments to your loved ones and possessions, as they will only divert you from your right path.
- ► Enter the path of the blue light of the human realm or the white light of the god realm.[62]

The summary instruction for what to do for yourself after death: relax, and recognize that it's all the play of your mind. Don't react to what's happening; practice equanimity. Think of your teacher, Amitabha, or Sukhavati with intense longing. Go toward the blue or white light.

6. What to Do for Others After They Die

Seeing into darkness is clarity.
Knowing how to yield is strength.
Use your own light
and return to the source of light.
This is called practicing eternity.
—Lao-tzu

The View

PEOPLE OFTEN FEEL helpless after someone has died, thinking there is nothing they can do to help. But this is actually the time when we can do the most, and when our help is needed the most. Unless the dead person is prepared, they're probably stumbling through bewildering terrain, buffeted by the storms of karma, facing the projections of their own mind, and feeling confused, alone, and afraid.

The bardo texts don't offer much consolation for those unprepared. Perhaps this is to inspire us to become prepared or to instill the wholesome fear of karma. Most people after death are as vulnerable as they were after birth. They need the same level of help. This is when those left behind should take advantage of the full force of Buddhist post-death practices.

As we have seen, when the mind is no longer restricted by the body, it becomes much clearer. It also possesses temporary psychic powers, including the powers of clairvoyance and clairaudience.[1] Dzongsar Khyentse Rinpoche says, "Bardo beings have very refined minds ... so the practice you do in the bardo will be much more beneficial, more powerful."[2] These powers can be used to benefit the bardo being. We can invite it into our mind space and then guide it.

When the mind is anchored by the body during life, it can be hard to get things moving. Spiritual progress takes time. But when the mind is set free in the bardo, rapid spiritual progress is possible. It's like taking a huge tree stump, which even a dozen people can't budge on land, and putting it in water. In this fluid new environment it's easy to move and guide.

The Tibetan Book of the Dead talks about why we should help, and the abilities of the dead person to respond. The book asserts that "it is impossible not to be liberated by these [instructions]":

> This is because: first, consciousness in the intermediate state is endowed with an, albeit corrupt, supernormal cognitive ability. Therefore, whatever one says [to the deceased] is heard by the deceased. Second, even if the deceased was deaf or blind [while in the human world], now [in the intermediate state], all the sensory faculties will be complete and therefore whatever is said will be apprehended. Third, since the deceased is continuously being overwhelmed by fear and terror, there is an undistracted concentration on what to do; therefore, what is said will be listened to. Fourth, since the consciousness has no [physical] support, it is easy to guide and it can penetrate to the essence of whatever is focused upon. [Additionally], since the power of retention is now many times clearer,[3] even the mentally weak will have, in the intermediate state, a lucid awareness, by virtue of their past actions. Hence, they will have the gift of knowing how to meditate on that which is taught and the gift [to assimilate] such points [of instruction]. These are the reasons why the performance of rituals on behalf of the dead is beneficial.[4]

This is all possible because karma is temporarily suspended. If we're prepared or properly guided, we can shape our mind into any imaginable form. This is why the bardo of becoming is also called the bardo of possibility or opportunity. As one close to the deceased, we can effectively guide the consciousness into this new form. Their next life can be shaped by what we do now.

The fluidity of the mental body is both a blessing and a curse. It's a curse in that the bardo being is highly unstable. With nothing to secure it, the mental body flickers about like a candle flame in the breeze.[5] And without a physical body, the bardo being can't retain new information as well. This is why instructions have to be continuously repeated.

But the blessing is that this fluidity allows those left behind to guide, and even forcefully move, the bardo being in the direction of a good rebirth.[6] We can direct the karmic gusts to blow in the right direction. This is especially true for those who have the strongest karmic connection to the dead person. The bardo being will be naturally drawn to you, so you are in a good position to help.

Because of the temporary psychic powers, bardo beings can see and hear you when you call out to them. They can also read your mind. If you're holding them with loving thoughts, that will settle their mind. Positive states of mind are contagious and can become states of reality for them, delivering them into the higher realms.

Conversely, if you're harboring hurtful thoughts, that can unsettle the bardo being and create negative states of mind. This could deliver them into lower realms. Here is an inner application of the power of "holding environments" discussed earlier. The first way to help them, therefore, is to hold them in your heart with love. Whenever you think of them, automatically add the mantra OM MANI PADME HUM, which frames your memories with meditation. In the bardo of dying we want to create the feeling of a warm physical hug. In the bardo of becoming we want to sustain that hug spiritually.

Some teachers say that we should try not to cry, but rather rejoice in a life well lived. If we can do this without placing undue pressure on ourselves, that can help the dying person let go. But the loss of a loved one is perhaps the most painful experience in life. The added pressure of conducting the perfect post-death emotional response can further add to our heartbreak. We should try to place their needs ahead of our own, but we should also remember that if we don't care for ourselves we won't be able to care for them.

Death is not an emergency. There's no need to rush and call anybody official. When my father passed on a Monday evening, I didn't contact hospice until the following morning. I didn't call the funeral home to pick up the body till Tuesday afternoon. That gave me eighteen hours to practice with him. It also allowed family and friends to be with him in an intimate setting. Even though he died without pain, his breathing had been labored, which was hard for the family to witness. Seeing him lying in repose put them at ease, softening the difficult memories of his final hours. Every family member who expressed doubts about keeping the body for so long said that sitting with him after he died changed that view. They felt grateful for the opportunity to be with him.

WHEN TO HELP

It's especially important to help those who have passed during the first three and a half weeks after death. This is when the bardo being is still in the shape of a mental body similar to its previous physical body and is lingering around familiar people and places. Due to habitual patterns, we continue to see ourselves the way we were. Consciousness comes into the bardos wearing its old habits, which literally shape the mental body.

As we progress through the bardo, some teachers say the mental body slowly morphs into the shape of the body it will fully become in the next life. Old habitual patterns fade and new ones take shape. Therefore the second three and a half weeks, or the second half of the bardo experience if the bardo being doesn't stay for the full seven weeks, is when the bardo being turns toward its next life. Karma takes control and locks the being into its next incarnation.

We should concentrate our efforts to help the deceased every week on the day that they died—in other words, on the seventh, fourteenth, and twenty-first days after death. This is because the dying experience is repeated every seven days. It's not a repeat of the dying process, since the physical body is already gone and the dissolutions cannot take place. Kalu Rinpoche explains,

> At the end of each week there is the trauma of realizing that we are dead and our minds plunge into another state of unconsciousness like the one immediately after death, but not quite as intense. After each of these very short periods of unconsciousness, consciousness returns, and once more the mandalas of the deities present themselves, but now in a fragmentary and fleeting way. The successive opportunities afforded by these appearances are not as great as at the first stage, but the possibility for Liberation does recur throughout the after-death experience.[7]

These are the days to focus on the rituals described below.[8] Jamgön Kongtrul writes:

> If the being is unable to begin the birth process within those first seven days, it undergoes a minor death, which is like fainting for a short time, and again is born in the intermediate state. It may

then begin the birth process within the [next] seven-day period. If even within that period, it still does not meet with the number of factors necessary for taking birth, it will inevitably [begin the process of] taking birth within forty-nine days [from the time of death].[9]

For example, if a person died on Sunday before noon, the first focus day would be on the next Saturday. If they died after noon, it would fall on the next Sunday. The fourth week after death is considered particularly important, because many beings don't stay in the bardo longer than four weeks. Forty-nine days is generally the longest one spends in the bardo, so rituals are often done then.[10] One year after death is another potent time to reach out.

In addition to the time of death, there's also a connection to the place of death. This is especially true if the death was traumatic. It's best if we can do our practices at that location, and on these special times. But if we can't, don't worry about missing the ideal situation. The ideal situation is our heartfelt motivation to help.

While these are special times to help, it's never too late. Space and time do not limit the power of compassion and the force of merit. Even after the bardo being has been reborn, merit dedicated to them still helps. Finally, your efforts to help the dead, especially if you have a strong karmic connection, can be as effective as that of a spiritual master. It's not just the spiritually elite that can benefit the dead.

Until the heart center cools, or some blood comes out of the mouth or nose (signaling that the red bindu has ascended and released the consciousness), don't touch the lower parts of the body. Wait until the dying process is complete so that consciousness isn't directed out of a lower exit. Direct your attention and contact to the top of the head. Remember that it takes about twenty minutes for the inner dissolution to occur. If the dead person is an organ donor, the generosity of offering their body supersedes these instructions. Organ harvesting should begin immediately.

For a few days after death, don't disturb any of the dead person's possessions. Their consciousness may be attracted to these items, and messing with their things could upset them. Although consciousness has left the body, the body still remains the main karmic link to this past life. The bardo being often hovers around it. Treat the body with reverence and respect. Bathe it, bless it, and tend to it with care.

The following sections offer rituals and meditations that benefit the dead. These practices also benefit those left behind. They help us say goodbye and give us the feeling that we're doing something to help. The Tibetan tradition is fabulously rich in things we can do. Some of these rituals are esoteric, even for students of Tibetan Buddhism. But they have been practiced for hundreds of years by the most realized beings on this planet. These are not empty rituals for social purposes. These are heart-practices of a wisdom tradition designed to benefit those in need. We would do well to surrender to this wisdom and trust in its methods. We will start with the simple practices then progress into more esoteric methods.

THE POWER OF MERIT

One of the most effective things we can do to help the dead is to gather and dedicate merit to them. Merit is the cosmic currency of Buddhism.[11] It's something we gather to benefit ourselves, and it's something we can transfer to benefit others. It's literally the stuff the world is made of. Learning about merit can strengthen our desire to gather and dedicate it.[12]

The Indian master Nagarjuna said, "By generating the thought of enlightenment for the benefit of all beings, a mass of merit is collected. If this merit took form, it would more than fill the expanse of space."[13] Buddhist scholar Luis Gómez writes: "The power of good deeds can be harnessed, directed, and transformed, so that through good deeds one becomes capable of affecting the life of others and even capable of working wonders. Good deeds can effect changes in reality; merit can produce wondrous deeds and events."[14]

In the Pure Land tradition, the power of merit literally creates world systems. Sukhavati was created by the oceans of merit dedicated by Amitabha in his previous lives. It's also the transfer of this merit from Amitabha's "account" into our own that helps us enter Sukhavati. According to the Kalachakra Tantra, it's collective karma (merit is a form of good karma) that transforms into world systems. These worlds then serve to contain the beings who generated that karma and who will now experience its fruits.

The cosmology of merit may be difficult to grasp, but the practice of collecting and dedicating it is easily understood.[15] Merit is gathered by performing good deeds. Delivering that merit to others is accomplished by dedicating it properly, which means doing so with conviction and loving motivation. If you just mouth the words, some benefit might trickle. If you really mean it, great benefit pours forth.

To transfer merit properly, do a good deed with the person you want to dedicate it to in mind. Perform the deed with them in mind, and then dedicate it to them when the deed is done. This can be as simple as saying: "I dedicate the merit of this action to all sentient beings, and especially to [insert their name]. May it bring them benefit and solace. May it guide them into the best possible rebirth."

The dying or dead person also gathers merit by being the cause for the helper's motivation to generate the merit. It's particularly helpful to perform dharmic deeds, because dharmic activity is considered the most valuable. Dharma is also the highest form of generosity. You can dedicate your spiritual practice, sponsor translation projects, send money to a dharma center, or sponsor someone in retreat. You can donate to the construction of a spiritual project, like a stupa, monastery, or shedra (monastic college). Vajrayana practitioners can perform or sponsor a feast (tsok) in the name of the deceased. A "saving of lives" practice is especially helpful. This involves rescuing animals that would otherwise die; for example, buying and releasing worms from a bait shop.

In Buddhist countries, butter lamps are frequently offered after someone has died, sometimes numbering over a hundred thousand. This is an offering of light, a symbol of wisdom, which is what a bardo being needs on their journey into darkness (confusion).[16]

You can give the possessions of the dead person to Goodwill (waiting a few days after they died to do so), contribute in their name to humanitarian projects like hospice, orphanages, or hospitals. You can give to a charity, volunteer for a worthy cause, plant trees, or pick up trash. The list of beneficial things you can do in their name is endless. The power of merit can also bring solace to those who wonder how a non-Buddhist might fare in the bardo. Any good person automatically accumulates merit and is taken care of by the force of that merit.

Proper dedication of merit is important because it multiplies the power of the good deed. Tulku Thondup says:

> In order to enjoy a peaceful and happy life and rebirths, it is essential to accumulate merits and cultivate positive qualities. Whatever happiness and peace you are enjoying today is the direct result of your meritorious behavior in the past. To further improve your future life, you must continue to make more merits by performing virtuous deeds. Just as you gain physical

well-being by providing your body with proper nourishment and exercise, so you must care for your spiritual health by making merits. Dedicating merits multiplies their power exponentially. The greater the scope of the dedication, the greater the power. So dedicate merits, not just to the deceased but also to *all* mother-beings, as the cause of their happiness and enlightenment. Then enormous merits will redound to them. Next make aspirations. This is a way to invest merits for a particular goal and further magnify them. Using your dedicated merits as the seed, make aspirations that all mother-beings may enjoy the fruits of happiness and rebirth in the pure land. Beings in the bardo in particular need us to dedicate merits and make aspirations for them. If we repeatedly dedicate whatever merits we and the dead person accumulated—no matter how meager—to that person and all mother-beings for their rebirth in the pure land, we can be sure that the merits will cause that result.[17]

Giving merit away doesn't work the same way as giving something material away. When you give your merit to all beings, not just to one, the merit doesn't lessen like a material offering might lessen. The merit ironically grows. So by dedicating it to all beings you're not watering the merit down—you're beefing it up. Khenpo Karthar says:

If you dedicate the merit to one person around one situation, then that merit will ripen only once and the merit will be exhausted. But if you dedicate the merit to all sentient beings, the merit becomes inexhaustible. Merit can also create affluence and wealth for you, but this karmic ripening happens just once and is exhausted. With the mind of enlightenment [dedicating the merit to all beings], the merit becomes inexhaustible.[18]

The merit of an act can be lost if it's not dedicated. If someone gets angry before the dedication, the anger can erase the merit. So you should dedicate the merit of your good actions every time you perform them. It's like hitting the "save" icon on your computer after you've written something important. Dedicate the merit from your meal, or your exercise. Dedicate the merit after you read some dharma, or after a day of work. Train yourself to dedicate the good that you do, and you may find yourself doing more good. B. Alan Wallace writes:

"Merit" can be understood as "spiritual power" that manifests in day-to-day experience. When merit, or spiritual power, is strong, there is little resistance to practicing Dharma and practice itself is empowered. Tibetans explain that people who make rapid progress in Dharma, gaining one insight after another, enter practice already having a lot of merit. By the same theory, it is possible to strive diligently and make little progress. Tibetans explain this problem as being due to too little merit. Merit is the fuel that empowers spiritual practice. . . .

Just as merit can be accumulated, it can also be dissipated by doing harm. In general, mental afflictions dissipate merit. The mental affliction that is like a black hole sucking up merit, worse than all the others, is anger.[19]

The classic way to gather merit is through the practice of the first five *paramitas* or "perfections" (literally "crossed over")—generosity, discipline, patience, exertion, and meditation. The paramitas are a Buddhist practice that culminates in the sixth paramita, *prajna*, the perfection of wisdom. Cultivating the four immeasurables—loving-kindness, compassion, sympathetic joy, and equanimity—also generates immeasurable merit. In daily activity, we can recite mantras and dedicate that recitation. There are endless liturgies to recite and dedicate, but one of the most powerful is *The King of Aspiration Prayers: The Aspiration for Noble Excellent Conduct*, by Samantabhadra.[20] According to Khenpo Tsültrim Gyamtso Rinpoche, this is an especially powerful liturgy to recite for people who have committed suicide. Rinpoche says that this prayer should be recited a thousand times by loved ones and dedicated to the one who committed suicide.

Because gathering merit is so simple, and because it's not material, we don't believe in its power. How can it be so easy to help others, especially the dead? But the power of merit is fathomless.[21] The esoteric practices below aren't necessarily more effective than gathering and dedicating merit. Indeed, one of the reasons to do the following practices is to gather, magnify, and direct the merit to the dead. If you don't connect to the following rituals, then relying on the power of merit alone will suffice.

We saw how powerful mindfulness is in preparing for the bardos. Merit has a similar potency. Along with equanimity, the baseline instruction for the bardos is mindfulness and merit. These practices alone can carry you, and others, through the bardos.

Aspiration prayers are connected to the dedication of merit. Aspirations are "forward prayers" that invest and amplify merit toward a specific goal. Dedication and aspiration are like lasers. They concentrate a diffuse beam of "light" into a powerful ray that can cut through anything and therefore reach anybody anywhere. The biggest challenge for skeptical Westerners is believing it. Dodrupchen Rinpoche talks about how aspirations have real force at the time of death:

> Buddha Shakyamuni told many stories to illustrate why someone had become his disciple or why someone in particular had become one of his gifted disciples. In many instances, the main cause he gave was that these people had made virtuous aspirations while they were dying. So, what wishes you make at the time of death will have a great impact on your rebirth.[22]

Tonglen is very helpful after someone has died. On the in-breath, absorb the dead person's confusion through every pore of your body. On the out-breath, send out light and love from the center of your boundless heart. Imagine that by doing so you are clearing their mind and illuminating their path through the darkness of death.

READING *THE TIBETAN BOOK OF THE DEAD*

As I describe the practices you can do to help, choose those that you, or the dead person, connect with the most. Your belief and heart-connection are what matters. Reading *The Tibetan Book of the Dead* aloud for the dead person is the first of our esoteric practices. In addition to the guidance provided by the book, reading it generates great merit and blessing through the force of the words themselves. These are the sacred words of the tantric Buddha Padmasambhava.

The inner reason to read *The Tibetan Book of the Dead* is that it stabilizes the mind of the reader. This stability provides a sense of ground for the dead person, which is what they desperately seek. By reading the book, or any sacred liturgy, the mind of the dying person is magnetized to the steady mind of the reader, and takes refuge in that stability.

Some teachers say that the book is so powerful that it should even be read to those who are not Buddhist. Most teachers, however, say that this is inappropriate. As a Buddhist, how would you feel if a well-intentioned Christian started to read the Bible at your bedside, or a good Muslim started reading the Koran? Always check your motivation. Trungpa Rinpoche said that reading the book aloud is probably not helpful unless you understand the text and can relay it in your own words. But if the dying person was familiar with *The Tibetan Book of the Dead* and requested that it be read, or if a teacher makes the suggestion, then we should honor that instruction.

You can start reading the book when the dying person stops breathing. Read it slowly and clearly. Some teachers recommend reading it loudly. Since we don't know where the person is in their journey, the instruction is to read it continuously for forty-nine days. You can buy a recording of the book and play it constantly, or read it on the seventh, fourteenth, and twenty-first days after the death.[23] The bardo being is easily guided but easily forgets, and our job is to remind them. It takes about three hours to read the book. If possible, it's good to read it at the place where death occurred.

The book itself says, "This teaching does not need any practice; it is a profound instruction that liberates just by being seen or heard or read. Even if the buddhas of the past, present, and future were to search, they would not find a better teaching than this."[24]

SUR OFFERING

The bardo being is called a "gandharva," or "scent eater." Gandharvas live off the smell of food, but only if it is dedicated in their name.[25] Without this sustenance they feel hunger just like us. The traditional way to feed the gandharvas is with the *sur*, or burnt, offering. Due to habit, your loved one may continue to visit during family meals, and wonder why there's no place setting for them. This is a good time to do the sur offering. Tenzin Wangyal Rinpoche recommends doing it every day for forty-nine days.

The sur is blessed with your meditation and motivation, and then burned. You can play a small set of hand cymbals, called "tingsha," to call the gandharvas. There's a classical recipe for sur, but you can also burn cookies or chips on small charcoal briquettes.[26] Don't use meat or foods that cause an unpleasant smell. Small pieces of new fabric or brocade can be included. Tulku Thondup says:

> In sur ceremonies, with the intensity of heartfelt compassion, the power of meditation, and the force of mantras, we *purify* all the impurities of the sur materials, *magnify* the materials into enormous amounts filling the earth, and *transform* them into

wish-fulfilling materials that the dead will enjoy and benefit from. Thus, the smoke will not only appear to the dead as food and drink, but also assume the form of whatever they wish for and need. Even if the performers cannot follow the meditations in detail, if they have devotion to the buddhas, bless the sur with prayers, and dedicate it to the deceased with pure love, then the sur offering will become a source of satisfaction and benefits.[27]

COMMISSIONING MONASTERIES

One of the most effective ways to help the dead is to commission a retreat center or monastery to perform rituals for them. This benefits you (you gain merit from making the request and paying for it), the monastery (the monks or nuns gain merit by doing the ritual and also make income for the monastery), and especially the dead person (who benefits from the vast accumulation of merit dedicated on their behalf). There are a number of complex rituals, some of which I will describe below, that are beyond the capabilities of the average Westerner. Having ritual masters, monks, and nuns perform these practices is more realistic than gathering all the materials, getting the necessary empowerments, and learning the intricate procedures. Bardo beings need our help *now*.

Contact the monastery. Tell them what you want, or ask for their advice. Then make a donation. Most monasteries have a set charge for standard practices, but there may be room for negotiation. For example, Thrangu Rinpoche's monastery in Kathmandu does shitro and Amitabha practices, and offers hundreds of butter lamps, for around one hundred dollars. When I have been fortunate enough to have a rinpoche do phowa for my loved one, I have sent five hundred dollars. If a fee isn't set, offer what feels right. They want to help more than they want to make money. And remember, the money is used to support the dharma.

Make the inquiries in advance so that when the person dies you can take immediate action.[28] Don't be disappointed if you can't get a master to do phowa for your loved one. Unless you have a connection to a lama, or contact them in advance, phowa is often not available.

In India and Nepal, most of the monasteries associated with teachers that visit the West are available to help. If you study with such a teacher, get the information for their post-death services now. I have asked a number of these monasteries, and they all confirm that this is beneficial to them, to the dead person, and to you. It's part of their job and we should take advantage of it.

On a personal note, the solace I have gained from having monasteries, my community, and my teachers doing practices for my loved ones has been immeasurable. Because I set it up in advance, it took minimal effort to start the rituals after my loved ones died.

MONASTIC RITUALS AND CEREMONIES FOR THE DEAD

On one hand, Tibetan Buddhism is practical, sensible, and down to earth. It's simply about waking up and helping others. On the other hand, Tibetan Buddhism can seem wildly esoteric, shamanistic, even superstitious. This is particularly true when it comes to the bardos. Buddhism is "super-natural" in both senses: very natural and fully of this world, yet sometimes totally out of this world. Some of the practices listed below stretch the mind. But they are part of the tradition and are widely practiced in Asia. The following is a sample of how much Buddhism has to offer in terms of helping the dead.

The world is a mysterious place, full of magic and wonder. And the wilderness of the dead is the ultimate mystery. The Tibetans have explored this terrain for centuries, offering a legacy of practices that can penetrate into the bardos and benefit those wandering in its bewildering landscape. The list of meditations and rituals designed to help the dead is vast.[29] A few of the standard practices are discussed below. If our faith is strong, and we trust the monasteries doing the rituals, we can leave it to them. But it helps to have an idea of what these practices are, and what they accomplish for our loved one. If you don't connect to these practices, skip to the summary comments on page 158.

The *Iron Hook of Compassion* is an advanced phowa practice that is performed by a lama for someone who has died. Most three-year retreatants have also had this training. This may not be easy to commission because a capable lama isn't always available. It's best to do phowa immediately after death, or as soon as possible thereafter.[30] For someone who is not highly accomplished, it's also best to do phowa at the bedside of the one who just died. For a master, distance doesn't matter. The longer someone spends in the bardo, the harder it is to find them.[31] If someone is approaching death and you have access to a lama who does phowa, contact the lama in advance to let him or her know death is imminent. The meditative power of a master can locate the bardo being, hook their consciousness, and send it to a pure land.[32]

Compassion is the essential ingredient in this practice. Even if signs don't occur, it doesn't mean the phowa was unsuccessful (see the discussion on phowa for these signs, page 54). You don't have to be highly realized to benefit another person with phowa. You simply have to do it at the right time and with the right attitude. Because the power of any practice is magnified in a group, it's helpful to have several people doing phowa for someone who has just died.

Phowa is the esoteric practice most frequently mentioned for the dead. This is because the best thing that most people can do in the bardo is transfer to a pure land, either through their own power or with our help. Chagdud Tulku quotes his teacher, Lama Atse, on the importance of phowa for the deceased, but his words apply to any post-death meditation:

> Think of the dead person. Remember that he has lost everything he held dear including his own body, that he is being blown about helplessly with no place to sit, no food to eat and no one to rely on but you to release him from the turbulence of the bardo or the possibility of a difficult rebirth. Think about the relatives who have lost their loved one. What they can do is very limited. Their hope is in you. Meditate from the depth of your love and compassion, and concentrate on the accomplishment of transference. Otherwise, you will fail the dead, you will fail the living, and you will fail yourself by breaking your commitment to them.[33]

Another common practice to benefit the dead is *dur*. Some Lamas say that in order to make the other practices more effective, dur needs to be done first. The reason for performing dur is that if someone dies before age seventy or so, it can be due to the negative influence of unseen malevolent beings, called maras.[34] The Tibetans describe entire classes of malicious beings that can adversely affect us, shortening our lives.

In Tibetan lore, the mara that contributed to the death can linger around the dead person's consciousness, obstructing their journey through the bardo. The dur ritual is designed to remove the mara, clearing the way for other beneficial practices.[35] Tulku Urgyen says:

The dur pertains to certain classes of spirits connected to each and every person's corporeal existence. In the main part of the ritual, the presiding master disengages nine devouring spirits from the vital energy of the deceased. The understanding is that unless these nine spirits are disconnected when a person dies, they can slow down or create obstacles to liberation in the bardo. . . . The dur rituals have both a peaceful and a subjugating aspect. Sometimes they involve ritual name-burning, a pacifying activity that summons the deceased's consciousness, purifies it, and sends it to a buddhafield. The subjugating aspect exorcises evil influences that may have taken possession of the deceased. These devouring spirits are demon ghosts, a type of sentient being. You hear a lot of HUNG and PHAT during the part of the ritual where the nine spirits are being chased from their various hiding places. This ceremony is necessary even for a great being . . . because such a master's splendor attracts many mundane spirits.[36]

Once the obstacles are cleared, then the following practices are more effective. *Sukhavati* is a common ritual usually performed three days after death, or after the onset of rigor mortis. This allows time for consciousness to exit the body. The practice comes in various forms, but the idea is the same: let the dead person go, direct them into Sukhavati, and supplicate Amitabha for help. This practice is done regularly at many Western meditation centers.[37]

The following practices can be done by yourself, if you have received the empowerments and trainings. If you haven't, then others can do them for you. Sogyal Rinpoche describes the practices of *né dren* (liberation from the six realms, literally "leading to places") and *chang chok* (effigy ritual):

Hand in hand with the reading of the *Tibetan Book of the Dead* goes the practice of *Né Dren*, the ritual for guiding the dead, or *Chang Chok*, the ritual purification, in which a master will guide the consciousness of the dead person to a better rebirth.

Ideally the Né Dren or Chang Chok should be done immediately after death, or at least within forty-nine days. If the corpse is not present, the consciousness of the deceased is summoned into an effigy or card bearing their likeness and name, or even a photograph, called a *tsenjang*. The Né Dren or Chang Chok derive their power from the fact that during the period immediately after death, the dead person will have a strong feeling of possessing the body of its recent life.

Through the power of the master's meditation, the consciousness of the dead person, roaming aimlessly in the bardo, is called into the tsenjang, which represents the dead person's identity. The consciousness is then purified; the karmic seeds of the six realms are cleansed; a teaching is given just as in life; and the dead person is introduced to the nature of the mind. Finally the phowa is effected, and the dead person's consciousness is directed toward one of the Buddha realms. Then the tsenjang, representing the individual's old—now discarded—identity, is burned, and their karma is purified.[38]

Né dren can also be performed as a person is dying. Either way, this practice purifies the negative seeds of the dying person that would otherwise lead them to a lower realm. It also accumulates positive seeds, which can send them into higher realms. Né dren brings the blessings of the buddhas, which can deliver the bardo being into the pure lands, or to complete enlightenment.[39]

Another practice is to have some of the remains of the deceased (ashes, hair, nails) blessed, and then put into little statues called *tsatsa*. These are buddha images made of clay or plaster. Tsatsa can be kept in your home, and offerings can be made to them in order to gather and send merit.[40]

His Holiness Khyentse Rinpoche said that the best purification practice for the dead is the *Purification of the Six Realms*. This practice cleanses the body of the six principal negative emotions (passion, aggression, ignorance, jealousy, pride, and greed) and therefore blocks the door to rebirth in their respective realms. This practice works directly with the root of rebirth. It can be done during life for ourselves, but here it is used to help those who have died. Sogyal Rinpoche says:

According to the Dzogchen Tantras, the negative emotions accumulate in the psycho-physical system of subtle channels, inner air, and energy [*tsa*, *lung*, and *tigle*], and gather at particular energy centers in the body. So the seed of the hell realm and its cause, anger, are located at the soles of the feet; the hungry ghost realm and its cause, avarice, rest at the base of the trunk; the animal realm and its cause, ignorance, rest at the navel; the human realm and its cause, doubt, rest at the heart; the demigod realm and its cause, jealousy, rest at the throat; and the god realm, and its cause, pride, rest at the crown of the head.

In this practice . . . when each realm and its negative emotion is purified, the practitioner imagines that all the karma created by that particular emotion is now exhausted, and that specific part of his body associated. . . with the karma of a particular emotion dissolves entirely into light. So when you do this practice for a dead person, imagine with all your heart and mind that, at the end of this practice, all their karma is purified, and their body and entire being dissolve into radiant light.[41]

Sogyal Rinpoche adds this caveat: "Traditional practices such as this require training and cannot be followed simply from this book [*The Tibetan Book of Living and Dying.*]"

The *shitro* practice discussed in chapter 1 is also used to help others. After doing the visualizations mentioned in chapter 1, imagine that the deities radiate light to the dead person, purifying their negative karma. Then recite the hundred-syllable mantra of Vajrasattva, who is the central deity of the shitro mandala. This is a mantra for purification and healing.

For those with a connection to female buddhas, there is a **Red Tara** meditation for the dead. Those familiar with Tara can invoke her blessing by calling her name while they're in the bardo. Her blessing then directs their consciousness into her pure land or into an auspicious rebirth. Again, it's best if the dead person did this practice during life so that the habit arises automatically in the bardo. Chagdud Khadro says:

Visualizing either Tara in the space in front of us, or ourselves transformed into the wisdom body of Tara, we meditate that rainbow light shines from Tara's heart throughout the six realms and the bardo and envelops the deceased wherever they are, "purifying their karma and infusing them with Tara's radiant blessing." The more profound our realization of emptiness, the deeper is our experience that this is actually the case—not merely imagined light washing over imagined figures of the deceased, but mind's unobstructed quality of sheer clarity encompassing the mindstreams of the deceased, purifying and blessing them, bringing forth their natural radiance, which dissolves into Tara's enlightened expanse.[42]

The English version of a Red Tara practice written by H. E. Chagdud Tulku Rinpoche contains this Red Tara meditation for the dead.[43]

Finally, Sogyal Rinpoche also offers practices that we can do at the cremation to benefit the dead:

> The crematorium or funeral pyre is visualized as the mandala of Vajrasattva, or the Hundred Peaceful and Wrathful Deities, and the deities are strongly visualized and their presence is invoked. The dead person's corpse is seen as actually representing all his or her negative karma and obscurations. As the corpse burns, these are consumed by the deities as a great feast and transmuted and transformed by them into their wisdom nature. Rays of light are imagined streaming out from the deities; the corpse is visualized dissolving completely into light, as all the impurities of the dead person are purified in the blazing flames of wisdom. As you visualize this, you can recite the hundred-syllable or six-syllable mantra of Vajrasattva.... The ashes of the body, and the tsenjang [see page 153], can then be mixed with clay to make little images called *tsatsa*. These are blessed and dedicated on behalf of the dead person, so creating auspicious conditions for a future good rebirth.[44]

GELUGPA RITUALS

For those with a connection to the Gelugpa tradition, Lama Zopa Rinpoche provides this list of practices to help someone who has died:[45]

- ▶ Perform Medicine Buddha *puja* [literally, "honor, worship"].
- ▶ Recite the eight prayers that are normally done in monasteries when someone passes away: *Confession of Downfalls to the Thirty-five Buddhas*, *General Confession*, *King of Prayers*, *A Daily Prayer to Maitreya*, the dedication chapter from the *Bodhicharyavatara*, *A Prayer for the Beginning, Middle, and End of Practice*, *Prayer To Be Reborn in the Land of Bliss*, and *Until Buddhahood*. The liturgies for all these practices are included in his book.
- ▶ Perform Vajrasattva tsog ["feast"] puja.

- Make many thousands of light offerings or other extensive offerings.
- Do *nyung né* practice [fasting practice to purify obstacles].
- Do a weekend of Vajrasattva retreat, Chenrezig retreat, or Medicine Buddha retreat.
- Meditate on tonglen together with recitations of OM MANI PADME HUM and dedicate for the person who has died.
- Recite the *King of Prayers* many times.
- Recite the *Diamond Cutter Sutra.*
- Recite and meditate on the *Heart Sutra.*
- Meditate on emptiness, dedicating for the person who died.
- Perform Dorje Khadro fire puja as a group, dedicating for the person who died.
- Make stupas or tsatsa. [The most important thing is to dedicate and say the name of the person who died as you insert the four powerful mantras. Doing this can change the circumstances of a person who is going to be reborn in the lower realms, benefiting them to have the causes to be reborn in a good rebirth.]
- Make Mitrugpa tsatsa.
- Make thangkas or statues and dedicate for the person's good rebirth.
- Publish dharma books or sponsor their publication on behalf of the person who died.
- Recite *Sang Chö, The Prayer of Good Deeds.*
- Recite the Namgyalma mantra twenty-one times.[46]
- Purify the bones, ashes, hair, or nails with the skillful Vajrayana meditation called *jangwa.*[47]

If the person who died practiced tantra, then one can do the following:
- Perform self-initiation and tsog offering of the person's main deity.
- Do a weekend retreat on the person's main deity.

One can also make offerings on the person's behalf, as follows:
- It is very powerful to make offerings to the Sangha on that person's behalf, as well as to make offerings to lay students who have the same guru as the person who died. This collects an inconceivable amount of merit that you can then dedicate for the person who has died.
- Also, one can make offerings to the person's gurus, or you can make offering to your own guru on that person's behalf.

- You can make charity or offerings to the center on the person's behalf, as the center is a place where people can meditate on the path, where they can learn Dharma, and where they come to purify their minds and collect merit.
- You can make charity on that person's behalf to sick people, homeless people, to solve other people's difficulties, to various charities, or to poor people.
- You can also make charity on the person's behalf to animals.[48]

Lama Zopa also describes the benefits of making small stupas for the dead.

Other Gelugpa rituals and liturgies include The Buddha of Purgation of the Inferior Realms (Sarvavid Vairochana); the Eliminator of the Lord of Death (Vajrabhairava); the Buddha of Compassion (Avalokiteshvara); the Buddha of Purification (Vajrasattva); the Buddha of Infinite Light (Amitabha); and the protector practice of Riwo Sangchö.

SUMMARY

These practices give us an idea of how much is available to help the dead. Knowing about these rituals also helps if they are mentioned when we contact a retreat center or monastery. While all these practices are wonderful, loved ones may be too numb to do anything but grieve. The last thing we need is the pressure of conducting the perfect post-death rituals. Feeling that we're letting the dead person down only adds further stress. This won't help us or the dead.

This is when we rely on dharma friends. If some of these practices resonate with you, tell your friends in advance that you would like to do them and ask for their help. If none of these practices speak to you, don't worry. Your love and compassion is what matters.

Summary instruction for how to help others after they die: think of them only with love. Perform good deeds and dedicate the merit to them. Commission monasteries or dharma centers to practice for them.

PART TWO

Practical Preparation

7. Before Death Approaches

Before everything else, getting ready is the secret of success.
—Henry Ford

Remembering that I'll be dead soon is the most important tool
I've ever encountered to help me make the big choices in life. Your time
is limited, so don't waste it living someone else's life.
—Steve Jobs

THE PRACTICAL PREPARATIONS for death are not always separate from the spiritual preparations. What we do about organ donation, euthanasia, or suicide will be dictated by our spiritual views. The essence of practical preparation is to get the affairs of our life in order before we enter the bardo of dying. Since that can occur in the next moment, this means we need to get our affairs in order *now*. Finishing our business well in advance of this final deadline is a spiritual practice.

Most people like the beginning of things but have a harder time with proper endings. We don't enjoy the messy affairs at the end of life, such as cleaning up our estate, resolving painful relationships, or facing the harsh reality of impermanence. But this is where "rock meets bone" as the Tibetans say, or where the "rubber hits the road" as we might say. We can tell more about a person's character by the way they say goodbye than by the way they say hello. Hellos are easy because they're full of the promise and potential of life. Goodbyes always have a tiny smell of death. The true colors of a person are revealed more in the grace they bring to a divorce than the sweetness brought to an engagement.

If you were to die today, what would remain unfinished that you really want to finish? Do you have any regrets? Have you found meaning in your life and meaning in your death? Are there any relationships you need to clean up? Do you need to express forgiveness? Have you written your will and advance directives, and have you drafted a medical power of attorney?

Attorney John Scroggin, who developed the "Family Love Letter," a comprehensive estate planning document, writes:

> Seventy percent of Americans do not have an estate plan. Failure to plan and a failure to provide basic information in virtually every case will create family conflict, cause the dissipation of assets you have spent a lifetime building, or result in the payment of income and estate taxes which might have been avoided easily. . . . The emotional turmoil and family pain [around death] is often magnified by the resulting confusion over the plans, assets and desires of an incapacitated or deceased family member. The mental fogginess that accompanies the family's trauma is exaggerated by the inability to make basic decisions—because of the lack of basic information. . . . Estate planning is not about death and taxes. Instead, it is about the legacy you leave behind when you no longer can help your family. Will you leave chaos? Or, will you leave a well conceived plan with information to help your family in its confused times?[1]

By dealing with the medical and legal issues in advance, we can better relax at the time of death. This preparation also benefits others because we're not leaving a medical or legal mess behind. I am continually amazed at how many financial skeletons people keep in their closets. These skeletons come out after death. If you're part of the clean-up crew, be prepared for some unexpected financial or legal problems.

The main purpose of estate planning is to protect our loved ones. Our disability and death will radically affect them. Give those who will be dealing with some of the most intense emotions of their life your final gift. Say to yourself, "For the benefit of others, I will prepare for the medical and legal issues surrounding my death. By doing so, others will be free of this burden when I die." As with our spiritual practice, we're not doing this for ourselves. It's the act of a bodhisattva to deal with these matters now.

Finally, unlike the timeless aspects of spiritual preparation, the practical facets are always in flux. Laws change, medicine advances, and new counseling strategies develop. The guidelines below will be modified as their respective fields continue to evolve. With the miracle of the internet, it's easy to stay current with the topics discussed below.

LEGAL ISSUES

An obvious preparation is writing our will. There's a spiritual basis for doing so. By settling our business, in particular by giving our possessions away (literally or through written intent), we will be removing some of the pain from the painful bardo of dying. Remember that the bardo of dying is painful because it hurts to let go. We're forced to let go of everything we have, and everything we think we are. Letting go of everything we think we are was addressed in chapters 3 and 4 above. Letting go of everything we have will be dealt with here.

When it comes to death, the legal issues are as omnipresent as the spiritual. The law applies to all three phases of what to do before, during, and after death. There are matters that need to be dealt with before death (creating and filing all the papers), during death (application of medical and durable power of attorney, living wills), and after death (implementation of wills and trusts). Just as our maxim "the mind leads all things" applies to the spiritual, the maxim "the law follows all things" applies to practical matters concerning death.

By giving things away, writing advance directives, and drafting a will, we're practicing a form of phowa. Recall that *phowa* means "transference, moving, or ejecting." In order to successfully move our consciousness forward, we have to cut the ties that hold us back. The term *advance directive* is wonderful when it comes to phowa. After death, *direct* your consciousness to *advance* by allowing it to—write the documents that help everyone to let go and advance.

The phowa discussed earlier is tantra phowa, which is a forceful method of transference. There are also sutra forms of phowa, which are more gentle methods of moving consciousness.

One such method is called "the application of the five powers." The second of these five powers is called "the power of the white seed." Buddhist scholar Glenn Mullin says of this, "Try to rid the mind of all forms of physical attachment. In order to effect this, give away all wealth, property and possessions to noble purposes, such as the poor and needy, the sick, educational institutes or hospitals, spiritual institutes, and so forth."[2] In other words, writing our will is a form of phowa.

We want to travel light through the bardos, with just the bare essentials. Most of us, however, lumber through death with lots of luggage. Just as in life, this baggage pulls us down. All kinds of physical and emotional attachments hold us back. In order to transfer your consciousness later, transfer your material possessions to others now.

Attachment binds us to samsara during life and holds us back during death. Hinduism says that when we die, we'll move toward whatever we were most attached to at the moment of death. We want to remove those attachments so we can move forward. Trungpa Rinpoche says, "You are capable of making your consciousness step outside of your body when the time comes. This again means cutting through a lot of possessiveness toward one's body, particularly the desire for possessions and entertainment. One has to have the power to remove clingings. You have to leave things behind, which can be very scary and very unsatisfying."[3]

Attachment also causes pain for those left behind. Our desire to fill a void, with physical or psychological stuff, occurs constantly. We're afraid of silence and space. So we fill it in conscious and subconscious ways. This urge is amplified when a loved one dies. What we once held so closely is gone, and the space left behind becomes unbearable. We long to fill that emptiness.

We have all seen pictures of spiritual teachers, or heads of state, being passed hand-to-hand above the heads of a crowd. People often snatch at bits of clothing, or any other memento. They want a piece of what's leaving. This human tendency to fill space is portrayed in some teachings on death as "grabbing possessions."[4] In our litigious society, even under the most loving conditions, a person's money and possessions are often a bone of contention. Family and friends try to fill a longing to remain connected with the one who died, or merely try to satisfy their greed. This urge to fill the void left by death can cause loved ones to grasp at the possessions of the dead, which results in negative karma.

As a dying person, offer a gift of kindness by dispersing your wealth and possessions through proper documentation. Be aware of this human tendency to grab, and make provisions to lessen it. There are stories of Tibetan masters who transferred their consciousness before the Chinese could kill them as a way to protect the Chinese soldiers from accruing enormous negative karma. Similarly, through legal means, we can protect our families and friends from the karma of conflict and greed. Protect them from collapsing into the hole of deficiency and from the grasping that often ensues.

Alex Halpern will explain most of the legal issues in detail below, but here is a brief summary that explains the legal terms:

A *will* or a *trust* disposes of your assets. It's your final statement of what should happen to your material possessions. If you have children who are minors, these documents also convey your wishes of what should happen to your family in the event of your demise. An example would be the guardianship of your children. A will identifies the people who will make decisions when you are gone. It can dramatically reduce conflicts between family and friends who may want your assets.

A will or trust can be used to make charitable gifts, to reduce estate taxes, and to help heirs who may be minors or who aren't able to manage the inherited assets. Although it doesn't carry legal weight, a *letter of instruction* can be a useful supplement to a will. It lists the names and contact information of your attorneys, accountants, and financial advisors for your executor (the person you named to implement the wishes in your will).

Included in the will or trust is a *personal property disposition list*. This is where you can specify who will receive items of your personal property (but not real estate or money). If you're married, it helps to list what possessions belong to you and what belongs to your spouse.

A *living will* expresses your choices regarding the use of life-sustaining treatments. It is used by your doctor or health care agent (see below) to understand and implement your end-of-life wishes. Making these wishes known can eliminate expensive treatment when there's no reasonable hope of recovery. It can also reduce stress when painful decisions around life support have to be made, such as whether or not to administer or continue artificial (IV) nutrition and hydration. "Five Wishes," a customizable living will created by the nonprofit organization Aging with Dignity, meets legal requirements in most states and simplifies the process of specifying how you are to be treated if you get seriously ill.

An *advance directive* is written instructions for caregivers that specify what actions should be taken if a person is no longer able to make decisions due to illness. All advance directives should be readily available. If you're dealing with a serious health condition, your living will—along with any other advance directives—should travel with you to any medical facility.

A *medical power of attorney* (MPOA) gives someone the authority to make medical decisions for you when you're no longer able to do so. This person is called your health care agent, surrogate, or medical proxy. An

MPOA assures that your chosen agents, not doctors who are strangers to you, have the final say on treatment. It's good to have two or three people as your agents. If the first person can't be reached, the second or the third can be contacted. Life and death decisions sometimes need to be made quickly. Your personal doctor should have contact information for your agents, and your agents should have copies of all your *updated* advance directives (as should your doctor). They should all be familiar with the contents of these directives, and they should discuss your wishes with you in advance. The need for thoroughness and clarity cannot be overstated. When emotions run high, fatigue and stress are rampant, and huge decisions are required, your agent needs to know what to do and when.

Here are some tips for choosing a health care agent. Choosing the person you are closest to may not be your best choice. Sometimes it's better to choose someone with more emotional distance who can therefore make clearer decisions. Is this person someone who would put your wishes ahead of their own? Do they have any medical knowledge, and are they comfortable in a hospital, ICU, or ER? Does your family know, and trust, them? Are they willing and able to stand up for you and fight for your end-of-life rights? If an agent has not been chosen, the next of kin usually become the de facto decision makers. And remember: if you don't appoint an agent, it's possible that a court could appoint one for you. Do you want a stranger making decisions for you?

Finally, be careful. Your agent may reverse your orders when you're no longer able to contest that maneuver. Be very clear to your agents (and your family, who may put immense pressure on your agent to change your written directives to suit *their* wishes) about the specific situations that might give your agent the freedom to change your written wishes (such as implementing life-sustaining measures until a relative can arrive). This is another reason why it's good to have more than one agent and essential that you're all on the same page. If one of them decides to go against your wishes, the other agents can challenge that decision for you. If you are chosen as an agent, remember that you have been entrusted to help that person die the way *he or she* has chosen. It's not the family's call, nor yours. How would you feel if others violated your final wishes?

It's also helpful to reinforce to family and loved ones beforehand that the directives your agent is implementing reflect your strong desires and are not something the agent is making up. When it comes to the really difficult issues (for example, whether it's time to pull the plug), it is very helpful to know that "This is her (the dying person's) decision, not mine. She's the one who doesn't want heroic treatments." This is why the MPOA is so important.

A *durable general power of attorney* identifies a person who will manage your assets when you're no longer able to do so. It's an authorization to act on your behalf in a legal and business manner (as opposed to medical matters) when you're incapacitated or not available. This document is written in as much detail as possible, so that your designee has as much authority as possible. Things can easily become confused when emotions run high or people are tired and stressed out. Being articulate and methodical with your directives infuses clarity at a time when it's needed the most.

Some estate planners recommend a *proof of ownership*. This is an informal document that lists what you own. It can also help you during life if you need to file insurance claims. In terms of death, if you don't inform your loved ones about these assets, they may never find out. Things to list would include homes (do you have rental properties?) and land ownership, vehicles, stock certificates and savings bonds, cemetery plots, a list of brokerage or escrow mortgage accounts, and any partnership or corporate operating agreements.

Unless family and friends do their own investigation—going through bank accounts for interest payments, or watching the mail for real-estate tax bills—these assets may go unclaimed. Keep a list of loans you have made to others. They can be included as assets in an estate. Keep a list of debts you owe, to avoid unwelcome surprises for your family (remember that creditors have a specific period of time in which they can file a claim against the estate). It also helps to have the last two or three years of tax returns available. They provide an overview of much of this information.

An *ethical will* is not a formal document and therefore has no standard format. This is where you leave your personal legacy behind. It's a philosophical portrait of the person who died. An ethical will can be written, tape recorded, or video recorded. There are a number of reasons for doing this: (1) the personal satisfaction of doing it, and the benefits of reflecting back on your own life; (2) it can help in the estate planning process by sharing your deeper views behind the legal documents which are required for estate disposition; (3) it leaves behind your intangible assets, so that others can decide if they want to "inherit" those assets. Things to include would be of this sort:

- ► I believe the most important things in life are:
- ► The values or traditions I want to pass along to my family and friends are:
- ► My core, or what I want to be remembered for, is:
- ► The most important thing I have done in my life is:
- ► When I am gone, I hope my family and friends will have learned this from me:
- ► Life has taught me these lessons:

These are the central ingredients in any estate plan. Your will or trust, along with your personal property disposition list and your durable general power of attorney, should be drafted with the counsel of a legal expert or attorney. You may want to discuss your living will with your physician or other health care provider, and/or your attorney. But in most states you aren't legally obligated to consult with either. Without professional advice, you run the risk of making mistakes. These mistakes can have significant repercussions as your loved ones try to sort through and implement your final wishes. You don't need professional advice for your ethical will or proof of ownership.

Estate planners recommend that these documents be reviewed and updated every few years, or when a major life change occurs, like the birth of a child, marriage, or divorce. These documents will change as your life circumstances change. Unless you die right after you create these documents, estate planning is an ongoing process, not a one-time event. Make sure your heirs and other empowered agents are aware of these documents and know where to find them. Sometimes people retain so many papers that loved ones can't easily find the important ones. Be considerate in that regard.

The consequences of not having these documents and keeping them updated are significant. According to the National Association of Unclaimed Property Administrators, state treasurers currently hold $32.9 billion in unclaimed bank accounts and other assets.

Finally, make sure your spouse knows where to find the marriage license, otherwise he or she may have to pay for a new one to prove your marriage. This proof may be needed before the surviving spouse tries to claim anything. If you're divorced, it helps to have the divorce judgment and decree available. If the divorce was settled without court involvement, make the stipulation agreement available. These papers document alimony, property settlements, and child support. They may also list the division of investment and retirement accounts.

MORE ON LIVING WILLS AND ADVANCE DIRECTIVES

The documents listed above reflect the core legal and medical issues that surround end-of-life and death. The following terms and forms supplement this information. They help us understand the scope, and complexity, of modern death. On first exposure, it's easy to get lost in the dizzying array of medical and legal forms, especially the ones that vary from state to state. But just as with meditation, you want to "become familiar with" these forms now. Remember: you are not doing this for yourself. You are wrestling with this material now so that you—and your loved ones—won't have to later.

Anyone eighteen years or older should have advance directives in place. The illusion of immortality provided by youth makes this unlikely for young adults. But there are many tragic instances of early death. If you are a young adult who wants any control over your coma, or any other medical end-of-life dilemma, talk to your parents or guardians and draft your own advance directives now.

There are many varieties of living wills available, such as the "Five Wishes" document mentioned earlier. You're generally asked on admission to a hospital if you have advance directives, so that your wishes may be honored. You are not required to have an advance directive in order to receive treatment or to be admitted to a facility. An attorney is not required to complete these forms, but if you have legal questions you should consult with one. If you spend a great deal of time in different states, it's good to have an advance directive that meets the requirements of the laws in each of those states, or to at least know the differences in the laws. In most states, advance directives are also legal documents.

These documents don't remove your right to change your mind at any time. You might change your mind due to fluctuating or unusual health care problems, or upon admission to a facility. If you're still conscious and coherent, your verbal wishes override any written advance directive. Advance directives go into effect when you can no longer communicate or are otherwise incapacitated. Alex Halpern defines below what "being incapacitated" legally means.

Once again, give a copy of these documents to your doctor, your family, and your health care agent. It is highly recommended to discuss your wishes with your proxy and your family, so they clearly understand what you want. Having it in writing makes it official but also emotionally distant. Talking directly about it makes it heartfelt and brings the message home.

Make sure that copies of your advance directives are included in your medical records. It's your responsibility to provide these copies to your care providers. Have a copy at home as well, and wear a "no CPR" bracelet if that's your wish. One of the most common causes of death is sudden cardiac arrest occurring outside of a health care facility. If that happens, an ambulance or other emergency team will respond. They don't have immediate access to health care records or advance directives and will therefore implement life-support measures unless clearly directed otherwise, for example by a "no CPR" bracelet.

A *cardio-pulmonary resuscitation (CPR) directive* allows you or your agent to refuse resuscitation, which would otherwise happen when your heart stops beating or you stop breathing. A DNR ("do not resuscitate" directive, discussed below) is the most common form of CPR directive. With a CPR directive you can also specify what components of CPR you want, which is where this form is different from the more usual DNR form. A CPR directive is more specific. For instance, you may want to have shock treatment and chest compressions but no IV medications. Most health facilities have a policy that requires resuscitation be implemented unless there are written physician orders or CPR directives to the contrary. If you don't have a CPR directive, your consent to CPR is assumed. Even if you do have other advance directives, a CPR directive is suggested if you don't want to be resuscitated.

Anyone over eighteen can sign a CPR directive for themselves. It can be cancelled at any time by the person who signed it. If you're unable to make decisions for yourself, it can also be cancelled by your health care agent. If you never want it cancelled, relate that to your agent. Inform your family and other caretakers of your wishes and where the directive can be found. If this directive isn't found, or you're not wearing a CPR necklace or bracelet, CPR will usually be initiated by emergency medical services (EMS)—that's their job. A CPR directive doesn't prevent you from receiving other care, such as treatment for broken bones, bleeding, or pain. This form may be obtained from your doctor, health care facility, or from the internet.

A *do not resuscitate directive* (DNR) is basically a "no CPR" physician's order. The term "allow natural death" is gaining favor—it's more natural. Doctors will write a DNR order, in consultation with the patient or health care agent, when they feel resuscitation is inappropriate. These circumstances include terminally ill patients and those who are frail. CPR in these situations may only partially work, leaving the patient brain damaged, or in a worse medical condition than before the heart stopped.

CPR training is offered widely today, and people often assume that CPR should always be administered—and that it usually works. But with the elderly, CPR almost always results in fractured ribs and crushing of the chest wall. When you consider that 93 percent of those who have a heart attack outside of a hospital die (the percentage is slightly lower if the cardiac arrest happens in a hospital), and of those who are resuscitated, around half will have permanent brain damage, CPR is a bad idea at the end-of-life or with the frail. Many of those who are revived end up on artificial life support. "Artificial life" is an appropriate term for what they are coming back to. Keep this term in mind when you are thinking about heroic measures to keep someone alive. CPR is good for the young and healthy, not for the old and fragile.[5]

A DNR is an order often written in hospitals, nursing homes, and other health care facilities, but it can be written at any time. A DNR is essentially a physician officially saying "No CPR for this patient." A DNR doesn't affect any treatment other than intubation or CPR (which could include cardiac needles, shock, breathing support, even open heart massage). As noted with the CPR directives above (again, a DNR is a CPR directive), you can still receive care by EMS for broken bones, bleeding, etc. And patients with a DNR can continue to receive antibiotics, chemotherapy, or other appropriate treatments.

A DNI (do not intubate) order is usually part of a DNR unless otherwise indicated. A DNR can be activated or revoked only by you—if you are still able to make clear-headed medical decisions—or by your health care agent, in the event you are not.

Each state accepts different forms, and DNR orders are only official on state-approved forms. They will not work if they're just in your living will. If you have a DNR form, and live at home, it's a good idea to have it visible—say, on your refrigerator (where it will then serve the added function of reminding you of impermanence). Placing a copy in your wallet or purse is also helpful. I have seen people who had "DNR" tattooed on their chest. Necklace, bracelet, fridge, wallet, tattoo . . . you get the point—and so will EMS.

Even with a DNR bracelet or necklace, if there isn't someone else (family or friends) to enforce the DNR, or EMS doesn't see the DNR order, EMS doesn't always comply. It's often a function of the paramedic's level of comfort in doing nothing—they are trained to act. A firefighter and paramedic I interviewed said:

> The biggest obstacle I ran into as a firefighter is that the family seemed to be confused and conflicted on what their dying loved one wants versus what they want for their family member. It is really hard for the family to let go of a loved one. We had situations where there was a DNR present but a family member was yelling at us to do something to save their loved one. It's a really tough call for EMS not to act. Our job is to saves lives, not to let them die.

This is why it's so helpful to have hospice involved from the outset. For end-of-life care situations, in an emergency, call hospice, not 911. But if hospice is not involved, then all the above tips are strongly recommended to ensure a DNR is respected.

A *medical order for scope of treatment* (MOST) is designed for chronically or seriously/terminally ill patients who receive regular medical attention. Different from a simple CPR directive, MOST forms list your preferences for life-sustaining treatment, such as artificial hydration and nutrition, or antibiotics. This form is completed and signed by the patient or their agent, together with a health care provider (a physician, physician's assistant, or advanced practice nurse).

MOST does not replace other health care directives, and it should always be aligned with the choices set out in a person's living will. It travels with the patient when they enter a hospital or transfer to another facility, so that their treatment choices are known and followed. While everyone over eighteen should have their advance directives (living will and MPOA) completed, MOST is only appropriate for people who recognize that their health situation puts them at risk for medical crises. It should be reviewed frequently to ensure that their choices continue to match their health changes and goals of care.

About a dozen states have adopted a form called *physician orders for life sustaining treatment* (POLST), which is a state-approved form establishing the medical orders that articulate life-sustaining wishes at the end of life. It's a blend of what's found in living wills and DNR orders, and goes into effect once signed by you (or your surrogate) and your doctor. Once signed, your wishes become medical orders.

Organ donation is a form of advance directive but is different in that it doesn't deal with medical care decisions for someone who is living. Organ donation is a directive about how you want or may not want your body's organs to be shared with others. See chapter 10 and appendix 1 for more on organ donation.

In conclusion, health care workers report that even legally binding documents become compromised, or even ineffective, when combative family members demand (to the point of threatening to sue the hospital unless their demands are carried out) aggressive life-sustaining treatment. To prevent this, discuss your wishes with your family, your health care agent, or anybody else who may be involved with your care. Be as specific as possible with your documents.

Without these directives, health care workers and family members tend to err on the side of sustaining life. This often means treatment that causes unnecessary suffering—and financial cost. It is estimated that 1.4 million Americans are so medically frail that they only survive with a feeding tube. About 30,000 people are kept alive in a comatose or a permanently vegetative state. Around twenty-five billion dollars is spent each year to keep people alive via ventilators. The cost to individuals and families is often backbreaking: 31 percent have lost most or all of their savings, even though 96 percent had insurance. And it is also bankrupting Medicare. You can dramatically reduce unnecessary emotional and financial burdens for your loved ones (and for your government) by filling out advance directives *now*.

Legal Concerns Before, During, and After Death
by Alex Halpern, JD

About once a year I receive a call from a dying friend who wishes to resolve their affairs at the last minute. I often tell my friend that his estate is quite modest, and a will is not necessary. Nevertheless, he will invariably request that we prepare a will for his peace of mind. Meetings at these times are particularly poignant and surprisingly cheerful. One friend, who was within a day of dying, asked as we shuffled through papers together if I remembered the movie *Beetlejuice*, where the first beings the dead couple met were paper-pushers in the post-mortem bureaucracy, and noted the equivalence to my role on this side. Another remarked as I left with his documents, "See you soon," to the amusement of his attending friends. In these situations, the imminence of death enhances the ritual quality of the seemingly mundane activity of signing off on some legal documents. Beneath the technicalities of disposing of one's property lies the satisfaction of bringing to a close those details that have consumed so much of the life we have led.

The distribution of one's property upon death was once governed entirely by custom, not formalized by law. There was no uniform prescription among peoples. My father, an anthropologist, told me that the Quechan native people in the desert Southwest concluded their funeral ceremonies by burning the dwelling and all the possessions of the deceased to the ground and never spoke his or her name again. By contrast, here is how Herodotus describes the burial practices of the nomadic Bactrians of present-day Afghanistan:

> Here the corpse is placed on a couch, round which, at different distances, daggers are fixed. . . . In some other parts of this trench they bury one of the deceased's concubines, whom they previously strangle, together with the baker, the cook, the groom, his most confidential servant, his horses, the choicest of his effects, and, finally, some golden goblets.

It is characteristic of our modern world, where, contrary to the Bactrians, everyone agrees "you can't take it (or them) with you," that our task is to distribute our money and property in accordance with our individual preference. The question of what happens to your property when you die is determined by the laws of the country and, in the United States, the state in which you were residing at the time of your death. In 1969, the Uniform Probate Code was proposed as part of an effort to align the laws of the fifty states, but today there are only eighteen states that have adopted that Code in its entirety. Thus, while the basic concepts are very similar among those systems rooted in the English common law, any general statement is at best a probability and must be verified by reference to the actual governing law.

At the broadest level of generality, the law permits a person (let's say "you") to direct the passage of your property by a written document, such as a will or a trust, provided that it meets certain formalities. But first, what happens if you die "intestate"—without a valid will? The law makes a will for you. Typically, your property will first be divided between your spouse and your children or, if they aren't there, to their descendants. If you have none of the above, your property will pass to your "next of kin" (parents, siblings, and so on by a set formula). And, if you should have no next of kin, your property will "escheat" to the state, to the benefit of all sentient beings.

Dying intestate is not necessarily a problem. The truth is that it is not uncommon for families to work these things out among themselves, particularly if there is a surviving spouse, and entirely avoid the intervention of the legal machinery. Further, the rules of intestacy may suit your purposes, particularly if you intend to leave your property to your spouse or your children and assuming there isn't an enormous amount of it (which is almost invariably a source of mischief). But note, in many states your intestate property may go one-half to your spouse and one-half to your children, which may not be what you (or your spouse) have in mind. Intestacy doesn't work if you want to make gifts to charity or to people other than your spouse or children. It also doesn't help you to address non-property issues related to your death, such as guardianship of your children or the disposition of your body.

Before proceeding to your will, we should understand that a lot of property passes or can pass outside of your will (or intestate estate). The most important and common example is real estate (your home) owned with your spouse in "joint tenancy with right of survivorship" or some equivalent. Your joint tenancy property will go automatically to your spouse when you die, whether or not you have a will and, if you do, no matter what your will says. The same is true of jointly owned bank and investment accounts. Also, if you have named a beneficiary on your life insurance or investment (retirement) accounts, those funds will go to the named beneficiary, again, no matter what your will says.[6]

Wills

This brings us to your will. In this context, you are the "testator" and the recipients of your bounty are the "beneficiaries." To begin, your will must be written and meet certain formalities. Unlike virtually all other documents today, the only valid version of your will is the one with the original signatures. So don't lose it; a copy is not sufficient. You must sign your will and, in addition, there are witnessing and notarization requirements. Typically, a will must have two witnesses who are not among your beneficiaries; you and your witnesses must all be present together when you sign the will; the witnesses must attest to your competence; and the signatures of the witnesses and the testator must all be notarized.

Many states do, however, recognize an informal, "holographic" will, which is any document that purports to be a will, the material provisions of which are written entirely in your own handwriting. If you decide to go that route, try to be as simple and explicit as possible about your wishes, and have a friend read it to make sure it is clear and unambiguous. A confusing homemade will can be worse than none at all. I recall the case of a woman who left $10,000 to charity and "all of my bank accounts" to her aunt. Of course, all her money was in her bank accounts—she had inadvertently given the same money twice.

In your will you will begin by naming your personal representative or executor. The personal representative is responsible to close out your affairs and collect and dispose of your property. This includes assembling your property, paying your debts, and distributing what's left to your beneficiaries. Usually, or half the time anyway, your surviving spouse will do this job, but if you don't have one, it will have to be somebody else. This can be a complicated and tedious task, including figuring out where your assets are, who you owe money to, and what to do with all of the stuff in your closets and basement. As a rule of thumb, your personal representative is somebody who owes you a big favor in this life or from a former one. Expect them to ask you to reciprocate in this life, or a later one.

If you have children who are minors, you may also name a guardian to continue rearing them and a trustee to manage their finances. These jobs can be filled by a single person, but they do call upon different skill sets. It may be obvious who should raise your children if you and your spouse are gone, but it can become controversial among your family and friends. Remember that the guardian will be taking on a lot of responsibility. Becoming the guardian for your child and bringing him or her into their family will change their lives. Among other things, your guardian will probably need financial help from you. This is a good reason for younger parents who haven't yet hoarded a lot of wealth to carry life insurance.

You may wish to leave instructions in your will for the disposition of your remains. Typically, funeral homes will follow the directions of a surviving spouse. However, if there is none, you can avoid confusion by specifying your wishes in your will. This is particularly important for unmarried people who do not live with or near their family. A friend who shows up and says you want special funeral arrangements may be viewed skeptically. In some families where religious beliefs conflict, leaving written directions can be very important if you are concerned that, for example, your parents will object to cremation or Buddhist rituals at your funeral. I have prepared the following form of funeral provision for use by members of the Shambhala Buddhist community:

> My funeral exercises and the disposal of my body shall be conducted in strict accordance with the practices and rituals of the Shambhala Buddhist Church, including, without limitation, that my body shall remain undisturbed and unembalmed, in state, for three (3) days after my death, or until otherwise directed by a qualified representative of the Shambhala Buddhist Church, and shall thereafter be cremated, preferably at Shambhala Mountain Center, Larimer County, Colorado [for example], or another dharma center or site of the Shambhala Buddhist Church. I further desire that after the passage of forty-nine (49) days from the date of my death, or such other duration as may be directed by a qualified representative of the Shambhala Buddhist Church, my ashes shall be buried at Shambhala Mountain Center [again, for example] or, if that is not practical, another dharma center or site of the Shambhala Buddhist Church.

I must tell you that if a close relative were to challenge this directive in court after your death, I am not certain that your wishes would prevail. This is one of the things that it would be best to work out while you are living. On the other hand, I have known more than one person who simply acknowledged that his parents would not be able to bear a cremation and conceded that things may not go his way after death any more than during life.

The topic of what happens to your body after you die requires a short digression concerning treatment of the body after "death." I use scare quotes because this digression stems from the different definitions of when you are really dead between civil authorities and the Buddhist understanding. In some Buddhist thought, the death process is not complete until your body has relaxed from rigor mortis. For most people, that is around three days after you are medically dead. During that period, Buddhist thought advises that the body remain undisturbed. Civil authorities, however, commonly regard the body as a public health hazard by twenty-four hours after medical death and require embalming or freezing. This difference in approach must be worked out with those authorities, usually through the intermediary of the mortuary. In addition, if you die from unknown causes, an autopsy will be required, again for public health purposes. I doubt that this can be avoided.

Disposition of Property

Now we come at last to the question of disposing of your property. Let's start with your personal property, including items such as jewelry, musical instruments, coin or other collections, paintings and sculpture, furniture, dharma objects and texts, and so on. Some states permit you to make (and change whenever you want to) an informal list of personal property that identifies who you want to receive it without requiring witnesses, notaries, or lawyers. Some people make detailed lists, but in my experience most do not. I suggest that this is an opportunity to make gestures of acknowledgment to family and friends that even if not of significant monetary value may be very meaningful to the recipients.

You may have a close friend who would be very grateful to receive an artwork from you; or a sibling who would like to receive a memento of your childhood. Also, it must be acknowledged that your surviving children may find it very stressful to attempt to divide your goods immediately after your death. Sibling relations are complex, and conflicts can occur at this difficult time that result in lasting ill will. It will be very helpful if you take the time to consider those possibilities and resolve them by this simple process.

Trusts

Gifts of property to children who are minors may require the creation of a trust. Trusts are used when you want to have a person or institution manage the funds of another person. Trusts have three principal parties—the settlor, the trustee, and the beneficiaries. The settlor in this case is you. The beneficiaries are your children (or whoever you wish), and the trustee is the person, persons, or institution you designate to be responsible to manage the trust assets and distribute them in accordance with your direction. The trustee has a "fiduciary" duty to act solely in the best interests of the beneficiaries and in accordance with the directives of your trust.

Particularly with children who are minors, the trustee may have a significant role in making decisions affecting their upbringing. The terms you set for distributing funds for the benefit of your children will vary according to the amount of money you leave them, but typically you will want to be sure to provide for their health care and education needs while they are dependent. All trusts come to an end at some time when the remaining funds are distributed to the beneficiaries, who are by then adults. When should that happen? It is difficult, maybe impossible, to foresee whether today's toddler will be sufficiently financially responsible to manage your hard-earned money by the age of twenty-one, thirty, or ever. Obviously, there is no definite formula. Reflection on one's own youth for guidance can be disconcerting.

In addition to your immediate family, you may wish to leave some portion of your estate to charity. This can be done by a specific bequest of a certain amount of money, but you may not know if the amount you are stating today will be too much or too little by the time you die. In that case, I recommend leaving a percentage of your estate to your preferred charities rather than a set amount of money. So, you could say in your will, "I leave ten percent of my estate to [your charity]."

Finally, after making specific gifts of personal property, to charity, and to other special friends or whatever, you conclude the process by making a gift of all the rest of your estate (referred to as your "residuary estate"), which is usually the majority of it. If you have a surviving spouse, it is common to leave your residuary estate to him (or her) and let him deal with what to do with it all when he dies. However, you can certainly distribute it more widely than that. Here again, it is a good idea to think in terms of percentages rather than dollar amounts. Decisions about who to leave how much are entirely dependent on personal circumstances, which are too variable to attempt to address in this context.

I should include a brief word on the lifetime or inter vivos trust. These trusts have the same cast as the testamentary ones, with a twist. There are the settlor (you), the beneficiary (you), and the trustee (you again!—at least while you're alive). You establish it during your lifetime (hence, "inter vivos") and transfer all your assets into it. Then, while you are alive, you manage your assets within your trust as your own trustee, for the benefit of yourself.

Why would you do all that? Because your lifetime trust also includes provisions for what happens after you die. This permits the direct transfer of your property to your heirs on your death without going through the hazards and delay of the dreaded "probate." Probate is the legal procedure for resolving your estate through the courts. Avoiding probate became popularized through best-selling how-to books back in the 1960s, when Americans started getting rich. In some states, probate is evidently intolerably expensive and difficult. In others, however, it is inexpensive and easy. I recommend that you think twice before putting everything you have into a lifetime trust that may not really be necessary. Typically, though, they are revocable, so you can undo them if you change your mind.

This is just an introduction to the topic of "what happens to my stuff when I die." It is basically enough to understand the territory for most people whose financial and property lives are relatively uncomplicated. For example, I have not attempted to delve into the arcanum of estate (or, for the Libertarian reader) death taxes, which can drive wealthier individuals to extreme states of mind. Other complicating conditions that I have avoided include ownership of a small business, artistic estates, children from multiple marriages, rights in trusts from preceding generations, incompetent or disabled family members, pets, and on and on.

Finally, I am required by the unwritten rules of the lawyers' union, and our insurance carriers, to remind you that all of the foregoing is not legal advice and that in considering the disposition of your estate you should consult with your own lawyer. Moreover, that is absolutely true. Everyone has individual life circumstances that require specific consideration well beyond the reach of an introductory discussion such as this one.

The Living Will and the Medical Power of Attorney

The reader is by now familiar with the idea that before death there comes sickness and old age, unless one is unfortunate enough to short-circuit the process by dying while young and healthy. In this section we discuss legal issues particular to sickness and old age, specifically the period of time when you are incapacitated by one or both of those conditions. While the disposition of property upon death is one of the most venerable of legal concerns and is well defined, legal issues related to medical decisions for people who become incapacitated due to sickness and old age have been, and will continue to be, the subject of significant social and legal controversy.

These issues have become sharpened by the relentless progress of medical science and technology in sustaining life (or some condition within medical understanding of that term), and the medical definition of death. Back in the log cabin days, people died at home. There were certainly difficult decisions to be made, but they took place in private, within the family, and beyond the ministrations of institutional medicine and the scrutiny of the law. It is far more common now, perhaps inevitable, for individuals approaching death to become engaged with sophisticated medical interventions that impact on their dying process and demand choices that never existed before. Significantly, these decisions occur beyond the immediate family in institutional contexts that implicate medical professionals, and the public interest in the form of state law. What had been predominantly a private matter has become increasingly public.

The development of new end-of-life choices poses new social questions addressing the problem of who can make what choices for whom. When these questions become conflicts, they wind up in the legal system, acting as society's arbiter of final resort. In that forum, the debate becomes framed as a matrix of competing "rights" and "interests," which is the way the law thinks. The protagonists include the individual (you, unfortunately), your immediate family, the state on behalf of the "public" interest, the medical profession, and, in the worst case scenario, the harpies of the media and mass politics.

The competing rights and interests include the individual's "right to privacy," the family's right to act in the interest of their dying relative (or perhaps dead relative), social and criminal proscriptions against suicide and euthanasia, and the physician's ethical obligation to sustain life. Much of the debate takes place within an environment of beliefs (experienced as highly vivid emotions) about death that are vastly different from the one presented in the work you are reading.

This is not the context for an extended discussion of this remarkable phenomenon. In the legal world, the "right to privacy" does not literally appear in the United States Constitution but was interpolated by the judiciary as a bashful creature lurking in the overlapping shadows (the "penumbrae") of various express guarantees in the Bill of Rights. It has yet to shake the stigma of the illegitimate stepchild. The "private" deaths of Karen Ann Quinlan, Nancy Cruzan, and, most recently, Terri Schiavo, all became the property of the law when they were unable to die (or live) due to this interaction of medical progress, family and societal conflict, and questions of humanity well beyond the depth of legal analysis.

In the thirty-five years since the case of Karen Ann Quinlan brought the matter of medical decision-making by and for the incapacitated (less graciously, the "brain dead") to the attention of the law, legislatures and courts have struggled to craft methods for people to avoid these end-of-life pitfalls. These are the subject of this brief note. They have become relatively accepted in our society and usually work as intended. But, as the Terri Schiavo controversy revealed, these methods remain contingent at best, and may prove to be unavailing in the wrong situation.

For our purposes, the practical point is to emphasize the critical importance of the durable medical power of attorney (MPOA) and its better known (but far less useful) counterpart, the "living will." Both of these documents have been designed by law to permit you to exercise now, while you are clear-headed, your presumed right to make decisions about medical care to be provided later (or not provided), when you are not so clear-headed. Here again, state laws differ, and generalizations are not necessarily a correct statement of the law that applies to where you reside.

Both of these documents take effect when you become mentally "incapacitated," or some similar term. What does "incapacitated" mean? Legal definitions vary according to the context. But where the issue is voluntary withdrawal of medical intervention, a working definition is: "unable to make or communicate responsible decisions concerning my person." Lacking this sort of "decisional capacity" refers to the inability to provide informed consent, or the refusal of medical treatment, or the inability to make an informed health care decision.

The living will is a direction to your physician that you want life-sustaining medical interventions to be discontinued in a very specific, and often extreme circumstance. You tell your physician that if you have been in a coma, or are unconscious (or the equivalent) for a period of time, commonly seven days, and are unable to communicate your medical treatment wishes; and if in the opinion of your physician(s) your condition is terminal and incurable; then you want all forms of life-sustaining procedures to be removed. You want them to "pull the plug" and let you die (which may actually mean discontinuing massive doses of antibiotics, or a continually growing number of other interventions).

You may have to specify whether, under those conditions, you also want artificial (intravenous) nourishment to be discontinued. On that point, some people say that if I'm that far gone, stop everything. Others say that if artificial nourishment actually keeps me alive, maybe I'm not as far gone as it looks and let's keep it going. There is probably no "right" answer. [See Dr.

Gershten's comments on this topic under "Hydration, Nutrition, and Pain Control" in chapter 8.]

As you can see, the living will is limited to one extreme situation. Think of it as a fail-safe to get you out of a really bad spot. The medical power of attorney is far more flexible, wide-reaching, and useful. You may become incapacitated in connection with your last illness long before seven days in a coma have elapsed. You may be incapacitated temporarily at any time in your life by an injury or illness. Or it is possible to be incapacitated for years due to mental deterioration. In all of those cases, a living will is useless, and a MPOA may be crucial. So whom does your health care provider turn to?

This is a particularly important question for people who do not have either a spouse (including gay couples), or adult children; in other words, someone who is capable of making decisions for them. If you are incapacitated and there is no recognized immediate family member to help, how will a treating physician know who has the right to speak for you? You do not want to leave a physician or a hospital in that position. They may feel forced to take steps to keep you alive based on ethical grounds, or on concerns for legal liability that you would not prefer.[7]

The MPOA involves you, the "principal," empowering some other person, your "agent," to make all medical decisions for you whenever you are incapacitated. Your agent has essentially the same power that you would have if you weren't incapacitated. In this way, there is always a person to whom your medical caregiver can turn when a medical decision has to be made and you can't make it. If you recover from your incapacity, you regain your own decision-making power and take control of your own situation.

Your MPOA includes your instructions to your agent concerning what you want them to know when they have to make those decisions. Your agent must comply with your directions and wishes. If your written instructions are not clear, your agent has the power to make the decision that they believe would be consistent with your wishes. You are able to say today what you believe you will want in the future. As an example, here is one rather legalistic phrasing of the wish not to be kept pointlessly alive:

> I direct my agent to make decisions concerning life-sustaining medical treatment with the knowledge that I do not want my life to be prolonged artificially nor do I want life-sustaining medical treatment to be provided or continued if such means are the sole source of my continued living.

At some point you will want to talk about your medical treatment preferences with your agent. It will help your agent if you can say something more specific than "I don't want to live forever," or "If I'm dead, let me die." Remember that your agent, who is probably somebody who loves you, may have to make decisions that are deeply painful. The "Five Wishes" is one popular system that provides an outline-style format to help you hold such a conversation, and the MPOA does so with greater coverage and clarity.[8]

DEMYSTIFYING HOSPICE:
AN UNDERUSED SERVICE AT END OF LIFE
by Beth Patterson, MA, LPC, JD

Many people hear the word "hospice" and think it means a place where a loved one goes to give up and die, alone and on too many medications. Nothing can be further from the truth. Hospice is not a place but a valuable service that supports dying patients and their family members to maintain hope, dignity, and quality in all domains of life—physically, emotionally, and spiritually. The services provided by hospice allow a patient to spend his or her final days among family and friends at home (wherever home is, from a private dwelling to a nursing home or assisted living facility, and even a homeless shelter or prison), as alert and comfortable as possible, and away from the hospital with its often dehumanizing high technology.

The History of the Hospice Movement

Although the modern hospice movement is relatively young, the word "hospice" has its historical origins in the Middle Ages. Hospices were shelters available to pilgrims traveling from Europe to the Holy Land. Today, they can be considered as way stations on life's travels from this plane of existence to the next.

Dame Cicely Saunders (1918–2005) is considered the leading pioneer of the modern hospice movement. Dame Saunders was a social worker, then a nurse, and then a physician. Observing patients dying in pain, she returned to school for specialty medical training in controlling pain for the terminally ill. Dame Saunders also observed that the terminally ill were dying depersonalized deaths, isolated from their loved ones, in hospitals with tubes and monitors in place that served no real purpose and which increased patients' and families' despair at the end of life.

With these observations in mind, Dame Saunders founded St. Christopher's Hospice in London in 1967. Her goal was to keep patients engaged in life and autonomous in their decision-making for as long as possible, while also attending to their physical, emotional, and spiritual pain. Dame Saunders sought to change the emphasis on the medical approach, where the needs of the dying were ignored once curative treatments were exhausted. Instead, she emphasized palliative, or comfort-oriented, care; pain management; emotional and spiritual care to enhance patients' quality of life; and help to maintain their own and their loved ones' hopes for a dignified end of life. Because of her, the final years, months, or days of mortally ill people have been transformed from what was often painful, fearsome, isolating, humiliating, and meaningless to a period in which they can discover intense creativity, reconciliation, intellectual and spiritual development, and peace. As Cicely Saunders wrote:

> To talk of accepting death when its approach has become inevitable is not mere resignation on the part of the patient or defeatism or neglect on the part of the doctor. For both of them it is the very opposite of doing nothing. Our work then is to alter the character of this stage [of life] so that this time is not seen as a long defeat of living but as a positive achievement in dying.[9]

Thus, hospice is about quality of life. When there is nothing more that can be done to cure a disease, there is still much that can be done to enhance the patient's life and to support the patient and the family.

The American Hospice Movement and the Medicare Hospice Benefit

Elisabeth Kübler-Ross (1926–2004) is another important pioneer of the hospice movement who brought the word "dying" out of the metaphorical closet and into the light of day in the death-defying culture of the United States, through her groundbreaking book *On Death and Dying*. Kübler-Ross and others observed that the medical profession viewed the dying as failures and not as simply those experiencing a natural and normal phase of life. Thus, they were often isolated from care, far from nursing stations, with care providers slow to respond to their needs and loved ones not informed of their conditions or needs. Through her work as a psychiatrist, Kübler-Ross researched the experiences of the terminally ill. "Her research provided poignant evidence of the great isolation and discomfort in which patients were dying at the time."[10]

The issues around death led to Senate hearings in 1972 on Death and Dignity. The hearings, which included testimony by Dr. Kübler-Ross, focused on the formation of an American hospice program. The first American hospice was founded in 1974 in New Haven, Connecticut, under the direction of Dr. Sylvia Lack from St. Christopher's Hospice in London.

Thanks to pioneers like Dame Saunders and Dr. Kübler-Ross, the emphasis in care for the dying has shifted from doctors and hospitals to care at home by those most involved in the patients' lives. "As with childbirth, the care of the dying is now influenced as much as possible by those main players, who receive as much information as they want and need. Dying patients are seen less often as passive targets for diagnostic tests and painkillers, and more often as individuals with control over their living and dying."[11]

Since the founding of the American hospice movement in the early 1970s, hospice has burgeoned and is available throughout the United States. As a result of the growth of the United States hospice movement, hospice care is now regulated by Medicare, and the costs of hospice care are largely covered under the Medicare hospice benefit (as well as under most insurance companies for those who are not eligible for Medicare).[12]

Buddhism and the Hospice Movement

It is worth noting that the emergence of the American hospice movement coincided in the early 1970s with the emergence of Buddhism in the West. The first Buddhist hospices were founded in the United States in the 1980s to care for AIDS patients. The most prominent of these is the Zen Hospice Project in San Francisco, which, in addition to providing hospice care, offers workshops to health care providers emphasizing the role of mindfulness meditation practices in caring for the dying.[13]

The Upaya Zen Center in Santa Fe was founded in 1990 by Roshi Joan Halifax. The Upaya Zen Center's Project on Being with Dying was founded "to inspire a gentle revolution in our relationship to dying and living, a means for people to explore the meaning of death in the experience of their own lives . . . and to develop an approach to death that is kind, open and dignified."

The Rigpa Fellowship, under the direction of Sogyal Rinpoche, is another leader in bringing together Buddhism and end-of-life issues. Sogyal Rinpoche is a Tibetan Buddhist meditation master and teacher who first came to teach in the United States in the 1970s. Like *On Death and Dying* by Kübler-Ross, Sogyal Rinpoche's *The Tibetan Book of Living and Dying* is viewed as a groundbreaking work in bringing death with dignity and awareness into modern Western consciousness.

The Services of Hospice

Under the Medicare benefit, hospice care is available to anyone who has a life-threatening condition or terminal illness with a prognosis of six months or less if the illness or condition were to run its normal course, as certified by the patient's attending physician and a hospice medical director. Nonetheless, many people stay on hospice for more than six months, as long as they continue to meet the foregoing requirement at the end of each certification period. Individuals are evaluated for re-certification at the end of the first ninety-day period, the second ninety-day period, and thereafter at the end of each sixty-day period. There is no limit to the number of sixty-day re-certification periods, as long as the individual continues to meet the six-month prognosis requirement.

In addition, in electing hospice care, the patient elects palliative or comfort care, rather than curative or life-extending treatment. In fact, as discussed further below, palliative or comfort care is a hallmark of hospice care, and hospice clinicians are expert in providing effective pain management. It should be noted that the patient and his or her family retain autonomy regarding medical decisions at all times, and the patient may elect to revoke hospice benefits at any time if he or she feels that curative treatment may be beneficial. The patient can re-elect the hospice benefit at any time, and will begin service in the next certification period.

In keeping with the hospice movement's mission to provide care in all domains of life, each hospice's program provides support to the patient and his or her family through the interdisciplinary team consisting of the medical director, nurses, social workers, home health aides, chaplains, bereavement counselors, volunteer coordinator, and volunteers. Also available, if necessary for comfort and quality of life related to the hospice diagnosis, are dieticians and speech, occupational, and physical therapists.

Under the Medicare benefit, the patient and family are considered the "unit of care." The care and support provided by the hospice interdisciplinary team recognizes this.

What Does Hospice Care Look Like?

Once it is determined that a patient is appropriate for hospice care, the patient, or his or her medical-proxy decision makers (those who hold medical power of attorney), will sign consent and insurance forms. This is often called the "EOB (or election of benefits) process," whereby the patient agrees to forgo curative treatment under Medicare benefits, and instead elects hospice benefits. One of the first things the hospice staff will do is contact the patient's attending physician to ensure that he or she agrees that hospice care is appropriate, and that he or she then agrees with the hospice plan of care, including decisions about medications and other care.

The hospice clinical team for the patient—registered nurse (the case manager), social worker, chaplain, and home health aide (HHA) or certified nursing assistant (CNA)—is then assigned. Each member of the team will meet with the patient and his or her family and assess initial physical, emotional, social, and spiritual needs, and develop a plan of care for the patient, which may change as the patient's condition changes. It is noteworthy that the patient and family, or other caregivers, are involved in formulating and changing the plan of care. Physical needs may include medications, or durable medical equipment such as wheelchairs and oxygen.

Psychosocial needs, including any needs for community services, are assessed by the social worker, who also assesses the need for volunteers to provide companionship or other support, including massage, music or art therapy, or respite for family caregivers. The chaplain will provide spiritual support, and also help the patient resource those in his or her spiritual community, as needed. The chaplain, in coordination with the social worker, will also help with funeral or memorial arrangements. The CNA or HHA will assist with bathing and grooming. The need for pre-bereavement support will also be assessed. The members of the clinical team are required to visit the patient at least once every other week (more often for HHAs and CNAs). Visits are often more frequent based on needs, and are likely to be daily as death is more imminent. Volunteers generally visit once a week.

The Medicare hospice benefit also requires that bereavement support be provided for at least one year after the patient's death to family members and others affected by the death. Many hospices provide this service for thirteen months, to guide the bereaved through the first anniversary of the death.

As a result of the growth of the American hospice movement, there are thousands of hospice programs throughout the United States, serving all regions of the country.

The Importance of Managing Pain

The management of pain—physical, emotional, and spiritual—is one of the most important missions of hospice care. Unrelieved physical pain results in unnecessary suffering in the terminally ill. In a hierarchical needs system, the first step in managing global pain is to manage physical pain. Indeed, Dame Saunders "saw how the futility of terminal pain drained life and a sense of meaning out of its sufferers. Chronic pain held patients captive. Dying patients living in pain could do nothing other than fear it and curse it as it demanded all of their energy and deprived them of their humanity."[14]

Unfortunately, misconceptions about pain and pain control continue to interfere with the acceptance of hospice care. Some picture loved ones dying in hospice alone and in abject pain. The picture of the terminally ill dying in pain is, unfortunately, historically accurate. Before the advent of the hospice movement, under-treatment of cancer-related pain was common, and the terminally ill did often die alone in hospital beds. "[T]hey were often handled as bundles of physical symptoms or simply as failures of the medical system, but lost in all this 'expert treatment' was a human being with fears, questions, desires, needs, and rights."[15]

Fears about over-medication and addiction also discourage the wider use of hospice services. Addiction is very rare in the use of narcotics to treat pain. Hospice clinical staff is specially trained in the effective use of narcotics and other pain-relieving drugs, as well as drugs to counteract the side effects (such as nausea and constipation) of those drugs. In addition, anti-anxiety and anti-depressant drugs are used as needed to enhance the terminally ill patient's quality of life.

It is impossible to work with a person's emotional and spiritual pain if he or she is experiencing unrelenting physical pain. Unrelieved physical pain can lead to feelings of hopelessness and fear, and can also cause the patient to isolate him- or herself from family and other support. With this in mind, Cicely Saunders developed the concept of "total pain": "an understanding of pain as the complex interaction between physical pain caused by disease and pain caused by mental, emotional, and spiritual malaise."[16] If the patient is in chronic pain, he or she may give up hope of a peaceful and dignified death. Effective pain control allows the patient to maintain a sense of autonomy and control and focus on quality of life issues, unfinished business, and spiritual concerns. Thus, the interdisciplinary team approach of hospice is indispensable for the treatment of "total pain."

Hospice chaplains, social workers, and bereavement counselors, as well as those in the hospice patient's spiritual community, play an important role in maintaining the patient's quality of life and helping to relieve spiritual pain. Those facing death commonly search for essence and connectedness. Concerns about essence include questioning whether one's life and death have meaning and purpose, questions about values, doubts, and beliefs. Concerns about connectedness stir questions about how one is connected to family and others in one's life, as well as to a higher being, and also bring to the surface the individual's unfinished business in his or her relationships.

Listening to a dying patient's fears and concerns is at the heart of the services provided by hospice. Fears cited by hospice staff in working with the dying include fear of the process of dying, fear of loss of control, fear for loved ones, fear of dying alone, fear that one's life has been meaningless, and fear of the unknown.

Conclusion

As the Buddhist teachings emphasize, impermanence and death are part of the natural order of things, not something to be hidden away in fear and despair. Death and dying are integral parts of human existence, and indeed, of human development and growth. Elisabeth Kübler-Ross has observed: "If you can begin to see death as an invisible but friendly companion on your life's journey . . . you can learn to *live* your life rather than simply passing through it."[17] Hospice care is available as a companion on that journey, enabling patients and loved ones to embrace this special and sacred stage of life with dignity, autonomy, and peace.[18]

8. Caring for the Dying

To the yogi death is the sauce that adds spice to life.
—B. K. S. Iyengar

The Needs of the Dying
by Christine Longaker

AFTER YEARS of listening to many people who are dying, hearing them try to articulate what they need during this most difficult passage of their lives, I will try to speak for them to you, their loved ones and caregivers. I will speak with one voice representing their many voices, communicating the emotional, practical, and spiritual needs of a human being facing imminent death.

I need to talk about my thoughts and fears. I am going through so many changes; I feel so uncertain about my future. Sometimes all I can see in front of me are those future things I am afraid of. And each day, my fear ignites a different emotion. Some days I can't take it in and I need to believe it isn't happening. So there might be days or even weeks that I will feel sad, or act irritated. If you can listen and accept me, without trying to change or fix my mood, I will eventually get over it and be able to relax, and perhaps even laugh with you again.

Until now, you may have always expected me to be emotionally strong and in control. Now I'm afraid that if I honestly reveal myself, you will think less of me. Because of the extreme stresses I am going through, it might happen that the very worst sides of my personality, the real dregs, will get stirred up. If that happens I need permission to be "lost in the woods" for a while. Don't worry, I will come back.

Do you know that I'm afraid to express my true thoughts and feelings? What if everyone I care about runs away and leaves me all alone? After all, you might not believe how hard this really is. That's why I need you to reassure me that you understand my suffering, and that you are willing to stay with me through the process of my dying. I need to know that you will listen to me, respect me, and accept me, no matter what sort of mood I am in on any particular day.

Here's the most important thing: I want you to see me as a whole person, not as a disease, or a tragedy, or a fragile piece of glass. Do not look at me with pity but rather with all of your love and compassion. Even though I am facing death, I am still living. I want people to treat me normally and to include me in their lives. Don't think that you cannot be completely with me. It is okay to tell me if I am making your life harder, or that you are feeling afraid or sad.

More than anything, I need you to be honest now. There is no more time for us to play games, or to hide from each other. I would love to know I am not the only one feeling vulnerable and afraid. When you come in acting cheerful and strong, I sometimes feel I must hide my real self from you. When we only talk of superficial things, I feel even lonelier. Please, come in and allow me to be myself, and try to tune in to what is going on with me that day. How healing it would be for me to have someone to share my tears with! Don't forget: we're going to have to say goodbye to each other one day soon.

And if we have a rocky history between us, don't you think it would be easier if we could start by acknowledging it? This doesn't mean I want you to rekindle the same old disagreements. I would like it if we could simply acknowledge our past difficulties, forgive each other, and let go. If we don't communicate like this, and instead stay in hiding from each other, then whenever you visit me we will feel the strain of that which remains unspoken. Believe me, I already feel much more aware of my past mistakes, and I feel bad about the ways I might have hurt you. Please allow me to acknowledge them and say I am sorry. Then we can see each other afresh and enjoy the time we have left together.

Now more than ever I need you to be reliable. When we make plans and you are late, or do not come at all, you don't realize how much you've really let me down. Thinking that I will have one visitor on a given day can make all the difference in how much I am able to bear my pain or emotional distress.

Each moment spent with a friend who really cares and accepts me is like a warm light shining in a very difficult, lonely, and frightening existence.

When you come into the room, can you meet my gaze? I wish you would take the time to really look into my eyes and see what I am truly feeling. I long for friends to embrace me, or at least touch my shoulder, hold my hand, or gently stroke my face. Please don't hold back your affection and your love. In the hospital, I sometimes feel more like an object or a disease rather than a human being. Please, bring in your humanity and kindness to ease my suffering. Because no matter how I might seem on the outside—gruff, withdrawn, cheerful, bitter, or mentally impaired—inside, I am suffering and I am very lonely and afraid.

Even though this is a difficult time in my own life, often my main worry is about how my condition is affecting my loved ones. They seem so lost, so burdened, so alone with all of the changes they are experiencing and all the responsibilities they shoulder. And what about *their* future? How are they going to cope after I am gone? I'm afraid I am leaving them stranded and alone. Some days, when everyone comes in with different emotions and needs, I am too weak to handle it all. I can't possibly listen to everyone and all of their burdens. I would be so relieved if someone could help my closest family members contact a counselor, or an organization like a hospice, who could support them, listen to their needs and their sadness, and maybe even help out in practical ways.

Saying goodbye is so very hard for both of us. But if we don't, and if you are resisting my death when I have begun the process of dying, it will be even harder for me to let go. I would like to live longer, yet I cannot struggle anymore. Please do not hold this against me, or urge me to fight when all my strength is gone. I need your blessings now, your acceptance of me and of what is happening to me. Tell me it is all right for me to die, even if I appear unconscious or in great pain, and tell me you are letting me go, with your warmest wishes and all the courage you can muster in this moment.

One of my deepest, most powerful fears is that I will be reduced to the situation of an infant, helpless and incoherent. I fear that you will forget who I am and treat me with disrespect. Even thinking about others taking care of my most intimate needs makes me feel ashamed. And every step closer to death makes me realize I will soon be totally dependent on others. Please try to understand when I resist giving in to one more change, one more loss.

Help me to take care of myself, even in little ways, so that it will be easier to tolerate the bigger changes which are coming. *Speak directly to me*, rather than over my head, or as though I were not in the room. Find out what my wishes are for my medical care during the time of dying while I can still articulate them. And please honor and respect my wishes, ensuring they get written down and communicated.

When everyone treats me as though they know what is best for me, I get so angry. *Aren't I the person who is ill?* Isn't this my life, and my body? Don't I have a right to know what is going on, to know if I am living or dying? I need to know what my condition is. I need to know, in the doctor's best estimate, how much time I have left. If you find the courage to tell me what is going on, then I can decide which type of care is right for me; then I can make decisions about my life. If we stop hiding the truth about my imminent death, I will be able to wrap up the details of my life and prepare my family to survive after I'm gone.

You know, the pain can be unbearable sometimes. On other days, the pain is just there, like a bad toothache, and I get tense and irritable. Please forgive me when I am in a bad mood; you may not know what it is like to live with constant pain and discomfort. What is hardest is when no one believes the amount of pain I am having; that makes me feel crazy. I need to be believed and I need to have my pain relieved. But please don't knock me unconscious to do it. I would rather experience a little pain, and still be conscious—to enjoy my life and my family, and to do my spiritual practice—while I am in the last few weeks of life.

One of the most important ways you could offer practical help would be to act as an advocate for my needs. When I am ill and weak, I may lose my ability to communicate what I want and need. Perhaps some hospital rules can be relaxed to accommodate my lifestyle, my family, and my personal needs. My loved ones might need reassurance, or encouragement to take a break from caregiving duties when they become too emotional or stressed. And legally, help me to plan ahead of time whatever practical arrangements are necessary so that I can prepare for a peaceful atmosphere at the time of my death.

And what happens if my mind starts to disintegrate? How long will you visit me then? I hope you will not give up communicating with me when my words come out garbled, or when I can't speak at all. Do not forget that underneath the seeming confusion—or unconsciousness—I am still there, I can still hear you, I can even feel the quality of our relationship. I might be feeling lonely and afraid, though. I always need your love and your reassurance. In order to help me, I hope you can learn to be deeply peaceful inside and receptive, so that you can sense what I am feeling and needing and know how to respond appropriately.

As my body and mind disintegrate, remember that inside I am still the person I was when my life was at its peak—and thus I am always worthy of kindness and respect. No matter how far gone I appear to be, trust that your love and heartfelt prayers do get through and deeply reassure my entire being. Please don't give up on me when the going gets rough. This is our last chance to heal our relationship, and to give to each other our last gifts of love, forgiveness, and wisdom.

Being in the hospital makes me feel so restricted. It's hard to give up the patterns of my normal lifestyle—my ability to enjoy the company of my friends, my favorite activities, and even my usual waking and sleeping patterns. It's hard to lose my privacy; in the hospital I feel so exposed and vulnerable. I miss the home-cooked meals, the family celebrations, and my favorite music. It's hard, in this controlled and public environment, to find a space to share our intimacy and our grief without fear of being interrupted. When I'm hospitalized, I yearn to have a connection to the outside world, to nature, to the beautiful changes of weather and seasons and wind. Do I have to be cut off from all that I love and cherish even while I am living?

I might prefer to die at home. If you called a hospice program, they could show you how to arrange for me to be cared for at home as long as you can manage it. Being at home would make the process of dying more bearable. I understand that if you have the responsibilities of work and raising your family, you might have to put me in a hospital. But please, do not abandon me there! Help make the hospital environment more like home; try and spend the night when you can. And, even if I have to be hospitalized for most of the period of my dying, I would be grateful if you could arrange with the hospice nurses to bring me home for at least the last few days of my life. What a relief that would be, to be cared for in my familiar surroundings, with family and friends keeping vigil—meditating, praying, or simply talking with me, to help relieve my fears and my loneliness.

I need help reflecting on my life, so I can make sense of it. What meaning did my life have? What have I accomplished? How have I changed and grown? I need to know you will not judge me, so that I can honestly face and reveal my life to you. Encourage me to acknowledge my regrets, so that I can make up with anyone I've neglected or harmed and ask for their forgiveness. Sometimes when I look back on it, my life seems to be one continuous string of mistakes, or a legacy of selfishness and disregard for others. Remind me of what I have accomplished, of any good I have done, so I can know that in some way I have contributed to your life.

Please don't feel you must have all the answers or wise words to assuage my fears. You might come to my side feeling anxious, not knowing what to say. You don't have to pretend or keep up a strong façade. To really offer me spiritual support, I need you to be a human being first. Have the courage to share with me your uncertainty, your fear, your genuine sadness for the immense loss we are facing. Going through these difficult feelings together, establishing a deep bond and trust, I will feel safe enough to begin letting go, and I'll be able to face my death with more equanimity and an open heart.

After you have listened to my painful stories or complaints, remind me that I am more than my fear or my sadness, my pain or my anger. Help me understand that whatever suffering I am going through is natural; it's part of the human condition. Remind me that my painful emotional or physical condition, no matter how seemingly solid and real, will pass.

If I seem to be lost in my own suffering, help me to remember that there is still one positive thing I can do: extend my love and compassion toward others. Tell me the ways my life has touched yours. In whatever way you can reach me, help me connect to the inner goodness which is the most essential part of my being.

How can my process of dying have meaning? When I am lying here, weak and helpless, I am tempted to feel that the remainder of my life is useless. Everyone has to do everything for me, and it's so hard to feel that I have nothing left to contribute. If you ask, you might find there is something I do have to offer you: the insights about life and about death that I've recently gained. Would you allow me to give you whatever final gifts I have?

Sometimes the thought of death terrifies. At the same time, I also feel strangely peaceful and even curious about the adventure that is ahead. Yet it is a journey for which I may not have prepared. It won't help if you try to give me your own beliefs and answers about death; I need you to help me discover my own philosophy, my own inner resources and confidence. But if you are grounded in a spiritual tradition which gives you strength, which helps you work through your own suffering, perhaps you can find ways to open windows and doors of hope for me. Perhaps all you need to do is tell me your own story, without any expectations attached. With time, if you give me your love and your trust, I will work something out deep inside me.

What will happen to me after I've died? What will count then? Help me find images of death which inspire rather than frighten me, so I can trust that what I am going toward is good. What I don't like is to feel I must simply "give up" and die. Perhaps you can help me find a way to meet death in a more positive way, calling on the best qualities of wisdom and authentic compassion within me. Maybe, like the prodigal son, I have been wandering far away from my home and my truth. Dying might be the process to help me find my own way home, so I can make my peace with God or my inner truth.

Perhaps you could learn which spiritual practices—prayers or meditations, sacred readings or music—are inspiring for me, and sit by my side and practice with me whenever you visit. Finding a spiritual practice that fills my heart with confidence, devotion, and compassion will help me to feel more prepared for death. I would be grateful if you could arrange whatever is necessary with the hospital staff and my family, so that the atmosphere when I am dying is loving and peaceful, and will be conducive to spiritual practice.

And please do not worry or feel bad if I die when you are not by my side. Sometimes your presence is soothing, but sometimes your being there makes it harder for me to leave. Please say and do whatever you need to early on, and then you won't have regrets if I should die unexpectedly soon. And when you learn I have died, please let go of any guilt! Remember that I am grateful for all you have done—and what I need most is your kindness, your sincere and heartfelt prayers, wishing me well and letting me go.

THE FIVE PSYCHOLOGICAL STAGES OF DYING AND MEDICAL ISSUES AROUND DEATH
by Mitchell Gershten, MD

The process of dying is neither easy nor simple. Disengagement from the body often requires significant effort and may be associated with pain or other discomforts that can limit our ability to be fully present for the process. For some, disentangling from the physiology that has supported and nurtured us is challenging, and those challenges frequently increase when clinging to this life is coupled with fear about what may happen after death.

I have observed many ways by which people undergo this process. In a medical setting, at least in America, it seems that the process begins when a person is informed about a diagnosis which will, in time, lead to their death. The knowledge of one's impending end rushes in unimpeded like water through a breached dam. There is no escape, and no method short of complete denial that can relieve such a person of that certainty.

The death process truly begins at the moment of conception. At the same instant that the processes creating life are initiated, the processes of dissolution are also set into motion. It is impossible to have one without the other.

In the absence of a defined disease process, people frequently seem incapable of grasping these fundamental truths, let alone allowing them to inform and guide their lives. While this may be acknowledged in the same fashion as the body's other needs, it is almost an afterthought, a subtle sensation that can, if one chooses, be ignored. Even in the face of observing the disease and death process in those around us, denial reigns supreme. The belief of our own exemption from this process guides our planning, our attitudes and our decisions, leading us to unrealistic expectations about living as well as avoidance of full participation in our own death.

The Five Psychological Stages of Dying

Failure to recognize this early in life leads to the full expression of the five psychological stages of dying that Elisabeth Kübler-Ross has written about. In my observations of patients confronted with the reality of their impending deaths, these five stages, while not always fully expressed, frequently manifest. These five stages form a useful framework with which we can look at the processes of death to better understand it in others as well as in ourselves.

The five stages are not necessarily a linear process. They can happen in any order, and one can skip back and forth between the stages. But the stages often follow their traditional sequence. These stages are longer or shorter in different people, largely on the basis of one's prior preparations for death, one's sense of satisfaction with how one's life was lived, as well as the depth of one's grasping to the memories of life. I have already mentioned the first stage, that of denial, and while this is clearly present when a fatal diagnosis is given, it is present more subtly long before such information is provided. The more powerful one's denial, the more intense are those feelings when the truth is fully grasped. This appears in different ways.

People often discuss their plans for the future, for meetings or excursions that will likely never occur. The planning can be so full of detail and verve that an observer can be lulled into feeling that there really is a chance that these events will occur. The dying individual works hard to convince everyone, and perhaps most importantly themselves, that their process of death is an error and that their efforts at long-term planning can erase the messages given them by physicians, or frequently by their own bodies. This often leads to the next stage, anger.

Anger develops when the truth of one's death is finally acknowledged. One's resistance appears with such force that the emotional outbursts can be intense and overwhelming, for the individual as well as for caregivers. Anger can be expressed externally, directed at others over minor issues. Nothing is right, and inconsequential concerns are blown out of proportion. To incredulous observers, and those unaware of this process, it can be frustrating and bewildering. The dying person often expresses exasperation at the fact that they themselves are in such a situation. They wonder how this could have happened, and how this can be happening to them.

This stage can go on for days or weeks. Gradually, as resistance is worn away by the relentless truth of their situation, the next stage emerges, that of bargaining. At this point, death is acknowledged, but attempts are made to reason with whatever power is perceived to be in charge or in control of these matters. Offers are tendered to gain more time to see a given event occur, to complete a project, to clean up old business, or to complete communication with others.

When it is realized that no amount of supplication can alter the fact of one's impending death, and particularly for the unprepared, the stage of depression develops. People withdraw from communication, choosing to relinquish any participation in life. There is risk of the depression becoming pervasive and permanent.

It is not necessary for this stage to be passed through before the last of the five stages is reached. Acceptance, the last stage, is generally achieved when all one's denial has been exhausted, when anger is shown to be of no use, when entreaties clearly fall on deaf ears, and when depression itself is unable to change the fact of one's death.

Here, at last, is a genuine opportunity for peace, for appeasing the disparate emotional forces that drove the prior stages. When the dying person is finally able to embrace the process, there emerges a more relaxed state, a tranquility, even joy. While the dying may not be pleased about their death, the certainty of the process is fully grasped, and with that comes acceptance.

The Five Stages in Loved Ones

Loved ones can go through similar stages. The healthier, the more open, and the more communicative is the relationship between the dying individual and the loved ones, the more relaxed is the process of release. However, this is often difficult for the loved ones. The stages described above for the dying are readily mirrored in loved ones and friends. As such, it is crucial that those caring for the dying remain in touch with their own emotional states, to be more present, compassionate, and helpful to the one dying. Each one of the five stages can powerfully influence the dying if the care-givers are ignorant of their operation, within themselves and within those dying. Indeed, unrecognized expression of these stages in loved ones and caregivers can make the dying process more difficult for the dying person.

Denial of death by a loved one can confer false hope or foster delusional ideas about survival in the dying. It can confuse the dying person if those around them do not support the reality of their death. Any anger expressed can be disturbing, a source of bewilderment, and deplete the energy of the dying person as they try to appease it.

Caregivers often do their own bargaining with some higher authority, to somehow stave off their loved one's death. They may attempt to bargain with the dying person themselves, as if they have enough control over their own death to delay or reverse it. Depending on where the dying are in their process, they may wish to participate in the covenant, however unreasonable or unrealistic. Caregivers may discuss future events that they hope the dying can attend, such as a wedding, a birth, or a graduation. There are often attempts to cajole the dying to linger so that unfinished emotional business can be completed.

At some point, this can give way to depression. The loved one fully realizes the loss, and this often leads to overwhelming sadness, a profound sense of impotence that for some never disappears. Those with some insight into this process will work through this stage to finally reach a place of acceptance. This is critical, not only to the individual left behind, but also for the dying. It can make the release from this life that much easier when a sense of responsibility for others can be relinquished.

Biological Changes

In addition to these emotional changes, there are many physical changes that are helpful to know. While there are similarities in each death, there are also vast differences. The process can be short, taking moments to hours, or it can be long, taking days to weeks. Most of the deaths I have observed reveal some discomfort. It is rare to watch someone die without distress. Those who die easily simply close their eyes and gradually breathe less, and eventually not at all.

There may be moments of lucidity, where they seem to awaken and engage whoever might be at their bedside. They may speak clearly about their lives, offering pearls of wisdom from what they have seen, both from memory and from their pre-death reveries. This phase may last moments, hours, or days before they lapse into unconsciousness.

From observing people die, I have often felt that whatever it is that forms personality, one's core being, one's spirit, departs at this time. As breathing decreases, the "death rattle," which sounds like the blowing of bubbles through a narrow tube, is often heard, and is the result of mucus, blood, or other fluid accumulating in the throat. After breathing stops, there may be random contractions of the heart, until it too ceases. After this, biochemical activity persists at the molecular and cellular level, and the body begins to decay and smell.

For months, or even years prior to death, the process that will ultimately lead to death labors at subtle levels, with only occasional glimpses seen on the surface. A person's color becomes sickly yellowish, their skin more dense or thickened. You may observe this for a few days or hours before the person recaptures the appearance you are more accustomed to, and you may wonder if what you saw was real. Their energy levels and zeal for activity, requiring more than a baseline level of input, may wax and wane. At those times, you may question how your dying friend or family member feels about you, as it can seem like they are becoming more aloof or withdrawn. And indeed many are, for the world that you are so engaged in no longer holds the same excitement that it does for you. As their bodies slowly disintegrate, so does their willingness to extend their spirits beyond the frontier of their skin. They become increasingly withdrawn.

With time, you may observe the effects of their dying process manifest more obviously on that skin. That yellow color is now undeniable. The yellowing of the skin or eyes in people with progressive liver failure, for example, becomes increasingly apparent. The tone of their skin darkens and sullies, or may begin to turn shades of blue as their skin becomes less oxygenated. With that loss of circulation, the skin may break down, in some cases seeming to dissolve before you, leaving an open wound that may become infected and draining, malodorous, or frankly putrid. This will become even more apparent to you should you be a caregiver, the one cleaning wounds and changing dressings. You may have to steel yourself against the possibility of retching, which you will not want to do for fear of offending or embarrassing the dying person. Even those most familiar with death are challenged by the harsh biological reality of dissolution.

Depending on the person's illness, there may develop a faint yet unmistakable odor. The smell may be sweet and fruity—like fermenting honey or rotting fruit, or slightly foul—noticeable but not yet overwhelming. Initially, the dying person may be aware of this, and perhaps even ashamed or apologetic for it. In time, this concern usually passes as just another inconsequential worldly concern, despite the increase of the odor.

Depending upon the underlying illness, a person becomes progressively weaker and less able to move, sit up in bed, to feed themselves, or to willfully urinate or defecate. The dying will frequently be unable to inform caregivers of any impending need to void, and will urinate or expel stool in the bed without warning. They may be unable to inform you that this has happened, and it is only the worsening of foul odors that alerts you to the need to clean them. At this point, they will be likely confined to bed, unable to care for even the slightest personal need.

We come into this world as infants, unable to control our bodily functions, and we often leave the world with the same lack of control. From the cradle to the grave, we rely on the kindness and understanding of our caregivers to help us.

Many dying people develop an astonishing lack of concern for things that seem so important to us. They may seem unconcerned with people or goings on around them. On the other hand, some may express an excessive concern about the moods, feelings, or needs of others. As caregivers, it is helpful to know the gamut of possible expressions.

At some point the person loses consciousness. We can think of this juncture in a number of different ways. Perhaps at the time earthly consciousness is permanently lost, the dying person's spirit, or soul, in some way leaves the body, or is present but disengaged, or perhaps hovering nearby. The disembodied consciousness is unable to apply any motive force to its former flesh, let alone communicate with those left behind. It may be useful to recall that this body we inhabit is a collection of finely tuned biochemical mechanisms, motivated by the force of physical energy (calories), and by the presence of "spirit." This spirit is both tightly bound to, and intimately interactive with, the body's physical processes.

Thinking about it in this way, it can be seen that once the dying person's spirit disengages and emerges from the body, all that remains is the residual energy in the body's biochemical stores, which will persist in expressing themselves through the common and familiar pathways they have moved through during life. This means, for example, that the diaphragm will still move up and down, sustaining the remnants of breath. So while it may appear that the dying person is breathing, this should not be construed as the taking of breath, or more esoterically as the mixing of prana with flesh. In my opinion, this only occurs when the spirit is present and the movement of breath consciously motivated. In this setting, that is not the case. At this point, it can therefore be useful to think of the dying body as merely expending its remaining stores of energy, much as a wind-up toy slowly becomes less animated as the spring gradually uncoils.

As the body loses energy, the eyes draw in and sink deeper into the skull, and the cheeks collapse. It is as if there is an internal vacuum, sucking away any energetic investment from the external appearance of the body. The skin becomes dull, acquiring the feel of unworked leather. The abdomen crumples inward and flesh hangs, listless and empty. Even in people who were heavy in life, there develops an obvious concavity at the belly as the bony lower ribs form a shelf from which hangs the now dull and heavy flesh. The weight of the musculature, pulled by gravity, stretches the skin downward. All remaining sphincter tone releases, and if there is stool remaining in the rectum, it often leaks out at this point. From here on, what was once imbued with life is now irrevocably and undeniably a corpse.

While I have described the simplest of death processes, the vast majority of deaths are not this predictable or straightforward. Regardless of the many events that can lead to death, there comes a threshold that leads irreversibly into death. This threshold can be mental, as in a resolute decision to die, but most often it is a physical threshold.

Depending upon the psychological and biological nature of the process of death, it can be a gentle unraveling or an unpleasant or even violent one. It is therefore useful for caregivers and loved ones to be aware of what can occur and thereby be prepared.

Hydration, Nutrition, and Pain Control

Family and friends often feel impotent around death, or constrained from interacting with the process of dying. Even if we are inclined to act, this process is so removed from our normal experience that we don't know what to ask, when to ask it, or what to do to help.

The first thing to know is that it is difficult to really injure a person who is already dying. This varies, of course, depending on the stage that the dying person is in. Early on, the dying person can acutely feel pain or thirst, but as the process progresses, things that we might consider noxious are perceived by the dying as either benign or they are not perceived at all. This is important because it can inform the caregivers in terms of what to ask for, and when. Questions regularly emerge about hydration, nutrition, and anxiety or pain control. When is it appropriate to give fluids? Do we need to be concerned about caloric intake or how to administer that? If we give narcotics to relieve the pain, will that accelerate death? The answers are specific to the individual who is dying, yet a few general comments can be made.

There has been much discussion about hydration. Many health care workers think that dehydration is uncomfortable for people and have advocated keeping intravenous fluids going as a patient dies. I have done this myself, and although I have been directly involved with many patients as they die, I have no way to assess whether or not it is true that they suffer from dehydration. This idea may come from our own memory of being dehydrated, and the ensuing discomfort, a feeling that we then unwittingly project onto the dying.

With this said, it is relatively benign to have an IV in place. Given that this may alleviate some discomfort, and is minimally invasive and nontoxic, it is reasonable to give fluids to a dying person. However, this does not mean that extreme measures need to be taken to gain IV access. If a simple buff cap (an IV catheter) cannot be maintained, I would not advocate more aggressive measures to obtain IV access. In these instances, moistened cotton washcloths applied to the lips, a few ice chips placed in the mouth from time to time or, if the person is able, a few sips of water may be all that can be offered, and all that is needed.

As for nutrition, in my experience this is not an area where invasive procedures have much value. There are basically three ways to provide nutrition for a dying person. It helps to know about these in case the doctors provide these options. First, a nasogastric tube (or a tube known as a Dobhoff, which is much thinner and more pliable than a standard NG); second, a PEG tube (percutaneous endoscopic gastrostomy), which is a device placed through the abdominal wall directly into the stomach. This is accomplished via a scope passed down through the esophagus into the stomach, at the same time that an incision is made through the abdominal and stomach walls. What amounts to a grommet is placed in that newly created hole and, with that in place, tubes can be threaded directly into the stomach for infusion of liquid nutritional supplements.

Third, nutrition is delivered intravenously through a technique known as TPN, or total parenteral nutrition. This requires placement of a central intravenous catheter which is either located in the internal jugular or subclavian vein. A more easily placed PICC line (peripheral intravenous central catheter) can also be used. With the exception of the first of these three options, these are all invasive techniques and (with the exception of the first option) carry considerable costs.

Prior to embarking on any of these approaches, a fundamental question needs to be answered: what is the ultimate goal of providing nutrition in this setting? If we can agree that the person is in fact dying, then from my point of view there is nothing to be gained by providing nutrition. Indeed, what we may be doing is unnecessarily prolonging their suffering.

In many instances, families or medical-proxy decision makers opt to provide nutrition when guidance from the dying person is not available. This is why advance directives are so important. Tell your family and friends before you die what you want them to do. Well-intentioned but misinformed loved ones, out of fear of doing the wrong thing, or of somehow being judged adversely (that their "wrong" decision not to provide nutrition contributed to an accelerated death), often request artificial nutrition. Always remember that the person is dying, and *none of our actions will ultimately change that fact.*

A guiding principle in making any of these decisions is this: is my decision going to contribute to my loved one's further pain and suffering? In other words, the decision to provide artificial nutrition can have the opposite of our intended effect: instead of relieving them of their suffering we may be contributing to it.

Consideration of pain and anxiety management is vital. Many caretakers are reluctant to give narcotics because of our culture's obsession with addiction and the stigma of opiates. Let me be very clear: this is not the time to be concerned with these issues. If a dying person is in pain, it is absolutely incumbent upon us to alleviate that pain.

This generally means one of the many forms of narcotics which should, in my opinion, be offered liberally. With this said, it is important to understand that narcotics can accelerate death.[1] They do so by directly suppressing the respiratory control centers in the brain, and in so doing reduce the rate and depth of breathing. This is the double-edge of pain control which must be understood by caregivers. We do not have to limit decisions regarding their use but rather to better understand the implications of their use.

Many of these decisions must be made with the assistance of doctors, some of whom will have differing views to your own, or to the previously expressed wishes of the dying person. This is where your advocacy becomes critical. Express clearly what you believe is needed. If you have been granted medical decision-making powers by the dying person, exercise those powers with clarity and wisdom. Think about what your loved one would want. Do not be intimidated into withholding your views and do not be shy about requesting what you believe is needed to best assist your loved one. But also don't be belligerent in expressing your views. Be firm yet gentle when dealing with professional caregivers. Doctors are human beings, often fallible, and often bringing their own views on mortality, including those informed by their religious beliefs or fears.

This is the time when the dying person's needs and requests, and your best understanding and advocacy of them, are the priority. It's not about the doctors, and it's not about you. Sometimes we need to remind ourselves and to remind them. As much as the dying person sometimes needs permission to let go, sometimes physicians require a similar insight. This is entirely about your loved one's process of dying, and how that can be eased or facilitated.

Physical Signs and Symptoms of Dying
by Andrew Holecek

Depending on a person's age, their disease, and a host of other factors, there are stages that a dying person goes through as they approach death. As with the spiritual stages of dying, not everyone experiences every stage or the signs and symptoms associated with it. They can also occur in a variety of sequences. *Signs* are objective indicators of a condition, like blood in the stool or a rash. They are visible to others. *Symptoms* are subjective, like fatigue or pain. They are often not apparent to others. If you're the one diagnosed with a terminal illness, ask your doctor how people usually die from this disease and how it tends to progress. Learn about the signs and symptoms you may experience.

Each sign and symptom is part of a natural process that occurs as the functions of various organs shut down. If decisions have been made not to alter this natural process, none of these signs or symptoms indicate a medical emergency or require treatments to reverse them. But steps can be taken to make them less painful. An increase in pain is common during the dying process, whether it's an existing pain or something new. The golden rule is that no one needs to suffer from physical pain at the end of life. This is the role of hospice care and palliative (or comfort-only) medicine.[2] If your doctor is not familiar or comfortable with aggressive pain management, find someone who is. Once again, don't worry about addiction. Worry about making the dying person comfortable. Many doctors say that when a dying person hints at suicide or requests euthanasia, it often comes from unmanaged physical pain.

In the case of sudden death—cardiac arrest, stroke or trauma—none of the following signs may occur. Someone may also die from a combination of gradual and sudden causes. A patient suffering from end-stage cancer, for example, may suddenly die from a stroke. In the case of sudden death, there is often greater confusion because there's less time to prepare. The main issue to prepare for with sudden death concerns resuscitation—do you rush the patient to the emergency room, do you perform CPR, or do you let them go? Because decisions have to be made quickly, it's important to have advance directives, especially documents like DNR (Do Not Resuscitate). Did the dying person empower someone with a durable medical power of attorney? Were advance directives communicated to family and loved ones? These uncomfortable issues should be settled in advance to lessen the shock of sudden illness and death.

In a gradual death, energy is slowly concentrated in the organs essential for life: the heart, lungs, and brain. Circulation to the extremities and to the skin, muscles, liver, stomach, kidneys, and bladder decreases. This causes many of the signs and symptoms discussed below: loss of appetite, concentrated or decreased volumes of urine, discoloration of the extremities, cooling, itching, and breakdown of the skin. Caregivers can offer comfort by first accepting these sometimes disconcerting events and then reassuring the dying person—if they are even aware of these changes—that this is a natural process.

As circulation to the digestive system lessens, the dying person loses interest in eating and drinking. A person with advanced illness may lose interest in food and drink weeks before they have circulatory changes, which may be one of the first signs that they are entering terminal stages. This is the time to discuss artificial nutrition and hydration.[3] But again, think about how these measures may only serve to sustain *artificial life*. Balance artificial life with authentic death.

The changes in body chemistry associated with no fluids or food is thought to have natural pain-relieving effects. The body has its own internal pharmacy and knows what to do and when to do it. It writes, fills, and administers the proper dosage of a host of natural prescriptions. While these sometimes need to be supplemented (especially pain medications), don't get in the way of the body's inherent wisdom.

Intravenous fluids are often administered near the end of life. I took my father to the hospital many times to get him rehydrated. This can be briefly effective, but not if one is nearing death. As the kidneys lose their function, IV fluids can worsen other symptoms, such as shortness of breath or choking due to increased secretions. These secretions also contribute to the disconcerting "death rattle." Swelling, or edema, is commonly seen in lower extremities, and sometimes throughout the body, as death approaches. Ankles and shins often get puffy. Artificial hydration can make this worse (diuretics can make it better).

As death approaches, what we perceive as dehydration is probably proper hydration that actually makes the dying person more comfortable. Artificial nutrition or hydration is sometimes strongly encouraged by nursing homes and other facilities that receive higher reimbursement for patients receiving this level of "care." Be polite but firm in enforcing your informed and genuine care. Swelling is abnormal in healthy people but normal for those who are dying.

As the process of dying progresses, it becomes harder to swallow and therefore easier to choke on fluids or food. Despite the urge to make someone feel better by trying to nourish them—often because we associate food with expressions of love—don't force the dying person to eat or drink. Doing so can cause distress to a system that's no longer functioning. The person may swallow but immediately vomit. Feeding them may make *you* feel better, but it can make them feel worse. Now is the time to switch from physical to spiritual nutrition.

Even though he or she may appear increasingly emaciated, the dying person is often not hungry. They're not starving to death—they're simply dying. The body's natural morphine, endorphin, is often released during this end phase of life and serves to lessen the pain of dying. Offering sips of water, or water on a swab, will keep the mouth, lips, and tongue moist and comfortable. I have used an eye-dropper to deliver water when the end is near.

A fever may develop as dehydration progresses. Tylenol suppositories can control the fever and prevent seizures. It helps to place a cool moistened washcloth on the forehead, or to sponge the limbs. Putting a humidifier in the room also helps. The body loses its ability to control its temperature, causing the person to feel hot one minute and cold the next. Add or remove blankets as needed, but avoid electric blankets, which can cause burns. Change perspiration-soaked garments and linens to keep the patient comfortable.

Because of the decrease in fluids and food, urine and stool amounts decrease. Urine becomes concentrated and dark, and several days may lapse between bowel movements. You don't want bowel movements to cease entirely, which could indicate the development of a painful bowel impaction. My father had to go to the emergency room to relieve this condition. Milk of magnesia or other laxatives should be used if a bowel movement doesn't occur within three days.

When someone stops eating, the body begins to metabolize muscle and tissue mass, eating itself in a sense, and feces continues to form. This later form of fecal matter may have little or no odor. New patterns of waste elimination can develop, and the consistency and color of the stool often changes. Loss of control over bladder or bowel functions may occur days or even weeks before death, or when the muscles relax at the moment of death. Protect the mattress with plastic, and provide waterproof padding under the patient for increased comfort. If they can't make it to the bathroom or commode (portable toilet), use a bed pan or pee bottle (which are separately designed for men and women). When they can no longer move, ask the hospice nurse about urinary catheters or disposable adult briefs.

Because the organs are shutting down, the dying person withdraws from the world and spends more time sleeping or resting with their eyes closed. They often become increasingly difficult to arouse, and we should avoid the temptation to do so. This is their time. They are doing what they need to do. Heed the natural wisdom of the body. Don't shake the body, speak loudly, or try to force a response. Talk to them in a normal voice, even though there may be no apparent response. Don't say anything in their presence that you wouldn't say to them when they're awake—don't assume they can't hear you.

These are all reasons why we should say our goodbyes early in the dying process. The dying person's withdrawal is a sign that their body is starting to say goodbye. We should use that sign to begin our own goodbyes. Missing the chance to say what's in our hearts can cause unnecessary regret. Death often happens faster than we might expect. Because it can be hard for the dying person to let go when a loved one is present, they often die when no one is around. They frequently grasp on to life because they feel the force of your grasping on to them.

As circulation to the extremities decreases, their arms, hands, legs, and feet become increasingly cool, and often manifest a purplish blotching, called mottling. This is frequently accompanied with breakdown of the skin, another indication of the decrease in blood flow. Moisturizers can be applied to the skin. If wounds or sores develop, use antibiotic ointment and nonadhesive bandages over the sores. Move or turn the body every few hours to prevent these bedsores. Dying people often love to be touched, so massaging in some lotion is usually welcome. They don't want to be viewed as an untouchable but as a human being just like you.

A yellowish pallor often manifests, which should not be confused with jaundice. The eyes often rest with lids partly open and can become dry. Artificial tear drops placed every few hours will keep the eyes moist. Even when seemingly unconscious, some dying people will suddenly have muscle spasms or even seizures.

Most hospice workers and professional caregivers are aware of these signs and symptoms. They are trained to manage them. Respect their work. Be sensitive if you offer suggestions or feel the urge to complain. There are times, however, when workers neglect their duties (and sometimes even abuse the dying person). As an advocate for your dying loved one, speak gently but firmly. Don't vent onto them. Always check your motivation, and remember that the intensity of the situation can trigger irrational emotions as you struggle to cope with your own pain. Angry outbursts are common from both the dying person and stressed-out loved ones.

As death approaches, blood flow to the brain decreases, which causes disorientation and drowsiness. Even family members may go unrecognized. The dying person may be confused as to where they are or what's happening. They may become restless, pulling at bed linens, trying to get up, or reaching for imaginary things. This often worsens in the evening. Sedatives, like Ativan (Lorazapam) in liquid form, can be used every four hours, or even hourly as needed. Sedatives calm not only the patient—seeing them tranquil will calm you.

The dying may report strange dreams or conversations with dead people. All kinds of unusual, nonsensical, and confusing statements can be uttered, even shouted. These indicate the loss of cognitive function and the loss of grounding in physical reality. The dying person is in a psychic place we do not comprehend, dipping in and out of varying states of consciousness, from dream-like internal mindscapes to confused waking landscapes. They are often unable to distinguish between the two. To get some idea of what the dying may be experiencing, remember those states of mind that are partly awake and partly asleep (hypnogogic and hypnopompic states associated with pre- and post-dreaming). Mix in some pain, emotional distress, and a vague or clear sense of losing everything you have and everything you are. How would you feel or react?

I have been with dying people who start to hallucinate, seeing strange beings as clearly as they see me. They are sinking into bardo-like realities— partly here and partly gone. You may be curious and ask about those perceived realities, but don't challenge them. For the dying person those states are real. Your efforts to rescue them, by pulling them back to your reality, may confuse them even more. If they're looking for reassurance, quietly remind them of where they are and who is present. Comfort them with casual conversation or gentle touch. As they continue to withdraw, however, they may not want to be touched. Be aware of their needs, and let those supersede your own.

Many of these signs are indications of delirium, a state of disorientation that can happen within a few hours or days before death. Classic symptoms include agitation and irritability, acute mood swings, seeing or hearing things that aren't there, sleeping during the day and staying awake during the night, and difficulty paying attention. Causes of delirium include extreme anxiety, oxygen deprivation, pain, infection, certain medications, and withdrawal from alcohol or medication.[4]

Whatever is happening, allow the dying to express themselves (unless they're hurting themselves or others). Provide the supportive environment to accept whatever arises—without judgment or panic. Reassure them that everything that's happening, as disconcerting as it appears, is part of a natural process. Once again, your stability and presence of mind, often without saying a thing, may provide exactly what they need.

I have seen people resist death, flailing about and even becoming violent. Under those extreme conditions they may need to be heavily sedated or even restrained. This will prevent them from harming themselves and others. Palliative care physician Dr. Daniel Matlock says, "This terminal agitation is common and can be very, very ugly. We use a lot of sedatives in these cases. Sedation is not euthanasia, or physician assisted suicide, because the *intent* of the sedation is to treat a symptom." It should be understood, however, that the use of sedatives can accelerate the dying process.[5]

Identifying yourself in a soft and clear voice helps the dying person reorient to waking reality. This may need to be done repeatedly but should never be done forcefully. Before you touch them to implement bodily care, inform them of who you are, what you are going to do, and why you are doing it. Because of the cognitive changes, and the decrease in oxygenation to the brain, disorientation is a constant companion for the dying person and for loved ones. Knowledge, patience, and understanding reduces the confusion. If the person is dying from a specific disease, learn about that disease and the symptoms that accompany it. Then practice empathy and imagine yourself on that bed.

The dying may enter a partial or full coma and no longer respond verbally. If they're not in a coma, their mouth may move as they try to speak but are unable to. They might communicate with eye movements, a slight nod, or a gentle squeeze of the hand. Reassure them that it's okay, that there's no need for them to talk. Remember that we're trying to help them relax. And keep in mind, as nurse Lynn Weitzel says, "The spirit does not get cancer or AIDS or Alzheimer's." The relative may be dying. The absolute never dies.

When circulation slows to the core, which is to the heart and lungs, the heart may speed up before it slows down and stops. Blood pressure may also spike to unusually high levels, then drop to very low levels. If the "death rattle" manifests, which again is simply secretions collecting in the airways, turning the body or head to the side helps gravity drain the fluids. Sometimes suction can be used. You can also wipe the mouth with a moist cloth to remove the mucus pooling there. Dr. Matlock says, "I often tell people that the "death rattle" is more distressing to us than it is to them. There are also medications, like scopolamine patches and atropine drops, that can dry these secretions." They might try to cough up mucus, and their mouth is often dry and encrusted with secretions. You can cleanse the mouth with glycerin or use mineral oil swabs dipped in cool water to relieve the dryness.

Breathing may become shallow and rapid before it slows down. Exhalations are often longer and more pronounced than inhalations. Breathing often becomes labored, accompanied with moaning, or even snoring sounds. Raise the head of the bed to help manage this, and remember that moaning is not always a sign of pain. It's usually the sound of air passing over relaxed vocal cords. If breathing is labored, ask the doctor to administer medications that can relieve the respiratory distress.[6]

If you're in a nursing home or hospital and do not wish to be intubated and placed on an artificial ventilator, you should have a DNI order in place (which is usually part of a DNR). Narcotics, such as morphine, also block the sensation of shortness of breath. Your loved one does not have to feel like they're suffocating or drowning. Cheyne-Stokes breathing can manifest, which is when there are several breaths followed by a period of no breathing. It's often unsettling for loved ones when the dying person suddenly stops breathing. This cessation can last from several seconds to over a minute.

If you're at home, supplemental oxygen (provided by hospice), and repositioning can help. If you're in a care facility, you could have a snug-fitting face mask attached to a breathing machine administered, which is designed to push air into your lungs. This set-up doesn't involve intubation. It's called *noninvasive positive airway pressure*, and is similar to the CPAP (continuous positive airway pressure) devices used for sleep apnea. The dying person is literally taking their last gasps of life. But we can ease those gasps.

People often want to die in the comfortable and familiar surroundings of their home, although fewer than 20 percent actually die this way. Even if hospice is involved, they usually don't visit every day. A typical routine might involve the hospice nurse and a home health aide (who deals with bathing and other hygiene concerns) visiting twice a week, either on the same day of the week or on alternating days. A hospice nurse is usually on call twenty-four hours a day, every day of the week. When a patient first begins hospice care, it's common to call on the nurses every day. The need for advice will diminish once things settle in and you learn how to care for your loved one. A hospice volunteer, whose principal role is emotional and practical support, might come by for a few hours each week. A social worker may visit once a week to coordinate all the above.[7]

Unless you have arranged for home health care services outside of hospice, be prepared for some challenging and intimate care.[8] Incontinence is common and can get very messy—even with adult diapers. Sleepless nights are common. The end of life is much like the beginning, but for most people it's easier to change, wipe, or bathe a baby than it is an adult. This is one reason why many people leave their dying loved one in a nursing home. It makes it easier for you but often harder for your loved one. Ask them beforehand if they're comfortable with you providing this intimate level of care. It could be too embarrassing for them.

As a summary, expect these changes: increased sleeping, decreased appetite, difficulty swallowing, decreased urine and fecal output, incontinence, changes in breathing, impaired senses, discoloration of the extremities, restlessness, disorientation, and withdrawal from the world.

Death occurs when the heart stops beating and respiration ceases. One can occur before the other, and several minutes can transpire before both finally end. There are two ways to define clinical death, which becomes important in terms of organ donation, i.e., when to start harvesting: (1) as an irreversible cessation of all the functions of the brain, including the brain stem, and (2) as an irreversible cessation of circulation, heartbeat, and breathing.[9]

Death is often accompanied by involuntary muscle movements and spasms as the tissues deprived of oxygen fully relax. Because of this relaxation, control of the bladder and bowel ends, often releasing urine and feces. The jaw often drops, and the eyes can remain partly open. Everything is "exhaling." The person is no longer responsive to verbal commands or to shaking. Blood pools in lower parts of the body, creating purplish bruises. If the body is to be viewed in an open casket, make sure the person is lying on their back. This keeps the face and other visible parts from becoming mottled.

Unless organ donation has been arranged, which needs to begin as soon as possible, the body doesn't need to be moved until you're ready. You can keep the body for twenty-four hours without dry ice, and up to three days with dry ice. Three days is pushing it, because the body starts to leak fluids.

The sense of peace that often pervades the atmosphere after death doesn't need to be filled with activity. *Death is not an emergency*. It is the end of a completely natural process. Rest in the profundity of what just happened. After my father died I waited twelve hours before calling hospice.

Although death is expected, it frequently remains a surprise. Think ahead about what needs to be done. If hospice is involved, call them and they will initiate post-death action. Once again, with some preparation you will be able to understand what's happening physically, what might be happening spiritually, and what needs to be done practically. All of which helps everyone relax.

It's difficult to predict the amount of time a terminally ill person has left. Hospice nurses and doctors frequently offer varying opinions. I have seen oncologists offer a prognosis of several months, while the general physician sees a few weeks or less. Some of the common indications of the impending death are outlined below.

A few months before death, the person begins to withdraw. They lose interest in worldly events—newspapers, magazines, news shows—and then they lose interest in neighbors and friends. Touching, and the simple presence of loved ones, becomes more important than words. They start to sleep more. Communication and energy decrease; weakness and fatigue increase. Restlessness and confusion can increase, along with the need to constantly move, or if in bed, to change positions. Monitoring or constantly assisting in this movement is trying for caregivers. Instead of following a two-year-old around to keep them from hurting themselves, you are now doing so with your elderly loved one.

Changes in breathing and the onset or increase of edema often occur. Appetite decreases, nothing tastes good, nausea is evident. Weight loss increases. Liquids are preferred over solids. Meats, vegetables, and other hard-to-digest foods lose their appeal. Eventually a taste for anything solid disappears. It's as if their inner loss of solidity is being expressed externally.

As weakness develops, there is an increased tendency to fall, which often results in broken bones and serious bruising. As the body fails, so does its ability to stave off infections and recover from new bodily stress. And so begins a negative spiral of disease, weakness, and an inability to recover— which leads to more disease, more weakness, and so forth. The list of problems often gets longer as death gets nearer. While we can try to lessen the effects of this spiral, we often can't prevent it.

There is often a need to settle unfinished business, practical or emotional. The plumbing needs to be fixed, the house painted, the garden weeded. Family heirlooms suddenly need to be passed along. People often have a deep intuition that something is off, and that they are dying. A few weeks before my father went to the doctor (at my urging), he told me over the phone, "I've aged a lot recently. I don't want to die, but I'm ready if I need to." It was a shocking statement, and totally out of the blue. But it was the first expression of his impending death, which happened only two months later. You may hear things like, "See you next week—if I'm still around." "This will probably be my last Thanksgiving." "Promise me that you'll take care of [insert name] when I'm gone." "I don't need this anymore, take it."

A few weeks before death, sleep is more common than being awake. It's difficult for the dying person to keep their eyes open. They're increasingly tired and weak. They may see and converse with loved ones who have died, or perceive things we cannot. They may talk about people and places unknown to others, becoming nonsensical and increasingly confused. Shorter sentences or single words replace full sentences.

A cane or walker is needed to move about, and supplemental oxygen may be required. They become wheelchair bound, and eventually bedridden. Toilet lifts (plastic doughnuts with hand rails, which extend the toilet rim and make it easier to sit down and get up), pee bottles (so they don't have to get out of bed), commodes, or bedpans may be needed. Shower benches, which allow them to sit under the shower, are often needed. At this stage it's easy for them to fall and break a bone, which would require hospitalization and probably a nursing home. Be gentle but firm in telling them that some activities are no longer possible.

Incontinence is common. Once bedridden, movements may become agitated. They might pick at sheets and bedclothes, or try to pull out catheters. Bed rails are often needed to keep them from falling out of bed. Hospice provides many of these aids, covered by Medicare—walkers, wheelchairs, oxygen, commodes, hospital beds (where the upper body can be raised and lowered), bedpans, protective coverings, adult diapers, bed rails, etc. A baby monitor, hand bell, or other signaling device is helpful so that you know what's going on in the room, or to help them reach out to you. Be prepared for lots of ringing at first.

Blood pressure, heart rate, respiration, and body temperature can fluctuate widely. Increased perspiration, coughing, and congestion may occur. Urine concentrates and bowel movements decrease. Skin color changes, mottling develops. Only soft foods or liquids are consumed.

A few hours or days before death, fluid intake may decrease markedly. Urine output is low and very dark. Not even soft foods are taken. The dying one may be sleeping or coma-like most of the time. Breathing may become labored, with long pauses (apneas). The jaw may weaken, opening the mouth more. Amazingly, sudden surges of energy may occur, called *rallying*. Favorite meals, requests to see certain people, and other desires seem to come out of nowhere. After some minutes, hours, or even a few days of this increased awareness and activity, a return to reduced energy and diminished consciousness occurs. If the sudden increase of energy and mentation occur, followed by a return to reduced energy and awareness, the end is usually very near. This final burst of energy can startle loved ones and create the illusion that a miraculous recovery is underway.

Restlessness often increases, then drops. Congestion can be marked, the "death rattle" manifests. Eyes are glassy and not seeing, or constantly closed. The person is unresponsive to speech or touch. Hands and feet become purplish and cool, and feel numb to the dying person. Just before death, "fish out of water" gasping may arise, and breathing becomes shallow or episodic. Since breath is the marker of life, breathing patterns are often the best indicator for impending death.

Spiritual Matrix

Lynn Weitzel's comment, "The spirit does not get cancer or AIDS or Alzheimer's," warrants a brief return to the spiritual matrix of all experience. Understanding the spiritual context in which even the most difficult physical events take place can reframe an entire illness or death. This can instill ease into a difficult situation.

It's easy for a person afflicted with a disease, and for those around them, to start to identify with it. While it's important to know about an illness for obvious reasons (what to expect, how to treat it, etc.), if we start to identify with the disease we may contract around it. We may convince ourselves that the pathology is now who we are, or if we're a caregiver, who the patient is. In a recent article on autism, a writer for the *New York Times* remarked that "the diagnosis [of autism] is in many ways central to their lives." Self-contraction, and the ensuing reification, is one of our most powerful habits. This is when a disease of the body spreads to infect the mind and spirit.[10]

I have seen many patients surrender, unintentionally or even willingly, to a diagnosis. They will tell me about their cancer, for example, and convey a sense of dangerous acquiescence: "What can I do about it? My doctor says the prognosis is bleak. This disease has taken control of my life." I'm not blaming doctors, for there are many who deliver their diagnosis with empathy and compassion.[11] There are also many patients who unconsciously enable their doctors, imbuing them with god-like powers of life and death. I'm also not saying that disease doesn't have the ability to overwhelm and adversely transform a person, profoundly changing their physical life. There are diseases where death is virtually guaranteed.

What I am saying is that doctors, patients, and caregivers need to be careful when it comes to the promise and peril of diagnosis.[12] It sometimes feels, for example, like some patients have the excuse they have been waiting for to finally get them off the hook of life. They may say to themselves: "I am no longer responsible for my life and my actions. This disease has taken over, can't you see that this pathology is who I am!?" They have become the victim, and surrender in a damaging way.

Dr. Candace Pert, one of the most eloquent exponents of mind-body medicine, says, "Take responsibility for your own health—and illness. Delete phrases like 'My doctor won't let me . . .' or 'My doctor says I have [name of condition], and there's really nothing I can do' from your speech and thought patterns."[13] There's a big difference between appreciating a diagnosis and identifying with it. When we talk about surrendering to reality, this is not the surrender we're talking about.

Disease may be a temporary physical reality, and living in ignorance of it could lead to the other extreme of living in denial, but this disease is not who we are. Our spirit, who we really are, will never get cancer and it will never die. Be present for your disease, but don't endorse it. Identify with your immortal spirit, not the malfunction of the body that temporarily contains it. Trungpa Rinpoche said:

> [B]y relating with the ordinary conditions of your life you might make a shocking discovery. While drinking your cup of tea, you might discover that you are drinking tea in a vacuum. In fact, *you* are not even drinking the tea [getting the disease]. The hollowness of space is drinking tea [is getting the disease] . . . . When you put on your make-up, you might discover that you are putting cosmetics on space. You are beautifying space, pure nothingness [when you get cancer or dementia, it is space, pure nothingness, that "gets" the disease].[14]

Doctors, as well as patients and loved ones, succumb to this temptation to pigeon-hole and to therefore dismiss. It's easy and convenient. What's being dismissed are the complex factors involved with a disease, the mysterious interplay between physical and spiritual, and the context of a larger spiritual identity.

In my practice of dental medicine, the staff will often tell me: "We have a biopsy in operatory one, we have an abscess in operatory two." No we don't. We have a human being, a sacred expression of pure spirit, dealing with a temporary physical hiccup. So when a patient gives me their health history and says, "I have cancer," I feel like replying, "Don't let it have you." Don't let it possess you. Never forget, as author Stephen Levine says, that we are spiritual beings with physical experiences, not physical beings with spiritual experiences.

This is why the teachings of part 1, our spiritual preparation, come before and contain the considerations presented in part 2, the practical preparation. While honoring the latter, we should always take refuge in the former. Like space itself, spirit easily contains, and remains unaffected by, anything that arises within it. Iyengar says, "Though the body is subject to sickness, age, decay and death, the spirit remains unaffected. Birth and death are natural phenomena but the soul is not subject to birth and death. As a man casting off worn-out garments takes on new ones, so the dweller within the body casting aside worn-out bodies enters into others that are new."[15]

Empty the Disease

We briefly discussed emptiness earlier, which is one of the most important teachings in Buddhism. A deep understanding of emptiness would completely transform the way we relate to disease and death.[16] Emptiness is the ultimate holding environment. Khenpo Tsültrim Gyamtso Rinpoche talks about the importance of emptiness in relation to disease:

> The reason we have trouble with illness is that we have the wrong view about illness, a mistaken understanding: we cling to it as truly existent and then it is difficult to heal ourselves. So remember this view. Look directly at the illness. If it did not exist before, how could it possibly exist later? This is another way of saying that the illness has no essence [it is *empty* of inherent existence]. But on the level of apparent reality, it arises as mere appearance, like a dream, an illusion, a reflection of the moon in water. With an understanding that illness is not truly existent, you could cure yourself.[17]

Rinpoche's last statement is a challenging one. It is not meant to burden the patient by making them feel that their disease, and its cure, is due merely to their views about it. This popular New Age notion, that we somehow create our disease with our bad thoughts and can cure it with good ones, is facile and careless. It puts undue responsibility and stress on the person already suffering from the ailment. The last thing a person suffering from a disease needs to hear is that they somehow created it. There's a place for the power of positive thinking, but there's a higher place for the power of accurate thinking. Buddhism teaches that thought affects physical reality. It doesn't create it.[18]

This New Age notion, that you create reality, can lead to what psychotherapist John Welwood calls "spiritual bypassing": "using spiritual ideas or practices to avoid or prematurely transcend relative human needs, feelings, personal issues, and developmental tasks."[19] This bypassing manifests in what Welwood calls "advaita-speak," where *advaita* is the Sanskrit word for nonduality, a state ascribed to God or the Absolute. This heavenly state can't be reached by reason or relativity. Because it's nondual, it's beyond dualistic and rational criticism. It's above the messiness of being human. It is the untouchable "superiority" of this view, the dismissive quality of the complexities of relative reality, that's so seductive to New Age thinking and a limitation of it.

If nonduality doesn't honor duality, it becomes sterile, disconnected, and dangerous. It becomes "a one-sided transcendentalism that uses nondual terms and ideas to bypass the challenging work of personal transformation. Advaita-speak can be very tricky, for it uses absolute truth to disparage relative truth, emptiness to devalue form, and oneness to belittle individuality."[20] In other words, it's a superficial view that engenders an escapist attitude about relative details and difficulties.

Understanding spiritual bypassing helps us avoid the other extreme of taking excessive refuge in the spiritual or the absolute. While we do want to identify with the spiritual, exclusive identification with it creates its own set of problems.[21] We can become disembodied, disconnected, elitist, apathetic, even nihilistic. In other words, literally and metaphorically out of touch. In an effort to find heaven on the spiritual path, we lose contact with earth. A complete and accurate identification with the spiritual, in the words of Ken Wilber, "transcends but includes" the material. It honors and integrates the relative while simultaneously transcending it.

Without this more complete view, a well-intentioned but misinformed "spiritual" person may visit the dying and bring an attitude that doesn't acknowledge the real suffering of sickness and death. An "absolute-only" view will not connect such a person to relative reality, as temporary as that reality may be. The result can be a disingenuous compassion, a lack of empathy, or an "understanding" that is patronizing.

Once again, if the dying person isn't open to your views, don't force your philosophy upon them. And be careful not to exude an advaita-speak aura:

"What's the big deal here? Can't you see that none of this is really happening, that everything is empty?" While it's important to take refuge in the spiritual, always acknowledge and honor the material. The ultimate view is to unite the two.

What Khenpo Rinpoche's statement therefore implies, yet again, is that while acknowledging the relative appearance of the disease, we shouldn't solidify it. If we examine the illusory and transparent quality, not only of the disease but of the body that temporarily expresses it, this helps to generate the proper holding environment. And while doing this investigation, we should always acknowledge the power of relative truth. Things do appear to be a certain way from a confused perspective but are not that way from a more realized one. The conclusion of such an analysis would be one of the central tenets of *The Tibetan Book of the Dead*: emptiness cannot harm emptiness. A disease empty of inherent existence cannot harm a body empty of inherent existence. An attack in a dream cannot affect a dream body.

Emptiness does not deny appearance. It challenges the status and solidity of that appearance. A true understanding of emptiness doesn't slip into spiritual bypassing, because while surpassing material reality, emptiness always respects and embraces it. Emptiness undercuts our propensity to identify with things, which is a central function of ego, even if those things are pathological. We have stressed that the ego is exclusive identification with form. Now we can see that it is exclusive identification with *anything*.

9. After Death

After-Death Care
by Karen Van Vuuren

WHEN KAREN C., a forty-six-year-old mother of two young children, died at home, family and friends were by her side. They lovingly tended her physical remains with a ritual bathing that honored her body as a sacred vessel and death as a spiritual transition.[1] They laid her out in a designated "wake" room, decorated according to her wishes by her children's elementary school teachers.

It is rare in our Western culture to find a dying person who will plan their own after-death care, but Karen participated in conversations about what would be meaningful for her transition. She helped create her own after-death care plan, right down to the type of clothing she wanted to wear for her wake and the sacred texts she wanted read at her vigil. Karen's family chose to conduct what, in contemporary language, has been called a "home funeral." This term has come to mean after-death care in which a family or community plays an integral role. It often involves a wake or vigil with people paying their respects by sitting with the body. The location may be the home, or a spiritual center, or it might also be a nursing facility where the staff supports families' rights to do things their own way.

An after-death care plan, created long before death, in the absence of crisis, should clarify funeral wishes. (Note that a recommendation to preplan is not an endorsement of prepayment. More on prepayment later.) Of course, we can never know the circumstances surrounding our death and so any plan must remain provisional. It is a template that can serve those who may otherwise flounder, but it should not preclude the ability of survivors to add their own personal touches to ritualizing a transition. Leaving no opportunity for the unique ideas of family and friends may deprive those left behind of a meaningful role that helps them creatively deal with their grief.

Before the emergence of the modern funeral industry in America after the Civil War, home funerals were the norm. The people who cared for you in life were there for you at its end. Death was visible as most people died at home, involving and affecting entire communities. The family parlor rather than the funeral parlor provided a familiar, intimate setting for mourners to pay their respects. Eastern traditions have carried on the practice of caring for the dead within the community, but now home funerals are also making a comeback in secular America (out of economy—they are cheaper—and for other reasons such as environmental consciousness and the desire to do it yourself).

My father used to say, "When I kick the bucket, just throw me in the furnace." For him, death was the end. It was matter that mattered. His generation had experienced war on a hitherto unprecedented scale and the trauma of the battlefield brought an inability to dwell on mortality and a disinclination to "drag it out" with ritual.

Today's conventional funeral is predicated upon handing over the care of our dead to professionals who take charge.[2] We may memorialize the one who has died, but the story of what awaits them after death, and our role in support of that spiritual process, is often missing. The modern "rites of passage" movement pioneered by the School of Lost Borders stresses the importance of the "no-name" period following a major transition. This is a time for being with the dramatic change in circumstances that is ushered in by death. Thus, wakes and vigils provide an opportunity for integration.

I recently heard from a woman whose in utero baby was without kidneys. The child, a boy, was not expected to live for very long after birth, and yet this mother was determined to celebrate his birth and mark his death by bathing and dressing him and keeping his body home for a wake. I was awestruck by this mother's fierce determination to provide a gentle, loving container for his birth and the same for his leaving. The child lived for a few hours after birth. The family cuddled him in bed, then bathed and dressed him for a wake, which lasted for a number of days. She was so grateful to have had this healing time.

Caring for Our Own Dead—Is It Legal?

In most US states, families may care for their own dead. Lack of knowledge about legal rights, as well as about how to care for the dead, tends to limit the role families play after death.[3]

Funeral Directors

Funeral directors can have a role to play, and there are good, sensitive people in the field. Families may lack resources to allow them to care for their own dead. They may be overwhelmed, and circumstances may be so challenging that a stranger stepping in to take over may be necessary. It can be helpful to have the funeral director handle things like the paperwork or the transportation, while leaving the more intimate task of caring for the body to those with a personal connection to the deceased.

Lisa Carlson, founder of the Funeral Consumers Alliance (www.funerals. org), has written a useful guide for the consumer on funeral law, on a state-by-state basis. Her book *Caring for the Dead* outlines the legal requirements for families conducting their own after-death care. For example, Carlson notes that embalming is almost never a state requirement. Certainly, funeral homes should obtain permission from the next of kin before embalming any dead body.

Each state has its own laws concerning procedures to follow after death and the time frame within which these should occur. Filing a death certificate is necessary in order to obtain a permit for cremation or burial. This is a legal record of what are known as the vital statistics of the deceased, including birth and death dates, place of birth and death, parents' names, and the cause of death to be determined by a medical examiner. If the death was unexpected, or occurred under unusual circumstances, a coroner is required.[4]

Carlson's book on caring for the dead outlines which states allow families to file death certificates themselves. In many states, families may be able to do everything, including transporting the body of the deceased in their own vehicle, burying on their own land (depending on the county zoning laws regarding land use), and even conducting open-air cremation on rural, agricultural property, with county permission and the cooperation of the local fire department. Eight states currently make it necessary to hire a funeral director: Connecticut, Illinois, Indiana, Louisiana, Michigan, Nebraska, New York, and New Jersey. It takes research ahead of time to find out what is possible, and when talking with officials, it is important to get more than one opinion and to ask for a referral to laws or regulations to clarify and confirm what is said.

I mentioned earlier that while each of us should certainly preplan (and this does mean familiarizing yourself with your state's laws, county regulations, and what is possible) it does not necessarily mean it is a good idea to prepay. The Funeral Consumers' Alliance has sage advice for families considering prepaying for funerals and signing up "pre-need" (the industry term for making and paying for arrangements before death occurs). The FCA's website (www.funerals.org) contains detailed information on the benefits and the dangers of prepayment. Insurance companies, for-profit cremation societies, and pre-need associations all market the benefits of prepaid, pre-need arrangements, but pitfalls do exist, and it is important to carefully scrutinize the fine print of any pre-need document.

In some states, plans may not be portable if you die traveling, or move. Providers may go out of business by the time you die. There may be restrictions on changes to the plan and penalties. And some of the biggest scandals in the funeral industry have involved misappropriation of pre-need funds that, by law, should have been held in trust.

The FCA also points out that insurance does not usually grow as quickly as money in the bank. Many families state that their reason for prepayment is to ensure there is money set aside for a funeral that will not be counted as assets. However, there are other ways to set aside money for funeral payments and, at the same time, allow your lump sum to accrue interest. Totten trusts, or pay-on-death accounts, are individual trusts or savings plans to cover funeral costs. You can designate a beneficiary who will have access to these funds on your death, without the delay of probate. Inquire about these at your bank, and remember, if you are prepaying, the rule is "buyer beware."

First Steps Following an Expected Death

By expected death, we mean death that follows an illness, as opposed to death in the wake of an accident. When hospice is involved at death, a home funeral represents a continuum of care. Family members who have been present for the dying of their loved one may continue, post-death, to cradle the deceased through transition. Even when a family is not conducting a home funeral, they should not feel that death is an emergency. I have seen scenarios in which multiple cell phones appear moments after the last breath. It is easy to be sucked into a maelstrom of frenetic activity, calling medical providers, relatives, the mortuary, etc. While there may be a few key people who deserve notification, it is far better to approach tasks with calm. It is helpful to designate someone to make calls or activate a phone tree. Death brings huge change. Honor the time of transition. When you are at the threshold of the realms of life and death, maintain peace and cultivate an atmosphere of serenity.

In some traditions, it is important not to disturb the body immediately following death, until there are indications that handling the body will not interfere with the spiritual process.[5] You might even wait a few hours before calling the hospice, if this is what you need to do. Note the time of death to convey it to authorities. A medical practitioner, or an official from the coroner's office, will come to officially pronounce death.

Care of the Body After Death

Rigor Mortis

People often ask questions about rigor mortis and when it sets in. Rigor mortis is the phenomenon of the stiffening of the body after death. It seems like a manifestation of the life forces leaving, and the contraction and expansion of death. The textbooks often say it will set in anywhere from one to three hours after death, but I have seen it where a body is rigid quite soon after death. Rigor mortis (caused by the build-up of lactic acid) comes in waves, and will relax on the second day. Families are often concerned that they need to dress their loved ones before it sets in. However, although a stiff body is harder to work with than a relaxed and compliant one, it has never presented an insurmountable problem for any of the families I have encountered caring for their own dead. Caregivers who have worked with stroke patients with inflexible limbs will know that there are techniques for dressing that overcome any challenges.

I once had the honor of assisting a family with a ritual bathing and dressing many hours after an elderly man died. He had died in a fetal position in bed, with considerable release from the bowels and bladder (part of the "relaxation" that is normal at death). The family had decided to wait to bathe him. What to the assembled care team seemed an extremely difficult task proved amazingly easy. His body cooperated to the degree that we were able to clean him up and dress him in his finest, three-piece suit. By the time we were done, this large-boned gentleman had straightened out and his feet were almost dangling over the end of his bed.

The body may be more unwieldy and seem heavier after death. However, the weight does not change. What we experience is literally "dead weight," where the body loses levity as life forces leave.

Don't Do It Alone

You may be working with the guidance of a spiritual teacher when someone dies, but if not, a general guideline for families tending their own dead is to center yourself before you begin the physical care of the body, so as to remain fully present. You may want to say a prayer, verse, or just sit in silent meditation before you begin. Do what you need to do to gather yourself. This will also help to ground you at a time when others are emotionally volatile and may even be turning to you for stability.

A Sacred Space

If we view death as a spiritual transition, then we will have created the most beautiful and sacred attitude, and a beautiful and sacred space can then manifest around the dying person. This can be facilitated by decorating the bedroom of the one who is dying in the most inspirational way, thereby inviting a peaceful transition. The accoutrements of end of life care—the oxygen machines, the commode—should all be removed at death to mark the change that has occurred and to transform the atmosphere of the space. Energetically, it is good if one feels uplifted walking into the room. Sometimes fragrant candles, incense, or the diffusion of essential oils can help achieve this.

A Suggested Checklist of Items for Physical Care of the Body

waterproof or plastic sheet (for under the body)
towels (to place under the body and for drying)
washcloths
draw sheets (2)
latex or similar protective gloves
pure soap
essential oils (favorite fragrances or oils that facilitate
   peaceful transition or release)
cotton balls
cornstarch (or other drying agent)
large bowls (2) (preferably ceramic)
protective tape for covering open wounds
Rescue Remedy
clothes for dressing the deceased

Bathing

Settle yourself before you begin, and perhaps say a prayer asking forgiveness for any unintentional clumsiness that may occur as you care for the body. Hospice staff or other caregivers can remove intravenous ports and catheters before you begin with the bathing. Start by cleaning the genital area. There is often a discharging of fluids from the bladder, and feces from the bowels at the time of death, and this requires attention for the sake of dignity. Protect the mattress with a waterproof sheet or towels, using the concertina method to position them under the body. The concertina method refers to how you fold the sheet—creating multiple pleats, before rolling your loved one to their side (at least two people should help with this, one supporting the head) and pushing the pleated sheet under the body as far as it will go. It is helpful if you can bend the knee of the deceased before trying to roll the body. Now roll the body to the other side and grab the folded sheet, pulling it out and straightening it under the deceased. It is easier to do this if the bed is accessible from all sides. If the deceased drank any liquid close to the time of death, it is possible that some is still in the mouth. Moving could dislodge it. Placing a towel under the head to catch any discharge is a good idea.

Bathing may happen organically, or follow a procedure dictated by a spiritual tradition. Even where it occurs without prescription, this washing with love can be a beautiful honoring of the body as caregivers reflect on their relationship to the physical in a ritual of blessing and letting go. Some families choose to bathe the entire body, but this washing is less of a sanitary measure and more of a ritual bathing. Applying cornstarch after patting the body dry with towels can help to dry the body. Remember that open wounds will remain unclosed after death, so you should cover these with tape.

Wear gloves when dealing with bowel and bladder movements. You can press down on the bladder region above the pubic bone to help evacuate any urine. Use warm water with a few drops of essential oils or pure soap for the cleanup. Afterwards, you may choose to place cotton in the anus to prevent any further discharge. Some families find this too invasive and choose to place a diaper on the deceased. At any rate, know that leakage is possible, so it is good to take measures accordingly.

Change the water once you have washed the genital area and rinse the bowl. Families sometimes choose to pour the water on a plant instead of flushing it down a drain. Continue with the bathing, patting the body dry with a towel and applying cornstarch if desired.

Dressing

If possible, choose clothing that stretches. Put on shirts, blouses, etc., by raising the deceased into a sitting position (supporting the head), and bringing
the garment down low, so that both hands can go into the sleeves at once.
Then pull the clothing up the arms and up the back. It is possible to cut
clothing items (blouses and shirts, up the back) which are too difficult to
manage. The cut will not be visible when the person is lying on their back.

Crematories usually request no shoes, so remember to remove these and
any jewelry before cremation takes place. If your loved one has a pacemaker,
it is necessary to remove this before cremation occurs because of possible
damage to the cremation chamber through explosion. Crematories may
undertake this or arrange it for you.[6]

Temporary Preservation Methods

Embalming is not the benign, spiritually rooted practice we associate with
the ancient Egyptians. It is a highly invasive procedure that involves punc-
turing the internal organs with a long, metal implement, draining the body
of fluids, and replacing them with a formaldehyde solution mixed with preservatives and dyes.[7] Its purpose is temporary preservation. The introduction of modern embalming techniques presaged the birth of the modern
funeral industry. During the Civil War, families hired embalmers to preserve bodies which were then shipped back to hometowns for public viewing and memorial services. Embalming became the vogue, and bodies that
would have stayed at home after death were removed for preserving, thus
taking death care out of the home and out of the hands of the family.

Embalmers also touted their practice as a sanitary measure. Notable physicians and pathologists such as Dr. Jesse Carr, chief of pathology at San
Francisco General Hospital and professor of pathology at the University
of California Medical School, is quoted in Jessica Mitford's *The American
Way of Death* as saying: "There are several advantages to being dead. You
don't excrete, inhale or perspire." He goes on to say that dying of a noncom-
municable disease is no health hazard whatsoever. Furthermore, nearly all
organisms need a live host to survive. Universal precautions when caring for
someone with a communicable disease (wearing protective gloves and hand
washing) are needed to care for the dead, in the same way one might care
for the living. Certainly, when after-death care is gentle and noninvasive, as
is the case with home funerals, there is no danger of contamination from
handling a corpse.

The kindly but fear-instilling funeral director who embalmed my mother just hours after her death told me that I would not want to look upon her body after death because of the unpleasant changes that occur. I don't think he had ever experienced an alternative to embalming, and I took him at his word. And yet my mother had chosen to stop eating and drinking in the weeks before death. She was a shrunken, emaciated figure when she died, and, I believe, her body would have changed quite gradually had she been placed on dry ice instead of being embalmed. When I viewed her body, she was waxen and childlike, with the coloration of neither the dead nor the living. I have heard that many embalmers regard their work as a form of art and their goal is to please. However, they should be duty-bound to explain the process and its environmental ramifications to consumers.

If the body is to remain lying in state, or "in honor" as one death midwife calls it, dry ice is the simplest and most effective method of preservation.

Dry Ice

Dry ice is usually available at the local supermarket (sold by the pound), or at liquor stores. Some states have guidelines for the application of dry ice for body preservation. Generally, anywhere from fifteen to twenty pounds per hundred pounds of body weight should suffice. It's important not to touch the ice with your bare hands because it burns. Wear heavy-duty gardening gloves to break the ice into small pieces with a hammer, and then place small amounts in pillowcases. Turn the body to one side and place these under the torso, rolling the body to the other side to do the same. This will elevate the torso, so that the head tilts back and needs raising up by the placement of additional pillows. Dry ice is frozen carbon dioxide that will evaporate. Because it sublimates (changes directly to gaseous form), it is important not to store it in confined spaces. Check every six to twelve hours to see if the ice has evaporated, and feel the body to ascertain whether it is really cold.

Sometimes it is helpful to place a beautiful comforter or quilt over the body, to insulate in the cold, especially if it is summer and the room is warm. An air-conditioner may also help keep the room cooler. I know of rural communities who have used regular ice when dry ice is not available, but the potential for mess makes it a less desirable method of preservation. Commercial ice-packs from the freezer are another possibility. A volunteer home funeral support group based in Crestone, Colorado, the Crestone End of Life Project, has been using a cooling pad, which is similar to an electric blanket, except it cools instead of warms. Another option in winter is simply to turn off the heat and leave the windows open. This might make the space less inviting for those who come to sit with the body, unless blankets and wraps are on hand to keep visitors warm.

Some funeral educators are now also recommending a cooling product used in the fish industry for preservation during transportation. One of the trade names used for this is Techni-ice and although not as cold as dry ice, it has been used effectively at home wakes and vigils. It comes in sheets that are immersed in water and then frozen for a number of hours before use. These can be washed and reused, and can be prepared for use ahead of death.

Caskets

Not too long ago, the local cabinetmaker, the town carpenter, also turned out caskets. Casket manufacturing became a separate industry as the new profession of undertaking took off. According to the Federal Trade Commission's Funeral Rule, families can provide their own casket even when they are working with a funeral home, and the funeral home may not charge a special handling fee. These days, it is possible to buy inexpensive caskets online. Families can also make their own, which can be a meaningful ritual. For cremation, crematories generally provide a cardboard cremation container, which the cremationist can then push more easily into the cremation chamber. I have known families who have decorated these cardboard caskets with beautiful images, poems, and statements in tribute to the deceased. This can be a creative outlet, especially for children dealing with grief and loss. Nowadays, biodegradable caskets with nontoxic finishes, made from sustainable materials, are growing in popularity. There are a number of companies offering models made from eco-plywood, wicker (a Moses basket for the dead), and recycled newspaper. A trend in the American funeral business is toward simpler and less expensive funerals, and that also means that consumers are shying away from the high-end, glossy, indestructible sealer caskets that some people mistakenly thought sealed out death and decomposition but which actually speeded up the process of putrefaction and exploded when they were not fitted with gaskets.

Unexpected Death

Where death comes out of the blue, for example through accident, sudden heart attack, or stroke, families may face the prospect of an autopsy to determine the cause of death. If the deceased has a medical history indicating a predisposition to the type of illness that caused his or her demise, an autopsy is less likely. Families may voice their opposition to autopsy on religious or conscientious grounds, but it is nevertheless within the coroner's power to approve the procedure.[8] The coroner is deemed to act on behalf of the deceased and in the interests of the law.

Coroners' offices generally return bodies with minimal suturing, leaving gaping incision wounds. This is because they are used to releasing bodies to morticians who then do the repair work before presenting the body to the family for viewing. If the plan is to later hold a home funeral with a viewing, and an autopsy is scheduled, it is advisable to notify the coroner's office as early as possible. There is no harm in appealing to the coroner's good nature in the hope that those conducting the autopsy may properly close the openings.

If a body is in bad shape following a car accident or similar occurrence, a family may not choose a home funeral, and may not choose to display the remains. They may also choose to hire a mortician to repair the body to make it suitable for viewing. I have known home funeral families, however, for whom it has been so important to conduct a wake in the presence of the deceased's body that they have chosen to keep the remains in the body bag they received from the coroner, using dry ice and keeping the room as cool as possible. For others, prayer and practice for the deceased can happen in absentia. When my own father died (of natural causes), a three-day vigil would have been my preference to assist with his transition, but because this was not possible, I withdrew into a three-day retreat of reflection and meditation while his body went to the mortuary cooler. The cremation happened on the fourth day following death. In my mind, whatever we do for the highest good and with the best intention will serve to assist the deceased in their transition.

Odors and Changes at Death

However little a body may change outwardly at death, particularly if the person has not eaten or drunk for quite some time and is emaciated, there is usually a smell of death. It may be subtle, or not. Diffusing essential oils, using scented candles or beeswax candles can help mask the odor, as can burning incense or filling the room with flowers. (Dry ice or another cooling method is also essential to retard decomposition and minimize odors.) I tell people that what they are experiencing is nature. The face may become more hollow looking. Eyes and mouths that have been closed at death may open. This is part of the natural process. As a society, we don't look upon death. We are used to hiding it or camouflaging it by procedures like modern embalming. More corpulent, fluid-filled bodies, or bodies of those whose life-forces were stronger up until death, may undergo more rapid change. If the changes are unsightly, a closed casket may be a solution.

Options for Final Disposition—Cremation or Burial

Burial at a Conventional Cemetery

Most cemeteries in the US were once not-for-profit entities. Nowadays, they are mostly for profit and often owned by funeral corporations rather than cities or churches. Some cemeteries, however, are still connected with particular religions; others offer burial to all, with sections for particular faith groups. Cemetery costs for burial in a conventional cemetery usually include the cost of the plot and a vault. This is a one piece unit, usually of concrete, metal, or fiberglass, which covers the casket to prevent the kind of ground sinkage that makes it hard to mow the lawn. A grave liner is a less expensive alternative to a vault. These are usually made of concrete and assembled on site. Cemetery fees will also include opening and closing the grave. Cemetery workers will do this, but families can often, with permission, participate in the lowering of the casket using ropes and the placing of dirt in the grave. Each cemetery will have its own standards for permissible grave markers and memorial stones. The term *perpetual care* refers to the upkeep of the gravesite, and this may or may not be included in the cemetery's fees.

Some cemetery managers are wising up to the growing demand for simpler and greener funerals by offering burial options that include burial without a casket (bodies wrapped in shrouds or blankets), although families will still need to purchase the vault for interment at a conventional burial ground. It is always good to ask what is possible.[9]

Green Burial in an Established Conventional Cemetery

Some cemeteries are turning sections of land over to green burial. These sections are more natural settings without the usual landscaping. Here, families may bury the unembalmed remains of their loved ones. The body returns to the earth in a biodegradable casket or without any container whatsoever. The cemetery may allow simple markers such as engraved stones, or plot the grave's location using a GPS system.

Green Burial at a Conservation Burial Site or Green Burial Preserve

Ramsey Creek Preserve in South Carolina was the first conservation burial site in the US. The modern phenomenon of preserving land by designating it as a burial site is immensely popular in the UK, a densely populated country with dwindling green, open space. In a bid to promote conservation and offer a more earth-friendly alternative to conventional burial, conservation burial sites are now springing up around the US. Some initiatives have been collaborations with land trusts. You may have a hard time spotting a grave if you happen to wander through one of these natural cemeteries. The vegetation is native and Mother Nature has free reign. The markers (if they exist) are unobtrusive, perhaps boulders or large stones with simple inscriptions. Most burial preserves have a central registry of grave sites, identified by their GPS coordinates. The Green Burial Council (www.greenburialcouncil.org) is a nonprofit organization that is a good source of information about conservation burial sites across the US.

Home Burial

Burial on private land, in the back forty, was the way of the homesteaders. In rural areas, home burial may be relatively easy. It is necessary to check local ordinances to establish whether or not it is possible, and which procedures you will need to follow. Your state Department of Health, Vital Records/Statistics division, is the place to start. As each death requires the filing of a death certificate, and each death certificate will state the location of final disposition (burial, in this instance), there will be an official record of the body's final resting place. You should also record on the property deed that there is a gravesite on the land. Families may want to consider how this could affect any future sale of the property, and how important it is to ensure access to the grave in the future, should the property change hands.

There are no established criteria for the depth of a grave or the location. According to popular mythology, it's "six feet under," but some cemetery managers have told me they go with two feet of earth on top of the body. Another guideline I have heard is to bury 150 feet away from a water source. Are wild animals likely to dig up your grandmother? Conservation burial experts tell me no. Home burial families I have known are often very involved in the care of their loved one and repeatedly testify to the healing nature of their participation. In particular, I have heard about how meaningful it has been for bereaved family members and friends to actually dig the grave. This especially applies to men, who may not assist with more personal, hands-on care of the deceased, but whose grief finds an outlet in this physical task.

Cremation in a Conventional Crematory

The cremation rate is on the increase in America. Cremation appeals to many families because it is cheaper and convenient. While many crematories are owned by funeral chains, there are still a few independent operators, and there is rising demand for what has been termed "direct cremation." Direct cremation providers offer no-frills packages at a cheaper cost. They will pick up the body, file the death certificate, and give you back the ashes. These services are often listed in the yellow pages as "simple cremation."

Newer cremation chambers complete the burn process within three hours. Crematories require the placement of the body in a cremation container (cardboard), which they usually provide. At the end of the cremation process, the cremationist will vacuum out the bones and the ashes, place them in a "grinder," and then transfer the "cremains," as they are called, into a container, usually plastic.

All crematories should place metal tags with bodies to ensure proper tracking of remains and avoid mix-ups. Families should have the right to witness a cremation, watching as the body is pushed into the cremation chamber and the door closes. For liability reasons, some crematories are now insisting that families view the cremation on a video screen in a room away from the cremation chamber. This is a shame because, for the bereaved, being there for this final stage in parting with the physical body can be of great significance.

Families sometimes receive misleading information about laws regarding the scattering or burial of cremains. It is worth checking the legal requirements for your state because claims about restrictive regulations may prove unfounded. Check with your state Department of Health–Vital Records/Statistics. Crematories sometimes refer to the plastic box containing the ashes as a "temporary container," but it is important to note that there is no reason to purchase and transfer the cremains to another (and more expensive) container, unless that is what you want. I have known families who have made their own cremains containers out of wood, created beautiful pottery, or used the family coffee can. On the internet, you will also find eco, biodegradable burial urns made from natural materials.

From an environmental standpoint, there's an argument that cremation releases pollutants, such as dioxin, hydrochloric acid, sulphur dioxide, and carbon dioxide, as well as mercury from dental fillings, into the atmosphere. The cremation process also uses natural resources. We all need to be aware of how our choices impact the planet. At the same time, I understand that families need to do what they feel allows them to honor their dead in their own way. As a side note, I do hear from a lot of people who would choose green burial over cremation if that option existed where they live.

Open-Air Cremation

In some parts of the country, Buddhist groups have their own cremation pyres for members of their community. Open-air cremation is labor and resource intensive, requiring a lot of wood and a fire tender to make sure the blaze remains under control. It may take the best part of a day for the physical remains to burn down to ashes and bone fragments. There is usually an annual limit imposed on the number of cremations that may take place in areas with established pyres. Open-air cremations should also only happen with the cooperation and consent of the local fire department.

The word "funeral" comes from the Sanskrit meaning "smoke," and, in India, the funeral pyre is the "sacred flame." For Eastern faith traditions, there are spiritual indications for cremation, which prescribe the consumption of the physical remains by the purifying flames of the pyre. Open-air cremations are certainly an incredible, inspirational spectacle.

I recently worked with a family who chose to conduct an open-air cremation on a friend's farmland. The land was designated as agricultural, and the owners had regularly held bonfires. Getting a permit for cremation from the local vital records office was not a problem. (This is not necessarily going to be the case everywhere, but never assume something is not possible until you know it is not.) During the last week of his wife's death, Chris began assembling the funeral pyre. This meant clearing the land of nearby trees, constructing a base of cinderblocks on which he laid a metal grate, and gathering a mountain of firewood.

During his wife's three-day wake, Chris put the finishing touches to the pyre site, working side-by-side with his brother-in-law and best friend. He was so proud of his construction, and when the day of the cremation arrived, drizzly and cold, Chris carried his wife down the stairs of their house, placed her in a home-decorated casket, and drove to the farm. The pyre grate had been covered with juniper boughs and flowers, the structure protected from the elements by a tarp covering. Friends had brought more flowers to cover Chris's wife in a floral blanket, on top of which they placed more wood.

After dousing the wood with ghee (clarified butter is often used for ceremonial burnings in Eastern traditions), Chris ignited the first log. He worked diligently for many hours, feeding the fire, while a circle of friends sang spirituals, their tears merging with the fine drizzle that fell. The smoke, initially white from the fragrant juniper, soon became clear. Within three hours, the layer of wood on the body had burned away revealing a white torso and skull; no limbs remained. When you talk to Chris now about his experience, he says, "It was the most beautiful day of my life." To some, this statement may seem incomprehensible, even crazy, considering the man had lost his wife. But if you had been there, you too would likely have been deeply affected by the potency of this fire ritual and awed by the dazzling brilliance of the sacred flames.

What to Do with the Cremains

Some people deposit the container with the ashes in their basement, its location forgotten until discovered on the occasion of their own death. Other families offer pride of place to the urn (the technical term for the receptacle containing the cremated remains), placing it on the living room mantelpiece. I understand that families of golfers often sneak onto golf courses to scatter cremains on the deceased's favorite green (usually without permission). Others hike to a favorite spot in nature. I am not giving these options a stamp of approval. It is certainly wise to remain within the law and respect private property. I am merely stating what happens in reality when families are passionately committed to doing what is most meaningful for them.

Many people bury cremains in their backyard. My father's partner sprinkled him on his prized rosebushes. In recent years there have been scandals involving aerial scattering services that fail to fulfill their obligations (the cremains are never airborne). Unless you accompany the plane, you will just have to trust it happened. And for former seadogs, there's the option of mixing cremains into large cement balls, which, dropped to the ocean floor, create artificial reefs, attracting myriad sea creatures, forming a living memorial to the dead.

Other Options for Final Disposition

People are coming up with more innovative alternatives to standard burial and cremation. Cryogenics, freezing bodies for posterity and possible future vivification, is familiar to many of us.[10] But now there's freeze-drying through a process developed in Sweden called *promession*. This involves the use of liquid nitrogen to turn us into human compost for the vegetable patch. Surfing the Internet will turn up many more, sometimes unusual, ways to deal with our bodies.

Donation

Educational teaching establishments, such as medical schools and medical research facilities, accept bodies for anatomical study. Donated bodies are super-embalmed with very strong preservatives, so students and researchers can use them for up to a couple of years. Donors generally give their bodies as an act of service to humanity, in order to further scientific knowledge. You will need to check whether a facility will cover all costs, such as body pick-up, death certificate filing, and cremation. It may well be that they will take care of all these details. If you want to donate your body for anatomical research, you will need to sign the authorization forms before death. (The same applies to tissue and organ donation.) When a body is no longer required for anatomical research, families will receive the cremated remains of the deceased. With organ and tissue donors, once the harvesting procedure is complete, families may conduct their own ceremonies with the body and arrange for final disposition (and may pay associated costs).

Exposing Children to Death

In denying our children the experience of death as part of life, we cloak it in unnecessary mystique.[11] Death will often remain a mysterious and frightening event, an unknown, until we are well into adulthood. Wyn, in his seventies, had never encountered a dead body until his stepmother's passing. He approached her deathbed with trepidation but was fascinated by the peace he saw on her face. On the second day of her wake, he even brought a camera to take photos, as once was the practice in bygone days. He even read old letters out loud that were comforting to him and to her.

Many families want to shield their children from death. They fear psychologically damaging them by exposing them to anything unpleasant. This stance applies before as well as after death. They will keep their children away from the patient ravaged by long-term illness and say, "I don't want the kids to remember him that way." My views on this issue stem from my own experience growing up with a very sick brother, who eventually died at age nine. The elder by two years, I witnessed and can recall my brother's suffering, and that of my family, but this experience was a profound teaching in unconditional love.

Far too often, our society has hidden away its sick, its disabled, and those who are dying. I believe that looking upon these people, and looking beyond the illness to the human being obscured by an ugly, declining physical body, is necessary to cultivate compassion.

I spoke with the ex-wife of a relatively young man who was dying of liver cancer. He had been hospitalized for a crisis and, now stable, was expecting to go home. But home was inconvenient, and there was no one to care for him there. I asked if she had thought of bringing him to her home, especially as death was considered imminent. She was keen, but her reservations centered upon their thirteen-year-old daughter and how she would handle seeing her father in his yellowed, emaciated state. There had also been tension in their relationship since their parting. Once we established that the family had resources to provide adequate care, I offered, "Think what a healing experience and lesson it could be for your daughter to experience you caring for your ex-husband at this difficult time. We will all meet death at some point, and it may not be pretty. It will likely be hard. You know, this experience of caring for a vulnerable human being will stay with her forever." I later heard that the ex-husband was transferred to his ex-wife's home where he died within twenty-four hours, having told his daughter that he would miss her. His ex-wife said she believed her daughter would treasure those words forever, and she was eternally grateful that he had been able to speak them.

When it comes to attending the funeral, and seeing the dead body, families can express similar qualms about having their children see the corpse. But the setting for the "viewing," especially when the deceased is laid out in his or her own bed, in familiar surroundings, can make a big difference. I have seen home wakes where children have wandered into the room with the body as if they were witnessing the most natural thing in the world.

Anne, an elementary school teacher, had a son in fifth grade when she died. At her wake, the entire elementary school filed through her small town-home. There were donuts and other goodies in the kitchen, and, upstairs, a thoughtfully decorated wake room that was a shrine to her vibrant existence. She lay on her bed, wearing her white satin bridal gown. While some children were hesitant, curiosity got the better of most, and they quietly or noisily entered the room to peek at her body. Anne didn't look great, and I'm sure her skeletal body was a shock to some, but the scene was death at its very best, the gold standard, if you like. What better exposure to mortality for a child than to witness it in these gentle, intimate surrounds, attended by a loving family and community of friends?

It can often be our own "stuff" projected onto children that removes them from proximity to the dying and death. We should be careful what we pass on to our offspring. Young children quickly pick up on our fears, making them their own. Our own relationship to death is key, as is how we prepare the young, emotionally and spiritually, for any encounter with the face of death. I believe young children are more connected to the world of spirit whence they came, and so their relationship to death is less complicated than ours. I have seen young children lovingly touch and talk to the dead without inhibition. With my own children, it has been important to talk about death as a transition that represents an end to the physical we know, but not an end to the essence of the being that we love. I believe that children (and adults) who have a spiritual framework for understanding the nature and meaning of death are able to integrate it in a healthier way.

There is nothing more life affirming, nothing that wakes us up more to our mortality, than bearing witness to death. It is a gift and a privilege to work with this threshold, and it is my belief that societies with more open and honest relationships to death operate less from a basis of fear. Our society still keeps death in the closet. But with the growth in hospice, we might now begin to reconnect to death as a natural part of the cycle of life. Caring for our dead is a final gift to our loved ones—and to ourselves.[12]

WORKING WITH GRIEF
by Kim Mooney[13]

A student asked his teacher, "How do I develop a spiritual life?"
The teacher replied, "Think of everyone you know, of all ages and
states of health, dying at random intervals."

We think of grief primarily as sadness and emptiness, but it is far more than that. Grief is alchemy—it cracks us open and creates opportunities for transformation. It insults the mind, taxes the body, and flings us into unpredictable contradiction. Grief exploits sorrow and wonder to break open our hearts. It offers us a glimpse of the ineffable and a doorway into our own profound spirituality. It upends our values and priorities and leaves no part of us untouched or unchanged. Grief makes us stop.

When someone or something we love dies, our bodies, minds, and souls are pushed upon to reassess all that we hold dear. By its very nature, grief is a rending of our assumptive world. We are often surprised at how deeply and relentlessly it persists, long after it has gotten old. And when we are deeply grieving, we can barely remember that there is more to the process than the pain.

A man once told his teacher, "My wife has died and the agony I feel is so deep, but I'm using my meditation practice to go down into myself and get through this." The teacher replied, "If you can still hold that thought, you're not down there yet."

In all grief—no matter what the loss—we swim in paradox. In one moment, our hearts lift up all the poignant richness of our insights. In the next moment, what was meaningful last week is now tiring. In the middle of a conversation, we may be suddenly overloaded and edgy. Relationships and things that were once compelling may now feel suffocating. Even our personal stories may feel vacant. Sometimes our vulnerability feels like a portal to something powerful and incomprehensible. At other times, we can't remember why we walked into the next room. We may be in agony, or furious, or not care about anything. Sometimes we are sad and relieved at the same time, or maybe we are strangely numb, only to suddenly plunge into a sea of wrenching emotions. And there are moments when we are brought to laughter, infusing our memories with song and color.

There are times when our feelings do not seem to be at all connected to our thoughts. To our amazement, we are caught in moments of soft wonder, as though we almost knew something we can't quite remember. Often we don't know how we will make it through. We may feel differently by tomorrow, or this afternoon. Nothing is quite right, and maybe we don't want to be here at all. We become grief soup. No wonder we often think we are going crazy.

Our brains, which consume a huge amount of energy, are not our best friends when we are in loss. They tell us to think, feel, and behave normally when we cannot. Then they shame us because we cannot. Our own tender experiences butt up against opinions from friends and families, the media, and our own enculturation about how it is supposed to go. Our bodies then carry the brunt of all the psychic energy it takes to grieve, as well as the anxiety and effort it takes to cram our grief into our ideas. No wonder we may have days when it is hard to get out of bed, when it is hard to open our eyes, when eating, sleeping or even breathing seems too much.

Often without warning, grief ebbs and flows, over days, months, and years. We think we are "getting better" only to be retriggered by a smell, a memory, or nothing we can put our finger on. We may find ourselves distressed, far beyond when we think it is acceptable. The shock wears off, and finality sets in. Time clarifies our experience, repeatedly giving us broader contexts in which to hold all our understandings. Then, in the distance that comes with time, the deafening silence can be full of a different kind of pain, and perhaps a seasoned gratitude and perspective. We need to remember that grief isn't an illness. It's a journey that changes us into people whose eyes are now more open.

We add to the very real burdens of grief by imposing our judgments upon them and by accepting or imagining the opinions of others instead of trusting our own. My favorite teaching story, the consummate description of full-bodied grieving in two sentences, is this:

A person, in conversation with a widow whose husband had
died seven months earlier, said incredulously, "You're still grieving?"
And the widow replied, "He's still dead."

Of the myriad expressions we may find, crying, anger, blankness, yearning, regret, sleeplessness, irritability, and sorrow are only a few. No wonder grief is marked by bone-deep exhaustion. It takes an incredible amount of time and psychic energy to digest what is happening, and to be completely rewritten as a person. In the middle of grieving, we are disoriented, skinless, unfiltered, and raw.

The profound exhaustion weakens our grasp on the illusion that life will stay as we wish. We may see into the number of ways we are not truly ourselves, or recognize the things and people that do not nourish us. We remember that death is not a distinct and occasional event but an unrelenting companion of life. With confusion and relief, we see that there is nothing absolutely true or untrue; grief unhinges our certainty about all manner of things. Here is the Buddhist "beginner's mind," or the Christian mystic's *nescivi*, meaning "to not know." Here, without defenses or explanations, is the chaos in which the world was born.

All of this is not simply a gaggle of wretched opportunities given to us to learn more about surrender. Grief is our human birthright, and it is our most powerful spiritual ally because it is embedded in the fabric of daily life and has the power to break our ego. The word *grief* comes from the Latin *gravis*, meaning "heavy," but it signifies the human condition that weights us to the earth and insists that we will not transcend the human experience without living through it. We pay mightily when we try to mask, ignore, or diminish it. Whether we choose to recognize it or not, grief is our messiest blessing.

Stephen Levine, a master teacher on death and grief, impressed upon me the recognition of both our personal grief and the grief of being human, and the need to hold both as sacred. "Render to Caesar what is Caesar's, and to God what is God's" seems another reminder of our obligation to honor our singular earthly life as much as we do our collective spiritual existence. While each person's grief is unique to that loss, that time, that person, the process of constantly letting go is unique to no one in a body. Clinging to one view or the other creates more pain than there needs to be, but when we allow ourselves to grow into this dynamic tension—between the individual and the collective, between the human and the spiritual—we discover the unfamiliar comfort of being home.

We can live through grief with grace, and we can help others to do so, but not alone. We gain purchase by opening to the wisdom of community. We carry on by remembering that we are all on the same journey, whether we are in the fire at this moment, have been, or will be.

For me, one of the most powerful visual metaphors for how community can help in grief is that of a plasma globe, the kind sold as a table decoration. It is a clear plastic globe about the size of a soccer ball, and when you turn the electricity on, lightning bolts explode freely and randomly inside the globe, constantly shifting direction and intensity. It is chaos, beautiful and endless, raging with no structure or pattern. But the globe, completely transparent, provides the perfect calm container for the cosmic storm within.

We can be the transparent holding environment for the chaos of another's grief. We can be the steady reflective human community—not closing in to intrude or redefine, to suffocate or impede the chaos—but also not pulling away to draw attention or energy from the natural course of things. Just holding, simply witnessing, and not assuming that we know how anyone should be, we can collectively create the opportunity for each person to manage the integrity of their solitary grief. In this conscious witnessing there is a willingness to be of service and a faith that what is happening is natural. We also bring endless patience and vast curiosity, which help us open to a deeper compassion for self and other.

In the Dagara tradition in Africa, grief rituals can go on for days and involve the whole community. In this culture, where self, family and community are all of equal importance, each death brings the whole community together to release anything old or new, creating a globe in which no one carries forgotten or unattended grief. In utter abandon, people are enfolded into a ritual space that works effortlessly in service to the deepest and most authentic forms of grief without flinching but does not admit the emotional distractions or mental constructions that we often interpret as "being in the chaos."

In the face of the absolute desolation of grief, our caring looks almost too simple. We help the grieving take care of their precious bodies. We bring them food, help them keep their environments calm and uncluttered, and remind them they need exercise and sunlight and sleep. We run errands for them, give them massages, or bring them a glass of water.

We listen, with curiosity and without supposition about their journey. We listen while they tell us about who and what they loved. We listen while they explore their inner world, and allow them to repeat themselves over and over, as each new heartbreak or awareness arises and seeks expression before finding understanding. We keep listening months and even years later, as they put color and meaning to their story, and as they move with how it is changing them.

We listen without needing ourselves to be part of the story, and we leave vast space for the grieving person to interpret their own experience. We remember not to distract them, and avoid giving advice about how to manage. We remember not to draw comparisons to other losses, or presume that we could understand what they are going through. And we try to discern when to ask how they are and when to simply bring our willing hearts into the room. We remember that sometimes there is extraordinary kindness in silence, and let people know we don't know what to do but we'll stay anyway.

We have enough courage to let them cry and rage and be dull without wanting them to be different—to let them be unpleasant and to not back away. We offer them permission to take care of themselves and reflect forgiveness when they cannot, and we validate the intensity of their reactions and assure them that they are not crazy. We allow them to hyperventilate into their own disequilibrium while in our hearts we breathe the words of the mystic, Julian of Norwich, for all beings: "All will be well and all will be well and all manner of things will be well."

And at some point, with consent, we lend our presence to help the grieving re-enter the world, trusting that they know how to find their way. We do all this from a seat of knowing that we carry within each of us the account of

246 — PRACTICAL PREPARATION

living with grief from every human throughout all time. We recognize that all losses, small and grand, teach the same lessons and that they feel merciless when we are alone but manageable when we are in community.

For each grief, no matter how leprous or how gently dispatched, is a pearl of impermanence held in our hand. With each experience—ours or another's—we learn more about how not to be surprised, insulted, or outraged by its demands. We learn more about how to accept grief's trials and challenges and discover that it holds precious gifts. We discern insights, awarenesses and secrets that we must then birth. And if we are able to recognize, respect, and protect grief in ourselves and others, then when it comes time to let go of our own bodies—whether we are frightened or ready—instead of being completely bewildered, some part of us will say, "Oh, this again. I know how to do this."

This time, like all times, is a very good time, if we but know what to do with it.—Ralph Waldo Emerson

WORKING WITH GRIEF FROM A BUDDHIST PERSPECTIVE
by Andrew Holecek

The Relative Approach

Because of the ferocity of grief, most bereaved people just want to survive the anguish and don't care about anything but getting through the day. After the death of my mother, I felt like I was injected with molten lead. Everything was so heavy. All I wanted to do was sleep. Many Buddhists, however, want to know how to work with these intense emotions from a spiritual perspective. The following are merely guidelines.

Death is the end of a body. It is not the end of our relationship with the person who died. In many ways, healthy grief is learning how to establish a proper relationship. Bereavement is a death-within-life and may be the closest thing we experience in life to the bardos themselves. Once again, learning about the bardos not only helps us with death itself but with the many painful transitions of life. Christine Longaker writes:

> In this transition [of grief], we are suspended between the past and the future. We may feel extreme anxiety and loss of control

as we experience the ground of our "known world" dissolving beneath our feet [the bardo of dying]. The new shape of our life has not yet manifested [the bardo of becoming], so we find no reassurance in the future. . . . Grieving challenges us to eventually die to our old way of life, letting go of our former expectations, identity, and all the associations we had with the deceased person.[14]

The first point is to practice *maitri*, or loving-kindness, toward yourself. Allow as much time as you need to process the loss. Don't feel pressured to feel better by some prescribed date, one that we might set for ourselves or that others set for us. Let yourself grieve fully. Grieving is not a sign of weakness but of real strength. It takes courage to feel this level of pain and to face the empty space left by the one who died. So maitri, as a critical component in healthy grief, includes both gentleness and fearlessness.

After the death of my parents, I felt stuffed with intense emotions and needed time to digest the enormity of what just happened. I couldn't eat any more experience. Returning immediately to normal activities would have made me sick. Daily problems were blown out of proportion, my irritability was at an all-time high. My neurotic tendencies were just below the surface, ready to bleed out with the slightest emotional scratch. So I hid from the world and gave myself permission to do nothing.

When I thought I was getting over it, a new wave of grief crashed over me. It felt like a plow had dropped deep into my heart and was dredging up all the unprocessed grief from previous losses. I was a wreck. But I allowed myself to be a wreck. I felt my pain without indulging it, and slowly digested this bitter experience.

It is better to face the grief and not suppress it, which requires fearlessness. Suzuki Roshi said that for any experience, it's best to be a good bonfire, not a smoky fire. Don't live your life on a pilot-light level. Live it with the gas turned on. One way or the other, the fire of experience must have its way. Experience must be lived fully—and therefore burned thoroughly—to be released properly. If we don't feel and therefore don't process the experience completely, instead of "cremating" it as we experience it, it tends to lodge in the body or mind and smolder. This creates all kinds of "smoke related" symptoms.[15] Longaker says, "If we have a deep aversion to entering this vulnerable state, we may suppress our grief for years and leave it unresolved.

Any subsequent losses are added to our burden of unfinished grief, and our hearts grow heavier—or worse, become numb. If we fear experiencing the deep pain of our grief, we will fear witnessing it in others."[16]

Other manifestations of unprocessed grief include overreacting to an insignificant new loss and living half-heartedly—partly in the past, partly in the present—unable to move on. Exaggerated behavior and emotional fragility are also markers of unresolved grief.

The temptation to avoid grief can be overwhelming. Infinite forms of entertainment are available to satisfy that temptation, which is the longing to fill the void left behind. There's nothing inherently wrong in turning on the television and distracting ourselves. Emotional masochism is not the point. The point is to be kind to ourselves. This means sometimes staying in the fire and sometimes stepping out. We do what we need to do. Understanding the process of grieving guides us in what to do.

When a loved one dies, part of us dies with them. Grief is about finding a way to come back to life. "Healing" is a difficult term when it comes to grief. On one level, we never completely heal. We learn how to live with the loss. We find a new place for our loved one in our heart.

The Power and Peril of Pain

If we relate to it properly, there is spiritual power in sadness. As Kim Mooney pointed out, the gravity of the emotion can bring us down to earth and help us contact reality. Reality is often touched through heartbreak, so we can let sadness guide us into it. We usually speak of enlightenment, which is the discovery of reality, as "waking up." It is just as viable to discuss it in terms of "waking down." Enlightenment is waiting for us in the depths of our body, and the gravity of a situation can plunge us into contact with that truth.

The heaviness of grief lends itself to profundity. The root "pro" means "advancing" [toward]; and "fundus" means "the foundation, base, bottom, depth." Grief has the power to drop us through the frivolities that obscure our true nature, our foundation, base, depth. It therefore helps us contact the bottom of our heart—which is where that nature lies.

But be careful not to indulge your grief and let sadness sink into depression. Depression is when our energy is turned inward against ourselves, in negative self-talk and damaging beliefs about ourselves and the world. It's good to come down, but don't stay down. Feeling our pain doesn't mean feeding it, which only gives grief an unhealthy life of its own.

There are many people who get stuck in grief and therefore in the past. If the love of our life is gone, it's easy to feel that our own life is gone. This is like driving down the road of life with our gaze stuck in the rear-view mirror. Everything is centered around yesterday, which is always dead, and therefore detracts from the experience of today. Only the present moment is alive. This is why teachers exhort us to always remain there. Use your memories, but don't let them use you.

If you find that your grief is turning into depression, seek the support of a grief counselor or grief therapist. A grief counselor acts as general support for uncomplicated grief. A grief therapist steps in when things get more tangled.[17] Find someone who knows about grief and is willing to work with you. Otherwise your busy medical doctor may send you home with an antidepressant, which rarely solves the problem. Sadness is not depression. Indulged sadness, however, can slip into depression.[18] As a final rule, grief is outward-oriented, toward the dead person or pet; depression is more inward-oriented, a more implosive and excessive preoccupation with ourselves.[19]

There are "three Ds" to look for that suggest grief is sliding into depression: *duration*, *distress*, and *dysfunction*. It's hard to put a time frame on these three, which vary from individual to individual, but here are some guidelines. To assess dysfunction: if after a month or so we just can't get back to life, and are lying in bed most of the time, a grief therapist could help. For distress: if after three months or so the intensity doesn't let up, and grief support isn't working, consider finding a grief therapist. For duration: if six months or so after the death all we can do is think about the loved one, we might ask for help.

Working with our own grief requires allowing ourselves to grieve fully and yet still finding our way back to life. If we come back to life quickly, we may be in denial, or revealing how little we cared about the person, or demonstrating an honest ability to process the grief. If we come back to life too slowly, we may be wrestling with issues of duration, distress, or dysfunction. Kim Mooney says, "Much of this depends on the type of death (homicide or suicide has a different trajectory than a spousal loss), and a professional assessment of strengths and stressors together. Someone may be very distressed after a death but, when counseled, find that their grief is appropriate."

If there is one central instruction, for those who are dying and for those left behind, it is to let go. Holding on is what makes death difficult for the one dying, and it makes life difficult for the ones still living. Grief is not about letting go of our *relationship* with our loved one. It's about releasing our *attachments* to them. Once again, it's about transforming our relationship. Maintain an emotional bond that doesn't bind. Sustain a relationship that allows us to move forward.

We should honor the past and the people who loved us. There is a noble place for our loved ones, as there is for history and tradition. But there is also a tipping point where this acknowledgment can slide into obsession or depression, and deny life instead of augmenting it. Treasure your roots and the beauty of the past, but don't plant yourself there.

This doesn't mean we have to tough it out and charge insensitively into the future. That's a gaze that's fixated too far down the road, which also doesn't exist. Use your mindfulness. Stay present with the feelings in your body. Don't indulge the thoughts spinning through your head. If we stay with our body, that automatically means staying in the present, for our body and its senses can only perceive the present.[20] It's the thinking mind that yanks us to the past or tugs us into the future. Our discursive mind takes the pain of grief, felt in the core of our body, and transforms it into unnecessary suffering. Healing always takes place in the present, no matter how difficult that present might feel.

Anticipatory Grief

A natural mourning often occurs when we are expecting the death of a loved one. This anticipatory grief has many of the same symptoms as post-death grief. Anticipatory grief doesn't mean that the person feels the same grief that's experienced after death. It also doesn't mean that the grief felt after the death will be shorter or less intense, although that's possible. There's never a set level or amount of grief that a person will feel.

If we relate to anticipatory grief properly, it connects us to the truth of impermanence. We can use it to treasure our loved one while they're still alive, and to prepare ourselves for their imminent death. Anticipatory grief is almost a subset of the four reminders discussed in chapter 1. The Thai meditation master Ajahn Chah once held up a glass and said, "Look at this. This glass does a wonderful job of holding water. It shimmers in the sunlight. When I tap it, it sings. But one day it will be blown off the shelf by a gust of wind, or my elbow will knock it off the table. If you really think about it, this glass is already broken. That is why I enjoy it so immensely now."[21]

If it's not related to properly, anticipatory grief can increase our attachment to the dying person and cause unnecessary hardship for them and for us. If the dying person senses too much premature grief, it might cause them to become withdrawn and depressed, "They're relating to me like I'm already dead!"

It helps to recognize anticipatory grief so that we can nurture its benefits and avoid its pitfalls. The key is to live in the moment. Acknowledge impermanence, but use it to empower the present—not to dilute it.

Compassion and Devotion

The middle-way approach to grief is the best. Feel your grief but don't indulge it. And remember that when we think and feel small, our emotions get big. Recall that thousands of people die every day. Countless people are grieving with us. Our grief can put us in contact with them and take us out of ourselves. Indulging grief, as painful as it is, is ironically selfish. Connecting with the pain of humanity puts us in touch with a larger reality. We are "suffering with" others. That's what compassion is, and that's what grief can engender.

The gift of grief is that it almost forces us to surrender. Crying out in anguish, longing, and unrequited love opens our heart and drops us into the core of our being. This ineffable feeling is similar to devotion, the most important feeling in Vajrayana Buddhism. Trungpa Rinpoche spoke about "the genuine heart of sadness," which is a doorway to both devotion and compassion.[22]

Compassion and devotion are centered around love. Love directed "up" is devotion. Love directed "down" is compassion. The force of grief can put us in touch with love, devotion, and compassion, three of the most powerful spiritual emotions. The weight of grief drops us into ourselves, which is where these noble qualities lie. In other words, grief can be profoundly spiritual. Kathleen Willis Morton, writing about the loss of her son, says, "Sorrow is a sacred blessing, a piercing awl. . . . Through that puncture wound we can choose to see only the loss, what is not there, or look at the opening it has made in us, the spaciousness to be filled up with natural great delight if we are receptive and patient."[23]

There is a beautiful irony in sadness. While it is born from loss, it can paradoxically instill a sense of fullness. "Sadness" comes from the same root as "satisfy" and "saturate." If grief is anything, it's a saturation of feeling.

Etymologically, feeling "sad" then developed to feeling that one had had "enough," which only later extended to "weary." In my experience, grief centers me (which is what gravity does). It puts me in contact with my inner self. When I feel into that center, I find that it's empty yet somehow full. It's strangely satisfying. Because it's so overwhelming, there's something about sadness and grief that is complete.

As with love, grief is intensely personal. It's part of what makes us uniquely human. It borders on the sacred. But with this said, and with all due respect, grief is an expression of our relative nature. It's not absolutely who we really are. If it was, it would never disappear. It may feel like grief will never end, that we will never find life or love again, and that the best part of ourselves died when our loved one died. But sooner or later, like everything else, grief will self-liberate. It too will die. New life will begin, for the one who died, and for loved ones left behind. Psychologist and grief counselor Judy Tatelbaum writes:

> As we journey through these painful experiences of living, we must never forget that we have an amazing resilience and capacity to survive. Just as whole forests burn to the ground and eventually grow anew, just as spring follows winter, so it is nature's way that through it all, whatever we suffer, we can keep on growing. It takes courage to believe we can survive, that we will grow. It takes courage, too, to live now and not postpone living until some vague tomorrow.[24]

The Absolute Approach

I was intimidated when I first thought of writing about grief. Although I have experienced it, I am not a grief counselor. Grief somehow seemed special, unique in its merciless intensity. But upon reflection, I realized that while grief is in a league of its own, it's also irreducibly just another experience. This perspective can help us relate to it better.

Even though grief and neurotic attachment are not the same, our level of pain when someone or something is taken away is directly proportional to our belief in the true existence of things. The more invested we are in something, the more it hurts when it's gone. Losing an unsaved paragraph on your computer doesn't sting as much as losing the computer itself.

There is a fine line between love and emotional addiction. Remember

Khenpo Rinpoche's advice on "love without attachment," or in our terms, love without emotional addiction. This is mature love. Attachment is the addiction part. It's the stickiness of love that causes so much torment. Our attachment and addiction to existence—to people and things—is never so painfully revealed as when existence is taken away. In other words, on an absolute level, *grief is a form of withdrawal.* It is the pain of withdrawing from our belief in the true existence of someone.

This is not to deny the raw and very human experience of grief, or the preciousness of love. It is meant to help us understand grief, to work with it by putting it in perspective, and to lessen the blow. On an absolute level, the best way to deal with grief is to study emptiness and to practice illusory form.[25] This is the way to prepare.

When we finally realize that nothing inherently exists, that everything that comes together must fall apart, that everything is just like a rainbow, then we won't be so devastated when yet another rainbow dissolves into the play of light and space from which it arose. If we understand emptiness, when another glass breaks or a loved one dies, we'll realize that that's just what rainbows do.

This view not only helps the ones left behind, it also helps the dying person. One of the most painful aspects of dying is the grasping of those who don't want to release the dying person. By letting the dying person go from our side, we are helping them to let go from their side. Likewise, from the side of the dying person, who would you rather have with you when you die: spiritual friends who understand impermanence, or loved ones who can't bear the thought of losing you?

Impermanence is the direct expression of emptiness, and emptiness is the best description of reality. In order to soften our grief we need to align ourselves with reality. We need to get past the mistake of seeing things as solid and lasting. In the words of Sogyal Rinpoche:

> The reason we become so fiercely attached to things—from our emotions, ideas, and opinions to our possessions and other people—is that we have not taken impermanence [emptiness] to heart. Once we can accept that impermanence is the very nature of life . . . then letting go becomes quite natural. With impermanence securely in our hearts, we'll see that if everyone were to realize its truth, then even in the thick of change and death and bereavement, we would not feel any great sense of loss. Our tears

then would not be because death and impermanence are facts of life, but because of something much deeper: we would weep with compassion, because we'd know that all the pain and hurt and suffering we go through do not need to be there. They are only there in fact because we fail to understand that everything, absolutely everything, is transient [empty].[26]

Over the past twenty years, I have spent considerable time with many lamas. I have observed these spiritual masters during times of great personal loss. It's difficult to say what they might be feeling, but they don't seem to feel grief. I have witnessed moments of sadness, but nothing that resembles the incubation of that sadness into grief. A number of veteran translators who have spent years at the side of these masters relate similar stories. Realized beings feel as much as we do (if not more), but they don't attach themselves to these feelings. In other words, they realize the truth of emptiness, which liberates them from the solidity of grief.

Marpa was a great master who was instrumental in bringing Buddhism from India to Tibet. One dark day his son was killed in an accident. Marpa wept inconsolably. His students were shocked. Here was an enlightened being, who had taught on emptiness and the illusory nature of reality, crying openly over the death of his son. Was he a liar or a fraud? Were his teachings on illusion wrong? When questioned, Marpa responded, "Yes, everything is an illusion, but the death of a child is the greatest illusion of all." When Trungpa Rinpoche heard about the death of his friend Suzuki Roshi, he cried out in anguish. But he didn't feed his anguish. He felt it intensely, and allowed it to self-liberate. He didn't give these feelings a place to land, take root, and blossom into grief.

Emptiness doesn't mean nothingness, which would be cold nihilism. It means no-thingness. It means that if we look closely at anything, or any person, we will discover there is no solid, lasting, and independent thing there. There's only a vast ecological network of causes and conditions, ceaselessly giving birth to appearances.

Realizing the empty nature of whatever arises does not negate the beauty or humanity of that arising. We still feel things. Indeed, the sensitivity of awakened beings (who have realized emptiness) compared to those still asleep (who have not realized emptiness), is like the difference between feeling a hair in your eye or on the calloused palm of your hand. When we wake up we feel more. But it hurts less. Emptiness cannot harm emptiness.

The Buddha first taught emptiness at Vulture Peak Mountain. It is said that the vulture flies the highest and therefore has the best view. The view of emptiness is supreme. It's the view of the enlightened ones. Vultures also prey on the corpse of existence. This is symbolic for the power of emptiness, which also devours existence.

We grieve because we think things exist. This is the view of a mole. To lessen our suffering, we need to increase our understanding of emptiness. We need to raise our gaze.

The Joy of Inter-being

Even though emptiness is the funeral for seeing things as truly existent, it is not a sad affair. Emptiness leads to the celebratory discovery of fullness. As Thich Nhat Hanh so beautifully writes, a piece of paper is empty of self-nature, but full of the sunlight and oxygen that nurtured the tree, full of the food and water that nurtured the logger . . . full of the universe. How much more so for a human being. We're not only full of physical things but of emotional and spiritual qualities. The loved one that we grieve, by returning to emptiness, has simultaneously returned to fullness. Their carbon, nitrogen, and oxygen have returned to the earth to sustain other forms of physical life. Their beauty, dignity, and love have returned to space to sustain other forms of mental and spiritual life—our own and other loved ones left behind.

This is not just a consoling metaphor. Every day we ingest and inhale countless atoms that once resided in countless beings of the past. Every day we excrete and exhale countless atoms that will one day reside in countless beings of the future. When we die, we're just returning these borrowed elements to their lender. They will be loaned, yet again, to sustain endless future lives. We are simply "returning to fiveness" (*pancatvam gatah*, "returning to the five elements"). More accurately, we are returning to infinity.

This is the way enlightened beings, and some scientists, see the world. It's a deep ecological view of the interpenetration of all things and all beings. Look at the world through the eyes of a buddha, and share in the joy of this clear vision. Realize that when your loved one dissolves into nothing, he or she is really merging into everything.

Because we limit a being to the envelope of the body, we suffer when that body disappears. Death is simply the opening of the envelope. It's a release of the sacred and deathless contents into new forms.[27] When great masters die, they become *more* available to their students. They're no longer restricted by their physical body. Their heart and mind and blessings become more available as they spill into space. Thich Nhat Hanh counsels someone who lost their mother:

> We can look deeply to see that our mother is not only out there, but in here. Our mothers and fathers are fully present in every cell of our bodies. We carry them into the future. . . . If you look deeply, you'll see already the continuation of your mother inside you and outside of you. Every thought, every speech, every action of hers now continues with or without the presence of her body. We have to see her more deeply. She's not confined to her body, and you aren't confined to your body. It's very important to see that. This is the wonder of Buddhist meditation—with the practice of looking deeply you can touch your own nature of no birth and no death. You touch the no-birth and no-death nature of your father, your mother, your child, of everything in you and around you.[28]

This is how to relate to our dead loved one. At the beginning of the chapter we saw that healthy grief is about establishing a new relationship with our loved one. The best relationship is to realize that while our loved one is relatively nowhere to be found, they are absolutely everywhere.

The breeze that you feel is the breath of your loved one, the warmth of the sun is their tender embrace, and the earth beneath your feet is the stability of their undying love. Before things crystalize into form, those things manifest as qualities. When those forms dissolve, they melt back into qualities. We've got it backwards. We usually attribute qualities to things, but things are actually frozen qualities.[29] Qualities, unlike things, never die.

Trungpa Rinpoche said that the ideal emotion is sad-joy. We can now extend his comment for a more complete understanding of the ineffable feeling, the emptiness-fullness, that is grief. A passage often attributed to Henry van Dyke expresses it this way:

> I am standing upon the seashore. A ship at my side spreads her white sails to the morning breeze and starts for the blue ocean. She is an object of beauty and strength, and I stand and watch her until at length she hangs like a speck of white cloud just where

the sea and sky come down to meet and mingle with each other. Then some one at my side says: "There! she's gone!" Gone where? Gone from my sight, that is all. She is just as large in the mast and hull and spar as she was when she left my side, and just as able to bear her load of living freight to the place of her destination. Her diminished size is in me, and not in her. And just at that moment, when some one at my side says: "There! she's gone!" there are other eyes that are watching for her coming and other voices ready to take up the glad shout, "There she comes!" And that is—dying.[30]

Conclusion

By allowing ourselves to be fully present to our grief, and with the wisdom of impermanence and emptiness as our guide, we eventually learn that it's okay to let go of the intensity of grief. This doesn't mean that we will forget our loved one. It means that the truth of impermanence and emptiness can open us to the possibility of transforming our grief into healing and into a new relationship with the one who died. With this understanding we have actually gained something from our loss.

Learning about grief, from an absolute and relative perspective, helps us make friends with it. It helps us to suffer consciously. By holding the view of emptiness (the absolute), and treating ourselves with kindness and compassion (the relative), grief becomes a sacred practice into dying.

10. DIFFICULT ISSUES

ORGAN DONATION, suicide, euthanasia, miscarriage, and abortion are complex and challenging topics.[1] They involve spirituality, psychology, politics, ethics, religion, gender, sexuality, economics, culture, and a host of intellectual and emotional responses that are highly charged. Because the subsequent emotional, medical, legal, and karmic implications are profound, we need to think deeply before we act. It is beyond our reach to thoroughly explore these topics. The challenge here is to offer sane advice in one brief section.

It's always best to consult with our spiritual teacher, or a lama well versed in these areas. It also helps to remember that the sometimes strong words from the Buddhist tradition about these matters usually don't come from judgmental people, or those out of touch with the times. At its best, this is advice from compassionate masters who act as representatives of reality. Their sole purpose is to relieve our suffering, now and in the future. Their counsel is based on a profound understanding of the laws of reality, in particular the immutable laws of karma, and the purest motivation to benefit others.

We may not always resonate with that advice. It's easy to convince ourselves that their words are too traditional or disconnected from modern life. It's like gravity. We may not like gravity and the way it constricts our life, and we may not like the laws of karma and the implications of our actions. But karma is as impersonal as gravity. In the end, we have no choice but to abide by the laws of reality. The more we know about them, the more skillful our actions become. Spiritual masters can point them out.

Buddhist scholar Judith Simmer-Brown says:

> The most important thing is for practitioners to study the tradition carefully, especially the Abhidharma, Madhyamaka, and

Yogacara–Buddha nature; to know karma well, both in the relative and absolute perspective; to respect and turn to the lamas for advice, and consider it; and to engage creatively with the tradition, making sure to understand one's own personal motivation. We are active participants here, not passive recipients of the tradition.[2]

Some spiritual masters may not fully comprehend our quirks and idiosyncrasies, our cultural and therefore superficial expressions. But they often understand the nature of mind and reality from which those superficial expressions arise. They get the heart of the matter. This itself is a charged topic. I'm not saying that spiritual masters are always the final word. But I am empowering their advice, and the motivation that gives rise to it. We are the final word. Our own wisdom, compassion, and motivation is where we take final refuge—and responsibility—for our actions. Author Scott Edelstein says:

> Part of our job as students is to give our teachers the right amount of power. This means allowing them to influence us, perhaps quite deeply—but not allowing them to brainwash us, control us, or make us smaller or less human. In practice, this means subjecting everything a teacher says to our own careful scrutiny. As you attend to a teacher's words and actions, do they seem right to your heart, your gut, and your head, or do they feel off the mark? Do they emphasize that the teacher is every bit as human as you, or do they imply that the teacher is more or better than human? Does the teacher consistently serve your (and other students') best interests, or do they appear to serve or gratify themselves? ... Scrutiny isn't an insult to any teacher. On the contrary, it's a way to take them—and yourself—seriously. The more insightful a teacher is, the more your scrutiny will validate what they say and the deeper their teaching will sink in.[3]

While the teachings of the four main schools of Tibetan Buddhism are in general agreement about the central aspects of death, dying, and rebirth, there are differences. Teachers themselves may not always be consistent. A master may offer advice to one person that doesn't even agree with what that master said to another person. The emotional and spiritual complexities around the difficult issues surrounding death, and the differing contexts in which they arise, invite disparate interpretations. Advice around these matters is very individual. Reality, especially around death, is not tidy.

Consult others, and contemplate fully, before karma is irrevocably set by your actions. The following sections point out some of the principal issues and offer the most general guidelines. They are not meant to be definitive, merely suggestive.

ORGAN DONATION

Organ donation is a common issue for Buddhists. This is because of *tukdam*, the meditative absorption that we discussed in part 1 (see page 82). It is traditionally taught that the body should not be disturbed for three days after death, so that tukdam can be honored and preserved. But other teachings say that donating our organs, which must be harvested immediately after death, is the final gesture of a bodhisattva to benefit others. What should we do?

As with any difficult issue, it is good to ask your teacher. Most of the lamas I consulted echoed these words of Khenpo Tsültrim Gyamtso Rinpoche:

> Organ donation is good. It is totally in harmony with the Mahayana practice of giving away parts of your body for the benefit of others, which the Buddha himself did many times as a bodhisattva. Some people say that it is not good to give organs if you are a Vajrayana practitioner, because it is not good to imagine the yidam deity as being dissected. However, you should simply dissolve your visualization of yourself as the yidam deity before giving away your organs. If you do it that way, giving away organs is not in any way contradictory with Vajrayana practice.[4]

Most beginning practitioners will not enter tukdam, so disrupting it is not an issue.[5] For advanced meditators who may be in tukdam, their practice is probably stable enough that it doesn't matter what happens to the body. Gross levels of mind are connected to the gross physical body. Subtle levels of mind are not. Khenpo Rinpoche's advice applies to practitioners somewhere in between.

Dr. Mitchell Levy, physician to Trungpa Rinpoche, says, "Trungpa Rinpoche said that, if during your lifetime you decide to donate your organs, and you make that decision while you are alive and able to think about it, then that is an act of generosity."[6] A general guideline, in life as in death, is that if you're in doubt about what to do, don't think about yourself. Think about the benefit of others. When you're just not sure what to do, open your heart, love, and give. By doing so your actions will benefit others, and your motivation will benefit you.

Eighteen people a day die in the United States while awaiting organ transplants. Over 108,000 people in America alone are waiting for heart, kidney, liver, lung, and pancreas transplants. Tens of thousands are in need of corneas, bone and other tissues, and skin (to heal burns). Each person who donates has the potential of saving or enhancing more than fifty lives. You also take up to eight people off the waiting list.[7]

If organs are to be donated, keep the body undisturbed for as long as possible without compromising the medical end of things. If it's necessary to harvest an organ right away, then do it.[8] Surgeons usually wait two to five minutes to make sure the person is dead before beginning to harvest any organs. Just before the organs are harvested, pull the hair or tap forcefully at the site of the brahmarandhra (the *brahmarandhra* is sometimes called the "tenth gate." It lies about eight finger-widths back from a normal hairline, and is considered the most auspicious gate for consciousness to leave at death).[9] Place the phowa powder or pill there if you have it. If consciousness hasn't left the body yet, this can facilitate the transference. According to the Dalai Lama, sand from the Kalachakra mandala, mixed with butter, can also be placed on the brahmarandhra.[10] Lama Zopa Rinpoche says that burning incense will help end the tukdam.[11]

EUTHANASIA

Euthanasia is another challenging topic.[12] Is it okay to pull the plug? The first issue is our motivation. If we're the one helping to euthanize a sentient being, why are we doing it? Are we doing it to remove their suffering, or to remove our anxiety around witnessing that suffering? Who are we trying to benefit, and why do we think it brings benefit? These kinds of questions help to reveal hidden motivations that can guide us through this complex issue. It's also imperative to realize that people rarely ask for euthanasia when their needs are met. If someone is feeling loved and valued, and has their physical symptoms managed, they generally won't ask to be euthanized.

There is a difference between active and passive euthanasia. Active euthanasia is actively ending a life, and the tradition is clear on this: Don't do it. Even though the motivation may be to end suffering, and that does soften the karmic consequences (see the four aspects of a fully constituted karma on page 266), active euthanasia still has significant karmic repercussions.[13] Active euthanasia, however well intentioned, is based on two fundamental misconceptions. The first is that experience ends with death. Although the purpose of euthanasia is to end suffering, not all suffering ends with death. Because we mistakenly identify mind with brain, we assume the mind dies when the brain dies. But mind continues. As religious scholar Huston Smith put it, "The brain breathes the mind the way lungs breathe the air."

As we have seen, when the body drops away at death, mind becomes reality. If the mind of the dying person was filled with suffering, that experience can initially be amplified. The physical pain from a diseased body disappears, but the suffering within the mind can spike. So the harsh reality is that euthanasia can *increase* suffering rather than end it.[14] It's like going to sleep full of bad thoughts. Our chances of having a terrifying nightmare, an experience far worse than the thoughts that seeded it, are high. Because of the law of proximate karma, the momentum of the last thoughts before death re-arises in the post-death bardos.

The second misconception is that the suffering that precedes death has no meaning. It seems rational for a dying person to ask, "Why should I endure this pain if the only way out is death? I'm going to die anyway. Why should I suffer so much?" But suffering can have great meaning and purpose. The suffering around death can be seen as the purification and exhaustion of past negative karma. That's exactly what death is, the final exhaustion of karma. This view can generate a new way to understand and transform our suffering, so that we bear it consciously.

To attain enlightenment we must purify karma in one of two ways: through meditation, or through experience. We can view the suffering in life —and death—as the purification of karma through experience. Someone who endures suffering with equanimity is making the best of a difficult situation, purifying karma, and progressing along the spiritual path. We should let karma run its natural course. A precious opportunity, however painful, is lost with active euthanasia. The Dalai Lama says:

> Your suffering is due to your own karma, and you have to bear the
> fruit of that karma anyway in this life or another, unless you can
> find some way of purifying it. In that case, it is considered to be

better to experience the karma in this life of a human where you have more abilities to bear it in a better way, than, for example, an animal who is helpless and can suffer even more because of that.[15]

Instead of trying to end suffering by prematurely ending a life, we should end our inappropriate relationship to suffering. Suffering comes when we contract around the pain, and lose our perspective. This is why we introduced the pain meditation in part 1 (see the "Reverse Meditations" section in chapter 1). With a proper relationship, the pain remains, but it's softened and infused with new meaning. Instead of resisting the pain, which only exaggerates it, we can embrace the pain and ironically prevent the suffering. We can practice equanimity.

Once again, putting hardship into perspective allows us to relate to it properly. Pack your bitter experience into a small mind, and it gets concentrated. It hurts. Make your mind as big as the sky, and that same experience is instantly diluted.

Passive euthanasia is allowing someone to die a natural death. If someone is in a coma with no hope of recovery, or kept alive by artificial means, then most teachers allow the removal of those means and the ensuing natural death. There comes a point when there's no need to prolong life and incur unnecessary emotional and financial burdens.

With the advent of palliative medicine, which doesn't try to cure the illness but instead lessens its hardship, fewer people need to opt for euthanasia. Through palliative care, and the proper view, we can transform a difficult death into spiritual practice.

Kalu Rinpoche says:

> The person who decides that they have had enough suffering and wish to be allowed to die is in a situation that we cannot call virtuous or non-virtuous. We certainly cannot blame someone for making that decision. It is not a karmically negative act. It is simply the wish to avoid suffering, which is the fundamental wish of all living beings. On the other hand, it is not a particularly virtuous act either. . . . Rather than being a wish to end one's life, it's a wish to end suffering. Therefore it is a karmically neutral act. When a healer is instructed by a patient to remove life-support systems, that puts the healer in a difficult position, because the instincts of the healer may be telling them, "If this person stayed

on the life-support system they would remain alive. If I take them off, they will die." The karmic consequences depend upon the healer's intent because the healer will be depriving someone of the means to stay alive, regardless of the fact that it was that person that told us to do it. If the basic motivation of the healer has always been to help and benefit that person and relieve their suffering, then from that state of mind it seems as though nothing karmically negative can develop.[16]

Tonglen is one of the best meditations for a difficult death, both for the dying person and for caregivers. The rugged quality of tonglen can meet and absorb any difficult death.

SUICIDE

The suicide of a loved one is one of the most painful events imaginable.[17] Even if we believe in reincarnation, the traditional Tibetan view concerning suicide doesn't comfort those left behind.[18] It's mainly in Pure Land Buddhism, especially the Japanese schools, that the Tibetan stance is softened. This is probably due to the theistic view of exoteric Pure Land doctrine. In this view, it's okay to leave a hellish experience on earth if we're heading to a heavenly pure land. This is another example of how one's view of the afterlife influences the actions we take during life—including the conscious termination of it.

Carl Becker, speaking in terms of the Japanese schools, writes:

> There is nothing intrinsically wrong with taking one's own life, if not done in hate, anger, or fear. Equanimity or preparedness of mind is the main issue. . . . The important consideration here is not whether the body lives or dies, but whether the mind can remain at peace and in harmony with itself. . . . the early Buddhist texts include many cases of suicide that the Buddha himself accepted or condoned . . . suicide is never condemned per se; it is the state of mind which determines the rightness or wrongness of the suicide situation.[19]

Matthieu Ricard, speaking on behalf of the Tibetan approach, offers this different view:

By committing suicide, you destroy the possibility you have, in this life, of realizing the potential for transformation that you have within you. You succumb to an intense attack of discouragement which, as we've seen, is a weakness, a form of laziness. By saying to yourself, 'What's the point in living?' you deprive yourself of the inner transformation that would have been possible. To overcome an obstacle is to transform it into an aid to your progress. People who've overcome a major trial in their lives often draw from it a teaching and a powerful inspiration on the spiritual path. Suicide solves nothing at all, it only shifts the problem to another state of consciousness.[20]

Scholar Damien Keown adds, "A person who opts for death believing it to be a solution to suffering has fundamentally misunderstood the First Noble Truth. The First Noble Truth teaches that death is the problem, not the solution. . . . What is significant is that through the affirmation of death he has, in his heart, embraced Mara!"[21]

To reconcile disparate teachings, and to address questions about the karmic implications of suicide, it helps to understand the four aspects of a fully established karma. What is a karmic action made of? How are the consequences of an act established? Even though the topic of karma has entered the public domain, it is perhaps the most complex topic in Buddhism. Only a fully enlightened Buddha can understand karma. We will limit our discussion to how karma can help us relate to suicide. Understanding the aspects of a fully constituted karma also helps us relate to any action and to its karmic implications. What is it that packs the karmic punch? How can I soften the blow?

In order for an action to have complete karmic repercussions, four components must be fully present. The first is the object, or target, of the action. If we take the extreme example of killing, the object would be the thing we're planning to kill. If the object is really clear, be it an insect, an animal, or a person, the first component is complete and the karmic impact is loaded.

The second component is our motivation, which is the most important. If we want to kill something out of malice, then that aspect of karma is clear and complete. If we kill with the intent to feed our starving family or ourselves, or to save other sentient beings, then the karma is softened. Because motivation is so critical, it is helpful, revealing, and tempering, to ask yourself before you do anything: what's my motivation? Why am I really doing this? This reality check can save you lots of trouble—and future lives.

The third constituent is the act itself. This is the clearest aspect. We either do it or we don't. Unlike the other three, this aspect is usually black or white, yes or no. We either step on the bug or not.

The fourth constituent is having no regret, or rejoicing in the act. If we look back upon what we did without remorse, if we're glad we stepped on the spider, we're in karmic trouble. But if we feel deep regret and vow not to repeat such an act, we have lightened the karmic debt.

If each of these four constituents is complete, then the karma around the act is heavy. If we want to kill something out of anger, the thing we want to kill is clear, and we celebrate the act of killing, then karma is fully loaded.

If we take these four aspects and apply them to suicide, or euthanasia, we can better understand the reality of such acts. If we want to kill ourselves, the first constituent is often unclear. Are we really trying to kill ourselves, or simply trying to kill the pain? Most suicide victims are terribly confused, and therefore the target of the act is not clear. The first constituent isn't complete, and the karmic implications aren't as heavy.[22]

The second aspect, our motivation, is also not clear. The motivation of most suicide victims is to remove suffering, which isn't a bad motivation. Sometimes people kill themselves to hurt others. In this case the second constituent would be complete, and the karma correspondingly heavier. But a fuzzy intention softens the karmic impact. Many suicide victims, because of the intensity of their suffering, simply don't know what they're doing. It's almost as if they're drugged or stunned by the intensity of their pain. If you've ever been shocked with overwhelming bad news, or immense trauma, you know the bewilderment that accompanies such a blow. You just can't think clearly.

The third constituent, the act of suicide, is complete. We either kill ourselves or we don't. There's nothing fuzzy here. This is where the karmic repercussions mostly arise. The fourth constituent, having no regret, or even rejoicing, is completely absent. There's nobody to rejoice in the act. Our action has cut off the last component.

Of the four aspects of a fully constituted karma, only the third is clear and complete. Two of the other three are hazy and incomplete, and the fourth doesn't exist. Does this mean it's therefore okay to commit suicide? No, the Tibetan tradition is clear on this. Understanding these four components is to comfort those left behind, not to instill a justification for suicide. There's a reason why the tradition speaks of dreadful karmic consequences. We should heed these warnings.

There are extraordinary stories of lamas in Tibet being led to execution by the Chinese and ejecting their consciousness by means of phowa before the execution, an act that would normally be considered suicide. Some masters have said that these lamas were doing phowa as a way to prevent their executioners from accruing the enormous negative karma of murder. In these exceptional cases, which only high lamas are even capable of performing, "suicide" is the best karmic act.[23] For the rest of us, no matter how we try to rationalize it, suicide is a negative act. Unless you are a realized being, whose every breath is taken to benefit others, you cannot kill yourself in a positive state of mind.

Buddhism cannot put the fear of God into us because it's a nontheistic tradition. There is no creator principle, no God in Buddhism, and therefore no one to judge our actions.[24] But Buddhism can put the fear of karma into us. This is wholesome fear, the recognition of the karmic implications of our actions.[25]

Suicide is a serious karmic act. But for those left behind, understanding the four aspects of a fully constituted karma can soften the pain and shed some light on a very dark event.

ABORTION AND MISCARRIAGE

According to Buddhism, three things are necessary to bring about life: sperm, ovum, and bindu (consciousness). Biology (sperm and ovum) is not enough. Consciousness must enter between sperm and ovum for rebirth to occur. This means that life begins at conception, even if it's in a Petri dish. The implications for miscarriage and abortion are immediate.[26]

The Dalai Lama, however, said that if science proves something that contradicts Buddhist doctrine, that doctrine needs to be reexamined and revised.[27] This famous statement suggests that if science ever proves a later entry or emergence of consciousness in the womb, the Buddhist stance on abortion should change. In 1992 the Dalai Lama also said that there are instances where abortion may be warranted—for example, when a fetus is severely malformed and would have to endure great suffering in life.

It is beyond our reach to explore why miscarriage takes place from a spiritual perspective. When asked, many teachers simply say, "karma." That may lead to helpful acceptance or to frustration. The point is that in miscarriage, stillbirth, or abortion, a death has taken place. The consciousness that entered the sperm and ovum now re-enters the bardos and begins the journey anew. All the practices associated with a normal death can be applied. At the least, a Sukhavati can be performed.

Dilgo Khyentse Rinpoche said:

> The consciousness of those who die before birth, at birth, or in infancy will travel once again through the bardo states and take on another existence. The same meritorious practices and actions can be done for them as are usually performed for the dead: the purification practice and mantra recitation of Vajrasattva, offering of lights, purification of the ashes, and so on.[28]

Abortion is a more complex issue because of the karmic implications of that conscious choice. To understand the repercussions, study the four aspects of a fully constituted karma (see page 266). As we have seen, the principal karmic force is motivation. With the purest motivation we can soften even the harshest action.[29]

When consulted by their students, many teachers will continue to support them even if they choose to go forward with the abortion. They may offer specific practices, like the purification practice of Vajrasattva, the recitation of sacred mantras, or the four opponent powers (see note 106 on page 349). Examine all the options, consult with wise advisors, know the implications, and act with the purest motivations. If one decides to abort, do so as soon as possible. Otherwise the consciousness will continue to identify with the growing fetus, and the abortion becomes more difficult for that consciousness.

Sogyal Rinpoche adds:

> In the case of an abortion, in addition to [the] usual practices, if the parents feel remorse they can help by acknowledging it, asking for forgiveness, and performing ardently the purification practice of Vajrasattva. They can also offer lights, and save lives, or help others, or sponsor some humanitarian or spiritual project, dedicating it to the well-being and future enlightenment of the baby's consciousness.[30]

Zen teacher Robert Aitken has written a Buddhist ritual to both mourn the loss of the fetus and to solace the parents.[31] There is also a famous Japanese ritual for abortion called *mizuko kuyo* that has been adapted by a Zen priest for Western women.[32]

DEATH OF A PET

The death of a pet can be as painful as the loss of a human loved one. There is research suggesting that many people view their pet as a kind of surrogate child.[33] As occupational and lifestyle choices have diversified, more people are opting not to have children. They find that a pet provides love and companionship much the way a child does. Pets become family.

Many of the instructions we've discussed can be applied to the death of a pet. The bardo literature is clear: these teachings work for all sentient beings, not just humans. Anyen Rinpoche says, "You can even place the mandala [of the takdrol] on the heart of a pet who is dying; the power of dependent arising—when causes and conditions come together—is so truly amazing that even such a thing as liberation for a dog is possible."[34]

Every animal, be it a worm, insect, snake, or your pet cat, goes through the same bardos as we do. When the animal passes through the painful bardo of dying, the mind that was encased in the animal's body is liberated from that temporary housing. From that point on, which occurs when the mind enters the luminous bardo of dharmata, it's no longer an animal's mind. It is now naked mind itself.

Physical form of any kind is stripped off during the bardo of dying. What remains is formless awareness. It's like plunging through that inconceivably narrow funnel of the hourglass. In the two post-death bardos, it's no longer a snake's mind, or an insect's mind, or Fido's mind. The snake, and the karma that hurled mind into that form, have been shed. The insect, and its karma, have been exhausted. Fido, and the habits that forced that continuum of mind to take the form of a dog, are left behind. The formless awareness that's revealed after death is the same awareness that you and I share when we reach that point in the bardos.

As we have seen, if it's not recognized, this awareness will be blown by the winds of karma into a new form. This signals the end of the bardo of dharmata and the beginning of the bardo of becoming. At this point, awareness starts to put on a new costume, assuming the habits from past lives that will result in a new body. But until it enters this karmic dressing room, every mind that passes through the bardo of dharmata is completely naked and identical in its nature.

We can look at this spiritual democracy from the opposite perspective. From our stance as a human, once our awareness drops this temporary human form in the bardo of dying, it could easily take on the appearance of a snake, an insect, or whatever shape expresses the karmic propensity at that moment. To become an animal in our next life, we only need to exercise an animal mind in this one. If we're pig-headed, stubborn as a mule, or full of dogged determination, we have acquired a karmic visa into the animal realm. You and your pet could easily switch roles.

This view of the common roots of awareness, that all sentient beings share a similar cosmic genealogy, instills respect for every form of life. It allows us to honor the animal world and to treasure the sanctity of life as it dances across the spectrum of manifestation. While I was in India a few years ago, I heard His Holiness the Seventeenth Karmapa give a teaching about com-passionate heart, or bodhichitta, called "the sevenfold cause and result of bodhichitta." The first of the causes, which build upon each other, is know-ing that all sentient beings have been our mothers. This is a classic teaching in Buddhism, easily dismissed as Buddhist hyperbole or mere metaphor.

But the Karmapa suggested this teaching be taken literally. His Holi-ness said that without the first cause, the second cause (let alone the other five) could not arise. This means that without viewing all sentient beings, including animals, as having once been our mother, we can't give rise to genuine compassion. The Karmapa then asked, "What is the measure that you have actually understood this first cause?" He answered his own ques-tion: "When you can hear a dog bark and instantly say to yourself, 'That's my mother,' or when you hear a cow moo and immediately respond, 'That's my mother.'" This is a humbling teaching. It shows us how far we have to go to attain this noble view of the animal kingdom.

With this elevated view of animals, it's easy to transpose the bardo meth-ods to our pets. Give them the best possible death and therefore the best rebirth. We never know—our treasured pet could someday be our mother again.

CONCLUSION

In matters of such magnitude, and with so many repercussions, it's impor-tant to do our homework. When it comes to karma, ignorance is never bliss.[35] Once we know the rules—medically, legally, karmically—we can intelligently work within them. Even the Dalai Lama, who maintains the tradition of Tibetan Buddhism with unwavering strength, says that every student is responsible for checking the guru's instructions against reason:

> What happens when the guru gives us advice that we do not wish to follow or that contradicts Dharma and reason? The yardstick must always be logical reasoning and Dharma reason. Any advice that contradicts these is to be rejected. This was said by Buddha himself. ["Accept my teachings only after examining them as an analyst buys gold. Accept nothing out of mere faith in me."[36]] If one doubts the validity of what is being said, one should generally push the point and clear all doubts. This should be done with respect and humility, however, for to show any negativity toward a teacher is not a noble way of repaying his or her kindness.[37]

This shows us just how complex these issues truly are. Even the advice for listening to the advice is challenging.[38] Gather as much information as you can, check your motivation, reflect deeply, and then trust your own heart and wisdom.

PART THREE

Heart Advice from Spiritual Masters

HEART ADVICE FROM SPIRITUAL MASTERS

THE FOLLOWING WORDS of wisdom are from Tibetan Buddhist masters who have taught in the West. I asked these teachers some version of the three questions that structure this book—three questions that strike the vital point:[1] (1) What is the best thing to do before death? (2) What is the best thing to do during death? (3) What is the best thing to do after death? When I had the time, I asked these questions in terms of what to do for ourselves, and then what to do for others. I gave each master the option of sharing whatever they felt was important. I didn't want to limit them with my formulated questions. The answers were directed to students of Buddhism, but many of these responses could be shared with anyone. Since Tibetan Buddhism is virtually synonymous with Vajrayana Buddhism, some of the answers emphasize the Vajrayana.

There is wonderful counsel in the following pages. I recommend reading and contemplating just one teaching at a time, to allow the depth of these words to soak in. In reading this treasure-trove of wisdom again and again, I find that my entire being relaxes. It's like being bathed in the liberating words of the Buddha himself. I know that if I have the luxury to die with my dharma friends around me, I will have them read these teachings to me repeatedly. I find the following advice to be the very embodiment of these masters. It feels like they're embracing me—the perfect spiritual holding environment.

ANAM THUBTEN RINPOCHE

Anam Thubten was raised in Tibet and received academic and spiritual monastic training in the Nyingma tradition. His main teachers include Khenpo Chopel, Lama Garwang, and the yogi Lama Tsurlo. Anam Thubten is fluent in English—he commands a prodigious vocabulary—and teaches frequently throughout America. He is the founder of the Dharmata Foundation, based in Point Richmond, California, and is the author of *No Self, No Problem* and *The Magic of Awareness*. This interview was conducted at Naropa University, in Boulder, Colorado.

What's the best thing to do to prepare for death? How would you advise your students?

Well, I don't know whether there's a Buddhist perspective versus a Hindu perspective, but the basic idea is that what you've got now is what you're going to get when you die. I'm very much a believer in this statement. This is what Buddhism says. There's an expression in Tibetan Buddhism that says, "Where you are going into the future can be known by looking at the color of your mind now." So I don't think there is a preparation for death separate from that of life. My advice is to become awakened as soon as possible, then at the time of death everything is taken care of. There is no advice separately for death and for life. Same advice for life and for death. If you don't know how to live then you don't know how to prepare for death either. So the question is: how do you want to live? Do you want to live as an awakened being?

When someone who is a student of Buddhism is actually in the dying process, what's the best thing they can do at that point?

Arise above the illusion of self. Not to identify with the self. Then no one is dying. And then reside in the luminous awareness.

What can sangha do to support someone who is dying, both during the bardo of dying and the bardo after death?

Pray, pray. The sangha can do sadhanas and prayers for them. Basically pray for the deceased one to discover their union with original Buddha. Pray for her or him to be awakened to their true nature as the dharmakaya, the unborn and undying Buddha.

It can be as spontaneous as just a heartfelt expression of that? It doesn't have to be a specific liturgy or practice?

No, no, no, not at all. You can use a particular liturgy, but it doesn't have to be. You can just pray out of your pure heart.

Is there anything else you would like to say to your students?

That's pretty much all.

ANYEN RINPOCHE

Anyen Rinpoche is from Amdo, Tibet, and has spent over fourteen years in study and solitary retreat, culminating in the khenpo degree. Rinpoche has taught in Tibet, China, Southeast Asia, Japan, and throughout North America. He lives in Denver, Colorado, and is the author of *The Union of Dzogchen and Bodhichitta*, *Momentary Buddhahood*, and *Dying with Confidence*. I talked to Rinpoche in Denver, and he responded to my questions via e-mail.

If practitioners want to be able to meditate in the bardo state, then it is essential to work at listening, contemplation and meditation now, during the bardo of birth and abiding. It is especially important to work at recognizing the dream state and at abiding in meditation in the dream state, since the dream state and the stages of death have similarities. Based on this preparation, you will have nothing to worry about during the stages after death. However, if you do not practice in this lifetime and just spend your time thinking that the bardo states are amazing or wondrous, this will not benefit you at all.

BARDOR TULKU RINPOCHE

Bardor Tulku Rinpoche was born in Tibet and fled to Rumtek Monastery, Sikkim, in 1959. At Rumtek he studied under the Sixteenth Karmapa, and was instructed by His Holiness to help establish Karma Triyana Dharmachakra in upstate New York (1978). Rinpoche is the founder of Kunzang Palchen Ling and the Raktrul Foundation. His publications include *Living in Compassion*, *A Practitioner's Guide to Mantra*, and *The Practice of Green Tara*. I interviewed Rinpoche in Woodstock, New York.

What's the best thing to do before death?
Basically, every practice during life is definitely a preparation for the bardo state. Nothing is different that you have to do. Whoever has their own teacher, whatever practices they give you, make a genuine effort to achieve that practice. If your teacher gives you Vajrayogini, Chakrasamvara, Hevajra, or Chenrezig, visualize those, focus on those. When you are passing away, you will recognize. That means you won't even have to go through the bardo state. You will be liberated. That's what practice is all about.
    If someone doesn't have that much strength, then the situation of the

second level is to focus on the root guru. That is the message. Among all the teachers and the deities, the closest one is your root guru, in human form. Because of your human contact, your history together, in the tantric practice, focus on the root guru. Imagine your mind is inseparable from the root guru. As soon as you know you are not going to make it, focus on this continuously: this is the key. You don't have to focus on too many deities—the root guru is all. The root guru is the yidam, lama, and dharmapala. By doing this, you will be able to save yourself.

Then, for the third situation. There are three different levels of the bardo. Bardo of the dharmakaya, of the sambhogakaya, and of the nirmanakaya. During these three different experiences, it all depends on how you are able to recognize them. If you are able to recognize the first experience, you will naturally dissolve into the dharmakaya. If you recognize the sambhogakaya, you will be able to dissolve into that, and if you recognize the nirmanakaya, you will dissolve into that. If not, you will have to take on a coarse form [and be reborn]. But still, if you are able to think of your teacher and consort as your yidam, and you merge into their mind, you will be able to take a good rebirth. But it is up to the individual's ability.

What's the best way for the sangha to help?
Read the *Bardo Thödrol* [*Tibetan Book of the Dead*] literature. Not the commentary literature, but the *Bardo Thödrol* literature. Start reading it when you know they are not going to make it. Try not to gather around the lower parts of the body, as much as possible. Gather around the top of the body, you can touch the top of the head, even pull on the hair [at the brahmarandhra], and recite different mantras, like Chenrezig's mantra, or Amitabha. Or if you are a Kagyupa, recite Karmapa Chenno, or if from a different lineage, your root guru's mantra. Things like that are sufficient. Then if someone has done the three-year retreat and has experience doing phowa, then doing phowa is very good.

If you can do this, then if the dying person was otherwise going to go to the lower realms, they will in essence not have to be reborn in the lower realms for the duration of this Buddha's teaching. In other words, Buddha Shakyamuni's teaching is still around, but it will someday disappear. Then the next Buddha (the fifth Buddha of this age) will appear, and the dying person will have avoided the lower realms during this entire time due to the power of phowa. It is therefore quite beneficial.

What's the best thing for us to do to help others after they have died?

We can offer butter lamps in front of a representation of the Buddha, along with the name of the person who has died. It depends on how much the family can do. The full forty-nine days is best, or seven days, or three days, or one day—it's up to the family. Doing this is very important. Then asking different teachers to do prayers for the dead is very important. Then the individual should do their own practice, even a little bit every day, for the forty-nine days, that is a good thing to do.

CHÖKYI NYIMA RINPOCHE

Chökyi Nyima Rinpoche was born in Tibet in 1951, the son of the great dzogchen master Tulku Urgyen Rinpoche. He fled to India in 1959 and studied at Rumtek Monastery, attaining the khenpo degree. In 1974 Rinpoche established Ka-Nying Sherab Ling in Boudhanath, Nepal, and serves as its abbot. In 1981 Rinpoche founded Rangjung Yeshe Institute for Buddhist Studies, and Rangjung Yeshe Publications, both designed to help Western students study Tibetan dharma. Among his many books are *The Union of Mahamudra and Dzogchen, Bardo Guidebook*, and *Indisputable Truth*. I interviewed Rinpoche in Boudhanath, Nepal.

What's the best thing to do before death?

Death is natural. Sometimes we live long, or short. The bottom line is we all will die. Each of us—there are no exceptions. Whether you like to talk about it or not, or think about it or not, it is very important to know about death and impermanence. We need to face that. We tend to think that death is ugly, not good. We ask ourselves, "Why should we talk about it, it's not necessary." This is not a wise way of thinking—we need to face it. We need to face sickness, old age, and death. Rather than hiding or being ignorant about these difficult topics, it's good to know about them.

No matter what religion or faith, people still want to die smoothly, easily. No one wants to die a horrible death. So what makes a peaceful death, what makes a difficult death? Difficult deaths are brought on by too much clinging. Clinging to self, or relatives, or what you have created in this world—name, fame, power, money. So much clinging, not letting go, leads to a horrible death. At the moment of death you realize you can't own anything. Even during life, if we lose little things, we feel uneasy: "Goodness, I lost my shoe, I lost my cat, I lost my camera, my car, my this or that." This is just a tiny piece. At death we lose *everything*. Everything that you created, anything physically, verbally, mentally is being taken away. All of it, suddenly, you need to give up. There is nothing you can take with you.

So, now, what is the method? Very simple: let go, let go. You need to let go. You need to know that if you cling, it only leads to more suffering. You need to give up. You need to let go, don't cling. Whatever you created— land, home, money, family, whatever—clinging is of no use. Especially to loved ones. Show them your love, care, respect, and let them go.

We also need to be kind to others during life. If we're not kind, suffering starts. Understand how kindness leads to happiness. Sometimes people may think you're naïve, "He's kind to everyone. This person has no discrimination." But the motivation to be kind to everyone is very important.[2] So now you need to give good and wise advice to your friends, family, whoever loves you, whoever trusts you—you need to give them very important and good advice: Don't be selfish.

What's the best way to help others as they die?
Phowa is very important. If you can't do that, try to be with them, and be simple and genuine. Tell them you love them, that you're here for them. Tell them not to overreact to anything, that the journey will be okay. Tell them not to be attached to anything. Meditate with them if possible, keep it simple, shamatha or vipashyana. Love them.

What's the best thing to do after someone dies?
Practice for them, and dedicate the merit to them. Ask your sangha to practice for them as well. Traditionally, every week, for at least the first three weeks, on the day that they died. If they died on Sunday, try to practice (and to have your sangha practice for them) the following Sunday, and then for the next few Sundays after that. That's the "emergency time," when they really need your help in the bardo, and you can affect their good rebirth. You can also contact monasteries here in Nepal, and the monks will do pujas for them.

DILYAK DRUPON RINPOCHE

Dilyak Drupon Rinpoche was born in Bhutan and trained by His Holiness the Sixteenth Karmapa. He is a graduate of the Nalanda Institute for

Higher Buddhist Studies, in Rumtek, Sikkim (India). Since 2000, Rinpoche has been serving His Holiness the Seventeenth Karmapa as his primary attendant, and in 2006 he was appointed his General Secretary. Rinpoche also maintains Dilyak Monastery in Nepal. He teaches in the West under the auspices of Nalandabodhi. This interview was conducted in Boulder, Colorado.

What is the best thing for students of Tibetan Buddhism to do to prepare for death?
In general, there are so many different methods to practice, so many different ways to prepare. Khenpo Tsültrim Gyamtso Rinpoche instructs that even though there are different meditations and visualizations that one can do, the simplest and best preparation is to practice lojong. Practice lojong in advance of death, and then again—to whatever extent you are capable—when you are actually dying. You can also think that whatever you have accumulated, whether it is merit or any other form of goodness and wealth, that is all given away to sentient beings on the medium of the out-breath. And then on the in-breath, take in whatever suffering, difficulties, and problems others have. In other words, practice tonglen.

What's the best thing someone can do when they are actually dying?
Usually we talk about looking at one's mind, as in mahamudra or dzogchen practice, but ordinary people can't do this right away. These practices need to be worked with for a long time, continually throughout one's life, then perhaps you can do this at the moment of death. If you are a mahamudra or dzogchen practitioner and are able to rest in the nature of your mind, that is the best. For others, lojong and tonglen are the best. Lojong is something you can think about, you don't necessarily need a great deal of experience. Ordinary people can simply think about taking the sufferings of others in on the in-breath, and then giving away their own accumulations and wealth on the out-breath. That is very simple. So therefore for normal people, even as they are dying, lojong and tonglen are the best practices.

If Rinpoche is at the side of someone who is dying and he is trying to help them, what is the best way to help?
In this kind of situation, if you are at the side of someone you know well, then help them according to the level of their own practice. If they have done mahamudra or dzogchen practice in life, then remind them of that.

If they happen to be a student of some lama, then remind them of their lama and help them nurture their devotion. Remind them of their guru. For example, if someone is a student of Khenpo Rinpoche, then just remind them of him. They already have their devotion and their own practice, so your job is to remind them of that.

After someone has died, and they wake up in the bardo and realize they are dead, what is the best thing they can do at that time?
It depends on the dead person. Some are good practitioners with good experience, and these people don't even need to go through the bardo. For others who have done a lot of practice and have some experience, but not a great deal of stability, the bardo can appear frightful. They may forget about their practice. These are the people you can help during the forty-nine days after death. For example, the *Bardo Thödrol* can be read to them. For each day, and for each week, there are explanations in this text of what they might be going through, so read the instructions and guidance from this book to help them. In our monasteries we have a tradition of doing pujas for them during this forty-nine day period. If possible, you can invite lamas to do this, or the sangha. If that can't happen, you can at least invite close friends to chant liturgies and practice for the dead person.

Because we often don't have access to lamas and monks who do these pujas, are there specific practices that Westerners can emphasize?
It is not necessary to have a big puja. For example, if your friend died, you can read the *Bardo Thödrol*, or other bardo books, and that will really help. In our tradition, we read very clear and slow, so they can hear what you are reading.

What is the place of the Pure Land teachings for Westerners?
Because the Buddha taught on the pure lands, there is great blessing in the Pure Land teaching. So it is indeed helpful to engage in Pure Land practice and study.

Does Rinpoche have any general comments for students in the West?
Generally, whatever we are doing as Buddhists is all preparation for death. The most important thing is that when you are getting close to death you should try to relax. Relaxation is really the most important thing.

DZIGAR KONGTRUL RINPOCHE

Dzigar Kongtrul Rinpoche was born in north India. He grew up and studied in a traditional monastic environment with Khyentse Rinpoche and Tulku Urgyen Rinpoche. In 1989 Rinpoche moved to the United States and taught at Naropa University. Rinpoche soon founded Mangala Shri Bhuti, and his retreat center Longchen Jigme Samten Ling, both in Colorado. He is an active teacher around the world and an accomplished artist. Rinpoche's books include *It's Up to You* and *Light Comes Through*.

Rinpoche's response, given at Ward, Colorado, is based on his teachings of the "five strengths" of Lojong, or the Mind Training slogans.[3] The order of presenting these five strengths is different from how the five are practiced during life (when they are practiced in this order: intention, familiarization, merit, critical intelligence, aspiration). His emphasis on cultivating bodhichitta as the best preparation, perhaps the most consistent advice given by all these masters, is eloquently driven home.

What's the most important thing we can do to prepare for death?
The most important thing we can do to prepare for death is to really focus on the practice of bodhichitta, as explained in the five strengths. When do you start the death-time practice of the five strengths? When the doctors tell you that you have so many months to live, when a terminal diagnosis is given. That is the time to really focus on this practice. In terms of the five strengths, we should practice them in preparation for death as follows:

(1) The strength of virtue, or merit. This is the power of good deeds and the accumulation of merit. Now is the time to get over your attachments, to let go of your assets, which only serve to bind you at death. Attachments are a real hindrance to a peaceful death and a hindrance in the bardo. Even in the bardo, the mind comes back to our assets, and we worry about who is using them, what is happening to our things. So before you die, increase the power of virtue by being generous. Offer your things to others. Be careful not to give your things to your family as an extension of yourself, but give to them, or others, as independent beings. This makes it cleaner, less sticky. Give "precisely"—with no strings attached. Otherwise, for sure, with one hundred percent certainty, it will come back to haunt you as you die or are in the bardo. It's good to give maybe 75 percent of your things to a charitable cause and 25 percent or so to your loved ones. But the really important point is to free ourselves of attachment.

Bardo beings have clairvoyance, they can see the state of mind of their loved ones left behind, they can see how they are caught up in your old possessions. So we want to give cleanly in advance and therefore not get caught up in the possessions we leave behind. If we are not attached, if we really practice generosity properly, then discipline follows more easily [generosity and discipline are the first and second paramitas, respectively]. If the mind is free of attachment, it is freer to do what it needs to do in the bardos. Giving also accumulates merit, and we want to accumulate as much merit as possible before we die.

(2) The power of aspiration, or prayer. Make the strong aspiration that we could take this time before death to really increase our bodhichitta practice, and to be able to continue from the last moment of this life into the bardo with bodhichitta practice, and then through the bardo and into our next life. In that way, all circles of life—however long it takes until enlightenment—can be a continuous practice of bodhichitta. Make a deep aspiration prayer in this way.

Also make aspirations to be born in favorable conditions, to find a real teacher, a real path, and the ability to practice bodhichitta until enlightenment. So even if we only progress 1 percent now, 99 percent is still to come. Make aspirations to meet this 99 percent in future lives, where positive seeds ripen and positive karma ripens, and where the practice of bodhichitta continues and leads to enlightenment. Make aspirations to actualize the practice of bodhichitta and to bring more benefit to beings than even the sun and moon. Pray in this way.

(3) The strength of critical intelligence. Any feeling at death, of fear, anguish, loss, confusion, anger, or despair, which are common at death, are all expressions of self-clinging that have not been remedied. At death, we have no choice but to remedy these feelings. If something is making you cling, you need to remedy it, to overcome it, now. You need to get over it so that you can die peacefully. Now is the time to relate to self-clinging, to use your critical intelligence against it. Let go as much as possible of these sets of thoughts and emotions, otherwise they will take over at death and completely dominate you. You need to summon the courage to make your last six months, or two months, or one month, or one week, the best preparation for death. You need to take this time to make the best use of your mind and not to get stuck in these self-clinging states of mind. Use your critical intelligence against your dark and gloomy self-centered states and emotions, letting go of all self-clinging.

(4) The strength of setting a powerful intention. Set the strong intention to really practice bodhichitta and not just pray to do so. Practice bodhichitta at the time of death and into the bardo, then into your next lives. Take the time of your remaining life into your hands with the intention to really use it to do the practice of bodhichitta. Know how this really works out, more than anything else. In other words, when you know you are really dying, instead of continuously and desperately seeking out more doctors, or comfort from the family, know how all that just leads to more disappointment, more despair and letdown. Make the strong intention to practice bodhichitta as much as possible, instead of doing these ultimately futile things. Know that the power of bodhichitta during the last week, month, or year will affect your mind in the bardo. Remember why you do this practice, the point in doing it, and how to do it. In other words, really set cause and effect in proper line. In this way, set your intention.

Set the intention that you are not going to waste your time—from now until your death. When you know you are going to die, you are not going to waste time on comforts or even cures. Know how the practice of bodhichitta affects the bardo state, and know how to practice bodhichitta in the bardo state, and know the point. Everything depends on what you do now with your practice of bodhichitta. Do not forsake bodhichitta during this charged period of time.

(5) The strength of familiarization. This is doing and becoming familiar with the two stages of bodhichitta practice: (1) the practice of relative bodhichitta, and then (2) the practice of absolute bodhichitta.

As strong emotions come over you when you are dying, acknowledge that you are dying. Acknowledge that this is the most painful thing for most sentient beings. The level of attachment we have to life will generate a proportionate level of fear of death. As much as we take life to be real, and cling to that, that much we will suffer. Before death, we haven't felt this level of attachment so much, but we really feel it when we are dying. We know that all who die go through this fear and suffering, so take this onto yourself. Take all the despair, confusion, hopelessness, anger, and suffering that occurs in relation to death—the feeling of loss and annihilation, of feeling like a victim—and bring this all into yourself. Then offer your own loving, compassionate, and sympathetic thoughts, along with your merit. In this way, do tonglen, taking and sending. Do this practice of relative bodhichitta when you are still alert and functioning.

Eventually this will wear out, and you will become less capable of doing this. At that point, transition into the practice of absolute bodhichitta and rest in the natural state of mind. Know that there is no sense of the realness of birth or death in the nature of mind—it's all illusory. Nothing affects the nature of mind, at all. Know this from your own experience. You can see that nothing changes the nature of mind, nothing changes the empty and luminous nature of mind. Death is only an experience in the mind steeped in illusion. Here there is no birth or death—there is no reality to death. Rest in that.

So at first, do more tonglen and relative bodhichitta practice. Later do more nature of mind practice, absolute bodhichitta practice. As brain function and the power of the body fades, do more resting in the nature of mind. Nothing can wear you out if you're resting in the nature of mind. This is how you want to die.

In this way, as Jamgön Kongtrul Lodro Thaye says, there are many forms of phowa and many death meditations, but there is nothing greater than this: a real way of living with bodhichitta and a real way of dying with bodhichitta. Do the five strengths from the moment you are conscious you are dying until death itself arrives, increasing this practice as much as possible.

What's the best thing to do during death?
[The three ways of dying:]
1. Be like a deer: animals always die alone. Wild animals die alone, so prepare to die alone.
2. Be like a bird: one never finds a bird's body after death. Die cleanly, don't leave a trace.
3. Be like a beggar on the street: a beggar has no relatives or anything for people to clean up afterwards.

Don't discriminate about where to die, how to die, or under what situation. Have no preferences. Always be prepared to die standing, sleeping, alone, or in a crowd, with no needs whatsoever.

What's the best thing to do after death?
Devotion. Devotion is the best thing for the intermediate state.

DZONGSAR KHYENTSE RINPOCHE

Dzongsar Khyentse Rinpoche was born in Bhutan in 1961 and studied extensively with His Holiness the Sixteenth Karmapa, Khyentse Rinpoche, and Dudjom Rinpoche. Rinpoche supervises his traditional seat in Tibet, Dzongsar Monastery, as well as new monastic colleges in India and Bhutan. He has centers in Australia, North America, and Europe. Rinpoche is the director of the acclaimed films *The Cup* and *Travellers and Magicians*. He is the author of *What Makes You Not a Buddhist*, and the founder of Siddhartha's Intent, which propagates his teaching throughout the world. Rinpoche replied to my questions via e-mail.

Before death, the most important thing a practitioner of Vajrayana Buddhism can do is remember the guru, the view, and the yidam.

During death, if you are not a good practitioner, it is good to have someone there to help you remember those three. This could mean having someone shout the name of the guru, or remind you of the view. They could also shout the name of the yidam or the mantra loudly, or show you a picture of the deity. However, if you are a seasoned practitioner, it helps to be left alone and undisturbed.

After death, for the first twenty-one or forty-nine days, the best way for others to help you is to do anything to remind you of those three. They can also accumulate merit through the two fields: buddhas and bodhisattvas, and sentient beings.

JETSUN KHANDRO RINPOCHE

Jetsun Khandro Rinpoche was born in Kalimpong, northeast India, in 1969, the daughter of Mindrolling Trichen Rinpoche. In India, she received monastic training as well as a Western education from St. Joseph's Convent, Wynberg Allen, and St. Mary's Convent. Rinpoche has been teaching actively in Europe, North America, and Southeast Asia since 1987. She established Samten Tse Retreat Centre in India to benefit Eastern and Western students of Buddhism. Rinpoche established the Lotus Garden Retreat Center in 2003 to propagate the teachings of all four schools of Tibetan Buddhism. She is the author of *This Precious Life: Tibetan Buddhist Teachings on the Path to Enlightenment*. Rinpoche replied to my questions via e-mail.

At the time of death there are many valuable and helpful things in the various traditions, and particularly in the Tibetan Vajrayana tradition there are so many practices. However, as many teachers have said, the really most important and most realistic help before death is virtuous conduct. At the moment of death the best help is supplicating to the guru and letting go. And after death it's back to the first: if your actions were free from harming others and you were genuinely kind, the merit accumulated in this way is the best help after death.

KHENPO KARTHAR RINPOCHE

Khenpo Karthar Rinpoche was born in Kham, Tibet, in 1925 and received traditional training at Thrangu Monastery. He fled Tibet in 1959, arriving in Rumtek Monastery in India. He has taught extensively in Bhutan. Rinpoche came to the United States in 1976, at the request of His Holiness the Sixteenth Karmapa, to found Karma Triyana Dharmachakra. Rinpoche has taught throughout the United States. His many books include *Dharma Paths*, *Wish-Fulfilling Wheel*, and the multivolume *Karma Chakme's Mountain Dharma*. The following interview was conducted at Rinpoche's monastery in upstate New York.

What's the best thing to do to prepare for death?
The best preparation for death must be done ahead of time, not right before dying. Take refuge in the Buddha, dharma, and sangha, do [aspiration] prayers, and accumulate merit through offerings, dharma activities, and practice. It is very important to prepare ahead of time.

What's the best thing to do during death?
There are two things involved. First, it would be great to have a master who can guide the person during their death and can give advice on how to concentrate during death. The other thing is that the practitioner may already have preparation, in terms of having read the bardo books or different commentaries, and therefore already know what to do. Again, I can't emphasize enough the importance of preparation before death. Without preparation, at the time of death, especially when going through the bardo, you won't be able to recognize the deities when they arise because you have not purified yourself and accumulated enough merit.

What's the best thing we can do after death?
Several things. The first is that the practitioner who has prepared well (they practiced well, read *The Tibetan Book of the Dead*, etc.) will be able to rec-

ognize the appearance of the deities of the bardo when they arise. Second, the relatives left behind, if they are Buddhist, can light butter lamps and practice for them. That really helps the person going through the bardo. Third, you can request great masters to do practices for them. Ask them to do phowa or other practices. With these practices the master is able to help them liberate from the bardo.

What's the best thing those left behind can do to help those who have died?
Sangha can help the dying person a lot. Especially if the sangha doesn't have any impure samaya with that person. They can gather together, even from a distance, and do prayers for that person. This will make it easier for that person to pass through the bardos.

Are there any specific ceremonies that you would emphasize?
They can do all kinds of practices, sadhanas, for the dead person. All of that will help. Amitabha practice is particularly effective and strongly recommended. The most important thing is that when they do this kind of practice for the dead person they should do so with heartfelt bodhichitta. This will help tremendously. The essence of preparation is like what you would do for a big trip. If you're going to travel into an unknown place you prepare ahead of time. You don't know the language, you don't know where to go, so study up on the language, learn about the country and how to get around. Even if you do all this, if you don't have money you can't go. Similarly, even if you know how to do the visualizations for the time of death, or after death, if you haven't gathered the accumulation of merit you will come up short. So the point, again, is to focus on our practice, to prepare during life.

LAMA THARCHIN RINPOCHE

Lama Tharchin Rinpoche was born in Tibet and is a dzogchen master who received his training at Dudjom Rinpoche's monastery. He fled Tibet in 1959 to live in India and Nepal, before arriving in the United States in 1984. He is the tenth lineage holder of the Repkong Ngakpas, a family lineage of yogis. Rinpoche is the founder of the Vajrayana Foundation and has established a monastic college and three-year retreat center. He teaches throughout the United States, and his gentle presence has endeared him to thousands. This interview was conducted in Boulder, Colorado.

What is the best thing for a practitioner to do before death?
We are now in the bardo of this life, which is from the moment of birth until the moment of a sickness that leads to our death. This is the time that is the best time to prepare. Dharma is how we can come to die professionally. That includes prostrations, circumambulation [around sacred sites and the gathering of merit], mandala offerings, Vajrasattva, taking refuge and generating bodhichitta, ngöndro, and then guru yoga. It is especially helpful to prepare with phowa practice. This is really powerful. We can practice phowa now, then when the time comes to actually do it, our chances for success are much greater. Reading Karma Lingpa's six bardo teachings is also helpful, along with the creation stage practices (of mahayoga). These deity and visualization practices are really wonderful. Then there are the completion stage practices and the Six Yogas of Naropa. This is all really important to do.

The main point is the recognition of your own enlightened buddha nature. When that wakes up in the bardo there is a chance you can be liberated at the level of the dharmakaya. The deity practices prepare you for the sambhogakaya. Any kind of practice is multiplied in the bardo, because consciousness is nine times smarter in the bardo. Therefore if we can practice in the bardo it's easier to attain liberation at that time.

What's the best thing one can do during death?
It is good if someone can read or remind the dying person to practice the teachings on the six bardos. In addition, try to remember these six things: remember the view, remember the deity, remember mantra, remember your samaya, remember your faith and devotion, remember love and compassion. It is also helpful to remember the Nyingma forms of liberation: liberation through taste (and the blessing substances, the relics), liberation through touching, through hearing, through seeing, through remembering, and through wearing. One can also read the Aspiration Prayer of Samantabhadra, or the Coppered-colored Mountain prayers—that can all be really helpful.

It is also very helpful to give teachings that will help the dying person recognize the bardo of dharmata, and to help them remember phowa. Practitioner or not, remind them to focus at the top of their head. You can also touch up there, or pull a little hair. Remember not to touch any lower parts of their body. Feeling directs consciousness, and it can make the consciousness exit from a lower door and take rebirth in a lower realm. You want consciousness to exit from the crown and merge with luminous emptiness awareness, so that your consciousness becomes vast like the sky. Reminding them of this is very helpful. There's also the recitation of all the Buddha's names, and the Chöying Dzö [Treasury of Dharmadhatu], by Longchenpa (which is what I usually recite). The root text is good to read.

What's the best thing to do after someone dies?
Each week, on the day that they died, they repeat the death experience, so this is a very special time for them and a time we can really help. You can do tsog (feast) offering on those days. Butter lamp offering is also special for those times, because the lamps represent clear mind—and help them find their way. If a practitioner is available, until the forty-ninth day, every day they could do the né dren ceremony, which is when you bring their consciousness into the support and then give empowerments and teachings and introduce the path that leads them to the pure land. You can also offer food and drink, and perform the sur offering. If you can do this every day until the forty-ninth day that is best (because seven weeks is the longest they can stay in the bardo), but especially in the first week, and then again for the third week. There is a phowa component in the né dren as well, so phowa is being practiced for them with this practice.

You can read also *The Tibetan Book of the Dead*, because bardo beings come back to hover around their loved ones during the bardo of becoming. This is the time when your prayers can penetrate and reach them directly, helping them. They can truly receive this help.

MINGYUR RINPOCHE

Mingyur Rinpoche was born in Nepal in 1975, the youngest son of Tulku Urgyen Rinpoche. He completed the traditional Buddhist training in philosophy and psychology before founding a monastic college in India. Rinpoche has a strong interest in Western science and has worked with neuroscientists on the effects of meditation on the brain. He teaches throughout the world and has retreat centers on four continents. Rinpoche is the founder of the Tergar Foundation, which propagates the dharma around the world. He is the author of *The Joy of Living: Unlocking the Secret and Science of Happiness*, and *Joyful Wisdom: Embracing Change and Finding Freedom*. Rinpoche replied to my questions via e-mail, then clarified some points in person in Boulder.

What someone should do during death:

- ▸ recognize mind nature—recognize ground luminosity during the bardo of dying
- ▸ bardo practice—for the bardo of becoming[4]
- ▸ phowa practice—so that consciousness doesn't leave through the wrong hole

What others should do for someone who is dying:

- ▸ Encourage the dying person.
- ▸ Remind them to think of their teacher.
- ▸ Remind them of their Dharma practice.
- ▸ Encourage them to recognize ground luminosity.

What others can do after death:
Do phowa during the first three and a half days. They can also read the *Bardo Thödrol* [*The Tibetan Book of the Dead*]. After three and a half days do the chang chok puja until the forty-ninth day [see page 153]. This can be done every day, which is best, or every week on the day that the person died, for seven weeks.

NAMKHA DRIMED RINPOCHE

Namkha Drimed Rinpoche was born in Tibet in 1938 and studied with the Fourteenth Dalai Lama, the Sixteenth Karmapa, and Dilgo Khyentse Rinpoche. In addition to his monastery, Rigon Tashi Choling, in Nepal, Rinpoche has monasteries in India and Tibet. His Eminence has taught in the West for years, most recently under the auspices of Shambhala International. He is a revered terton, or treasure discoverer, and an expert on the legendary Gesar of Ling. This interview was conducted at Rinpoche's home in Kathmandu, Nepal.

What's the best thing to do before death?
First and foremost, since we have this precious human life, it's very important that we really use this golden opportunity in a better way. Whether you go to the upper realms or to the lower realms depends totally on how you deal with your precious human life. How you are going to use this life in a better way—whether you go up or down—depends on what you do now.

It's very necessary that while we are healthy and living we should accumulate virtuous actions and not get involved in nonvirtuous actions with our body, speech, and mind. This is an important preparation—living in a good way, with pure motivation and virtuous action. One has to practice a great deal, starting from the preliminary practices (ngöndro) all the way to dzogchen. These are very necessary to do as a Buddhist. Don't skip, don't jump to dzogchen. Do the stages properly and thoroughly, step by step. If you practice like this, it will be very beneficial. If you practice in a really good way, you will be prepared. You will be content at the time of death.

But we are ordinary people, we have lots of things to do, so we don't get much time to practice. For these kinds of people, those not really prepared, when they are dying it will probably be panicky for them, they won't be sure how to deal with it. So for people like that, ordinary people engaged in lots of activities in daily life, phowa instruction is extremely beneficial. This is something you can do yourself, it is not complicated. If you practice well, then during death you will remember the instruction, even if you have been engaged in lots of nonvirtuous action.

At the end of your life, even if you really regret what you have done, you still have a chance to go to the Pure Realm. That's why phowa is considered so important. Phowa is something that anyone can do, that's why phowa for Sukhavati is considered "the most excellent one." That's why getting instruction for phowa is such an excellent thing and provides so much benefit. You don't have to meditate much on it, you will get enlightened by not doing much meditation. That is what is said. But we still do have to meditate on phowa, it still must be practiced prior to death.

We should abandon nonvirtuous action and try to do more virtuous action. We should pray to our root guru always, and arouse strong faith and devotion to Guru Rinpoche. These should always be there, unchanging. Then, of course, faith in the dharma altogether, and finding the time to practice more. Why phowa is so important is that when you are about to die, you remember all the instructions, and where you go after death depends on this time and what you do. We have everything in this body. Whether we go to the lower realms or the upper realms, we have this jewel, which people don't know sometimes. They are confused when they are about to die, they really don't know what to do. But with phowa instruction, we really know where to go. That is why phowa instruction is extremely important. And the easiest pure land to go to is Sukhavati. By the blessing of Guru Rinpoche and

Amitabha and Chenrezig, this is something very powerful, and also made easy for all ordinary people. That's why phowa—doing it when we are about to die—is extremely beneficial.

What's the best thing we can do for each other when we die?
Death is the separation of the mind and the body—they go separate ways. We normally visualize, while doing phowa practice, that consciousness is sent up, and sending it up is like going into the three upper realms. If you send your consciousness down while you are about to die, that means you are going into the three lower realms. That is why we need to make sure to send it up. During that time it is very important how you concentrate your consciousness and where you send it. If you are confused and send it down, it will go into the three lower realms. So we have to be sure to send it up to Amitabha's pure land.

Once again, this is why phowa instruction is extremely important and beneficial. We are preparing not to send our consciousness downward. The importance of phowa cannot be overstated. Everybody has the crown opening [brahmarandhra], but so few know about it, until and unless you practice phowa. Once we do phowa practice, this crown area opens, so consciousness can go easily up. When it opens up, you can actually feel it, you feel an itch, slight unease at the top of the head, then it becomes very loose, and you can actually put something in that opening, like a piece of straw. So suppose that you are about to die, and you get the signs that you are about to die, during that time you must remember where to send your consciousness.

If you have received the instructions on phowa, that is good, but you are not allowed to do phowa for others. It is said that only the high masters who have really powerful and skillful means can do that, but not ordinary people who do phowa. [Rinpoche is referring to strict phowa, "The Iron Hook of Compassion," not the essential phowa of Sogyal Rinpoche that anyone can do.] What you can do, since you are not allowed to do this phowa for others, is to contact a qualified master and ask them to do phowa for the dying person. You can go near the dying person and feel compassion, immense compassion, and pray to your root guru, pray to whoever you have a wisdom connection with. This immense compassion is extremely beneficial for the dying person.

It is said there are four things you can do: if you have a statue of Guru Rinpoche, keep it in front of the person who is dying. Show it to him or her. Just seeing it can eliminate the person's suffering and prevent them from going into the three lower realms. Secondly, one can read *The Tibetan Book of the Dead*. Let the person hear it—this is extremely beneficial. Don't be shy about reading it loudly so they can hear it. They can still hear it, even if they may be in a coma. Make sure they can hear what you are reading, which can bring about liberation. That is the meaning of *bardo thödrol* ["the great liberation through hearing in the bardo"].

When you are dying you have to be very careful. Reading the book will help them know what is going on and what they need to do. They have to know that they are dying. Thirdly, one can place the *takdrol* [liberation blanket] when they are about to die, and then cremate or bury them with it. Fourth, give them the pills [*dutsi*] from the high masters—this is very good to do. Now they have something to taste, and to hear, and to feel, and to see [four of the six forms of liberation in the Nyingma tradition].

By reading *The Tibetan Book of the Dead* to them when they are dying we can remind them: "Now you are going to encounter this kind of experience, so you have to be careful. You may encounter hallucinations; there is no need to be afraid. Do not get attached to the hallucinations that arise or be afraid of them." This is telling them to prepare for what they may see and experience, which is very important. Before the person dies, make sure you read the instructions of this book to them.

Once the person dies, the outer breath ceases, but the inner breath continues for about ten or twenty minutes. The sign that the inner breath continues is that they remain warm. If you can reach your spiritual masters during this time of the inner dissolution, this is the best time for them to do phowa for the person. This is when it is most effective because consciousness is still in the body and it makes it easier for a Lama to eject the consciousness.

After the person dies, consciousness dissolves into the heart, and at that moment the person faints, like falling into darkness. It depends on the individual, some people faint for one hour, others for half an hour. During that time, phowa is very effective if done by a high master. If there is no phowa, consciousness will eventually go away from that darkness. Then it is very difficult for the master to do phowa. If the dead person doesn't receive phowa, they wake up after death and often do not know whether they are dead or not. Because we are habituated to all the things we do normally, we continue to try to do the same old things after death.

Tukdam is something different. Masters do tukdam because they have not completed what they have to do, so they go into meditation again. Because they have not totally completed their practice [they were unable to finish everything before they died], during death they re-enter meditation and do what they would do normally. When they come out of tukdam, they become normal again [the body begins to decay and smell]. In tukdam, the body does not stink, and they have not totally died. During this time they are completing their practice.

What's the best thing to do after someone has died?
After death, the person experiences a great deal of fear, because there is so much that is unfamiliar. Therefore, shitro practice, if done prior to death, helps them recognize what is happening. They remember the shitro practice. Without this sort of preparation, there is a great deal of fear. If we know the deities, they are peaceful. If we do not [recognize them] they become wrathful, and we feel like they are going to attack us.

[Rinpoche then spoke on the ritual of *shendur*, or *dur*, and entered deep into the mysteries of Tibetan Buddhism. I hesitated to include the following, but Rinpoche felt it was important for students of this tradition.] If the person who dies is eighty years old or so, their life span has really finished. If people are younger when they die, perhaps seventy years old, it is fairly certain that you are dying because of obstacles, the maras. We all have maras but we do not see them. There are maras who want to take your life. Because of their negative influence, a person may die. If this kind of death occurs [you are under eighty years or so at the time of death], then it is very necessary to do a certain kind of puja called *shendur*. *She* is the mara who has taken the life of that person. [Shendur is done] in order to subdue that mara who has taken the life of that person. It is very necessary that this puja be done, otherwise this mara who took the life of the person creates lots of problems for that person.

Problems arise because you cannot separate the mara from that person, the mara always tries to bring obstacles to that person. Whatever puja you might perform for that person is not effective because that mara is causing obstacles. So it is extremely helpful to do the shendur to remove the mara, making all subsequent pujas more effective. So by doing the shendur puja first, all other pujas will be much more effective. Otherwise, the mara will try to stop the benefit of the other pujas and continue to create obstacles.

Then you can do pujas every week for forty-nine days, and they will be of even greater benefit. We should do whatever we can during these forty-nine days, because the bardo being is truly suffering. They are wandering, not knowing what to do, where to go—they are lost. This is the bardo. They need our help.

If you are unable to perform any pujas to help the deceased person during these forty-nine days, then it is very difficult to help the person in the bardo. It is almost certain they will descend into the lower realms. This is why people perform many pujas during the forty-nine days.

If you don't do shendur, people tend to come back as spirits or ghosts into other people's lives. So shendur is very important. It is important because in our local community, people die and become ghosts. I have seen many non-Buddhists in Orissa [India], and when someone dies in their family, because that person does not have a body, his spirit comes and eats everything, whatever they cook. They experience this sort of thing. The bardo being is wandering like a ghost. You can hear that person but you do not see them. I have seen this even in the Tibetan community. Because they have not performed the shendur puja, the spirit comes back to the family, hovering around, stuck as a ghost.

Shendur is something you cannot do by yourself. You have to sponsor a monastery to do it because you need many ritual implements to perform it. Ask a monastery to do it for the deceased. You need practitioners who have some power to do this. Without spiritual power, one is unable to subdue the maras. So contact a monastery, give them the name of the person who died and ask them to do the shendur puja. This way it is easy. Shendur is something that has to be done in a monastery with a more realized master, someone with more power.[5]

DZOGCHEN PONLOP RINPOCHE

Dzogchen Ponlop Rinpoche was born at Rumtek Monastery, India, in 1965. He graduated from the nine-year monastic college in Rumtek and studied closely with the Sixteenth Karmapa, Khyentse Rinpoche, and Khenpo Tsültrim Gyamtso Rinpoche. In 1994 Rinpoche established Nitartha International to integrate computer technology and traditional Tibetan scholarship. In 1995 he founded Nitartha Institute, a systematic training for Western students. In 1997 Rinpoche established Nalandabodhi, his network of centers around the world. His many publications include *Rebel Buddha*, *Mind Beyond Death*, and *Wild Awakening*. The interview was held in Seattle.

What would you tell your students is the best thing to do before death?
Live your life fully. And use every moment, every opportunity, in a way that is beneficial for oneself and for others. If we live every moment the same, in a positive, peaceful, and kind way, then death is also another moment—the same. So there's no difference. If we're not living our life in that way, and always preparing for something to come in the future, at the end, then our preparation is a little bit contradictory with what we're trying to do. How can we expect something positive to happen in one instant, at some point in the future, when we are not living that in every moment? So I think that's the most important thing. So people are talking about preparing for death and dying but actually how can we prepare? How do we know—are we going to die in an accident, are we going to die from a terminal disease, are we going to die in some unusual way, or usual way? There's nothing to predict. And if we can't work with every moment then we will definitely not be able to work with that moment. So setting our mind in that direction, setting our mind in that way, preparing and working with every moment is the best way to prepare for death. And don't make death a big deal.

What's the best instruction for someone who is actually in the dying process?
Reminding them of that, and creating a peaceful environment. An environment where openness, kindness, and love fill the space. The most important thing is to help anyone who is dying to relax. Doesn't matter what religion, or no religion. That's the most important thing. Help them relax and have some kind of positive environment, and positive thought processes.

One thing is that we have this Judeo-Christian culture which is sometimes negative, in that you have to confess everything before you die. Anything that you did wrong in this life, you have to remember that, and make it straight. This view causes more turbulence. Because you're always reflecting and looking at something you did wrong, you're regretting it, or trying to find the person to confess to, and to make it straight. That kind of thing is actually good to do in this life, not in that moment [of death]. That moment is the moment where you relax.

What's the best thing the spiritual community can do to help someone who has died?
If it's a sangha brother or sister, then I think it's helpful to do some practices and speak directly to that deceased person, reminding them. Remind them

of their mahamudra instructions, which you can also do just before they are dying. Remind them how to look at the nature of mind. And remember that. Help them to remember the instructions for the nature of mind. Help them to remember their guru. Remind them to think of their guru, to think of the buddhas and bodhisattvas, and to connect with their own practice. That's the key thing. The main practice is that of reminding them, of helping them connect with that.

If it's your family or someone else, then it's important to do something that's beneficial for the world and dedicate the beneficial activity for that person. When I was living in Vancouver, I thought many times of those park benches that were dedicated for those who had died. Something like that. It's really very beautiful. Do something that's good for the community, good for people, good for beings.

If the dead person had any money, or any possessions, then dedicate those things to a good cause. If the dead person intentionally gave instructions on what to do with their possessions, then of course we need to follow that. But if there are no instructions, we should try to do the best we can with their things. Those objects of attachment could be used in a positive way, so that the object of attachment is transformed. By so doing, the attachment itself will be transformed.

The idea is to generate good causes. A lot of times we don't see that [the objects can generate bad causes of attachment and suffering], and so we try to use the objects for personal benefit. If the surviving family members are really poor and need something, then definitely there's no doubt about it: use the possessions to benefit them. But if that's not really necessary, then it's good to use their possessions for a positive cause.

TENGA RINPOCHE

Tenga Rinpoche was born in Kham, Tibet, in 1932. He fled to Rumtek Monastery in India after the Chinese invasion, where he spent seventeen years as Dorje Loppon. Rinpoche settled in Kathmandu, Nepal, in 1976 and established Benchen Monastery, a large monastic complex that continues to thrive. Rinpoche taught extensively in Europe and the United States, and is the author of *Transition and Liberation*. This interview was held in Swayambhunath, Nepal. I felt very fortunate to meet with Rinpoche. He was elderly and not in good health. Sadly, he passed away on March 30, 2012.

What's the best thing to do to prepare for death?
Generally speaking, how to prepare for our death very much depends on the practice of bodhichitta, the altruistic mind, and the lojong mind training. So this should be trained with in certainty before one dies.

What's the best thing we can do when we are in the process of dying?
At the time of death, it is very important to hold on to this practice. In other words, if one can remain within the attitude of bodhichitta, the altruistic mind, at the moment of death, this is extremely helpful. And of course, if one is a practitioner, especially practicing the nature of mind, at the moment of death it is very important to remain in the state of the practice that is known as mahamudra, or the nature of mind. Then that person might have the possibility to achieve the state of dharmakaya at the time of death. If not, then at least if one is engaging in the practice of any kind of divinities, or yidams, that person will have the chance to achieve the state of enlightenment in the bardo in the form of the yidam, in other words, in the form of the sambhogakaya.

What's the best thing we can do for the person who has died?
As part of the sangha, it's definitely good to engage in our individual practices, and make aspirations, or wishing prayers for the dead person (or even the person who is dying), and dedicate the merit of our practice to them.

Tenzin Wangyal Rinpoche

Tenzin Wangyal Rinpoche was born in Amritsar, India. After completing eleven years of traditional studies, Rinpoche received his geshe degree (equivalent to a Western PhD). He is a leading exponent of the Tibetan Bön tradition as well as a master of Tibetan Buddhism. Rinpoche is the founder and spiritual director of the Ligmincha Institute in Virginia, an active teacher in the West, and the author of many books, including *The Tibetan Yogas of Dream and Sleep*; *Wonders of the Natural Mind*; *Healing with Form, Energy, and Light*; and most recently, *Awakening the Sacred Body*. This interview was conducted at Shambhala Mountain Center in Colorado.

What's the best thing to do to prepare for death?
The main thing, the best thing is to just let go of everything. Don't worry

about anything. Whatever is remaining, whatever you have left behind, people will take care of it. You need to be free from loved ones, from possessions, from your own ideas and thoughts. Try to do what you have been trained to do on the path. Everything you have done over the spiritual path in this life is about letting go. At the end just let go of everything possible. If that is not possible, then you do need to take care of things. But to prepare oneself the point is to step by step just let go of whatever you are able to let go of, and gradually work your way into what you are not able to let go of, and then try to release that. There will always be challenges at the last minute—some people still don't want to let go of things—but do your best in advance to let go.

What's the best thing to do during the bardo of dying?
It varies from person to person. There are different paths and people believe different things. Generally, there will be a lot of experiences after death, so try to become familiar with what is going to happen so that you are more prepared when the different visions come. It's like preparing to recognize a dream to be a dream. When you recognize that you are dreaming, you are no longer afraid of what happens in the dream. You can guide it, you can grow from it. It is the same thing with the dying process. If you understand, if you have the knowledge of the bardos—what the bardos are, what the visions are, what they mean—then you will have confidence. So during life you should learn about the bardos and practice for the bardos, become familiar with them. And even test some of those experiences in the dream, using dream yoga to prepare, so that when you encounter these visions after death you will be ready.

It is also good to resolve any family conflicts before death. You don't want to carry those conflicts into the bardo. This conflict resolution is probably even more important than drawing up legal wills.

What's the best thing to do for someone after they have died?
Those left behind should do the *sur* offering, the smoke offering, for forty-nine days. Every day if possible. Then every seven days family and friends could do some special transition ceremonies, to help the person go from one step to the next step in their journey. It's also good to burn lots of candles, as a light offering, an offering of wisdom, that can illuminate their journey. That is considered important. And also to do phowa. If they were a believer, it's good to have someone, a lama, do phowa for them. This is my heart advice.

THRANGU RINPOCHE

Thrangu Rinpoche was born in Kham, Tibet, in 1933, and received his traditional monastic training at Thrangu Monastery. Rinpoche became the abbot of Rumtek Monastery in India and eventually moved to Nepal where he maintains a number of nunneries, monasteries, retreat centers, schools, and clinics. Rinpoche founded a monastic college in Sarnath, India, and heads hundreds of dharma centers around the world. His many books include *Buddha Nature*, *Open Door to Emptiness*, and *Journey of the Mind*. This interview was conducted in Boudhanath, Nepal.

What is the most important thing to do before death?
In teachings on the bardo, the period of this life is called the natural bardo of this life. It is important to do spiritual practice and meditation in this life. In particular, the teachings on mind training [lojong] and the tonglen practice of sending and taking are the most important. So the best way to prepare for the bardo is to place good tendencies on your mind now. If you have a good heart and a very stable mind right now, then that will naturally extend into the bardo.

What is the most important thing to do during death?
At the time of death, you should try to meditate on bodhichitta and maintain an attitude of kindness. You should not be attached to your wealth, possessions, friends, or family, and those around you should not talk about inheritances or your possessions. It is best if you can study the bardos in advance and prepare for what you will encounter when you die. There is a great deal of literature on the bardos, and by spending time with it now you will know what to do when you are dying.

What's the best thing we can do for someone after they have died?
The best things for people to do on behalf of someone who has died are to make aspiration prayers, meditate on bodhichitta, and do phowa practice. In general, there are people who believe in Buddhism and the bardos, and those who do not. For those who do believe in the bardos, it would be very good if you could help them recognize how the bardo appears, what actually appears in the bardo. For those who don't believe in the bardos, it is helpful to have good heart for them, to generate the bodhichitta mind.

Are there any particular ceremonies or rituals that can help them?
It's good if one can recite aspiration prayers, virtually any of them. In the
Tibetan world we also have the tradition of doing the puja of shitro, the
peaceful and wrathful deities.[6]

If you [Rinpoche] had a student who was dying, and you were at their
side helping them, is there anything else that you would do for them?
When someone is dying, it is helpful to give them the blessing pills [*dutsi*].
You can also remind them about the dharma, the sangha, and the teachings.
In other words, remind them about taking refuge in the three jewels.

TSOKNYI RINPOCHE

Tsoknyi Rinpoche was born in Nepal in 1966 and did his monastic training in India. He returned to Nepal in 1990 to establish Ngedon Osel Ling
Monastery. His Western seat is Yeshe Rangsel in Crestone, Colorado. Rinpoche heads fifty-five monasteries in Tibet, and is the abbot of two nunneries in Nepal as well as the largest nunnery in Tibet. His books include
Carefree Dignity and *Fearless Simplicity*. Rinpoche has a facility with Western ways and is deeply committed to working with Western students. The
following is from a phone interview.

What is the best thing a student can do before death?
Refresh the teachings. Whatever you have received, go through your data-
base of teachings and refresh it. There are a lot of teachings, but try to capture the essential points of what you have received. The main points are to
be detached and to refresh your recognition of the nature of mind.

What is the best meditation to do before death?
[*This being a phone interview, Rinpoche heard "medication" instead of
"meditation," to which he replied:*]
It's best to have medications that reduce the pain but that don't interfere too
much with cognitive functions, that allow the person as much mental clarity as possible. [*After I clarified the question, Rinpoche continued:*] For older
students, find the nature of mind, which is mind beyond death and dying.
This mind doesn't die. Find that mind and rest there. For newer students,
they can rest in meditation. Mostly it depends on each person, according

to their belief, to create some hope. It's okay to connect to your own belief to find some peace.

What is the best thing to do when someone is actually dying?
There are several options here. One option is that if you have a yidam [meditation deity], you can grab on to that. By doing so, the yidam binds your mind. Again, whatever is happening, whatever is dissolving, the best thing is to maintain the unborn mind, the recognition of the nature of mind. Don't be afraid of the dissolution. Things may be dissolving, but you are resting in the nature of mind which is beyond dissolution and death.

What's the best thing for sangha to do to help the dying person?
If you know the person's yidam, that is very good. Invoke the mind of the yidam, and mix your mind, the mind of the dying person, and the mind of the yidam together—then rest in the nature of mind. That is a very big support for the one who is dying.

Should the sangha do the yidam practice along with the dying person?
Yes. If the helping person is familiar and understands yidam practice, then they can remind the dying person of the qualities of the yidam. It is also helpful to recite the mantra of the yidam. The dying person can recite it, and sangha at the side of the person can recite it with them. Think of the person's mind, the mind of the yidam, and your nature of mind, mingled together. Rest in that state. That is very helpful. It is also good to read vajra songs and dohas of fearlessness. Beginner practitioners can also do this. Read teachings on mahamudra, dzogchen, and other inspiring readings, along with *The Tibetan Book of the Dead*.

The helping person has to have some kind of intuition and be able to adjust according to the person who is dying. If they are Christian, say something to connect them to God. If they are Buddhist, then say something to help them connect to the underlying mind. If they are a free thinker, then help them connect with the peace in their mind and to let go of fear. You have to see and understand the person in order to know how to best say: Relax, let it go.

Provide what gives them hope beyond life—whether it's God, the pure lands, or the undying and unchanging mind. Most importantly, the helping person needs to use their intuition and wisdom to properly convey what they understand, and to match the belief of the dying person.

What's the best thing to do when someone wakes up in the bardo after death?

The first thing is for you to recognize that you are dead. Secondly, you should know that all the phenomena that you are experiencing now are bardo phenomena. Know that everything is the expression of your own mind. Think to yourself: "I'm not going to go crazy with the expressions of my mind. I'm going to try to find the nature of my own mind, which is beyond the delusion." Everything that is happening is the expression of your mind. It is better not to get caught up in that expression but to capture the royal seat of the nature of mind.

What is the best thing that sangha can do to support someone after they have died?

In a general way, every week you can do practices for them, because every week they have a chance to change their life, to change the course of their bardo experience.[7] The most important thing for changing in the bardo is to know that they have lived their life properly and can therefore let go of that life with confidence. On those days, you can do more pujas or prayers, or you can go through *The Tibetan Book of the Dead*, day by day. If you can read it in the house where they lived, where they spent the most time, that is best, because they usually come back to familiar places. They will probably not recognize that they are dead, so when they come back and hear the reading, they may recognize or remember that they are dead, and then they may click onto some good things—like remembering the teachings and what they should do.

Any final comments, Rinpoche, if you were at the side of someone who was dying?

Two things. First, if they are willing to hear your advice, then give them hope. Tell them that the relative is dying, the ultimate is not dying. Give them hope that they can recognize the ultimate, the nature of their mind, the mind that is unchanging and undying. You have to give a little promotion on the deathless side. Secondly, then the phenomena of this life that they are leaving, that they used properly—just let it go.

What is the role of Pure Land teachings for students in the West?
It depends on the student. In Tibet they have a very strong belief and trust that the pure land is there, so they have hope to be reborn there. It's case by case. I can't tell someone who has spent their entire life not believing in pure lands to suddenly start to believe in them at the time of their death. That's very hard to do. But Western practitioners tend to believe in the nature of mind as something special, so make that the doorway.

TULKU THONDUP RINPOCHE

Tulku Thondup Rinpoche was born in Tibet in 1939. He fled to India in 1958, and taught at Lucknow University and then Visva-Bharati University. In 1980 he went to Harvard University as a visiting scholar. Rinpoche works at translating and preserving Tibetan texts under the auspices of the Buddhayana Foundation. He is the author of many books, including *Hidden Teachings of Tibet*; *Enlightened Living*; *Buddha Mind*; and *Peaceful Death, Joyful Rebirth*. After I spoke with Rinpoche in Colorado, he e-mailed his response.

The Tibetan Book of the Dead and other esoteric (tantra) teachings have taught the ways of attaining buddhahood by realizing one's own nature of innate wisdom and wisdom lights while we are dying or while we are traveling in the bardo. These teachings are the most profound instructions for those who are highly accomplished meditators.

However, it is very important for us to know that for ordinary people like ourselves—who have been drowning long and deep in the ocean of samsara with hardened habits of dualistic concepts, emotional afflictions, and sensational feelings, and who have little or no high meditative experiences in advance—it is hard to realize and maintain one's wisdom nature and attain buddhahood at the junction of such a traumatic period of life—death and bardo. For such realization, we must transcend our samsaric mentalities and awaken the innate wisdom nature and qualities of nirvana, the buddhahood.

But there is also another way. If we accumulate a good amount of merits and make heartfelt aspirations to take rebirth in a "manifested pure land" (nirmanakaya-ksetra), such as the Blissful Pure Land (Sukhavati) of the Buddha of Infinite Light (Amitabha), taking rebirth in the Pure Land will become much easier. For taking rebirth and living in such a pure land, there is no need to transcend dualistic mentalities, emotional afflictions, and sensational frictions—because in manifested pure lands, we live with positive thoughts, positive emotions, and positive feelings. Furthermore, in such a pure land we will not be experiencing any sufferings or committing any cause of sufferings, so that the attainment of Buddha is assured for us before very long.

Therefore, it might be practical and feasible for many of us to work toward taking rebirth in a manifested pure land, or at least a happier and helpful rebirth in a healthier human or god realm, by accumulating merits and making aspirations. Making merits and aspirations is the way of gaining peace, joy, and enlightenment for oneself and sharing them with others. It is the heart of Tibetan Buddhist trainings, and the esoteric teachings such as *The Tibetan Book of the Dead* elaborate on them extensively.

Acknowledgments

It is impossible to write a manual of this scope without a village behind you. Many people gave generously to create this book. In addition to the offerings of my co-authors, Dr. Mitchell Gershten, Alex Halpern, Christine Longaker, Kim Mooney, Beth Patterson, and Karen Van Vuuren, the following people provided valuable feedback: Jeremy Hayward, Renita Jolley, Lindy King, Carole Lindroos, Eileen Malloy, Judith Simmer-Brown, and Jeffrey Stevens.

Special thanks to Darci Meyers, a professional in this field who co-directed a course with me that provided the framework for this book. And a deep bow of gratitude to Sogyal Rinpoche. No one has done as much to introduce the splendor of Buddhist teachings on death to the West.

For the section on physical signs and symptoms of death, I called on the advice of Dr. David Berman, Dr. Mitchell Gershten, Dr. Daniel Matlock, Dr. Gail McDonald, Dr. Greg Raybold, and the words of Lynn Weitzel, RN, BSN. Beth Patterson and Kim Mooney stepped in yet again to help me with the section on working with grief from a Buddhist perspective. Thank you to the noble translators who helped me interview the Buddhist masters included in part 3. They were often monks who happened to be available at the last minute, and whose names were not given to me. And to the masters themselves, thank you for your profound wisdom.

A deep thank you to my editor Susan Kyser, who provided invaluable insight and support. Dominie Cappadonna, Sebo Ebans, and Kimberly Roberts went beyond the call of duty in providing editorial help. And Cindy Wilson, an angel who came into my life, supported me in ways that only pure spirits can.

Finally, I want to thank Sakyong Mipham Rinpoche, who encouraged me to write this book. His beacon of light in this dark age has been an unceasing source of inspiration. And his message that *now* is the time to put meditation into action has given me the courage to write.

My version of an ideal death would be to have these people at my side. When I hold this book, I feel like I am holding each of their caring and capable hands. With their wisdom as it is embodied in these pages, and the warmth of their love as it is held in my heart, I am certain that my final journey—and hopefully yours—will be a good one.

Appendix 1: Checklists

The following checklists are offered as a help, not as a burden. Don't feel that the death is imperfect or that you're letting the dead person down if you can't do everything listed below. If you're the one dying, don't pressure yourself or others into doing everything. Take what you need and ignore the rest. If you need help implementing these suggestions, call on your friends. Talk through these lists with your entrusted dharma friends, and choose the items that are important to you. Finally, even though these lists are in separate categories, there is some overlap.[1]

Spiritual Checklist

- If the person has a lama, teacher, or strong spiritual friend, contact that person in advance and let them know what's happening. If they can't be present at the moment of death, let them know as soon as possible that the person has died. They can then begin phowa, or other rituals, from afar. If you're fortunate enough to have a lama or other teacher perform a ritual, be sure to send a donation for their services. Many masters will not be available to help you or your loved one. But you can let them know of the impending death and ask for their blessing.
- If you're going to have a monastery or spiritual center perform rituals, contact them in advance. Discuss the rituals, and arrange for donations for their services. Contact them as soon as possible after the death so they can begin the practices.
- Contact any entrusted spiritual friends or other spiritual helpers. You can keep dharma friends updated via an e-mail list, and ask for their practice (merit) or other assistance. Begin any prearranged bedside practices.

▸ If they left a dharma box and dharma will, implement the directives of that will, and employ the other contents in the box.

FAREWELL CHECKLIST

Think about the holding environment you want as you die. Do what you need to do to prepare that sacred space. If you don't have a dharma will, you could dictate your wishes to your spiritual friends when you realize you are going to die. Ask them for help in implementing your wishes. Here are suggestions for what to put into your dharma will:

▸ Who do you want to be with you when you die? Is there anyone you feel may disturb your death and should therefore stay away?

▸ Do you want many people coming through, a very quiet space, or something in between?

▸ What do you want the space to look like—a shrine, photos of your teachers, of loved ones? What other sacred objects do you want? Do you want candles or incense?

▸ Do you want something near you that you can touch, smell, feel or even taste?

▸ Do you want music, recordings of teachings, or inspirational verses read to you?

▸ It's good to die at home, in comfortable and familiar surroundings. If this isn't possible, instruct your friends and the hospital or hospice staff that you strongly request the TV not be on. Replace the TV or radio with recordings of teachings, or remain in silence.

Richard Reoch, in his book *To Die Well: A Holistic Approach for the Dying and Their Caregivers*, offers this advice, which is similar to Anyen Rinpoche's dharma will suggestions:

A simple gesture that you can make to your family to ease matters for them after your death is to create a file with all the information they will need about you in the event of your death. Make sure you regularly update it. Your file should contain: birth certificate; details of passport (you might die abroad), your will, Living Will, an enduring power of attorney, your organ donor approval, details of your bank account and credit cards, investments and other details, insurance policies, prepaid or other funeral plans, people you want notified, including employers, any specific requests or wishes not in your will. You can maintain the file lovingly since you are doing this for the people you care most about."[2]

Richard offers this additional checklist:

- ► What do you want done with your body—burial, cremation, or donation to medical science?
- ► What do you feel would be the most appropriate way for people to say goodbye to you after your death?
- ► Do you want people to be able to say goodbye in ways other than a funeral or memorial service? How?
- ► If you are a great lover of nature, would you like your friends and family to gather outdoors, at one of your favorite locations?
- ► Is there anything you want said or read at your funeral?
- ► Would you prefer silence?
- ► Do you want someone in particular to lead the gathering?
- ► Is it to be a party or some other form of celebration?
- ► Are there particular values or human qualities you want emphasized?
- ► Is there an important cause or charity you want to benefit?
- ► If you want to be cremated, where would you like your ashes to be scattered?[3]

Do you want the service video recorded? The eulogies, poetry, music, and other offerings are often so beautiful that people want to see them again. You can copy these recordings and send them to loved ones who were unable to attend, or save them for grandchildren.

The following are some of Anyen Rinpoche's suggestions, along with my own, for what to put in your dharma box:

- ► a copy of legal papers (wills, medical directives, etc.)
- ► a copy of your dharma will
- ► a copy, recording, or even video of any final message you want read at your service or left for your family or friends
- ► instructions to entrusted dharma friends for how to spiritually care for you
- ► instructions to non-Buddhist family members for what you want as you die
- ► copies for yourself and your spiritual friends of liturgies you want read or practices and rituals to perform
- ► copies of general prayers for non-Buddhist family and friends

- photographs of teachers or deities you may want near you as you die
- any ritual items you want near you
- *amrita* pills (*dutsi* in Tibetan) that can be given to you, with instructions for their use. *Amrita* means "immortality" in Sanskrit. These "deathless pills" can be ingested at any time, but general bardo instructions are to take them when the signs of the outer dissolution begin. You can put one pill in a bottle of water each day and then sip it. You can place the pills under the tongue or behind the lip and let them dissolve. Dutsi can also be placed on the brahmarandhra, with a bit of lotion to make it stick. You can get dutsi from a lama or from spiritual friends.
- recordings of teachings from your favorite teachers, or of mantras or liturgies
- a copy of the mandala of the peaceful and wrathful deities from *The Tibetan Book of the Dead*. This can be placed at the heart center.
- any of the contents of the bardo package listed below
- sur kit

BARDO PACKAGE

Khenpo Karthar Rinpoche offers a "bardo package" to be used at the time of death. In the Nyingma tradition there are six forms of liberation associated with the bardos: liberation through sight, touch, taste, remembrance, wearing, and hearing.[4] Khenpo Karthar Rinpoche's bardo package works with a number of these and includes the following:[5]

- a recording of *The Tibetan Book of the Dead* (the *Bardo Thödrol Chenmo*—"The great liberation through hearing during the bardo"—which is also included in the category of liberation through remembrance). This can be played continuously during the forty-nine day period following death to guide the deceased.
- amrita pills (liberation through tasting). These can be placed in the mouth during serious illness, at the time of death (approximately three days before death), or in the mouth of a corpse after death
- liberating sand (liberation through touch), which is placed on the brahmarandhra after death, and acts as a form of phowa[6]
- the takdrol (liberation through touch and through wearing), or "death shroud." This is placed over the body after death like a blanket, and burned or buried with the corpse.[7]

PRACTICAL CHECKLIST

The following checklists will help you prepare for the many practical details that accompany any death. They can ease the onslaught of things to do before and after someone dies. You could circle the ones that apply to you. The point is to provide suggestions, not to overwhelm you with things to do. In addition to contributions from the authors of this book, the following checklist was compiled in part from Philip Kapleau's "The Wheel of Life and Death."

► Take the time you need with the person after they die. If you have not already done so, find the person's final arrangements with respect to body donation, organ donation, and mortuary arrangements.

► If the person died at home, and the death was *expected*, call the physician or hospice nurse, and have a death certificate signed. If the deceased was not receiving hospice services but was nevertheless under the care of a physician, calling the physician would be the first step. If someone is not under the care of a physician, then the coroner or medical examiner will be involved to determine the cause of death. Medical providers should notify the coroner or medical examiner of any deaths, but it's good to check that this procedure has been followed. (See page 383, note 4, for the difference between a coroner and a medical examiner.)

► If the death is *unexpected* (or suspicious), with no hospice or personal physician care involved, call 911 and they will call the coroner. On discovery of a person who is seemingly dead, most people would dial 911 as an initial reaction anyway. (Questions to consider: do you know if the person is beyond resuscitation or not? If the person is elderly and frail, and therefore might not survive CPR anyway, would they want the disturbance of the attempted resuscitation?) The coroner will come out, investigate the death, determine its cause, and sign the death certificate. If the dead person has a doctor, the doctor could be called instead of 911. The doctor would then notify the medical examiner or coroner as needed.[8]

► Contact people who may want to spend time alone with your loved one. You can spend time with the body before notifying anybody. But be reasonable. Extensive delay in reporting a death is frowned upon by officials who might have to investigate it. The point at which you contact anyone mostly affects the official time of death on the death certificate. On the death certificate there is a time of death, and a time of pronouncement. The time of pronouncement is when the doctor or hospice nurse confirms the death. The time of death may be reported by the family as a different time.

▸ Turn off any electrical equipment attached to the body, but leave tubes in place for the professionals to remove.

▸ If the death occurs in a hospital, nursing home, or other facility, advise the nurse that you believe the person has died. The nurse will call the doctor to have the person declared dead. Generally, unless organs are to be donated, the family will have plenty of time to say their final farewells before the body is removed. Ask the facility how much time you can have with the body. Don't feel rushed.

▸ While each state has its own regulations and eligibility requirements for organ donation, there are some general guidelines. Check with your physician or a local hospital for the details in your state. To register as a donor, contact the donor registry in your state (visit www.organdonor.gov), or fill out an organ donor card when you get or renew your driver's license. If you are planning to donate organs and are in a hospital when death approaches, let the hospital know your intention. The hospital will contact a transplant coordinator who will get in touch with you. The organs of a person who dies at home are usually not suitable for donation.

Generally, the patient must be on a ventilator until such time as the organs are removed because the organs need oxygen to remain viable. If death is unexpected and happens at home, the only way organ donation might be possible would be if emergency services were there when death occurred, and they were able to pump air into the body. Some facilities place organ donors on a heart-lung machine, called ECMO, even before their hearts have stopped beating. This nourishes the organs, prevents lots of organs from being wasted, and thus saves more lives.

If coroners are involved, and if the person was a registered donor, it would be up to the coroner to act quickly, approving the contact with the organ procurement organization. Donation is always done in a sterile facility, not at home. When organ donation is not possible, you can often still be an eye and tissue donor. A donation organization will come to remove the body and bring it to the facility (and answer most of your questions). This must happen within a certain time frame, which varies on whether a body is refrigerated or not. Families can get the body back afterwards if they want.

▸ If the body is being donated to a medical school, call the school, inform them that the donor has died, and arrange for transportation. Not all bodies are acceptable for donation. If the deceased person is obese, for example, many schools will not accept the body. Be prepared for a rejection.

▸ If funeral arrangements have already been made, notify the mortician as to when you want the body to be transported. If hospice hasn't already removed the catheters, tubes, and syringes, the mortician will. They will then transport the body to the mortuary.

▸ Notify anyone who is to have a role in the services. Pallbearers could be selected before death and incorporated in a plan when death is expected.

▸ Arrange for family members or friends to take turns answering the phone, responding to e-mails, and answering the door at the home of the deceased. You may want to keep a record of these contacts.

▸ To those who phoned, sent flowers or other memorials, as well as those who helped with food or child care, consider sending appropriate acknowledgments. Include any other health care professionals who helped care for the person. On a balancing note, many people elect not to send thank you cards to anyone. Most people would understand.

▸ Coordinate the supply of food for the next few days, and take care of other things that need to be done, such as cleaning. When dealing with food, keep in mind the presence of possible out-of-town guests.

▸ Arrange for child care, if needed.

▸ Arrange for accommodations for out-of-town guests.

▸ Decide where memorial gifts can be sent if flowers are to be omitted. If flowers are to be accepted, decide what is to happen to them after the funeral.

▸ Write an obituary for the papers. A funeral home often does this as part of their services. Ideally, this could be done before the death occurs. Obituaries usually include the age, place of birth, cause of death, occupation, college degrees, military service, organizational memberships, any outstanding accomplishments, names of survivors in the immediate family, and names of any memorials set up in lieu of flowers. Deliver the obituary to the newspapers. There may be a charge to print it, per column inch. (In some cities, this can be expensive.) You can include a photo for a small additional charge. Try to get it into the papers early in the day, as soon as you know the time and place for the service. Simple death notices can be placed by the mortuary or by families, and are usually free of charge. Go to the newspaper's website and fill out the information required. The newspaper staff will make sure that the death occurred by asking for confirmation by the funeral home. In the case of a death at home, they may want to see a copy of the death certificate (as a nasty joke, death notices have been placed for someone still alive).[9]

▸ If the person died at home, arrange for return of any rented materials. Some unused material cannot be taken back by hospice but could be donated to local senior centers.

OTHER CONTACTS TO BE MADE AFTER SOMEONE DIES

▸ post office, to forward mail

▸ landlord and utility companies, to stop or alter services

▸ newspapers and magazines, to end subscriptions (and get refunds, if possible)

▸ agencies providing pensions, to stop monthly checks and obtain claim forms

▸ insurance agents, to obtain necessary death claim forms for life insurance and other assets

▸ police, to inform that the home of the deceased will be vacant and request them to periodically check the house

▸ Social Security (800-772-1213), to learn about benefits and stop monthly deposits

▸ Veterans Affairs, to learn about benefits and stop monthly checks

▸ investment professionals, to obtain information about assets owned by the deceased

▸ employer or business associates, to notify them of the death and learn about benefits

▸ attorney and executor of the estate, to discuss probate process (if needed—how to transfer assets, deal with heirs, and implement the will)

▸ accountant, to determine what tax returns should be filed

▸ guardian, conservator, or agent under a power of attorney, to notify of the death and end their responsibilities

FINANCIAL RESPONSIBILITIES AFTER DEATH

Find the will. Wills are found with the attorney of the deceased, in a safe deposit box, hidden in a safe place in the home, or with the court in the county where the person lived. Lodge it within ten days with the probate court in the county where they lived. If a will cannot be found, a probate attorney will guide you through the intestate probate process. In some states, a letter to a family member, handwritten instructions, or similar documents may constitute a will.

The following is a list of things that may need to be done within a few months after death:

▸ Death certificate: You will need certified copies for banks, insurance companies, and financial institutions to transfer property and assets. The easiest way to obtain death certificates is through the funeral director (about $10.00 per copy). Six to eight copies is usually adequate. You can get more later through the Vital Statistics Department of the county in which the death occurred (or the County Clerk).

▸ Credit cards: Cancel any credit cards held in the name of the deceased. This is best done sooner rather than later. Payments due on any card should be paid by the estate.

▸ Changing title or ownership: You may want to change these documents into your name: bank accounts—change the title and signature card on accounts; automobile policies—if the deceased had a car, the title needs to be changed; insurance policies—change the beneficiary; safe-deposit box—a court order may be required to open a safe-deposit box if you are not on the list of people who can enter it. The bank that holds the box can help. As with bank accounts, the signature card should be changed.

▸ Insurance policies and death benefits: Investigate possible insurance and death benefits for survivors. Insurance benefits may include life, accident, mortgage or loan, benevolent, auto, credit card, or employee benefits. The proceeds from an insurance policy are usually processed quickly and paid directly to the named beneficiary. A certified copy of the death certificate is often required.

Types of death benefits may include Social Security, credit union, trade union, fraternal, or military. The funeral director may contact the Social Security Administration (SSA), or the survivors can contact them at 1-800-

772-1213 (have the Social Security numbers at hand for both the surviving spouse and the deceased). Contact the employer of the deceased about any benefits for survivors, and contact past employers to see if survivors are entitled to any benefits from a pension plan.

Veteran's benefits. If the deceased is an eligible veteran, they may be entitled to burial benefits, like a burial at a National Cemetery, a grave marker and a flag. If the deceased was receiving disability benefits, other financial benefits may be available. Call the Veteran's Administration (VA at 1-800-872-1000).

Review all debts and installment payments. There can be delays in the transfer of assets and in other financial settlements at the time of death. If such delays occur, make arrangements with creditors to delay any payments that do not carry insurance clauses that would cancel further payments outright.

IN THE EVENT OF SUDDEN DEATH

Keep this list in a secure location, but where family members can get to it quickly. Let them know where you keep this list, which could be in your dharma box, or elsewhere. It's mostly a summary of what is listed above.

- ► Here are the account numbers for
  - credit cards (plus the toll-free numbers of companies)
  - bank accounts (plus the PIN numbers or passwords, toll-free numbers)
  - investment accounts (plus online passwords, toll-free numbers)
  - insurance policies (plus toll-free numbers)
- ► Here is where the following are kept:
  - wills
  - living will
  - power of attorney
  - property deeds
  - insurance policies
  - company benefits
  - safe deposit box key and location of box
  - list (or photos) of valuables and their worth

Be Aware

The funeral industry is big business. While there are many compassionate funeral directors, and funeral homes do provide a community service, they are a commercial industry taking in over fifteen billion dollars annually. On the noble side, I have heard of funeral homes that have buried babies for free, or acted selflessly during community disasters. But there are also ignoble stories, some of which are mentioned below.[10]

Funerals can be expensive—about half the cost of weddings, which average around twenty-seven thousand dollars. There's the casket, embalming, cremation, make-up, viewing charges, dressing, music, headstone, urn, chapel service, graveside service, memorial DVDs, flowers, limousine, etc. The best way to control funeral expenses is to plan ahead, but this is rare in a culture that denies death. Planning also prevents emotional shopping, which always means over-spending. When you're in shock over the death of a loved one, it's easy to be taken advantage of. You want the best for your loved one, and emotion trumps reason. You may feel that you don't want to cut corners in your final offering to them, and it seems petty to quibble over quality and price.

To avoid emotional shopping, you can hire an independent funeral planner, or work with a funeral home's pre-need plan. Pre-need planning includes things like buying a casket and cemetery plot, and making funeral arrangements well before the time of death. Approach the funeral industry as if you were buying a car. Shop around and compare prices. Ask if the person offering you their funeral services works on a commission. Many funeral homes charge a nonnegotiable fee for basic services, but lots of add-ons can be negotiated.

With funeral homes, it's easy to skim over the details of the services you're paying for, let alone whether or not you really need them. Bring a non–family member when costs and services are discussed, or bring several family members. Your friends and family will act as your advocate, catching things you might miss. Karen Van Vuuren says, "The Federal Trade Commission's 'Funeral Rule' is meant to prevent funeral service providers from engaging in deceptive or unfair practices. Funeral providers are required to provide a General Price List (GPL) and an itemized statement of services." Make sure you see the GPL and itemized statement. If you're getting prices over the phone, and doing some comparative shopping, the funeral home is required by law to inform you of their fees over the phone.

My father was a practical, funny, and frugal man. When I asked him what he wanted after he died, he said, "I want to go swimming with mom in Lake Michigan [he dispersed her ashes in the lake several years prior]. Just cremate me and toss me into the lake." He had researched the least expensive cremation service in the area, and left us that information. When my brother and I went to discuss his final wishes with the funeral home, the funeral director tried to sell us the most expensive casket. Mind you, this was not a casket to be buried in, but one to be taken (maybe?) to the furnace. The cost for this casket was $7500.00. When we kindly declined, he then presented the entire spectrum of other cremation caskets. We finally settled on the least expensive one, a simple but acceptable cardboard casket for $200.00. From a Porsche to a Pinto—I'm sure my father was proud of his assertive kids.[11]

If you do choose a casket, you don't need to buy it from the funeral home. Funeral homes, under law, must accept any casket that is delivered to them, and they cannot charge you a handling fee if you have one shipped in. You can go online and have a casket shipped overnight, which can save you up to fifty percent of what the funeral home would charge. If the body needs to be moved to another location (for the final service, etc.), and you have a vehicle large enough to accommodate a casket, you can drive it yourself. This can save you hundreds of dollars in airline fees.[12]

While funeral directors are not malicious, they generally will not inform you of cost-cutting measures. If you did order the casket online, don't tell them about it until after all the other services and prices have been discussed and *put in writing*. My brother and I had some scratchy moments with the funeral director once he found out how much we were going to do ourselves. "It's never been done this way before!" is not a satisfactory response from the funeral home, and doesn't mean it can't be done this way. Be informed, kind, yet assertive.

Several friends have shared stories of how they felt pressured by their funeral director to embalm the body of their loved one. In most states *the body does not need to be embalmed*, even if there is a viewing. It just needs to be refrigerated, put on dry ice, or kept in an air-conditioned room. I have seen many nonembalmed bodies that look *better* than other bodies that were embalmed. If you do get a person embalmed and cosmeticized, ask to see the final work a day or so before the viewing. If it's not acceptable, ask them to redo it, or to explain the limitations. Get the service you are paying for. While they may not be able to "bring her back to life," the cosmetologist can know that you will inspect their work *before* the viewing. It might inspire them to do their very best. My mother was cosmeticized before the showing (at my father's request), and she didn't look anything like what we thought. It almost felt like there was a stranger in the casket. When my father died five years later, we didn't embalm or prepare him, and elected to do a closed casket "viewing."

There is a long list of itemized services and charges associated with funeral arrangements. Take your time and make sure you know what you're paying for. Don't let the mortuary sell you unnecessary services, which they will almost certainly try to do. Most funeral homes will make nice DVDs of your loved one from photos and music you give them. But they often do so for outrageous fees. Find a friend who is comfortable with iPhoto or other computer-generated slide shows. You don't even need to take your photos to a store to burn them onto a disc (if you do, Walmart is the least expensive I have found). You can take a digital photo of the hardcopy photograph (use the camera on your smart phone) and transfer it directly into your computer. If you want to send the slide show to loved ones who couldn't attend the service, it's easy to burn copies onto a DVD disc and send them out. This is much easier than you think and can save you money.

There have also been a number of documented cases of morticians removing and selling the gold dental work from corpses—without informing the relatives of the deceased. When questioned, some funeral homes claimed they removed gold dental work, sold it, and donated the money to charity.[13] With the price of gold over $1,600 an ounce, this can start to add up. If your loved one had gold dental work, discuss this matter with your family and with the funeral director. Gold crowns can easily be removed and taken to a jeweler for cash.

Approach your funeral home with an open but careful mind. There's no need to be paranoid or combative. But there is a need to be firm and clear. Err on the side of caution. Ask questions. Let the funeral director know, through your thoughtful questions, that you are not a pushover. Are you actually getting what you paid for? Do you really need these services? How much of this can you, or your friends, do for yourselves? Remember Karen Van Vuuren's words:

> In many states, families may be able to do everything, including transporting the body of the deceased in their own vehicle, burying on their own land (depending on the county zoning

laws regarding land use), and even conducting open-air cremation on rural, agricultural property, with county permission and
the cooperation of the local fire department. . . . It takes research
ahead of time to find out what is possible, and when talking with
officials, it is important to get more than one opinion, and to ask
for a referral to laws or regulations to clarify and confirm what
is said.

Finally, thieves read obituaries and death notices. They can prey on others
during times of vulnerability and confusion. Be wary of phone solicitations
or other requests for information. Don't offer addresses or other private
information. Fake invoices may appear, so review all such documents carefully. Authentic creditors may get aggressive, but don't feel pushed. If you
need legal help sorting through financial responsibilities, seek it.

Appendix 2: Things You Can Write to Prepare for Death

Letters of Forgiveness, and Saying Goodbye

As discussed earlier, one form of phowa is contacting people with whom you have unfinished emotional business. If you don't, this unresolved baggage can drag you down during death, or distract you in the form of regret. If you knew you were going to die next week, who would you reach out to? Do it now. If you don't feel comfortable talking to someone, write to them. Do so without expectation. Don't expect to heal deep emotional wounds, even if you really are dying. Clean it up from your end. Express your feelings in the spirit of reconciliation, then let it go. You can't be responsible for what other people do. The idea is to lighten your load.

You can also send appreciation letters to those who have touched your life. Let them know how they helped you. If someone you know is seriously ill or dying, sharing your heart can benefit them, and you. It's the bodhisattva's gesture of generosity.

Writing these letters isn't always easy. If it's difficult, write the letter, then send it when it feels right. Sometimes just writing the letter helps, even if it's never sent. Don't think too much about yourself. Think about others.

Writing these letters can teach you how to live without residue now. You may find yourself relating to people every day as if this was your last day, treating them with more kindness and respect. It can help you to live cleanly so you can die cleanly. This doesn't mean we have to make everyone like us. It means we can free ourselves of emotional baggage before we die, and ease our journey through the bardos.

Writing Your Own Eulogy and Obituary

Writing your own eulogy and obituary is a powerful contemplation to remind you of impermanence. As with many death-related exercises, this one can bring you more fully to life. It will help you appreciate the preciousness of what you have. The eulogy and obituary can be left in your dharma box. They could help others in writing your official obituary, or their own eulogies to commemorate your life. They can also help you with your ethical will.

An obituary includes your age, place of birth, cause of death, occupation, college degrees, military service, organizational memberships, any outstanding accomplishments, names of survivors in the immediate family, and names of any memorials set up in lieu of flowers.

As for a eulogy, contemplate these questions:

- How would I like to be remembered?
- What life experiences will I always treasure?
- What am I proud of?

Then write with these guidelines:

- I will be remembered for ...
- What do I value about myself?
- How have I impacted the world?
- Who has been closest to me?
- What adjectives best describe me?
- What has been most worthwhile in my life?
- What has given me purpose and meaning?
- My treasured life experiences are ...

After you have written your obituary and eulogy, read them every year. Notice how things shift in your life, which is another reflection on impermanence. You can also place your obituary in a drawer frequently opened, and use it as a reminder of your impending death.

Appendix 3: Depression and Grief[1]

Grief and depression are different. It is possible to grieve without being depressed, but many of the feelings are similar. Grief encompasses the emotional, physical, behavioral, spiritual, and cognitive responses to loss. Depression is a medical disorder, like diabetes or heart disease, which can be diagnosed and treated. Depression, like grief, affects people holistically, involving the body, our moods, and our thoughts.

Classic signs of depression include sadness and crying; fatigue; difficulty thinking clearly or paying attention; loss of appetite and weight loss; withdrawal; feelings of worthlessness, guilt, or hopelessness; and lack of interest or pleasure in normal activities.

When someone has been living with depression prior to a loss, it's important to deal with the depression and bereavement as separate issues. Depression can deepen and complicate an individual's response to loss. It limits one's ability to have insight into the grieving process, and increases the likelihood of overwhelm. This sense of paralysis can prevent a person from getting support. To progress in the bereavement process, it's essential that the depressive symptoms be recognized and treated.

Symptoms That Suggest a Bereaved Person Is Also Depressed

These include
- intense feelings of guilt not related to the bereavement
- thoughts of suicide or a preoccupation with dying
- feelings of worthlessness
- markedly slow speech and movements, or lying in bed doing nothing all day
- prolonged or severe inability to function—unable to work, socialize, or enjoy any leisure activity

- ▸ prolonged hallucinations of the deceased, or hallucinations unrelated to the bereavement

WHO IS AT RISK FOR DEPRESSION AFTER A LOSS?

It is difficult to judge who will or won't suffer depression after a significant loss. When symptoms of worthlessness, hopelessness, guilt, apathy, or expressions of depressed mood persist beyond two months, get evaluated for depression. If complicating factors such as alcohol or drug use, severe anxiety, suicidal ideation, or poor self-care emerge, seek immediate psychiatric evaluation. Risk factors thought to increase the chance of depression include

- ▸ a previous history of depression
- ▸ current substance abuse problems
- ▸ history of significant past trauma
- ▸ intense grief or depressive symptoms early in the grief reaction
- ▸ few social supports
- ▸ little experience of death

TREATMENT FOR GRIEF AND DEPRESSION

The support of family and friends is invaluable to a bereaved person. Sadness after bereavement is natural. It's normal to want to discuss the deceased and to become upset while doing so. Sharing responses to a loss can support the grieving process.

Without a thorough history, physicians, counselors, and psychiatrists sometimes make the mistake of assuming that a bereaved person is depressed. It's important for bereaved people to share their history of loss when seeking treatment or support.

Grief counseling can help the mourning process by allowing someone to work through the stages of grief while being properly held. Healthy holding environments apply not only to those dying but to those left behind as well. The goals of grief counseling include

- ▸ accepting the loss and talking about it
- ▸ identifying and expressing feelings related to the loss (anger, guilt, anxiety, helplessness, sadness)
- ▸ living without the deceased and making decisions alone
- ▸ separating emotionally and forming new relationships
- ▸ the provision of support

- identifying ways of coping that suit the bereaved
- explaining the grieving process

If depression is thought to be present, then antidepressants can be an effective part of treatment. Antidepressants can treat the depression, but they don't have an effect on the underlying grief. Untreated depression, however, makes it extremely difficult to grieve effectively.

Depressive Grief vs. Depression

At times during a grief process, the bereaved may experience depressive grief, which acts as a time out for grieving persons. It slows everything down, and gives the person valuable time to digest experience. Depressive grief differs from clinical or chronic depression in the following ways:

Depressive Grief	Depression
mood varies	consistently low mood
able to experience some pleasure	unable to experience pleasure or withdrawn
responds to comfort and support	rejects any/all comfort or support
can express anger appropriately/ openly	anger is turned inward; may complain but does not directly express anger
relates depressed features to loss	does not correlate depression with any particular life event
preoccupied with the loss	preoccupied with self-blame
has *transient* physical complaints	has *chronic* physical complaints
expressed guilt over some aspects of loss	pervasive feelings of guilt about everything
personality remains intact	dramatic, prolonged personality change
self-esteem is intact	lack of self-esteem is pronounced
can feel hopeful at times	feels hopeless, helpless

What Might I Expect When I Am Grieving? Common Dimensions of Grief[2]

The following list can help you realize that you are not alone in your difficult feelings, and that these feelings are normal after a loss. Because grief is unfamiliar, we don't know what to expect, or the range of possible reactions.

Feelings
- shock, numbness, denial, disbelief
- anxiety, fear, panic
- loss, emptiness
- loneliness
- sadness, depression
- loss of pleasure
- hurt, frustration
- helplessness, hopelessness
- explosive emotions—anger, hate, resentment, jealousy
- guilt, regret
- disorganization, confusion
- relief, emancipation
- reconciliation, re-establishment

Thoughts
- disbelief
- confusion
- preoccupation with the deceased
- sense of presence
- lack of concentration
- trouble remembering things

Behaviors
- absent-minded behavior
- crying and sobbing
- restlessness, inability to sit still
- trying to "stay busy"
- visiting places or carrying objects which remind you of the deceased
- treasuring objects belonging to the deceased

- avoiding reminders of the deceased
- experiencing "grief attacks"—sudden acute upsurges of grief
- dreams of the deceased

Social Dimensions

- social withdrawal
- fearful of being alone
- dependent, clingy behavior
- surrounding yourself with others as a form of distraction
- irritable
- moody
- attempts to replace the loss
- changes in role, status, family system

Physical Dimensions

- fatigue, lack of energy
- hollowness in the stomach, stomach-ache, or other gastrointestinal problems
- sleep difficulties—too much or too little; interrupted sleep
- weight loss or weight gain, with associated appetite changes
- feelings of emptiness and heaviness
- heart palpitations, trembling, shaking, hot flashes, and other indications of anxiety
- nervousness, tension, agitation, irritability
- shortness of breath
- headache
- muscle aches and pains
- chest pain, pressure, or discomfort

Spiritual

- searching for meaning
- asking the "why" questions
- mystical experiences
- reassessing values, beliefs, and priorities
- if you believe in God, feeling anger toward him-her, or feeling abandoned
- exploring new dimensions of faith

And finally, Beth Patterson shares what not to say, and what is helpful to say, to those who are grieving.

- ► What not to say: "He's better off." "It was her time." "Don't cry, be strong." "It was the will of the divine." "The universe doesn't give us more than we can handle."
- ► What is helpful to say: "It's okay to cry." "This must be so hard for you." "I don't know what to say." "Just know how much we love you." "I will call you tomorrow."

Notes

Introduction

First epigraph drawn from Anyen Rinpoche, *Dying with Confidence: A Tibetan Buddhist Guide to Preparing for Death*, translated by Allison Graboski (Boston, MA: Wisdom Publications, 2010), 3. Second epigraph from William Shakespeare, *Measure for Measure*, Act III, Scene I.

1. "Bardo" is translated as "gap," "interval," "intermediate state," "transitional process," or "in between."

2. In *The Tibetan Book of the Dead: Liberation Through Understanding in the Between*, composed by Padma Sambhava, discovered by Karma Lingpa, translated by Robert A. F. Thurman (New York: Bantam Books, 1994), 28–29.

3. Death is therefore viewed as the greatest obstacle in life for it is the termination of it. If we can relate to death properly, however, this greatest obstacle transforms into the greatest opportunity. There are four classic obstacles in Buddhism, four *maras*. *Mara*, sometimes called the Buddhist "devil," means "murder," or "destruction," and is the embodiment of death. Mara represents anything that interferes with the spiritual path and as *mrtyu-mara* (the Lord of Death) is the second of the four maras—*skandha-mara* (mara of the aggregate factors of experience), *mrtyu-mara* (mara of death), *klesa-mara* (mara of disturbing emotions), and *devaputra-mara* (mara of the son of the gods). If approached properly, however, death doesn't interfere with the path. It *becomes* the path.

4. Lama Zopa Rinpoche, *Advice and Practices for Death and Dying for the Benefit of Self and Others* (Portland: FPMT, Inc., 2003), 5.

5. *The Tibetan Book of the Dead: The Great Liberation Through Hearing in the Bardo*, by Guru Rinpoche, according to Karma Lingpa; trans. Francesca Fremantle and Chögyam Trungpa (Boston: Shambhala Publications, 1975), 78.
   "This" refers to distraction. "This" can also refer to the bardo altogether. Relating to the bardos without distraction is the dividing line that separates buddhas from sentient beings.

6. Of the many texts dealing with karma, one of the principal source texts is the *Abhidharmakosabhasyam* by Vasubandhu (translated from the French by Leo

M. Pruden in 4 volumes; Berkeley: Asian Humanities Press, 1988). See vol. 2, pp. 551–690. For teachings on rebirth and realms of existence, see vol. 2, pp. 365–473. For a brief but elegant argument about the logic of reincarnation, see the Dalai Lama's introduction to *Meditations on Living, Dying and Loss: Ancient Knowledge for a Modern World, from the first complete translation of The Tibetan Book of the Dead*, edited by Graham Coleman and Thupten Jinpa, translated by Gyurme Dorje (London: Penguin Books, 2005), xxi–xxviii.

7. For views of other ancient and modern traditions, see Christopher Jay Johnson and Marsha G. McGee, eds., *How Different Religions View Death and Afterlife* (Philadelphia: The Charles Press, 1998); and see Gary Doore, ed., *What Survives? Contemporary Explorations of Life After Death* (Los Angeles: Jeremy P. Tharcher, 1990). For different views within Buddhism, see Carl B. Becker, *Breaking the Circle: Death and the Afterlife in Buddhism* (Carbondale: Southern Illinois University Press, 1993).

   Thrangu Rinpoche was once asked why Buddhism talks so much about pain, suffering, and death, which the questioner found depressing. He asked Rinpoche why Buddhism couldn't be like other religions, or even New Age schools, who paint a more cheerful picture of life and the beyond. After listening to the young man complain about this dark side of Buddhism, Rinpoche simply replied, "Suffering, pain, and death are not Buddhist inventions."

8. Carl Becker writes, "[T]he heavens, judgments, and ghostly scenarios described by other religious traditions have equal claims to validity; the afterlife is culturally relative insofar as its imagery is projected by the perceiver, and the perceiver has been conditioned by the culture in which he was educated" (*Breaking the Circle*, 103).

9. For a study on cultural translation, see Dzogchen Ponlop Rinpoche, *Rebel Buddha: On the Road to Freedom* (Boston: Shambhala Publications, 2010).

10. Becker, *Breaking the Circle*, 87.

11. On her website www.inspirationandchai.com, palliative care nurse Bronnie Ware summarizes her book *The Top Five Regrets of the Dying: A Life Transformed by the Dearly Departing* (Bloomington, IN: Balboa Press, 2011) in these five points:

    1. *I wish I'd had the courage to live a life true to myself, not the life others expected of me.* This was the most common regret of all. When people realize that their life is almost over and look back clearly on it, it is easy to see how many dreams have gone unfulfilled. Most people had not honored even a half of their dreams and had to die knowing that it was due to choices they had made, or not made. . . . Health brings a freedom very few realize, until they no longer have it.

    2. *I wish I hadn't worked so hard.* This came from every male patient that I nursed. They missed their children's youth and their partner's companionship. Women also spoke of this regret, but as most were from an older genera-

tion, many of the female patients had not been breadwinners. All of the men I nursed deeply regretted spending so much of their lives on the treadmill of a work existence.

3. *I wish I'd had the courage to express my feelings.* Many people suppressed their feelings in order to keep peace with others. As a result, they settled for a mediocre existence and never became who they were truly capable of becoming. Many developed illnesses relating to the bitterness and resentment they carried as a result.

4. *I wish I had stayed in touch with my friends.* Often they would not truly realize the full benefits of old friends until their dying weeks and it was not always possible to track them down. Many had become so caught up in their own lives that they had let golden friendships slip by over the years. There were many deep regrets about not giving friendships the time and effort that they deserved. Everyone misses their friends when they are dying.

5. *I wish that I had let myself be happier.* This is a surprisingly common one. Many did not realize until the end that happiness is a choice. They had stayed stuck in old patterns and habits. The so-called 'comfort' of familiarity overflowed into their emotions, as well as their physical lives. Fear of change had them pretending to others, and to their selves, that they were content, when deep within, they longed to laugh properly and have silliness in their life again.

12. Michel de Montaigne, *The Essays of Michel de Montaigne*, translated and edited by M. A. Screech (London: Allen Lane, 1991), 95.

13. Sogyal Rinpoche, *Glimpse After Glimpse: Daily Reflections on Living and Dying* (New York: HarperOne, 1995), 28.

CHAPTER 1: WHAT TO DO FOR YOURSELF BEFORE YOU DIE

First epigraph from Sakyong Mipham Rinpoche, talk at Shambhala Mountain Center, June 22, 2011. Second epigraph from Sogyal Rinpoche, *The Tibetan Book of Living and Dying* (San Francisco: HarperCollins, 1993), 14.

1. The Dalai Lama, *Kindness, Clarity, and Insight*, translated and edited by Jeffrey Hopkins (Ithaca, NY: Snow Lion Publications, 1984), 20.

2. *Bodhichitta* means "awakened heart-mind" and is the heart of Mahayana Buddhism. It is compassion, love, and kindness toward self and other, likened to the unconditional love a mother has for her child. Bodhichitta is expressing this kind of love for all beings. Dilgo Khyentse Yangsi Rinpoche said, "If you put all the Buddha's teaching into one word—it's to have a good heart."

3. Lama Zopa Rinpoche, *Advice and Practices for Death and Dying for the Benefit of Self and Others*, 5.

4. Tenga Rinpoche, talk at Karma Dzong, Halifax, Nova Scotia, December 6, 1991, translated by Karma Tsültrim Palmo.

5. The Dalai Lama, *The Path to Enlightenment*, edited and translated by Glenn H. Mullin (Ithaca, NY: Snow Lion Publications, 1995), 31.

6. Sakyong Mipham Rinpoche, talk at Shambhala Mountain Center, "Hearing, Contemplating, Meditating," July 6, 1999.

7. What we know as *The Tibetan Book of the Dead* is the translation of only three of fourteen chapters. Coleman edited the first complete translation, a seminal contribution. These fourteen chapters are themselves part of a greater cycle of teachings (associated with the Guhyagarbha Tantra) that extends to more than sixty-five individual texts. See *The Tibetan Book of the Dead: The Great Liberation by Hearing in the Intermediate States* by Padmasambhava; revealed by Terton Karma Lingpa; edited by Graham Coleman and Thubten Jinpa; translated by Gyurme Dorje (New York: Viking, 2006).

8. Coleman, *Meditations on Living, Dying, and Loss*, xiv, xv.

9. Ibid., xxvii, xxviii.

10. Mindfulness is the meditation common to all schools of Buddhism. It is the ground meditation upon which all subsequent meditations are based. Without a solid foundation in mindfulness, all the other practices become shaky. Shamatha instruction, as the way to cultivate mindfulness, is best received from a qualified meditation instructor, but there are many books that describe the process. See Sakyong Mipham Rinpoche's *Turning the Mind into an Ally* (New York: Riverhead Books, 2003). B. Alan Wallace is one of the principal advocates of shamatha from a Tibetan perspective; see *The Attention Revolution: Unlocking the Power of the Focused Mind* (Boston, MA: Wisdom Publications, 2006) and *Stilling the Mind: Shamatha Teachings from Düdjom Lingpa's Vajra Essence* (Boston, MA: Wisdom Publications, 2011). See also Jon Kabat-Zinn's *Wherever You Go, There You Are: Mindfulness Meditation in Everyday Life* (New York: Hyperion, 1994).

    Khenpo Tsültrim Gyamtso Rinpoche teaches about three forms of mindfulness. The first is "contrived mindfulness," which is one of the mental factors, and as such does dissolve when the mental factors dissolve into luminosity (see "Inner Dissolution" in chapter 3). The second, more evolved type is "effortless mindfulness," which is the mindfulness that is aware of the true nature of mind. As realization increases, mindfulness matures even further into the third type, "spontaneous mindfulness," which is nonconceptual and aware. It is these latter two forms of mindfulness that do not die. In this section, formless shamatha is the gateway into these later two forms of deathless mindfulness.

11. An equation for suffering, which suggests one way to work with it, is: suffering equals pain plus resistance. Subtract the resistance, and complex suffering dissolves into simple pain.

12. The bardo of dharmata occurs between each and every thought (the silent gap between thoughts), between each and every day (deep dreamless sleep), and between each and every life. Death is like an extended pause between two

breaths. See also figure 3, the hourglass, and how the fourth moment is the timeless point in the center. In this context, the top of the hourglass can also represent the past, the center point represents the present (and the portal to the fourth moment), and the bottom represents the future. See Padmasambhava's *Natural Liberation: Padmasambhava's Teachings on the Six Bardos*, commentary by Gyatrul Rinpoche, translated by B. Alan Wallace (Boston, MA: Wisdom Publications), 62, for reference to "the fourth time."

13. B. K. S. Iyengar, *The Concise Light on Yoga* (New York: Schocken Books Inc., 1980), 9.

14. When we become so absorbed in something other than ourselves that we lose ourselves in some task, it is because we have found some degree of the fourth moment. David Brooks writes: "Fulfillment is a byproduct of how people engage their tasks . . . . Most of us are egotistical and most are self-concerned most of the time, but it's nonetheless true that life comes to a point only in those moments when the self dissolves into some task. The purpose in life is not to find yourself. It's to lose yourself." (*The Denver Post*, June 1, 2011). The trick is to lose yourself properly. If you get lost in thoughts, memories, anticipations, or an entire life, that is just distraction, the opposite of shamatha. To lose yourself properly is to find the fourth moment. This puts you on the spot of reality, not off of it.

15. See note 10 above on the three stages of mindfulness and its fruition as spontaneous mindfulness, the nonconceptual zone of presence. Also see Mihaly Csikszentmihalyi, *Flow: The Psychology of Optimal Experience* (New York: HarperCollins Publishers, 1990). There are nine stages of shamatha. Achieving shamatha means reaching the ninth stage.

16. Jamgön Kongtrul, *The Treasury of Knowledge: Esoteric Instructions*, trans. Sarah Harding (Ithaca, NY: Snow Lion Publications, 2007), 200.

17. See Sakyong Mipham, *Turning the Mind into an Ally*, 36–114, for meditation instructions, or www.andrewholecek.com.

18. This is why dream yoga, discussed below, is a diamond of a practice for preparing for the bardos, and why shamatha-vipashyana is the best way to prepare for dream yoga. This is also our first glimpse of the power of equanimity, a topic we will return to many times. Everything that arises is equal in being mind only. See Karl Brunnhölzl, *Luminous Heart: The Third Karmapa on Consciousness, Wisdom, and Buddha Nature* (Ithaca, NY: Snow Lion Publications), 14–78, for more on the subtleties of "mind only."

19. These brief liturgies, also called the "four reversals," were composed by Padmasambhava. They can be viewed as representing the excursions Prince Siddhartha took outside his palace that eventually transformed the young prince into the Buddha. During these trips Siddhartha encountered old age, sickness, and death, developing the renunciation that transformed him from a "*chipa*," or "outsider," into a "*nangpa*," or "insider." *Nangpa* is the Tibetan word for

"Buddhist." Until we enter the spiritual path, we are all "outsiders." We are infatuated with materialism and lost in samsara. The four reminders turn the mind in, facing it in the proper direction. The Buddha discovered that enlightenment is an inside job. For more on the four reminders, see Thrangu Rinpoche, *The Four Foundations of Buddhist Practice* (Boulder, CO: Namo Buddha Publications, 2001).

20. Distraction manifests moment-to-moment (microgeny) or life-to-life (ontogeny).

   Alan Wallace writes about how easy it is to get lost: "Well, there was this really cool video game . . . then this really good movie came on . . . then their friends wanted to go out for a beer and they said, 'Why not?' . . . and then there was this really interesting relationship they got into . . . and then, and then . . . and then their life is over." *Stilling the Mind*, 41.

21. Composed in English by the Vidyadhara the Venerable Chögyam Trungpa Rinpoche. Copyright 1974 by Chögyam Trungpa and used with special permission. All rights reserved.

22. Sogyal Rinpoche says, "Ask yourself these two questions: Do I remember at every moment that I am dying, and that everyone and everything else is, and so treat all beings at all times with compassion? Has my understanding of death and impermanence become so keen and so urgent that I am devoting every second to the pursuit of enlightenment? If you can answer "yes" to both of these, *then* you *really* understand impermanence." *Glimpse After Glimpse*, 27.

23. Anne Carolyn Klein, *Heart Essence of the Vast Expanse: A Story of Transmission* (Ithaca, NY: Snow Lion Publications, 2009), 88.

24. Sam Harris, *The End of Faith: Religion, Terror, and the Future of Reason* (New York: W. W. Norton and Company, 2004), 38.

25. Of the five paths leading to enlightenment, most serious practitioners "save" their lives on the first path, the path of accumulation—the path of investment. This turning from squandering (this life) to investing (in future lives) is a manifestation of turning from a *chipa* (outsider) to a *nangpa* (insider). Outsiders splurge; insiders invest.

26. Lama Zopa Rinpoche and Kathleen McDonald, *Wholesome Fear: Transforming Your Anxiety about Impermanence and Death* (Boston: Wisdom Publications, 2010), 52.

27. Sakyong Mipham Rinpoche, talk at Shambhala Mountain Center, "Introduction to the Twelve Nidanas," July 2, 1999.

28. The three kinds of suffering, along with the four reminders, should be contemplated by those left behind: the suffering of suffering, the suffering of change, and all-pervasive suffering. These seven reflections deflate any samsaric aspiration. They can be viewed as subsets of the unpopular but uncompromising first noble truth, the truth of suffering, which says that if you take a close look, there is no happy ending in samsara.

The four reminders are reminiscent of the Christian practice of *memento mori*, "remembering your mortality." Remembering that you will die helps you live to the fullest. Memento mori is itself part of the "four last things," the Christian awareness of the ultimate realities awaiting humanity and the universe: death, judgment, heaven, and hell.

29. In the first phase of the bardo of dharmata, when the nature of mind is laid bare, Buddhism asserts that what is *revealed* is the same for everyone, but it is not *experienced* the same way. The nature of mind is the experience of emptiness, which means that the experience is empty of any surface structures. It is formless. There is nothing but formless awareness, raw and naked mind itself, before any conceptual or cultural clothing is placed upon it. No-thing is obscuring the nature of mind. For most people, this no-thingness (emptiness), even though it is revealed, is actually not experienced. Unless you have some familiarity with emptiness before you die, it is "experienced" as no experience, i.e., you black out. It's the same thing that happens when we fall into deep dreamless sleep, which for most people is simply unconsciousness. It's only when the mind moves away from its naked, empty, and formless nature and starts to put on the clothes of habitual pattern that experience becomes conscious.

This is where the difference between consciousness and wisdom is important. Consciousness is always dualistic; it always perceives something "other." Wisdom is nondualistic. The reason we go unconscious in dreamless sleep and death is because these domains are nondualistic—there is literally no-thing to experience. Formless awareness either recognizes itself, which is wisdom, or it does not. Dualistic consciousness (ego) goes blank when nondualistic wisdom is revealed. We will return to this difficult but important theme when we discuss the bardo of dharmata in chapter 3, and again in the introductory section of chapter 4.

30. Thrangu Rinpoche, *Journey of the Mind: Putting the Teachings on the Bardo into Effective Practice* (Vancouver, B.C.: Karme Thekchen Choling, 1997), 107.

31. Ibid., 115.

32. For the serious student, additional doctrinal preparation can be gained by reading the books in the bibliography. For the academically inclined, Dzogchen Ponlop Rinpoche's *Mind Beyond Death* (Ithaca, NY: Snow Lion Publications, 2006) and Francesca Fremantle's *Luminous Emptiness: Understanding the Tibetan Book of the Dead* (Boston: Shambhala Publications, 2001) are indispensible. For a more accessible study, Sogyal Rinpoche's *The Tibetan Book of Living and Dying* is without peer. *Journey of the Mind*, by Thrangu Rinpoche, is pithy and practical, as is Chökyi Nyima Rinpoche's *The Bardo Guidebook* (Kathmandu: Rangjung Yeshe Publications, 1991) and *Peaceful Death, Joyful Rebirth* by Tulku Thondup Rinpoche (Boston: Shambhala Publications, 2005).

33. For tonglen instruction, see *Start Where You Are: A Guide to Compassionate*

Living by Pema Chödrön (Boston: Shambhala Publications, 1994), or go to andrewholecek.com for a guided audio instruction.

34. Lama Zopa Rinpoche and Kathleen McDonald, *Wholesome Fear*, 27.

35. This term comes from the mahamudra tradition. Bon dzogchen, according to Tenzin Wangyal Rinpoche, has practices similar in spirit: "For example, the A-Tri system of dzogchen offers a group of successive practices in which one learns to maintain awareness while engaging in various virtuous, neutral, and nonvirtuous activities." See *Tibetan Yogas of Body, Speech, and Mind* (Ithaca, NY: Snow Lion Publications, 2011), 85.

36. These practices are considered tantric in spirit because tantra, or Vajrayana, is about transforming poison into medicine. A tantric practitioner is an alchemist, transmuting lead into gold, confusion into wisdom. Nothing is rejected in tantra. Everything is brought to the path and transformed into awakening. At higher levels of tantra, a practitioner will perform activities that would normally bind one to samsara and transform them into activities that liberate one from samsara.

37. Jon Kabat-Zinn has dedicated much of his life to bringing mindfulness into pain, or pain into mindfulness. See his book *Full Catastrophe Living: Using the Wisdom of Your Body and Mind to Face Stress, Pain, and Illness* (New York: Delacorte Press, 1990).

38. Dzogchen Ponlop, *Mind Beyond Death*, 191–193.

39. Ibid., 192.

40. Korde Rushen, a preparatory practice to dzogchen, is another reverse meditation, and a way to prepare for the bardo of becoming. Part of this practice involves diving into each of the six realms (god, jealous gods, human, animal, hungry ghost, and hell), exaggerating these six principal expressions of samsaric mind. By voluntarily doing so we can establish a new relationship to these states of mind now, which, without such preparation, will become states of reality as we take literal birth in one of those realms at the end of the bardo of becoming.

Charnel ground meditation is a tantric reverse meditation. If you can stay in the charnel ground and practice, you can arise as a siddha and transform the charnel ground into a pure land.

41. This very fear, which hurls us into our next rebirth, becomes the basis upon which we then unconsciously live our entire life. Horror movies work with a gross level of this fear but provide one place to start. Fear is the primordial samsaric emotion, the mood of the self-contraction, that runs our life and that has its genesis in the bardos. Establishing a relationship to fear, especially the fear of groundlessness—the truth of our nonexistence—is of critical importance.

42. There are twenty-seven states of samsaric existence, divided into three realms: desire, form, and formless. (Sometimes the three realms are divided into more than twenty-seven states, and sometimes less.) Entry into each realm, the form we will take in our next life unless we are born into a pure land, is gained by

cultivating twenty-seven respective states of mind. Pure Land practice cultivates elevated states of mind as a more enlightened alternative to these twenty-seven samsaric states.

43. These are just a few of the benefits; see *Peaceful Death, Joyful Rebirth* by Tulku Thondup for one of the rare Tibetan treatments of this subject.

44. As a student of Shambhala Buddhism, I asked Thrangu Rinpoche, who is familiar with this tradition and is a dear friend of Chögyam Trungpa Rinpoche (the Druk Sakyong) who founded it, if students of Shambhala Buddhism should go to the pure land of Shambhala or to Sukhavati. After reflecting at some length, Rinpoche replied that those who have a strong connection to this earth should aspire to be reborn in Shambhala, and everyone else should aspire to go to Sukhavati. My own feelings on his response is that those who have a strong desire to serve and protect this earth are the ones who should aspire to be reborn in Shambhala. When Tulku Thondup was asked about Shambhala as pure land, he said, "It is the closest pure land to earth." The Sakyongs who head the Shambhala lineage are literally "earth (*sa*) protectors (*kyong*)." Students of this tradition have their own liturgies for rebirth into Shambhala, composed by Sakyong Mipham Rinpoche. (Traditionally, one gets to Shambhala via the Kalachakra empowerment, not via phowa.)

On a recent trip to Nepal, some of the lamas I consulted said that the Seventeenth Karmapa has been talking about, and writing practices for, a "new" pure land with the same level of access as Sukhavati. Some of the unique characteristics of this pure land are that the buddha who presides over it (each pure land has a presiding buddha) is married and a householder. The vision of this pure land is mostly secular, similar in this regard to Shambhala. There is also a unique connecting principle of this pure land. If a person has to appear in court, for example, the judge and the police in the court are the same age and size as that person; or if a person goes to the doctor, the doctor also manifests as the same age and size as the patient. There are no power hierarchies, and communication and connection are easy. (Personal conversations with Lama Tenam and Ari Goldfield.)

The first bhumi, or "ground," is when one has a direct realization of emptiness. This is also the third path, the path of seeing, where you first see emptiness. Some teachers state that with the attainment of the first bhumi, one attains immortality. The remaining nine bhumis are developing an increasing familiarity with emptiness, and this constitutes the fourth path, the path of meditation, or literally, the path of familiarity (*gom*).

45. Kalu Rinpoche, *Secret Buddhism: Vajrayana Practices* (San Francisco: ClearPoint Press, 1995), 102.

46. Some teachers assert that you must receive the Amitabha or Chenrezig empowerments in order to arrive in Sukhavati. See Kalu Rinpoche, *Secret Buddhism*, 102. See Tulku Thondup's *Peaceful Death, Joyful Rebirth*, appendix A, on the

four causes for rebirth and a liturgical practice. The Pure Land sutras are available from the Numata Center for Buddhist Translation and Research.

A friend of mine was at the bedside when a sangha member was dying. She told me that just before he died his face lit up and, beaming with a smile, his parting words were, "The taxi to Sukhavati has arrived."

47. See "The Power of Merit" later in this book. Merit is virtually synonymous with good karma and is a cornerstone in Pure Land doctrine. Merit is what created Sukhavati and what is transferred to us by Amitabha that enables us to be reborn there. Good deeds are the best way to accumulate merit. See the many references to merit in Luis O. Gómez, *The Land of Bliss: The Paradise of the Buddha of Measureless Light* (Honolulu: University of Hawaii Press, 1996).

48. Tulku Thondup, *Peaceful Death Joyful Rebirth*, 239.

49. You can order it in a nicely formatted version from Karma Triyana Dharmachakra at www.namsebangdzo.com, or download it online.

50. "Vajrayana," or "indestructible vehicle," is the third of the three yanas, or vehicles, of Buddhism. It has the same view as the second vehicle of the Mahayana, or "great vehicle," but more methods for realizing that view. It is virtually synonymous with Tibetan Buddhism, and is the guiding yana of this book. The first vehicle is the Hinayana, the "lesser, or narrow," vehicle. See Part Four of *The Buddhist Handbook: A Complete Guide to Buddhist Schools, Teaching, Practice, and History* by John Snelling (Rochester, VT: Inner Traditions International, 1991) for a brief summary, or Reginald Ray's *Indestructible Truth: The Living Spirituality of Tibetan Buddhism* (Boston: Shambhala Publications, 2000) and *Secrets of the Vajra World: The Tantric Buddhism of Tibet* (Boston: Shambhala Publications, 2001) for a comprehensive exploration of the three yanas.

51. They lie at the center of the Wheel of Life, and are represented by a pig (ignorance), rooster (passion), and snake (aggression), each feeding on each other and emerging from each other. Fundamentally, aggression emerges from passion, which emerges from ignorance—the root of the other two roots. See figure 4.

52. Scholars estimate that Pure Land teachings comprise over 13 percent of all the scriptures in the Chinese canon. Over 290 sutras and shastras deal with Pure Land doctrine. This does not include all the teachings on Sukhavati found in the tantras. See *Approaching the Land of Bliss: Religious Praxis in the Cult of Amitabha* (Honolulu: University of Hawaii Press, 2004), edited by Richard Payne and Kenneth Tanaka, chapter 1, and the series of articles I wrote for *Bodhi* magazine, beginning in the Fall of 2007.

53. When Thrangu Rinpoche was asked about the symbolic interpretation of Sukhavati, he was adamant that it's not just a symbol. He asserted that Sukhavati exists and dismissed the cleverness of viewing Sukhavati as merely a heuristic. From a tantric Pure Land point of view, any environmental manifestation, good or bad, comes from the mind. It does not truly exist externally, from its own side, out there, and independent of us.

54. Each syllable in this mantra is associated with one of the six realms and can block rebirth into these realms. OM blocks entry into the god realms; MA blocks the jealous god realms; NI, the human realm; PAD, the animal realm; ME, the hungry ghost realm; and HUM, the hell realms. This mantra, perhaps the most famous in Tibetan Buddhism, also serves to block entry into each of the psychological states associated with the six realms, thereby preventing moment-to-moment rebirth in samsara: OM blocks pride (of the gods); MA blocks envy (of the jealous gods); NI blocks passion (of humans); PAD blocks ignorance (of animals); ME blocks greed (of hungry ghosts); and HUM blocks aggression (of hell realm beings). If left unchecked during life, each of these six psychological realms can propel a person into its corresponding ontological realm after death. See "The Benefits of Powerful Mantras," in *Advice and Practices for Death and Dying for the Benefit of Self and Others*, a commentary by Lama Zopa Rinpoche, for the unimaginable benefits of reciting this mantra.

55. This is one reason we visualize deities on top of our head in deity yoga. As usual, there are variations in the preparation for sudden death. For example, you can replace Chenrezig's mantra with that of Amitabha, OM AMIDEWA HRIH. Instead of closing the wrong doors, with this mantra you open the right one. The point is to keep it simple.

56. This is an exercise in prospective memory, which is remembering to do something in the future. It is a central practice in lucid dreaming/dream yoga, where one trains to remember to wake up while dreaming. Dzogchen Ponlop Rinpoche recommends that one prepare for sudden death by repeatedly flashing onto mahamudra or dzogchen awareness throughout the day. This can be tied to a prospective memory exercise. For example, every time you hear a plane, or a car honk, sensitize yourself to open your mind to pure awareness. Just instantly relax and open.

57. What about dying in your sleep? Is there any disadvantage to that? The only disadvantage for a practitioner is that they lose the opportunity to employ the law of proximate karma—unless they happen to be lucid dreaming or lucid sleeping when they die. (See note 60 below on the four forms of transitional karma.) So *nirmanakaya phowa* (what we usually think of as phowa) would not be an option. The practitioner also loses the opportunity to engage any other death practice that requires conscious awareness, like mantra recitation. For most people, dying in their sleep means the remaining three laws of karma would take over and play out: heavy, habitual, or random karma. However, there are four other forms of phowa which could be engaged if the person was a good practitioner. *Dharmakaya phowa* is essentially resting in the nature of mind, and takes place spontaneously for one versed in the formless meditations. *Sambhogakaya phowa* is the fruition of generation stage practice, and could also arise naturally as a result of the person's yidam practice. *Guru yoga phowa* is a devotion phowa, which would require more conscious effort. The fifth form of phowa, *celestial*, or *kechari phowa*, is a lucid dreaming phowa (associated with dream yoga in the

Six Yogas of Naropa). If you are trained in lucid dreaming/dream yoga, this is the phowa to use if you die in your sleep. See Thrangu Rinpoche, *Journey of the Mind*, 42–52.

Many people die in coma-like states or in sleep. It does not mean a second-class death. Strong practitioners will be fine no matter how they die. Other people will have to take refuge in the strength of their karma and in their ability to wake up in the bardos. This, yet again, is why proficiency in dream (or sleep) yoga is of such benefit. If the person can wake up to the fact that they are in the bardos, they can then use any of the techniques mentioned later in this book for negotiating those bardos skillfully. If they can't, they have to rely on their good karma.

58. The Four Noble Truths are (1) the truth of suffering; (2) the truth of the origin of suffering; (3) the truth of the cessation of suffering; and (4) the truth of the path leading to the cessation of suffering. The first two truths are the bad news truths; the second two truths are the good news truths.

59. Chögyam Trungpa, *The Truth of Suffering and the Path of Liberation*, ed. Judith L. Lief (Boston: Shambhala Publications, 2009), 22.

60. This tenet is based on the power of proximate karma, the second of the four types of karma that operate in any moment of transition, any bardo, and that dictate the form of the next moment or next life. Phowa, Pure Land practice, and dream yoga all take advantage of this second form of transitional karma. A Pure Land practitioner, for example, will recite countless Amitabha mantras as a way to pave the road for rebirth in Sukhavati. If you have Amitabha on your mind now, that can transport you to his pure land when you die.

These four types of karma are listed in order of power and importance: (1) heavy, or weighty karma, the karma that is the most intense; (2) proximate karma, that which is the nearest, or most immediately precedes the next moment or life; (3) habitual karma, the karma of our habits; (4) random karma, from past lives, or past moments. Proximate karma, and therefore phowa and Pure Land practice, works with the principle that the last thing on your mind before you enter a bardo tends to be the first thing on your mind when you come out of it. Working with proximate karma is like leaving a nice welcoming gift for yourself that greets you on the other side. See Jack Kornfield, *A Path With Heart: A Guide Through the Perils and Promises of Spiritual Life* (New York: Bantam Books, 1993), 277, for more on these four types of karma.

61. Sogyal Rinpoche, *The Tibetan Book of Living and Dying*, 224.

62. Milarepa, quoted in Sogyal Rinpoche, *Glimpse After Glimpse*, July 5.

63. Sogyal Rinpoche, *Glimpse After Glimpse*, April 13.

64. B. Alan Wallace, *Stilling the Mind*, 52.

65. Khenpo Karthar Rinpoche, talk on "Dying, Death, and the Intermediate State," given at Karma Triyana Dharmachakra, September 16, 1981, translated by Ngödup Tsering Burkhar.

66. To balance these assertions, I asked Thrangu Rinpoche how much we need to

worry about our next rebirth, and what to do about it. He said that if we are sincere practitioners with good hearts, and that if we help others and do our practice and study well, we will be fine. But even here, Thrangu Rinpoche is talking about the power of karma, and that if we create enough good karma then that karma will take good care of us.

67. Chögyam Trungpa, *Crazy Wisdom* (Boston: Shambhala Publications, 1991), 132.

68. Sogyal Rinpoche, *Glimpse After Glimpse*, February 24.

69. Anam Thubten, *No Self, No Problem* (Ithaca, NY: Snow Lion Publications, 2009), 50.

70. The trikaya was introduced by the Sarvastivada school of the Hinayana but developed in the Mahayana. The trikaya can be viewed as a *vertical* mandala or organizing template. They can be described in a progressive fashion or as manifesting simultaneously. When viewed simultaneously, the dharmakaya is seeing the openness, the emptiness, of whatever arises; the sambhogakaya is seeing the energetic, almost emotional or "color" quality; and the nirmanakaya is the clarity of the appearance itself.

71. Some masters place liberation at the level of the dharmakaya in phase one of the luminous bardo of dharmata, and liberation at the level of the sambhogakaya in phase two. The trikaya is also associated with realizing the twofold benefit: realizing the dharmakaya is the ultimate benefit for oneself; realizing the rupakayas (form kayas) of the sambhogakaya and nirmanakaya is the ultimate benefit for others.

72. Padmasambhava, quoted in Tsele Natsok Rangdrol, *The Mirror of Mindfulness: The Cycle of the Four Bardos* (Boston: Shambhala Publications, 1989), 73.

73. *Mahamudra* ("great seal") is the awakened nature of mind, and one of the highest teachings in Tibetan Buddhism. *Trekchö* ("cutting through") is a practice and teaching for cutting through to the awakened nature of mind. The *prajnaparamita sutras* are a vast body of teachings that describe emptiness from a Mahayana point of view, and *Madhyamaka* ("middle way") is a Mahayana tradition that rigorously explores the topic of emptiness.

74. Deity yoga, or yidam practice, is also called creation and completion phase meditation. Lama Yeshe refers to it as "evolutionary stage" practice. The creation phase (when you and your world arise out of emptiness and are visualized in a pure form) is designed to purify birth; the completion phase (when everything visualized dissolves back into emptiness) is designed to purify death.

Deity yoga lifts us into a more refined and complete sense of who we actually are. In essence we are a body of light and sound (the sambhogakaya), not just a clunky flesh and blood body (the nirmanakaya). See Jamgön Kongtrul, *Creation and Completion: The Essential Points of Tantric Meditation* (Boston: Wisdom Publications, 1996), 14–20, and Geshe Ngawang Dhargyey, *Kalacakra Tantra* (Dharamsala: Library of Tibetan Works and Archives, 1985), 94–95.

75. Forty-nine days is the amount of time most of us spend in the bardo of becoming. Forty-nine days is also the amount of time the Buddha spent after attaining enlightenment under the bodhi tree, before going into the world to teach. It was a period when he was deciding whether or not to teach (he thought his insights were so subtle and profound that no one would understand), and how to manifest in the world. His enlightenment was akin to the bardo of dharmata, the forty-nine days before he began to help others was akin to the bardo of becoming, and stepping into the world to teach was akin to the bardo of life.

   For more on the dark retreat, see *Wonders of the Natural Mind* by Tenzin Wangyal (Barrytown, NY: Station Hill Press, 1993); *Heart Drops of Dharmakaya: Dzogchen Practice of the Bon Tradition* by Shardza Tashi Gyaltsen (Ithaca, NY: Snow Lion Publications, 1993); or Trungpa Rinpoche's introduction to *The Tibetan Book of the Dead*. This is a practice you do not want to consider without preparation as well as direct permission and supervision by a qualified master. There is a fine line between enlightenment and madness, and this practice takes you to that line. The psychiatrist R. D. Laing said, "The mystic swims in the same ocean where the psychotic drowns."

76. Khenpo Gangshar, quoted in Khenchen Thrangu, *Vivid Awareness: The Mind Instructions of Khenpo Gangshar* (Boston: Shambhala Publications, 2011), 202.

77. Ibid.

78. Ibid., 204.

79. B. Alan Wallace produced a short video that goes through the shitro deities, with a background reading from the supplemental verses associated with *The Tibetan Book of the Dead*. See *Natural Liberation Through Contemplating the Peaceful and Wrathful Deities*, available from www.vimalavideo.org/other.html.

80. The lojong slogans are an entire path unto themselves. Dzigar Köngtrul Rinpoche's contribution in part 3 focuses on how these slogans apply to death.

81. Khenpo Karthar Rinpoche, *Bardo: Interval of Possibility*, translated by Yeshe Gyamtso (Woodstock, NY: KTD Publications, 2007), 55.

   Sleep and death are closely related. In Greek mythology, Morpheus (the god of dreams) and Thanatos (the god of death) are brothers. They are the sons of Hypnos, the god of sleep, who also represents ignorance. In other words, ignorance gives birth to death and dream. Because buddhas don't sleep at night, they also don't die. Sleep, dream, and death also share the same Sanskrit root, *svap*.

82. Khenpo Tsültrim Gyamtso Rinpoche, talk on "Dream Yoga" at Karme Chöling, June 1998, translated by Jim Scott.

83. Some teachers assert that the number seven is not to be taken literally, and that it implies the ability to regularly have lucid dreams. See Padmasambhava, *Natural Liberation*, 161.

   B. Alan Wallace, Lama Tharchin Rinpoche, Tenzin Wangyal, and Stephen LaBerge conduct dream yoga programs, as do I. There is a difference between dream yoga and lucid dreaming. Lucid dream practice shows you how to wake up in your dreams, which often results in all sorts of samsaric activities. Dream yoga goes a step further: after becoming lucid, you start to practice in the dream, not indulge it.

For instructions on lucid dreaming and dream yoga, see B. Alan Wallace, *Dreaming Yourself Awake: Lucid Dreaming and Tibetan Dream Yoga for Insight and Transformation* (Boston and London: Shambhala Publications, 2012), and Tenzin Wangyal, *The Tibetan Yogas of Dream and Sleep* (Ithaca, NY: Snow Lion Publications, 1998).

84. Khenpo Karthar Rinpoche, *Bardo: Interval of Possibility*, 56.
85. Spoken extemporaneously by Rinpoche and translated by Ari Goldfield. Illusory form may seem like a contrived practice, but it's actually seeing things as they truly are. Gyaltrul Rinpoche says, "By training yourself in seeing the whole of the animate and inanimate world as being without inherent existence, it is not that you are simply superimposing this upon the world. Instead, this practice merely acts as a catalyst for gaining insight into the nature of reality. It begins as an imaginary process, but it leads to a direct perception of reality." In Padmasambhava, *Natural Liberation*, 149.
86. Sogyal Rinpoche, *Glimpse After Glimpse*, January 28.
87. Sakyong Mipham Rinpoche, talk on "The Four Dignities," Tatamagouche, Nova Scotia, August 2003.
88. The twenty-seven states comprise four in the formless realms, seventeen in the realm of form, and six in the realm of desire (which can be further subdivided into six god realms, four human realms, and at least sixteen hell realms). See Hisao Inagaki, *The Three Pure Land Sutras* (Berkeley: Numata Center for Buddhist Translation and Research, 1995), 116–118; or Patrul Rinpoche, *The Words of My Perfect Teacher*, translated by Padmakara Translation Group (San Francisco: HarperCollins, 1994).
89. For more on sutra phowa, see Glenn Mullin, *Living in the Face of Death: The Tibetan Tradition* (Ithaca, NY: Snow Lion Publications, 1998), 83. Qualified masters offer Vajrayana phowa transmission and instruction to the public. See *Dying with Confidence*, by Anyen Rinpoche, 83–91, for tantric instructions on phowa. There are other, more dubious "masters" offering similar programs, and one should be careful. If you're not sure, talk to someone who knows and whom you can trust.

In *The Tibetan Book of Living and Dying*, Sogyal Rinpoche describes "essential phowa," which is a general form of transference easily learned by anyone. See *The Tibetan Book of Living and Dying*, 214–217. Also, see "Finding a Spiritual Practice" in chapter 4 of this book.
90. Kalu Rinpoche, *Secret Buddhism*, 99.
91. Leaving from the anus leads to the hell realms; from the genitals leads to animal realm; from the navel, desire gods; from the mouth, hungry ghost; from the nose, human; from the ears, jealous gods; from the eyes, form gods; from the

top of the head, four fingers back, formless gods; from the top of the head, eight fingers back, pure lands. Chagdud Tulku Rinpoche said that dzogchen practitioners exit through a point in the forehead just above the eyes. For Shambhala Buddhists, this makes the practice of *lungta* more compelling.

92. What actually leaves after death is called the *indestructible bindu*. This is a very subtle "wind" (*prana*) supporting a very subtle mind. It's a sort of mind pearl. At death, the outer body collapses into the inner body, which is made up of channels (*nadi*), the winds (*prana*) that flow through them, and the "drops" (*bindu*) that ride on the wind. Trungpa Rinpoche said that bindu is consciousness. See chapter 3 of this book on the inner dissolution, and see Francesca Fremantle, *Luminous Emptiness*, 184–193.

93. The brahmarandhra is associated with the posterior fontanelle, the "soft spot" in infants that lies between the two parietal bones and the occipital bone of the skull. It is also associated with the *sahasrara chakra* in Hindu tantra, which symbolizes detachment from illusion. This is the most subtle chakra, related to pure consciousness, from which the other chakras emanate. When kundalini rises to this point, samadhi (union with God in Hinduism) is experienced.

94. These signs include itching, a pointed headache, loss of hair at the brahmarandhra, oozing of blood, pus, or lymph from that point, and eventually the ability to stick a piece of kusha grass (thin straw) into the top of the head. A number of people who have returned from near-death experiences, or out-of-body experiences, report having had a sucking sensation out the top of their head as they exited the body.

95. There are differing views about when to perform phowa. The most common teaching is to do so at the end of the outer dissolution, when you still have some breath control left. Others say phowa can be performed when any of the outer signs of death are occurring. You don't want to do it too early, for that amounts to suicide. Even though phowa is considered a "forceful method of liberation," once the signs occur (which tend to occur more rapidly if phowa can be practiced in the presence of a master) it can be performed at the moment of death through intention alone.

Tibetans believe that having animal skins or furs in the same room as the dying person can present an obstacle to phowa, and that smoking tends to block the central channel, making phowa more difficult.

96. Anyen Rinpoche, *Dying with Confidence*, 90.

97. Vajradhara, as quoted in Patrul Rinpoche, *The Words of My Perfect Teacher*, 356.

98. Guru Rinpoche, as quoted in Patrul Rinpoche, ibid.

99. Naropa, as quoted in Patrul Rinpoche, ibid. Naropa may be referring to a different way of counting the openings, the two ears and the two eyes generally count as one opening for each of the two (i.e., two instead of four). How he arrives at nine samsaric exits versus the usual eight is unclear.

100. Milarepa, as quoted in Patrul Rinpoche, ibid., 357.

101. Ibid., 365. For more on phowa see Patrul Rinpoche, *The Words of My Perfect Teacher*, 351–367; Chagdud Khadro, *P'howa Commentary: Instructions for the Practice of Consciousness Transference as Revealed by Rigdzen Longsal Nyinpo* (Junction City, CA: Padma Publishing, 1998); and Dzogchen Ponlop, *Mind Beyond Death*, 142–159. What we've been discussing here is *nirmanakaya phowa*. See note 57 above on the five classic forms of phowa.

102. Lama Yeshe, *Life, Death, and After Death* (Boston: Lama Yeshe Wisdom Archive, 2011), 95.

103. For more on these deities, see "The Peaceful and Wrathful Visions," page 83.

104. Thrangu Rinpoche, *Journey of the Mind*, 105.

105. Francesca Fremantle, *Luminous Emptiness*, 367.

106. The four opponent powers are another way to purify karma. They can be remembered as the "four Rs": (1) reliance: before a sacred object, teacher, or even visualization of such, you express your sincere and intense (2) regret for the negative act. You then make the firm (3) resolve never to repeat such a negative act. You then perform (4) the remedy of mantra recitation, merit accumulation, or any other positive act of purification. Some say this process can even be used to purify the karma of others. See Karma Lekshe Tsomo, *Into the Jaws of Yama, Lord of Death: Buddhism, Bioethics, and Death* (Albany, NY: State University of New York Press, 2006), 130, and Tulku Thondup, *Peaceful Death, Joyful Rebirth*, 214.

107. Mis-taking things to be truly existent is the biggest source of new karma. Because we take things so seriously and solidly, as being truly real, we react to things in a negative way, which creates negative karma. By seeing things as illusory, or empty, we no longer react so negatively, karma is cut, and liberation ensues. The entire Second Turning is about this purification, so the study of the Prajnaparamita and Madhyamaka is a principal form of purification. See "Blocking" in chapter 5 on what to do after death.

108. Along with these esoteric Vajrayana practices, I must mention the many longevity practices available in the Tibetan tradition, like Amitayus or Tara. These practices are not in preparation for death but to defer untimely death, for ourselves and even for others. See Glenn H. Mullin, *Living in the Face of Death*, 149–170, "The Longevity Yogas of the Bodhisattva of Life."

Even more esoteric is the virtually extinct practice of *drong-juk*, or "forceful projection to a new residence." In this practice, an older or ill person can eject their consciousness into the corpse of a recently deceased younger person, and like dropping old clothes and putting on new ones, take on a new life form and continue to practice the dharma. One can also evacuate one's body and project the consciousness of someone else into it. See Glenn H. Mullin, *Readings on the Six Yogas of Naropa* (Ithaca, NY: Snow Lion Publications, 1997), 68–69. I hesitate to mention these practices, fearing that their unbelievability may throw into question the other practices of the Tibetan tradition. But these practices, as mind-stretching as they are, have a place in Tibetan thanatology. Here one can understand why tantric methods are considered secret, for without proper preparation they are too far beyond the limits of conventional mind.

109. Thrangu Rinpoche, *Journey of the Mind*, 133.

110. Dodrupchen Rinpoche, quoted in Tulku Thondup, *Peaceful Death, Joyful Rebirth*, 213.

111. There are a number of inspirational CDs and DVDs of masters giving advice on how to die, oral teachings that are "louder than your thoughts." See *Heart Advice for the Moment of Death*, and *Approaching Death*, by Sogyal Rinpoche; and *Advice for a Dying Practitioner*, by Kyabje Trulshik Rinpoche and Sogyal Rinpoche (available from www.tibetantreasures.com). These uplifting talks can elevate the mind of the dying person and act as a form of sutra phowa.

112. Anam Thubten Rinpoche, talk on "Music and Silence," Point Richmond, California, March 11, 2012.

113. Anam Thubten, *No Self, No Problem*, 43, 49.

114. See Anyen Rinpoche, *Dying with Confidence*, 22–40. This is a practical short book on how to prepare for death.

115. Appendix 1 offers further suggestions for what to put in this will (see "Spiritual Checklist" and "Farewell Checklist").

116. Anyen Rinpoche, *Dying with Confidence*, 34.

117. In addition to the three death bardos, there are three bardos related to life: the bardo of living, the bardo of dream, and the bardo of meditation. We are always in a bardo, always *between* two different states of consciousness.

118. *The Tibetan Book of the Dead*, trans. Francesca Fremantle and Chögyam Trungpa, 98.

Chapter 2: What You Can Do for Others Before They Die

Epigraph drawn from Chögyam Trungpa, *The Heart of the Buddha* (Boston: Shambhala Publications, 1991), 178.

Chapter 3: What to Do for Yourself As You Die

First epigraph drawn from Stanislav Grof, *The Ultimate Journey: Consciousness and the Mystery of Death* (Ben Lomond, CA: MAPS, 2006), 77. Second epigraph drawn from Tulku Thondup, *Peaceful Death, Joyful Rebirth*, 1.

1. For a fascinating view of the play of life and death see www.poodwaddle.com/worldclock.swf.

In terms of reincarnation, people often wonder why there are more people coming into this world than leaving it. Why isn't the number the same? They forget about the other twenty-six states of samsaric existence and that embodied life recycles through any of these realms. See chapter 1, note 88 for more on the twenty-seven states of existence.

2. Sogyal Rinpoche, *Glimpse After Glimpse*, March 29.

3. Stanislav Grof, MD, PhD, is an innovative psychiatrist who has developed a radical approach to helping people transition into death. With over fifty years of experience in psychedelic therapy, Grof helps dying people dislodge from this world by shifting and expanding their consciousness with agents like LSD. "Individuals who experienced psychospiritual death and rebirth saw this experience as a foretaste of what would happen to them at the time of biological death. They reported that as a result they no longer feared death, and they now viewed dying as a fantastic journey, an awe-inspiring adventure in consciousness" (Grof, *The Ultimate Journey*, 292).

   People who have taken DMT (dimethyltryptamine) also report a certainty that consciousness continues after death. Anything that can shatter our exclusive identification with form will help us die. See Rick Strassman, *DMT: The Spirit Molecule: A Doctor's Revolutionary Research into the Biology of Near-Death and Mystical Experiences* (Rochester, VT: Park Street Press, 2001); and John Horgan, *Rational Mysticism: Spirituality Meets Science in the Search for Enlightenment* (New York: Houghton Mifflin Company, 2003), 141–233. Whether the experiences brought on by these psychotropic agents are authentic spiritual experiences or merely drug experiences remains an open question. Drugs are not a spiritual path but at their best could lead someone to a genuine path.

4. For more on these topics, see the Third Karmapa Rangjung Dorje's *The Profound Inner Reality* (*Zabmo Nangdön*), chapters 3 to 5; or the tantric volumes in *The Treasury of Knowledge* series by Jamgön Kongtrul (Ithaca, NY: Snow Lion Publications, 2003–2012): *Systems of Buddhist Tantra*, *The Elements of Tantric Practice*, and *Esoteric Instructions*. See also Khedrup Norsang Gyatso, *Ornament of Stainless Light: An Exposition of the Kalacakra Tantra*, translated by Gavin Kilty (Boston: Wisdom Publications, 2004), which is a commentary on the Kalachakra Tantra. See also Fremantle, *Luminous Emptiness*, 173–193, for a description of these three bodies.

5. To play with the double meaning of the word "habit": our bad habits return till the end of time to clothe, to place a habit upon, the very subtle body. It is naked formless awareness, the indestructible very subtle body, that travels through the bardo of dharmata and gets dressed up for a new life in the bardo of becoming. This is what relative truth (*kundzop*, "all covered up") does to absolute truth (*dharmata*, naked reality). And finally, this is what the karmic bardo of becoming "does" to the luminous bardo of dharmata—as we will see.

6. Lama Yeshe, *Life, Death, and After Death*, 84.

7. See note 4 above on the inner yogas.

8. See *Luminous Emptiness* by Francesca Fremantle; *Mind Beyond Death* by Dzogchen Ponlop; *Journey of the Mind*, by Thrangu Rinpoche; *The Tibetan Book of Living and Dying*, by Sogyal Rinpoche; *Bardo Guidebook*, by Chökyi Nyima Rinpoche; *Kalacakra Tantra*, by Geshe Ngawang Dhargyey.

9. The Dalai Lama, *Consciousness at the Crossroads: Conversations with The Dalai Lama on Brain Science and Buddhism*, edited by Zara Houshmand, Robert B. Livingston, and B. Alan Wallace (Ithaca, NY: Snow Lion Publications, 1999), 105–106.

10. Tibetan divination systems can reveal dozens of signs portending death. See "Self-Liberation by Knowing the Signs of Death," 130–148, in *Living in the Face of Death* by Glenn H. Mullin.

    The secret signs also occur to practitioners in deep meditation. One sees these signs during meditation and therefore comes to recognize them at the moment of death.

11. Eckhart Tolle, *A New Earth: Awakening to Your Life's Purpose* (New York: Penguin Group, 2005), 284–287.

12. The five *skandhas* ("heaps," "aggregates") are five components, or aspects of experience, that give rise to a sense of self, the ego. From gross to subtle, they are form, feeling, perception, formation, and consciousness. See Chögyam Trungpa, *Glimpses of Abhidharma* (Boston: Shambhala Publications, 1987).

13. The mundane, or dualistic, level of each wisdom is what dissolves. In order: mirror-like wisdom; the wisdom of equanimity; discriminating awareness wisdom; all-accomplishing wisdom; and dharmadhatu wisdom. For more about these wisdoms, see Chögyam Trungpa, *Journey Without Goal: The Tantric Wisdom of the Buddha* (Boston: Shambhala Publications, 1981) or *Transcending Madness: The Experience of the Six Bardos* (Boston: Shambhala Publications, 1992); and Irini Rockwell, *The Five Wisdom Energies: A Buddhist Way of Understanding Personalities, Emotions, and Relationships* (Boston: Shambhala Publications, 2002) or her *Natural Brilliance: A Buddhist System for Uncovering Your Strengths and Letting Them Shine* (Boston: Shambhala Publications, 2012).

14. For Yogachara in general, see Janice Willis, *On Knowing Reality* (Delhi: Motilal Banarsidass, 1979). For more on the eight consciousnesses, see Thrangu Rinpoche, *An Ocean of the Ultimate Meaning: Teachings on Mahamudra* (Boston: Shambhala Publications, 2004), *Pointing Out the Dharmakaya* (Ithaca, NY: Snow Lion Publications, 2003), *Everyday Consciousness and Buddha Awakening* (Ithaca, NY: Snow Lion Publications, 2002), and *Transcending Ego: Distinguishing Consciousness from Wisdom* (Boulder, CO: Namo Buddha Publications, 2001). See also the introduction to *Luminous Heart* by Karl Brunnhölzl.

15. Their order of dissolution is navel chakra; heart chakra; throat chakra; secret chakra; crown chakra. The corresponding winds are equal wind; life wind; descending wind; ascending wind; all-pervading wind. See *Luminous Emptiness* by Francesca Fremantle, 224–233. *The Profound Inner Reality*, by Rangjung Dorje, is the central text on subtle body anatomy and physiology.

16. Anyen Rinpoche, *Dying With Confidence*, 53.

17. Each element is associated with a female buddha, and by recognizing the dissolution of the element as it occurs some teachers say we can attain liberation

in the pure land associated with these female buddhas. By recognizing the dissolution of the earth element, we can be liberated into the pure land of Buddha Lochana; recognizing the dissolution of the water element, the Buddha Mamaki; fire, the Buddha Pandaravasini; wind, the Buddha Samayatara; space, the Buddha Dhatvishvari. This correspondence of elements with buddhas also helps us cultivate pure perception, or sacred outlook.

18. The "death rattle" is when fluids accumulate in the respiratory system and breathing starts to sound like gurgling.

19. Kalu Rinpoche, quoted in Sogyal Rinpoche, *The Tibetan Book of Living and Dying*, 253.

20. For students of deity yoga, the appearances of sacred world, the mandala of their deity, can manifest at this time, along with the blessings of that deity.

21. The *Heart Sutra*, as the ultimate sutra on emptiness, is a sutra on death: "no eyes, no ears, no nose, no tongue, no body, . . . [and eventually] no mind." For the ego, emptiness is death. The mantra is a death, or liberation, mantra: OM GATE GATE PARA GATE PARA SAMGATE BODHI SVAHA, "gone, gone, gone beyond, gone completely beyond, so be it." Gone beyond the nightmare of existence into the liberation of emptiness, spaciousness, openness. Gone beyond the relative and into the absolute.

22. Lama Yeshe, *Life, Death, and After Death*, 47.

23. Ibid., 62–63.

24. Namkha Drimed Rinpoche is one of these masters. Sogyal Rinpoche also says that it is safest to begin phowa during the dissolution process, and to repeat it several times as the outer dissolution takes place.

25. The "space" that consciousness will dissolve into is not physical space but the space of the mind. It is the dharmadhatu, the space of reality. Consciousness dissolving into space really means that consciousness is dissolving into wisdom. "Wisdom" in Sanskrit is *jnana*, and "consciousness" is *vijnana*. The prefix *vi* means "divided," or "bifurcated," and therefore *vijnana* is divided or bifurcated wisdom. It is wisdom that has been split into two—self and other. At the end of the inner dissolution, vijnana melts back into jnana. The fracture is finally healed.

26. It is common parlance to talk about "attaining enlightenment," a view that resonates with our overachieving Western mentality. This is a subtle but critical misnomer. How can we attain something we already have? We don't attain enlightenment—we dis-cover it. Sustaining the view that we have to achieve enlightenment can paradoxically prevent it. One can say provisionally that we achieve merit and wisdom (the "two accumulations"), but everything we attain on the path fundamentally serves to help us relax. Relax into the natural state, don't struggle for it. Trungpa Rinpoche said that striving is the only obstacle.

27. To get a feel for the outer and inner dissolution, try this "gathering the mind" mudra. Stand up and close your eyes. Settle your mind by feeling into your body.

Once you feel settled, stretch your hands out to your sides, and slowly bring your outstretched arms up over your head until the plams touch. With your palms joined (in anjali, or prayer, mudra), slowly bring your hands down till they rest in front of your heart, as if you were praying. Bringing your hands together above your head simulates the outer dissolution (and gathering of winds into the central channel). Bringing your hands down to rest at your heart gives you a feel for the peace of the inner dissolution (and gathering of the winds at the heart center). The mind has been gathered and centered—just like it is at death. Rest in peace.

28. This is akin to the "butterfly effect" in chaos and complexity theory, or sensitive dependence on initial conditions. The idea is that a very small change at one place in a complex system can have large repercussions at another place. The image is that of a butterfly flapping its wings in the Bahamas; the wind of that flapping develops into a hurricane in the Carolinas. A tiny puff of confusion inflates into the hurricanes of passion and aggression.

29. This is the ignorance of the first *nidana*, or link of dependent arising, in the Wheel of Life. It is depicted by a blind grandmother, stumbling around in the dark, worn out from giving endless birth to the blind children of samsara. Ignorance, blindness, and darkness are synonyms in Buddhism.

30. The basis of samsara is just this: we lose the essence (of the mind) in the display (of the mind). We forget (*marigpa*) that all thoughts and all things, whatever appears (the display) is forever saturated with the essence (*rigpa*, dharmakaya). Not recognizing the dharmakaya, not seeing the nirvana in samsara, gives birth to suffering. This is why there are practices like "pointing out the dharmakaya," which points out the dharmakaya in stillness, movement, body, and appearance. A synonym for this is "pointing out nirvana"—in the midst of samsara. These practices remind us that every wave is forever made of water. Everything is seen to be saturated with the goodness of enlightenment.

31. Passion is when the waves are moderate in size and the sense of other is not too strong, which is why we want the objects of our passion. These are objects or people that are the most like us, or that we would like to be like us. They help create and augment our sense of self. We long to possess these waves. We want to make two into one, but into *my* one, which is what makes this passion neurotic.

Aggression is when the sense of other is fully reified and really strong. Because the winds are big so are the waves. Things are solid and out there, duality is more pronounced. When there is other, there is fear, so we tend to push (the objects of) fear away, aggressively. Because we have forgotten our common wetness, we hate these waves. They are too different from us.

32. Those who experience near-death often talk about going through a tunnel toward a white light. This report would correlate with the white bindu (consciousness) descending through the central channel (the tunnel). The white light could be the self-radiance of the white bindu itself.

33. The eighty thought states are associated with the three poisons, going from gross to subtle: aggression, passion, and ignorance. They are defined as the gross, medium, and subtle movement of the wind of mind toward its object. These three poisons are the spark plugs of samsara that are unplugged at this stage in the bardo. They don't spark anymore, the inflammable karmic winds of mind are no longer ignited, and the engine of samsara comes to a grinding halt. See the Dalai Lama, *Advice on Dying and Living a Better Life* (London: Random House, 2002); and Lati Rinbochay and Jeffrey Hopkins, *Death, Intermediate State, and Rebirth in Tibetan Buddhism* (Ithaca, NY: Snow Lion Publications, 1979), 39–46. Appearance, increase, and attainment are described in *Mind Beyond Death* by Dzogchen Ponlop, 135–137, and extensively in Jamgön Kongtrul, *The Treasury of Knowledge: Systems of Buddhist Tantra* (Ithaca, NY: Snow Lion Publications, 2005).

34. The indestructible bindu is eternal and unchanging, continues from life to life, and is very subtle mind and prana. It is luminosity, bodhichitta, our buddha nature. See *Luminous Emptiness* by Francesca Fremantle, 192–193; 230–232.

35. The three experiences of the inner dissolution are the three classic *nyams* (experiences) of bliss, clarity, and nonthought. These *nyams* are partial experiences of enlightenment, which become increasingly complete as we descend into the dharmakaya at the end of this dissolution. Death is the dharmakaya, which is why it is such an opportunity for awakening. Each kaya can be associated with each *nyam*, which suggests we descend from the nirmanakaya (clarity) back into the sambhogakaya (bliss) back into the dharmakaya (nonthought). For more on *nyams*, see Traleg Rinpoche, *Mind at Ease: Self-Liberation Through Mahamudra Meditation* (Boston: Shambhala Publications, 2003), 198–200; B. Alan Wallace, *Stilling the Mind*, 124–136; and Reginald Ray, *Secret of the Vajra World*, 250–254. According to Khyentse Rinpoche, the practitioner should recognize the white essence as the nature of the buddha's nirmanakaya, the red light as the essence of the buddha's sambhogakaya, and black attainment as the essence of the buddha's dharmakaya. See Dilgo Khyentse Rinpoche, *Pure Appearance: Development and Completion Stages in Vajrayana Practice* (Halifax, Nova Scotia: Vajravairochana Translation Committee, 1992), 42–43.

    Some texts refer to stage eight as "black near attainment," as distinguished from what would then be stage nine, or "black full attainment." Black *near* attainment would be all seven consciousnesses dissolving (relaxing) back into the eighth, the alaya vijnana; black *full* attainment would be the alaya vijnana dissolving back into alaya jnana—the ninth "consciousness," or wisdom.

36. The luminosity yogas are associated with this moment and allow us to transform blackout into bright light. Deep dreamless sleep and death are dense clarity, and recognizing that luminosity, either at the moment of going to sleep or during death, is considered by many to be the highest accomplishment of a yogi. See Dalai Lama, *Sleeping, Dreaming, and Dying: An Exploration of Con-*

sciousness with the Dalai Lama, edited by Francisco Varela (Boston: Wisdom Publications, 1997), 40; and Tulku Urgyen, *Blazing Splendor: The Memoirs of the Dzogchen Yogi Tulku Urgyen Rinpoche*, as told to Erik Pema Kunsang and Marcia Binder Schmidt (Boudhanath: Rangjung Yeshe Publications, 2005). This is not a physical light, but the light of the mind, which is even more dazzling. Light is the best analogy for an experience that's ineffable.

The relationship of external light to the internal light of the mind is intimate and profound. The dharmakaya can be seen as this internal light. And just as with external light, if there are no objects placed within it, it is paradoxically invisible. It is that which sees (forms), but itself cannot be seen (because it is formless). Physicist Arthur Zajonc writes of external light: "[W]ithout an object on which the light can fall, one sees only darkness. Light itself is always invisible. We see only things, only objects, not light." See Zajonc's *Catching the Light: The Entwined History of Light and Mind* (Oxford: Oxford University Press, 1993), chapter 1.

In deep outer space, even though light is present everywhere, if it doesn't fall on an object nothing is seen. Only darkness. As without, so within. In the deep inner space of mind, if there are no objects of awareness, there is no consciousness. In other words, with no objects in the luminous bardo of dharmata (phase one, the emptiness phase), or in deep dreamless sleep (where only formless awareness itself, the light of the mind, shines), nothing is seen. Hence, until we learn how to identify with this formless—and therefore deathless—awareness, the luminous emptiness of the dharmakaya, we black out when we go to sleep and when we die.

We black out, but the yogi lights up, because he or she identifies with the light. Remember Tagore's quote: "Death is not extinguishing the light, it is only putting out the lamp because dawn has come." In Shambhala Buddhism, this is the return to the dawn of the Great Eastern Sun. Lao-tzu says: "Seeing into darkness is clarity / Knowing how to yield is strength / Use your own light / and return to the source of light / This is called practicing eternity" (quoted in Arthur Zajonc, *Catching the Light*, 182).

37. Some teachers say it occurs at the very end of the bardo of dying, others say it signals entry into the bardo of dharmata. One way to delineate the three bardos altogether is that they are separated by a moment of unconsciousness, or black out. At the end of the bardo of dying, we black out as we go unconscious. If we're lucky, we wake up in the bardo of dharmata and attain enlightenment. If we do not, we black out in terror as the wrathful deities aren't recognized and wake up in the bardo of becoming. If we don't attain liberation in this bardo, we black out as we dive into our next body. There is therefore a "black line" that separates each bardo.

While not directly related to *tukdam*, another sign of accomplishment at death, especially for dzogchen masters, is the appearance of a perfectly pure sky, with perhaps a rainbow or two. The bardo literature is also replete with stories about "rainbow body," of which there are several types (great transference rainbow body, great rainbow body, small rainbow body). In these instances, a master will literally dissolve into rainbow light after death, leaving behind hair, fingernails, and teeth. Or they will shrink into the size of a small child, while retaining their adult proportions and features, finally disappearing without leaving a trace. Many realized masters, however, also die very ordinary deaths. We are in no position to judge the realization of a master based on how they die. See B. Alan Wallace, *Mind in the Balance: Meditation in Science, Buddhism, and Christianity* (New York: Columbia University Press, 2009), 183–186, for more on these forms of rainbow body. See also Tulku Thondup, *Incarnation: The History and Mysticism of the Tulku Tradition of Tibet* (Boston: Shambhala Publications, 2011), 78–83 and 91–93.

38. Rabindranath Tagore, translated by Deepak Chopra and quoted in his *Life After Death: The Burden of Proof* (New York: Three Rivers Press, 2006), 17.

39. Tsele Natsok Rangdrol offers this important caveat: "According to some scholars and adepts, although the general presumption is that all people who remain in the body for a longer time after death are in meditation [*tukdam*], that is not always certain: Some may be clinging to their bodies out of attachment" (quoted in Tulku Thondup, *Peaceful Death, Joyful Rebirth*, 219). Also, rigor mortis doesn't always occur in the dead.

40. The reason we see a sun and a moon now, and experience time, is because we have a sun and moon within us, i.e., because we have red and white bindus. When those bindus are gone, and the subtle body that houses them dissolves, so does our conception of solar days, and time altogether. Even though *The Tibetan Book of the Dead* talks about the visions that arise over twelve "days" in the bardo of dharmata, time doesn't exist as we know it. Bardo beings experience a kind of twilight haze and do not sleep. There is no night and day.

41. There are two forms of nirvana that relate to tukdam and can dictate the time one spends in it. At the level of the "hearers" (shravaka), one can attain the blissful state of *complacent* nirvana, and remain absorbed in various forms of samadhi, of which tukdam is one, for almost as long as one wishes. Because the extinction (*nirvana* literally means "blowing out") of ego is so blissful, it's easy to get attached to this egoless bliss. You don't want to move.

Nonabiding nirvana is the nirvana of the buddhas, and is more evolved. Your compassion moves you out from the dharmakaya (complacent nirvana) and into the rupakayas so that you can benefit others. A buddha doesn't actually leave the dharmakaya, for the dharmakaya remains as the ultimate benefit for oneself (which is realizing that there isn't one). The dharmakaya is the empty enduring quality of the awakened mind. It is the rupakayas that manifest in the world of form as the ultimate benefit for others. In this regard, the rupakayas are literally wisdom in action, or compassion. As the master Kamalashila said:

> The Buddhas have already achieved all their own goals, but remain in the cycle of existence for as long as there are sentient beings. This is because they possess great compassion. They also do not enter the immensely blissful abode of nirvana like the Hearers. Considering the interests of sentient beings first, they abandon the peaceful abode of nirvana as if it were a burning iron house. Therefore, great compassion alone is the unavoidable cause of the nonabiding nirvana of the Buddha. (The Dalai Lama, *Stages of Meditation*, by Kamalashila; translated by Geshe Lobsang Jordhen, Losang Choephel Ganchenpa, and Jeremy Russell [Ithaca, NY: Snow Lion Publications, 2001], 44)

42. Most teachers say that the luminous bardo of dharmata occurs when one is still in the body, which makes the most sense, since the hundred shitro deities reside in the body. A few say that it arises once the bindu has left the body.

43. The bardo of dharmata is principally a Nyingma contribution. You won't find it in many Kagyu, Sakya, or Gelug bardo texts. *The Tibetan Book of the Dead* that describes this bardo was written by Guru Rinpoche, the founder of the Nyingma tradition. To review: preparation for this bardo consists of the formless meditations for phase one (the emptiness phase): mahamudra, trekchö, prajnaparamita, and completion stage meditations. Preparation for phase two (the luminosity phase) consists of thögal, yidam, or generation stage meditations. We can also receive the shitro empowerment and do the associated practices. These meditations prepare us to recognize the dharmakaya and sambhogakaya respectively.

    Luminous Emptiness, by Francesca Fremantle, is the best commentary on *The Tibetan Book of the Dead*. Of the many translations of the *Bardo Thödrol*, the state-of-the-art is Gyurme Dorje's translation. It is beyond our scope to explore the hundred deities in detail, but Fremantle does so in her book. In brief, Thrangu Rinpoche says that when the eight consciousnesses are released from the body, they manifest as the forty-two peaceful deities, and when the fifty-one mental factors (the motion of coarse thoughts) are released from the body, they appear as fifty-one wrathful deities.

44. Sogyal Rinpoche, *Glimpse After Glimpse*, January 27.

45. The Dalai Lama, *Sleeping, Dreaming, and Dying*, 211–212.

46. Ibid.

47. Wind is just space, emptiness, or mind, in motion. It is the dynamic quality of mind. Fire is the illuminating nature of mind; water is the continuity and adaptability of mind; and earth is the stability of mind. From these five elemental qualities of mind, the five elements of the body arise, and then the five elements of the external world. See Kalu Rinpoche, *The Dharma That Illuminates All Beings Impartially Like the Light of the Sun and the Moon* (Albany: State University of New York Press, 1986), 57–59.

48. There are at least four kinds of subtle body: the subtle body in dreams, the subtle body in the bardo of becoming, and the subtle body (also known as ultra pure illusory form) that arises out of the deep samadhi of completion stage meditation (the body of the deity). Then there is the impure and pure forms of the subtle body as described in the inner dissolution. In the trikaya scheme, where dharmakaya is the *very* subtle body, and nirmanakaya is the gross body, all forms of the subtle body can be realized as the sambhogakaya.

49. It's a technical point, but the eighth consciousness (alaya vijnana) is actually the first consciousness, in the sense that all the other seven consciousnesses arise out of it.

50. The ultimate union, of which sexual union is but a symbol. "Great bliss" is the spiritual orgasm where not only male and female unite, but self and other, emptiness and luminosity. It's the ultimate release—of duality. This is what tantric sex, or *yab-yum* (mother-father) deities represent: the ultimate state, nondual enlightenment.

51. In yogic theory, everyone comes into this world with a certain number of breaths available to them. If you use them up quickly, you end your life quickly; if you can hold on to them longer, you live longer. B. K. S. Iyengar: "The yogi's life is not measured by the number of his days but by the number of his breaths" (*The Concise Light on Yoga*, 34). It is said that some are so skilled in breath control that they can live hundreds of years. Pranayama (*a-yama* means to remove the constraints upon) develops this breath control. I find this theory challenging to reconcile with the health benefits of aerobic exercise, which increases heart rate and respiration, and would seem to suggest a shortening of life based on this yogic view. Perhaps these teachings are referring to prana, how to hold the inner breath, and not to physical respiration, or the outer breath.

52. In cosmology, the entire physical universe began when a single point of infinitely dense and infinitely hot matter, smaller than the head of a pin, exploded with an unimaginable burst of energy in the Big Bang. The Big Crunch is the Big Bang in reverse, posited by many astrophysicists as how this universe could end. Is the bardo of dying an analog to the Big Crunch, and the bardo of becoming an analog to the Big Bang, both centered on the infinitely dense point of reality that is the bardo of dharmata? This provocative description from science writer Michael Lemonick is resonant with descriptions of phase two of the luminous bardo of dharmata, and stimulates the imagination in matters analogical:

> [About half a million years after the big bang] according to the widely accepted standard model of cosmology, our entire cosmos had swelled from a space smaller than an atom to something 100 billion miles across. It was then a seething maelstrom of matter so hot that subatomic particles trying to form into atoms would have been blasted apart instantly and so dense that light couldn't have traveled more than a short distance before

being absorbed. If you could somehow live long enough to look around in such conditions, you would see nothing but brilliant light in all directions. (Michael D. Lemonick, *Time* magazine, May 4, 1992)

Eventually the maelstrom cooled enough to create our manifest universe.

According to both dzogchen and modern physics, the relative world is made of frozen light. Absolute reality, dharmata, is too hot to handle (too bright, too empty) from ego's point of view, so we ice it down in the bardo of becoming, and moment-to-moment, so that we can get a grip on it—conceptually and literally. If you think the world is cold and cruel, it's because you have made it so.

53. Francesca Fremantle, *Luminous Emptiness*, 193.
54. Nothing whatever but everything arises from the dharmakaya (the bottom half of the hourglass); and nothing whatever but everything returns to it (the top half). As the mantra of the *Heart Sutra* declares, it is "gone, gone, gone beyond, gone completely beyond"—any form or concept. It is the primordial womb and tomb, the condensed heart of reality, of which nothing can ultimately be said.
55. *The Tibetan Book of the Dead*, trans. Francesca Fremantle and Chögyam Trungpa, 99.

CHAPTER 4: WHAT TO DO FOR OTHERS AS THEY DIE

Epigraph drawn from Sogyal Rinpoche, *The Tibetan Book of Living and Dying*, 210.

1. Be aware of the seduction of death. Death is uncompromising, like dharma itself, and vigorously reminds us of the path. This is the gift of being around death. The problem is that we can become a "death junkie." This is someone who gets high off of the intensity around death. There can also be a subtle sense of superiority in being around dying people, an unconscious need to boost yourself up by being around those who are down. "My life may be bad, but at least I'm not dying. This person is much worse off." Instead of compassion, there can be a covert sense of self-aggrandizement, almost delighting in the misfortune of others. While rare, these anomalies do occur. Always check your motivation.
2. A good book on Alzheimer's is *Shaking Hands with Alzheimer's Disease: A Guide to Compassionate Care for Caregivers*, by Maria Pertik and Zora de Bodisco (Seattle: CreateSpace, 2011).
3. On the problem of "helping prisons," see *How Can I Help? Stories and Reflections on Service*, by Ram Dass and Paul Gorman (New York: Alfred Knopf, 1986), 122–148.
4. Joan Halifax, *Being with Dying: Cultivating Compassion and Fearlessness in the Presence of Death* (Boston: Shambhala Publications, 2008), 66.
5. Frank Ostaseski, quoted in *Buddhadharma* magazine, Spring 2009.
6. *Being with Dying* by Joan Halifax; *Facing Death and Finding Hope* by Chris-

tine Longaker; and part 2 of Sogyal Rinpoche's *The Tibetan Book of Living and Dying* offer indispensable advice on how to be with the dying.

7. Translated by Jim Scott and Ann Bucardi.

8. Joan Halifax, quoted in *Gifts of the Spirit: Living the Wisdom of the Great Religious Traditions*, by Philip Zaleski and Paul Kaufman (San Francisco, Harper-Collins, 1998), 98.

9. Sogyal Rinpoche, *The Tibetan Book of Living and Dying*, 211.

10. For how to create holding environments for people of varying faiths, see Kenneth J. Doka and Amy S. Tucci, eds., *Living with Grief: Spirituality and End-of-Life Care* (Washington, D.C.: Hospice Foundation of America, 2011).

11. Animal-assisted therapy, which uses registered and certified "canine cotherapists," is finding its way into hospice care. A number of hospices allow and encourage hospice volunteers to bring their pets along for those dying people who connect to the unconditional love of an animal. If you or a dying loved one have this connection, find a hospice that works with pets.

12. Khenpo Karthar Rinpoche, talk on "Dying, Death, and the Intermediate State," given at Karma Triyana Dharmachakra, September 19, 1981, translated by Ngödup Tsering Burkhar.

13. Marie de Hennezel, quoted in *Shambhala Sun* magazine, July 1997, p. 49.

14. Christine Longaker, *Facing Death and Finding Hope*, 193.

15. *Vajradhatu Practice Manual*, p. 8, accessed on May 18, 2009 at http://www.halifax.shambhala.org/aging.php.

16. Music thanatology is a professional field under the umbrella of palliative care that has been developed over the past thirty years, principally by Therese Schroeder-Sheker. It unites music and medicine in end-of-life care. As a musician (pianist) and care provider, I can attest to the power of music in creating wonderful holding environments. In addition to playing at the bedside, musicians sometimes play soothing music in chemo wards. From the Music-Thanatology Association International:

> The music thanatologist utilizes harp and voice at the bedside to lovingly serve the physical, emotional and spiritual needs of the dying and their loved ones with prescriptive music. Prescriptive music is live music that responds to the physiological needs of the patient . . . by observing vital signs such as heart rate, respiration and temperature, the music-thanatologist provides music that is tailored to each specific situation. This music can help ease physical symptoms such as pain, restlessness, agitation, sleeplessness and labored breathing. It offers an atmosphere of serenity and comfort that can be profoundly soothing for those present. Difficult emotions such as anger, fear, sadness and grief can be relieved as listeners rest into a musical presence of beauty, intimacy and compassion. (www.mtai.org/index.php/what_is)

17. This may seem to contradict the central teaching of staying in the present. But we can still remain present while holding this view of the future. What about the terrifying visions of the wrathful deities—how does one look forward to that? We need to remember that for most of us the visions of the bardo of dharmata are a mere endnote, just like this one—they flash by in an instant completely unrecognized. If we are lucky enough to experience and recognize these visions, that will be due to our practice in learning how to recognize them during life. In that case, the wrathful visions are seen for what they are: a louder alarm clock to shock us into awakening. In other words, they are no longer terrifying.

18. Sogyal Rinpoche, *The Tibetan Book of Living and Dying*, 173.

19. Ibid., 174.

20. Woody Allen: "In my next life I want to live backwards. You start out dead and get that out of the way. Then you wake up in an old people's home feeling better every day. You get kicked out for being too healthy, go collect your pension, and then when you start work, you get a gold watch and a party on your first day. You work for forty years until you're young enough for retirement. You party, drink alcohol, and are generally promiscuous, then you are ready for high school. You then go to primary school, you become a kid, you play. You have no responsibilities, you become a baby until you are born. And then you spend your last nine months in luxurious spa-like conditions, with central heating and room service on tap, larger quarters every day, and then, Voila! You finish off as an orgasm. I rest my case."

Mr. Allen also says: "I find it (aging) a lousy deal . . . I'm seventy-four now. You don't get smarter, you don't get wiser, you don't get more mellow, you don't get more kindly . . . . Your back hurts more. You get more indigestion. Your eyesight isn't as good. You need a hearing aid. It's a bad business getting older, and I would advise you not to do it."

For a funny and fascinating book about death, see Mary Roach, *Stiff: The Curious Lives of Human Cadavers* (New York: W. W. Norton, 2003).

21. Sogyal Rinpoche, *The Tibetan Book of Living and Dying*, 174.

22. Ibid., 174–175.

23. Ibid., 176.

24. Ibid., 176.

25. Ibid., 177.

26. Ibid., 177.

27. Elisabeth Kübler-Ross, *On Death and Dying* (New York: Collier, 1970), 50.

28. Sogyal Rinpoche, *The Tibetan Book of Living and Dying*, 178.

29. Ibid., 179.

30. Ibid., 180.

31. Trungpa Rinpoche and Rigdzin Shikpo write about the origin and dissolution of the sense of self, and the fear that is associated with that:

The overpowerful creative energy breaks away from the alaya [which is frequently equated with ultimate reality, the dharmakaya] and becomes avidya (or moha) [ignorance], which ignores or forgets the alaya. This is the first establishment of the ego, and from it fear springs when one realizes that one is an individual and alone. . . . Just as fear was the first reaction to arise when the breaking away from the alaya took place, so it tends to be the last barrier to the return to the alaya [in deep meditation, or death]. As one begins to return to the alaya, fear may arise due to a sensation of impending annihilation, and this fear must be fully entered into before the return can be accomplished. (Chögyam Trungpa, *The Collected Works of Chögyam Trungpa, Volume Six* [Boston: Shambhala Publications, 2004], 552–554)

See chapter 9, note 18 on the origin of fear and the cascade into depression.

Hope and fear are the parents of the eight worldly dharmas, the polarities within which we live our entire lives: praise and blame; fame and shame; pleasure and pain; gain and loss. We hope for the former and fear the latter.

32. Sogyal Rinpoche, *The Tibetan Book of Living and Dying*, 181.

33. Ibid., 212.

34. Ibid., 181.

35. Ibid., 183.

36. Ibid., 185–186.

37. See ibid., 214–217.

38. Ibid., 218.

39. Ibid., 211–212.

40. Ibid., 219.

41. Cognitive science has shown that the brain cannot tell the difference between something that is directly perceived and something that is visualized. Buddhism goes even further, asserting that what we do with our mind radiates out to touch the cosmos. See the section on the power of merit in chapter 6 below. On how mind affects "matter," see Maitreyanatha/Aryasanga, *The Universal Vehicle Discourse Literature* (New York: American Institute of Buddhist Studies, 2004), xli–xliii. See also *The Maharishi Effect: A Revolution Through Meditation: Scientific Discovery of the Astounding Power of the Group Mind*, by Elaine and Arthur Aron (Walpole, NH: Stillpoint Publishing, 1986).

42. Sogyal Rinpoche, *The Tibetan Book of Living and Dying*, 221.

43. See the section on anticipatory grief in chapter 9 below.

44. Sogyal Rinpoche, *The Tibetan Book of Living and Dying*, 225.

45. Ibid., 223.

46. Ibid., 236.

47. Ibid., 236.

48. Ibid., 237.

49. Ibid., 238–240.
50. Ibid., 187.
51. Jonathan Franzen, writing in the *New York Times*, May 29, 2011.
52. Lama Zopa Rinpoche, *Advice and Practices for Death and Dying for the Benefit of Self and Others*, 146.

CHAPTER 5: WHAT TO DO FOR YOURSELF AFTER YOU DIE

Epigraph from Sogyal Rinpoche, *The Tibetan Book of Living and Dying*, 212.

1. Etymologist John Ayto writes: "In Old English times, *ghost* was simply a synonym for 'spirit' or 'soul' (a sense preserved in *Holy Ghost*); it did not acquire its modern connotations of the 'disembodied spirit of a dead person appearing among the living' until the fourteenth century" (*Dictionary of Word Origins* [New York: Arcade Publishing, 1990], 254).

2. It takes an average of forty-nine days for karma to sort itself out and the next life to therefore take shape. If karma is really good or really bad, the force of that strong wind blows us into a higher or lower realm instantly. For most of us, the four forces of karma (strong, proximate, habitual, random—see chapter 1, note 60) that work during any moment of transition have to play themselves out.

    Just as it is difficult to predict outcomes in complex weather patterns, with the winds, temperatures, humidity, and pressure systems that combine to create them, it is even more difficult to predict how karmic winds will play out in the bardo. So many factors come into play, so many different forces of karma, so many different jet-streams and breezes combine to create our experience now—and after death.

    Ken Wilber's elegant AQAL (all quadrant all level) model is one of the best current maps of this complexity as it manifests moment-to-moment in daily life. Every occasion can be described from four perspectives, and arises from the interdependent influence (winds) of those four quadrants. The four quadrants simultaneously describe and produce everything. The NW wind is individual interior (mental states); the NE wind is individual exterior (brain states); SE wind is collective exterior (social); SW wind is collective interior (cultural). How much more complex in the bardos, when it is not just the winds from this life but those of countless past lives that converge to create our reality. See *Sex, Ecology, Spirituality: The Spirit of Evolution* (Boston; Shambhala Publications, 1995) and *A Brief History of Everything* (Boston: Shambhala Publications, 1996) by Ken Wilber for more on the four quadrants. It is no accident that a few of the scientific disciplines that try to describe dependent origination from a conventional point of view are called Chaos Theory and Complexity Theory. From a spiritual point of view we can start to get a feel for why it is said that only a buddha can fully comprehend karma.

3. Kalu Rinpoche, *The Dharma*, 62.

4. The bardo of dharmata occurs within the realm of *rigpa*, or *yeshe* (wisdom); the bardo of becoming occurs within the realm of *sem*, or *namshe* (consciousness). If your practice is exemplary, it is possible for the soft lights that appear in the bardo of becoming to appear as the five wisdom lights, so wisdom may not be entirely over for a select few.

5. There are five paths on the way to enlightenment, which are actually five stages along one extended path: the path of accumulation, path of union, path of seeing, path of meditation, and the path of no more learning. The path of seeing is the pivotal path right in the middle, often traversed in one meditation session. Life prior to the path of seeing is like living in a dark room and knowing that somewhere in this room is a large snake. The darkness represents ignorance, and the snake represents the fear that accompanies, and is virtually synonymous with, ignorance. The path of seeing is like a flash of light that suddenly illuminates the room. You have enough time to see that what you thought was a snake is actually a rope. The light goes off (due to the power of karma, or your habituation to darkness), but your relationship to your world has irreversibly changed. You will never *see* things the same way again. Even though the light is gone, the fear that is the primordial emotion of darkness (samsara) dissolves.

   The snake represents seeing things as solid, lasting, and independent, in other words, as *other*. And where there is other, there is fear. Discovering that the snake is merely a rope is stripping away the projections, the imputations, that ego constantly throws upon a groundless, impermanent, and nondual world (the rope). Prior to the path of seeing, the world is infested with snakes and we live our life based on fear (of other); on the path of meditation the snakes are seen to be harmless ropes and we now live with fearlessness (and compassion for those who still believe in other). We have finally seen that emptiness cannot harm emptiness. The path of meditation, borrowing Huston Smith's words, is to transform these flashes of illumination into abiding light. Enlightenment, the path of no more learning, is when the light never goes off.

6. Who you really are is discussed in many different ways. Perhaps the most irreducible description, both for yourself and for reality, is that whatever appears is the union of luminosity and emptiness. You are therefore simultaneously nothing (emptiness) and everything (luminosity). The entire second and third turnings of the wheel of dharma are devoted to exploring emptiness and luminosity. From the Mahayana perspective, you are the trikaya. The dharmakaya is your empty nature; the rupakayas (the form kayas of the sambhogakaya and nirmanakaya) are your luminous expression.

7. Sogyal Rinpoche, *Glimpse After Glimpse*, February 22.

8. The snakes reappear.

9. According to many spiritual traditions we are currently in a dark age, what the Hindus call the "kali yuga," said to have begun in 3102 B.C.E. The overt manifestation of this darkness is seen in our ecological devastation, wars, and the

many obvious problems facing the world. The covert manifestation, of which the overt is merely an epigenetic expression, is the darkness infecting our minds. At this covert level, the dark age refers largely to the epidemic of distraction, which is getting worse. At the electronic level, a few generations ago we were entertained and distracted by merely the radio, then the TV. With the invention of the computer, and the countless gadgets spawned from this technology, we have entered an unprecedented age of distraction—and danger. With so many new weapons of mass distraction (smart phones, iPods, iPads, Facebook, Twitter, etc.), the discursive mind is running out of control. The most successful new weapons (products), those that sell the best, are the products that are even faster, or that allow you to multitask, breeding ever higher velocities of discursiveness. In the bardos, our absolute virtuosity in distraction will turn into an absolute nightmare.

Nicholas Carr, author of *The Shallows: What the Internet Is Doing to Our Brains* (New York: W. W. Norton, 2010), says that the Net is remaking us in its own speedy image. The problem is that we don't see ourselves caught in this net. We are all infected with varying levels of ADD (attention deficit disorder) and ADHD (attention deficit hyperactivity disorder), a natural consequence of jamming more information into a limited amount of time. Furthermore, we confuse information for experience, and end up living in our heads and not in reality. When the contents of that head turn into reality in the bardo, we're in trouble.

In this information age we are eating the menu instead of the meal and then wondering why we're still hungry. Living to such an extent in a virtual reality, we are reaching escape velocity from true reality, an ominous sign of the Dark Age. The average American spends at least eight and a half hours in front of a screen every day. We are literally screening ourselves from reality. The average teenager sends or receives seventy-five text messages a day. Author Pico Iyer says, "We have more and more ways to communicate but less and less to say." There is obviously nothing inherently wrong with information—it's a vital component of life and evolution. But uncontrolled information, and its insidious breeding of uncontrolled minds (rampant distraction), is an impending disaster. This runaway Information Age is turning into a euphemism for the worsening Dark Age.

10. Thrangu Rinpoche, *Journey of the Mind*, 51.

11. Five years ago my beloved mother died, as did my marriage. It was one of the most painful episodes of my life. I remember coming home in the dead of winter to a cold and empty house, lonely and grief-stricken. I longed to find refuge in a new relationship, a new "body." As I returned night after night to face my pain alone, I realized I wanted someone to save me. But from what? I wanted someone to save me from myself. The contents of my heavy mind and broken heart were too much to bear, and I wanted out. Distractions did help, but only temporarily. The greatest help was finally having the courage to face my mind

directly, which I did in extended meditation. I then remembered Trungpa Rinpoche's teaching: "There is no way out. The magic is to discover that there is a way in." This allowed me to develop a deeper relationship to the painful contents of my mind, which I did by just being with them, then by dropping below them. I took ultimate refuge in the empty *nature* of the thoughts and feelings, and not the thoughts and feelings themselves. It was like diving below stormy seas to take refuge in the depths of the silent ocean below. I also realized that if I couldn't be with myself, how could I expect anybody else to be with me?

12. Kalu Rinpoche, *Secret Buddhism*, 102.

13. *The Tibetan Book of the Dead*, trans. Francesca Fremantle and Chögyam Trungpa, 78.

14. Thrangu Rinpoche, *Journey of the Mind*, 110.

15. This capability is used in several of the ritual practices discussed later, when the consciousness is summoned and directed. See chang chok and né dren on page 153 below.

16. See note 40 to chapter 3 on why we don't see the sun or moon. There are also six indefinite signs that you are dead: location, resting place, behavior, sustenance, companionship, and mental condition. See *The Treasury of Knowledge: Esoteric Instructions* by Jamgön Kongtrul, 199 and 411–412.

17. *The Tibetan Book of the Dead*, trans. Francesca Fremantle and Chögyam Trungpa, 74.

18. Dzigar Kongtrul Rinpoche, talk in Ward, Colorado, July 18, 2009.

19. *The Tibetan Book of the Dead*, trans. Francesca Fremantle and Chögyam Trungpa, 74.

20. See *Peaceful Death, Joyful Rebirth* by Tulku Thondup, 85–163, for more on the experiences of this bardo.

21. Ibid., 92.

22. B. Alan Wallace, *Stilling the Mind*, 45.

23. Sogyal Rinpoche, *Glimpse After Glimpse*, January 7.

24. These teachings proclaim that the body does not give rise to consciousness (which is the standard view of epigenesis and epiphenomenalism of Western science). It *restricts* it. When the mind is liberated from the body, it is clearer and sharper because it is no longer encased and limited. The equation of mind to brain is a byproduct of Western materialistic and reductionist science, and does not accord with many spiritual views. British physicist Stephen Hawking speaks for the scientific world when he says: "I regard the brain as a computer which will stop working when its components fail. There is no heaven or afterlife for broken-down computers. That is a fairy story for people afraid of the dark" (*Time* magazine, May 30, 2011). His view is that of those who live in the dark.

25. Tulku Thondup, *Peaceful Death Joyful Rebirth*, 95.

26. Since Chenrezig is considered an emanation of Amitabha, we are keeping it all in the family of Amitabha and his pure land.

27. Chökyi Nyima Rinpoche, *The Bardo Guidebook*, 159.

28. *The Tibetan Book of the Dead*, trans. Francesca Fremantle and Chögyam Trungpa, 99.

29. *Yidam* is sometimes translated as "binding deity"—using the visualization of a deity to bind you to your innate awakened nature.

30. Yama, the Lord of Death, is the Judgment scene in this bardo, where all your good and bad deeds are presented in front of this judge, who then sentences you into your next life. There is no literal judge, of course, but only your propensity to judge, both yourself and others, that manifests at this time. Yama appears in a terrifying form, huge and dark, sometimes with the head of a scary bull or buffalo. In his presence you cannot make excuses. You cannot bribe him, seduce him, or mess with him in any way. He is a cold uncaring mirror that reflects your karma. Yama represents your deepest conscience, those secret motives that you try to hide from yourself and others.

    Yama teaches this lesson: when it comes to karma, you can't get away with anything. Everything is recorded in your substrate consciousness, which is exactly what is revealed after death. Every motivation is "photographed" by the seventh consciousness, stored on the film of the eighth, and developed in the dark room of the bardo of becoming for you to finally see. This process also happens in dreams. Most of us don't appreciate this display. But mind has become reality, and at this point that includes our deepest subconscious mind, so we have no choice. It's time to fess up. There's a reason we stuffed our dirty motivations so deeply away—we do not want to see the refuse of our subconscious mind. But Judgment Day has arrived, and you are about to sentence yourself to your next life. Karma is taking over. See *Peaceful Death, Joyful Rebirth* by Tulku Thondup, 88–90.

31. Mahamudra is the nature of mind, virtually synonymous with the dharmakaya. Secret names are the names students receive from their teacher when they formally enter the Vajrayana. It is said that your guru, or another representation of wisdom, will call to you in the bardo by using your secret name. They will therefore draw you to them—to wisdom instead of confusion.

32. *The Tibetan Book of the Dead*, trans. Francesca Fremantle and Chögyam Trungpa, 86.

33. Thrangu Rinpoche, *Journey of the Mind*, 119.

34. Francesca Fremantle, *Luminous Emptiness*, 357.

35. This could be the primordial expression of Freud's famous Oedipus complex. What we are fundamentally attracted to are the red and white essences embodied in the father and mother, and specifically sperm and ovum. In vitro conception occurs when we are karmically attracted to the union of these essences. Thrangu Rinpoche says, "The final experience of the bardo of becoming is the moment at which you identify with the sperm and ovum . . ." (*Journey of the Mind*, 109).

36. *The Tibetan Book of the Dead*, trans. Gyurme Dorje, 292.

37. *The Tibetan Book of Living and Dying*, 298.

38. Dzogchen Ponlop, *Mind Beyond Death*, 219.

39. *The Tibetan Book of the Dead*, trans. Francesca Fremantle and Chögyam Trungpa, 85.

40. Ibid., 75.

41. See Vesna A. Wallace, *The Inner Kalacakratantra: A Buddhist Tantric View of the Individual* (New York: Oxford University Press, 2001), 56–109, "The Cosmic Body."

42. *The Tibetan Book of the Dead*, trans. Gyurme Dorje, 286.

43. Tulku Thondup, *Peaceful Death, Joyful Rebirth*, 179.

44. Thrangu Rinpoche, *Journey of the Mind*, 113.

45. The reason the human realm is considered even more auspicious for rebirth than the god realm is because the god realm is too blissful. The first noble truth of suffering is hard to come by, and therefore there is no reason to pursue the path (the fourth noble truth). The human realm, poised in the middle between the lower realms (where suffering is too intense) and the higher realms (where pleasure is too intense), is considered ideal for spiritual practice. Not too tight; not too loose.

    There are different "continents" within the human realm, and of all these continents the Land of Jambu, which includes this earth, is considered the best. Jambu is called the "land of actions" because the actions performed in one life tend to bear their karmic fruits in that same life. In most other realms, part of the karma accrued in those realms comes to fruition in that life, and the rest of it in countless future lives. Therefore the inhabitants of Jambu are the best candidates for attaining enlightenment in one lifetime and in one body. See Jamgön Kongtrul, *The Treasury of Knowledge: Systems of Buddhist Tantra*, 433.

46. Francesca Fremantle, *Luminous Emptiness*, 364.

47. *The Tibetan Book of the Dead*, trans. Francesca Fremantle and Chögyam Trungpa, 87.

48. See pages 294–300 of Gyurme Dorje's translation, or 87–93 of the translation by Francesca Fremantle and Chögyam Trungpa.

49. For those who must know: god realm—we may feel we are on a high floor in a mansion, or see visions of pleasant multistoried houses; demigod—we feel we are in a wheel of fire, or have visions of a forest, ring of fire, or rain; animal—we feel we are in an empty cave or hut, or have visions of fog; hungry ghost—we feel we are in a dry cave, or have visions of dry river beds or dark, dusty places; hell—we have visions of red houses or dark land, a dark pit, or a dark path. See Tulku Thondup, *Peaceful Death, Joyful Rebirth*, 90–91 and 181–183.

50. See *Peaceful Death, Joyful Rebirth*, 90; Tsele Natsok Rangdrol, *Mirror of Mindfulness*, 71–72; and Dzogchen Ponlop, *Mind Beyond Death*, 208–217.

51. Tsele Natsok Rangdrol, *Mirror of Mindfulness*, 72.

52. Tulku Thondup, *Peaceful Death, Joyful Rebirth*, 90, 181.

53. Dzogchen Ponlop, *Mind Beyond Death*, 209.
54. Normally, to be born as a god one must have achieved the ninth level of sha-matha. This is the gate into the seventeen levels of gods of the form realm and then the four levels of gods in the formless realm (associated with the four dhyanas). See *The Three Pure Land Sutras* by Hisao Inagaki, 116–117. See also Dudjom Rinpoche, *The Nyingma School of Tibetan Buddhism* (Boston: Wis-dom Publications, 1991), 14–15, and for a detailed discussion, see Vasubandhu, *Abhidharmakosabhasyam*, vol. 2, 365–495. Again, the mind leads all things: a heavenly state of mind leads one to a heavenly abode. This also points out the limitations of meditative absorption, or samadhi, and the trap of the *nyams* of bliss, clarity, and nonthought. Samadhi has its obvious place, but if you feel it is THE final place, you are stuck. As many masters assert: the way to enhance your samadhi is to destroy it. Don't get attached to blissful states of mind, which are the most subtle of snares.
55. No one is really chasing you and instilling such fear. Your own actions, your karma, are always coming after you. Knowing this can prevent the fear of exter-nal pursuit—just as in a dream. As James Joyce put it: "History is a nightmare from which I am trying to awake." At this point it is *karmic* history that is creat-ing the nightmare.
56. *The Tibetan Book of the Dead*, trans. Gyurme Dorje, 295, 296.
57. This assumes you will be reborn from a womb. There are three other forms of birth: spontaneous, from an egg, and from moisture. "Womb" represents any form of birth in any realm.
58. *The Tibetan Book of the Dead*, trans. Gyurme Dorje, 299.
59. The bardo being enters through the top of the head of the father, or his torso, and travels into the womb of the mother. According to Buddhism life begins at conception. See the section on abortion in "Difficult Issues" below, as well as *Into the Jaws of Yama, Lord of Death: Buddhism, Bioethics, and Death*, by Karma Lekshe Tsomo.
60. Khenpo Karthar Rinpoche, *Bardo: Interval of Possibility*, 21, 71.
61. Francesca Fremantle, *Luminous Emptiness*, 360.
62. Tulku Thondup, *Peaceful Death, Joyful Rebirth*, 182–183.

CHAPTER 6: WHAT TO DO FOR OTHERS AFTER THEY DIE

Epigraph drawn from Arthur Zajonc, *Catching the Light: The Entwined History of Light and Mind*, 182.
1. The psychic powers (*siddhi*) are karmically generated and therefore not stable. Real siddhi, generated through meditation, is stable.
2. Dzongsar Khyentse Rinpoche, talk at Karma Dzong, Halifax, Nova Scotia, August 1, 1989.
3. This assertion in *The Tibetan Book of the Dead* is in contrast to what Tulku Thondup says, that without a body it is hard to retain and remember.

4. *The Tibetan Book of the Dead*, trans. Gyurme Dorje, 293.

5. Look at your mind now to see how things will be in this bardo, or look at your dreams. If you have an unstable mind, you will have that same mind in the bardo. You will dart around at the speed of thought. Such is the power of unmediated thought in the bardo, and such is the sense of groundlessness that ensues upon that freedom. Unless we're prepared to handle this freedom, we will contract away from it—and back into samsara. As sociologist Erich Fromm suggested, we will escape *from* freedom. Fyodor Dostoyevsky echoes this sentiment from a political stance in the Grand Inquisitor parable in *The Brothers Karamazov*.

6. Forcefully moving the bardo consciousness refers to the Iron Hook of Compassion. This form of phowa for others can even help a person with strong negative karma, but only if that person has a close connection with the master who performs it, if they have faith in the teachings, and if they have truly asked for purification. Forcefully moving also refers to the rituals of né dren and chang chok, discussed on page 153.

7. Kalu Rinpoche, *Secret Buddhism*, 62.

8. Some say that after each small death every seven days, the consciousness enters into a second, third, and up to a seventh new intermediate state, after which rebirth must take place. See Zopa Rinpoche, *Advice and Practices for Death and Dying*, 14.

9. Jamgön Kongtrul, *The Treasury of Knowledge: The Elements of Tantric Practice*, 110.

10. Again, these are general guidelines. Some bardo beings are reborn almost instantly after death, while others can spend years in the bardo, getting stuck as a type of hungry ghost. Sogyal Rinpoche refers to these beings as "bardo VIPs," those with really good, or really bad, karma. The force of that karma is such that these beings are instantly born into higher or lower realms respectively. Those destined to be born in the formless god realms also do not experience this bardo. The "wind" is so powerful that they are immediately blown into their next life. For the rest of us, it takes time for karma to sort itself out and our next life to take shape.

11. "Merit" is a translation of the Tibetan word "sonam" (*bsod nams*), and the Sanskrit *punya*. It's a charged word, difficult to translate, loaded with thorny Western connotations. Tibetan scholar Alexander Berzin translates it as "positive potential" and speaks about the accumulation of merit as "strengthening the network of positive potential."

   On a personal note, near the end of my three-year retreat, which I did with a small group, Mingyur Rinpoche came in to address us. We were all expecting a teaching on mahamudra, dzogchen, or the Six Yogas of Naropa—advanced topics befitting "advanced" students. We were a bit stunned when he spent his entire time talking about merit, a topic we deemed so simple. Rinpoche skillfully put us in our place, and showed us how vast and profound merit really is.

12. The Pure Land texts are a valuable resource for learning about merit. See *The Land of Bliss*, by Luis O. Gómez; *Approaching the Land of Bliss*, edited by Richard K. Payne and Kenneth K. Tanaka; *The Origins and Development of Pure Land Buddhism*, by Mark L. Blum (Oxford and New York: Oxford University Press, 2002); and *Living in Amida's Universal Vow: Essays in Shin Buddhism*, edited by Alfred Bloom (Bloomington, IN: World Wisdom, 2004). Merit, and its transfer (*punya parinamana*), is at the heart of the Pure Land tradition. To hint at the importance of merit, consider the following: the perfection of the dedication of merit only occurs at the eighth bhumi, a high level of realization. Of the five progressive paths to enlightenment, the first path, which is the one most of us spend our entire lives on, is the path of accumulation. This refers to the accumulation of merit and wisdom. Dharma practitioners spend most of their lives accumulating merit, and this currency then transforms into wisdom (insight into the nature of reality). Of the two veils obscuring enlightenment (conflicting emotions and ignorance), merit removes the first veil, and wisdom the second. And since merit is what transforms into wisdom, merit is at the heart of enlightenment.

One can think of merit as a kind of energy and metaphorically use Einstein's famous equation of matter and energy to show how mental energy can be transformed into matter.

Khenpo Karthar Rinpoche relates this surprising consequence about merit:

> People often wonder why so many rulers of the past had the power to create so much suffering and destruction in our world. This power and destructiveness shows the power of their individual prayer. Why were they so powerful? Why did they have the power to destroy half of the world? It is because of the merit that they had accumulated. Without the merit, they would not have been able to have that kind of power. But while the merit was there, their prayer was what we call a "reverse prayer," or negative prayer, which caused them to use their power to create great harm. This is why we must be cautious, as Buddhists, to always add to any accumulation of merit a proper, wholesome prayer for the well-being of ourselves and of all other beings. . . . Whenever you are accumulating merit, you accumulate it with a particular wish in mind. And that wish, that prayer, becomes the most important factor in how merit comes to fruition. (Khenpo Karthar Rinpoche, "Explanation of the Long Amitabha Sadhana," talk given at Karma Triyana Dharmachakra, Woodstock, New York, September 1999, translated by Chojor Radha)

Ponlop Rinpoche adds:

> [T]ulkus are very powerful. If they do something good, it's very beneficial and influential; but if they do something bad the power is equal [because

that force of merit can be directed in either direction, and with the same impact]. So sometimes it can be very dangerous. If the tulku does not develop the power given to him [by his merit] in a positive way it can be very destructive for many people, and he can even destroy himself. (Mick Brown, *The Dance of 17 Lives: The Incredible True Story of Tibet's 17th Karmapa* [New York: Bloomsbury Publishing, 2004], 30)

13. Dharma Publishing Staff, *Ways of Enlightenment: Buddhist Studies at Nyingma Institute* (Berkeley: Dharma Publishing, 1993), 252.
14. Luis O. Gómez, *The Land of Bliss*, 30.
15. The power of merit can only be fully appreciated by understanding that the nature of reality is not material but mental-spiritual. If we sustain the view that our tiny mind is up against a world of solid matter, then what we do with our mind (our merit) has little impact on this hard external world. But if the world and my mind is made of the same stuff, then what I do with my mind can indeed impact the world. The substrate of mind and reality is the same. Robert Thurman writes:

How difficult it seems to make such a [bodhisattva] vow in the mind and heart if one is thinking of the "universe of beings" as an infinite, substantial, external, dense, and heavy bunch of objects! How overwhelming the prospect of transforming all of it into a buddhaverse! But, if the nature of all beings and things is mental, mind-constituted, and mind-created, then a radical transformation of the inner mind, in intersubjective interconnection with other minds, could very well be able to effect a total transformation of everything that exists with a semblance of greater ease. One could then take up the bodhisattva vow [and the collection and dedication of merit] with a sense of possibility empowering the compassionate emotion and messianic determination. (Maitreyanatha/Asanga, *The Universal Vehicle Discourse Literature*, xli–xliv)

See also *The Inner Kalacakratantra* by Vesna Wallace, chapter 5.
16. For students doing visualization practice (tantra), you can multiply the power of merit through the power of your samadhi visualization. This is the spirit behind mandala offering. Oceans of merit are accumulated when the student visualizes offering the entire universe.
17. Tulku Thondup, *Peaceful Death, Joyful Rebirth*, 215–217.
18. Khenpo Karthar Rinpoche, talk at KTD, Woodstock, New York, August 19, 1996, translated by Yeshe Gyamtso.
19. B. Alan Wallace, *Buddhism With an Attitude: The Tibetan Seven-Point Mind Training* (Ithaca, NY: Snow Lion Publications, 2001), 208.
20. This is available at www.lotsawahouse.org/words-of-the-buddha/samantabhadra-aspiration-good-actions.

21. Of the twofold benefit attained at enlightenment—the benefit for self and benefit for other—it's the accumulation of wisdom that leads to the ultimate benefit for oneself, the realization of the dharmakaya; and it's the accumulation of merit that leads to the ultimate benefit for others, the rupakayas, or form kayas. Once again, what we perceive as form, matter, is the result of merit.

22. Dodrupchen Rinpoche, quoted in Tulku Thondup, *Peaceful Death, Joyful Rebirth*, 218.

23. Shambhala Publications has a recording of Richard Gere reading Trungpa Rinpoche's translation. In the "bardo package" offered by KTD (see appendix 1), it is read in Tibetan. It is said that due to the temporary powers of supercognition, the reading will be understood in any language.

    Tulku Thondup Rinpoche has written a user-friendly distillation of the essence of *The Tibetan Book of the Dead*: see *Peaceful Death, Joyful Rebirth*, 202–206.

    The Tibetan Book of the Dead, or what is more accurately translated as *The Great Liberation Through Hearing in the Intermediate State* (*Bardo Thödol Chenmo*), is one of six forms of liberation in the Nyingma tradition. The six are liberation through sight; through touch; through taste; through remembrance; through wearing; and through hearing. *The Tibetan Book of the Dead* also belongs to the categories of liberation through sight (just seeing the text can arouse a flash of liberation) and liberation through remembrance (by remembering the instructions in the bardo you are liberated). See *Luminous Emptiness* by Francesca Fremantle, 51–52. For more on this seminal text, see Bryan J. Cuevas, *The Hidden History of the Tibetan Book of the Dead* (New York: Oxford University Press, 2003) and Donald S. Lopez, Jr., *The Tibetan Book of the Dead: A Biography* (Princeton: Princeton University Press, 2011).

24. Francesca Fremantle, *Luminous Emptiness*, 367.

25. Gandharvas are also a different class of being in Buddhism, one of the lowest-ranking devas. This is when they are known as celestial musicians. Gandharvas also exist in Hinduism, as male nature spirits. In the bardos, gandharvas are a special type of hungry ghost. The bardos are not in any of the six realms (this is one reason why it is called *bardo*, or "gap"), but if one remains in the bardo for a long time one may become an actual hungry ghost.

26. *Sur* is made up of the "three whites" (butter, yogurt, and milk) and the "three sweets" (honey, sugar, and molasses) mixed with barley or flour. One can order *sur*, or an entire *sur* kit that includes everything you need, from www.tibetantreasures.com.

27. Tulku Thondup, *Peaceful Death, Joyful Rebirth*, 222. A short liturgy for the sur offering may be found on 259–263.

28. Use any internet search engine to obtain information for centers in America and Asia. Centers that do this include Vajra Vidya in Crestone, Colorado; Karma Triyana Dharmachakra in Woodstock, New York; the Chagdud Gonpa Foun-

dation in California; the Phowa Foundation, and the Foundation for the Preservation of the Mahayana Tradition.

29. For a description of some of these practices, see *Peaceful Death, Joyful Rebirth* by Tulku Thondup; *The Tibetan Book of Living and Dying* by Sogyal Rinpoche; *Oracles and Demons of Tibet* by René de Nebesky-Wojkowitz (New Delhi: Paljor Publications, 1998), chapter 26; and especially *Advice and Practices for Death and Dying* by Lama Zopa Rinpoche. For universal meditations that Buddhists and non-Buddhists can do to help, see Sogyal Rinpoche, *The Tibetan Book of Living and Dying*, 214–217, on "Essential Phowa"; and Tulku Thondup, *Peaceful Death, Joyful Rebirth*, 201, on "Universal Meditation for All."

30. There are websites that now offer this form of phowa: see the Phowa Foundation at www.phowafoundation.org/PFrequest_services.php.

31. Many teachers say it is never too late to do phowa. Even if the being has already taken rebirth, the merit of doing phowa for them will still reach them. Most teachers say it never hurts to do phowa for others. Other lamas say that only masters should do phowa for others, and that those who have not reached the first bhumi are not equipped to perform this practice for others.

32. There are some very high lamas who can locate a consciousness even after it has taken rebirth. The Karmapas are famous for this, as are the Tai Situs. They specialize in locating tulkus, the voluntary incarnations.

33. Lama Atse, quote in Chagdud Tulku, *Lord of the Dance: The Autobiography of a Tibetan Lama* (Junction City, CA: Padma Publishing, 1992), 36–37.

34. Subsumed under this classification are dozens of malicious unseen beings: *senmo, gyalgong, don, gek, barche, mamo,* and *rakshasa,* to name just a few.

35. Lama Pagyel informed me that *dur* originated with Karma Chagme Rinpoche at a time when *rolangs,* what we might call zombies, became a problem in Tibet. Dur was therefore a kind of exorcism, removing the negative spirits and liberating the rolangs. See Tulku Urgyen Rinpoche, *Rainbow Painting* (Hong Kong: Rangjung Yeshe Publications, 1995), 176–188. For more on *dur,* see Namkha Drimed Rinpoche's comments below in part 3.

36. Tulku Urgyen Rinpoche, *Blazing Splendor,* 245–246.

37. In appendix B of *Peaceful Death, Joyful Rebirth,* Tulku Thondup Rinpoche offers eight esoteric death rituals for the dying and the dead, the essence of which is to perform phowa for the dead person and to send their consciousness to Sukhavati.

38. Sogyal Rinpoche, *The Tibetan Book of Living and Dying,* 306.

39. For a description of this ritual, see *Peaceful Death, Joyful Rebirth* by Tulku Thondup, 221–224.

40. See Lama Zopa Rinpoche, *Advice and Practices for Death and Dying,* 18.

41. Sogyal Rinpoche, *The Tibetan Book of Living and Dying,* 306–307.

42. Chagdud Khadro, *P'howa Commentary,* 79–80.

43. See Chagdud Khadro, *Red Tara Commentary: Instructions for the Concise*

Practice Known as Red Tara: An Open Door to Bliss and Ultimate Awareness (Junction City, CA: Padma Publishing, 1999), 78–80. Contact chagdud@snowcrest.net for more information or to request this practice be done for the dead.

44. Sogyal Rinpoche, *The Tibetan Book of Living and Dying*, 308.

45. See Lama Zopa Rinpoche, *Advice and Practices for Death and Dying*, 34–36 and 44–50 for more details.

46. Lama Zopa lists the powerful mantras for liberating beings from the lower realms (ibid., 121–129), and then the extensive benefits of reciting them (132–148). For example,

> These five mantras have unbelievable power; they have unbelievable power to purify negative karma. If you recite these mantras, blow on sand, and then sprinkle the sand on someone's grave or cremation site, you can affect that person's consciousness, no matter where they have been reborn. You do not even have to touch the body. Simply sprinkling the blessed sand on the grave or cremation site can purify that person's negative karma and bring them a good rebirth . . . simply touching these mantras to the body of a dying or dead person purifies their negative karma, and they are not reborn in the lower realms. (Lama Zopa Rinpoche, *Advice and Practices for Death and Dying*, 133)

47. For definitions and explanations of these many terms and practices, see ibid., 343–344.

48. Ibid., 35–36, 44–50.

CHAPTER 7: BEFORE DEATH APPROACHES

1 The "Family Love Letter," created by John J. Scroggin and coauthored with Donna Pagano, 2010, available at www.familyloveletter.com. Excerpt drawn from booklet pages i, iii.

2. Glenn H. Mullin, *Living in the Face of Death*, 83–84.

3. Chögyam Trungpa, *Illusion's Game: The Life and Teaching of Naropa*, edited by Sherab Chödzin (Boston: Shambhala Publications, 1994), 51.

4. A Channel Islands auction house, in the UK, auctioned off a vial of blood from Ronald Reagan for over $11,000 this week. Articles of clothing and other personal possessions that belonged to famous people are routinely sold at high prices.

5. The statistics for survival with CPR, at any age, vary widely (and from study to study): from 3 percent to 16 percent. The odds are still low—even for the young and healthy. The same rule for DNR apples to major surgery for the elderly. Many families often regret having done invasive surgery for their elderly loved ones, who may never recover from the surgical trauma.

6. John Scroggin and Donna Pagano offer this important warning:

> Perhaps one of the most common mistakes in estate planning is naming the wrong beneficiaries of life insurance policies and retirement funds. You may not remember who you named as beneficiary or previous designations may be no longer valid because of changes in your wealth or family circumstances. Have you taken your ex-spouse off of your retirement plan or life insurance beneficiary designation? Every three to four years obtain a written confirmation from your life insurance carrier and retirement plan administrator of your designated beneficiaries. Do not designate minor children as beneficiaries (even as contingent beneficiaries), because they may inherit the assets at age 18. Instead, pass the assets into a trust to be held until the heirs have reached sufficient maturity to handle the money. ("Family Love Letter," created by John J. Scroggin and coauthored by Donna Pagano, 2010; excerpt drawn from booklet page iv)

Copies of life insurance policies are among the most important documents for your family to have. They need to know the name of the carrier, the agent associated with the policy, and the policy number. Be careful with policies granted by an employer upon your retirement, since these are the ones usually missed. The state of New York alone is holding more than $400 million in life insurance related payments that have gone unclaimed, and just since 2000. If your heirs are not aware of these kind of accounts, they will not be able to lay claim to them. [Andrew Holecek]

7. Included in your medical POA, and discussed in advance with your entrusted Dharma friends, should be instructions on how to handle pain medications. You want to be as conscious as possible when you die, not overly sedated with narcotics or other agents, but also not under-sedated and in extreme pain. Palliative care providers are trained in titrating (managing) levels of narcotics. Give your care providers specific guidelines in advance, through these legal documents, and the trusted friends who can implement them. [Andrew Holecek]

8. Some online legal resources include Aging with Dignity's *Five Wishes* (www.agingwithdignity.org), The American Hospital Association's *Put It in Writing* (www.putitinwriting.org), www.scrogginlaw.com, www.naepc.org, and www.estateplanninglinks.com.

9. Shirley du Boulay, *Cicely Saunders: Founder of the Modern Hospice Movement* (London: Hodder and Stoughton, 1984), 233.

10. K. Garces-Foley, "Buddhism, Hospice and the American Way of Dying," *Review of Religious Research* 44, no. 4 (2003): 344.

11. Maggie Callahan and Patricia Kelley, *Final Gifts: Understanding the Special Awareness Needs and Communications of the Dying* (New York: Bantam Books, 1997), 25–26.

12. In general, individuals are eligible for Medicare if they are United States citizens,

or have been permanent legal residents for at least five continuous years, and they are 65 years or older; or they are under 65, are disabled, and have been receiving either Social Security benefits or Railroad Retirement Board disability benefits for at least 24 months from date of entitlement (first disability payment), or get continuing dialysis for end stage renal disease or need a kidney transplant, or they are eligible for Social Security Disability Insurance and have amyotrophic lateral sclerosis.

The Medicare program was created in 1965 under Title XVIII of the Social Security Act. The original Medicare program has two parts: Part A (Hospital Insurance), and Part B (Medical Insurance).

Medicare Part A covers inpatient hospital stays, including semiprivate room, food, tests, and doctors' fees, and also covers stays in a skilled nursing facility if certain criteria are met.

Part B medical insurance helps pay for some services and products not covered by Part A, generally on an outpatient basis. Part B is optional and may be deferred if the beneficiary or their spouse is still actively working. However, there is a lifetime penalty (10 percent per year) imposed for not enrolling in Part B unless the beneficiary or spouse is employed. Part B coverage includes physician and nursing services, x-rays, laboratory and diagnostic tests, influenza and pneumonia vaccinations, blood transfusions, renal dialysis, outpatient hospital procedures, limited ambulance transportation, immunosuppressive drugs for organ transplant recipients, chemotherapy, hormonal treatments, and other outpatient medical treatments administered in a doctor's office. Part B also covers medical equipment such as wheelchairs as well as prosthetic devices and oxygen.

Under the Balanced Budget Act of 1997, Medicare beneficiaries were given the option to receive their Medicare benefits through private health insurance plans instead of through the original Medicare plan (Parts A and B). These programs were known as "Medicare Plus Choice" or "Part C" plans.

Pursuant to the Medicare Prescription Drug, Improvement, and Modernization Act of 2003 (MMA), prescription drug coverage was added to Part C coverage and became known as "Medicare Advantage" (MA) plans. Medicare Part D was also enacted under the MMA in 2006, and provides comprehensive drug coverage for all Medicare beneficiaries.

There is no income threshold for Medicare as there is for Medicaid (discussed below). For those who qualify for both Medicare and Medicaid, Medicaid will pay the beneficiaries' Part B premium and also pay for any drugs that are not covered by Medicare Part D.

Neither Part A nor Part B pays for all of a covered person's medical costs. The program contains premiums, deductibles and coinsurance, which the covered individual must pay out-of-pocket. Some people may qualify to have other governmental programs (such as Medicaid) pay premiums and some or all of the costs associated with Medicare. It should also be noted that Medicare does not pay for any item or service that is not reasonable and necessary for the diagnosis or treatment of an illness or injury. The notable exception to this requirement is hospice care, where coverage is provided for palliative care connected to the patient's hospice diagnosis.

Medicaid was created on July 30, 1965, through Title XIX of the Social Security Act to provide health care for individuals and families with low incomes and resources. It is a means-tested program that is jointly funded by the states and federal government, and is managed by the states. Medicaid is the largest source of funding for medical and health-related services for people with limited income in the United States. Because of the aging population, the fastest growing aspect of Medicaid is nursing home coverage.

In contrast to Medicare, Medicaid is a means-tested program that is not solely funded at the federal level and is a needs-based social welfare or social protection program rather than a social insurance program. Medicaid covers a wider range of health care services than Medicare.

Having a limited income is one of the primary requirements for Medicaid eligibility, but poverty alone does not qualify a person to receive Medicaid benefits unless they also fall into one of the defined eligibility categories. These other requirements include age, pregnancy, disability, blindness, and one's status as a U.S. citizen or a lawfully admitted immigrant. Special rules exist for those living in a nursing home and disabled children living at home.

13. See BuddhaNet (www.buddhanet.net) for a list of Buddhist-oriented hospices, hospice support programs, and training programs in English-speaking countries.

14. Gordon Brown, *Courage: Portraits of Bravery in the Service of Great Causes* (New York: Weinstein Books, 2008), 185.

15. Maggie Callahan and Patricia Kelley, *Final Gifts*, 25–26.

16. Gordon Brown, *Courage*, 190.

17. Elisabeth Kübler-Ross, *Death: The Final Stages of Growth* (New York: Simon and Schuster, 1975), x.

18. The National Hospice and Palliative Care Organization offers further helpful information: www.caringinfo.org.

CHAPTER 8: CARING FOR THE DYING

Epigraph drawn from B. K. S. Iyengar, *Concise Light on Yoga*, 20.

1. And rebirth into an animal realm. This is where the physical interfaces with the spiritual. Excessive narcotics can predispose the mind toward rebirth into an animal realm. A heavy, thick, and even stupid mental state is a quality of the animal realm, and excessive narcotics can bring about that state of mind. A sensitive caregiver will manage the amount of narcotic provided, removing the pain

but not unnecessarily dulling the mind. It's the middle way again: not enough pain medication can create a hellish state of mind and predispose the person to rebirth in a hell realm; too much of a narcotic can direct them into an animal realm. [Andrew Holecek]

2. Hospice has the goal of not curing the disease, while palliative medicine takes a broader view where patients can receive palliative care (which is about relieving pain or alleviating a problem without dealing with the underlying cause) and at the same time receive curative treatments, for example chemotherapy. One of the best books on the medical issues around death is Dr. Sherwin Nuland's elegant *How We Die: Reflections on Life's Final Chapter* (New York: Vintage Books, 1995).

3. My family had to make these decisions around the death of my mother. Prolonging unnecessary suffering and incurring unnecessary financial burdens led us to choose against artificial nourishment. A 1992 study reported that having a medical power of attorney, or a living will, saved more than $60,000 per patient during their final stay at the hospital. Twenty-seven percent of Medicare's annual $327 billion budget goes to the final year of life, with that percentage increasing dramatically as the final months and weeks approach. It is estimated that by 2050, the cost of treating Alzheimer's alone will be $1 trillion annually in America. The *New York Times* columnist David Brooks said this about the national budget: "This fiscal crisis [that began in 2008] is about many things, but one of them is our inability to face death—our willingness to spend our nation into bankruptcy to extend life for a few more sickly months" (*The Denver Post*, July 16, 2011).

   Many of these costs are unnecessary. They are due to doctors and family continuing to view death as a defeat. They want to keep patients alive at all costs, so that they can win what they perceive as a battle. The prolonged emotional costs are even higher. Examine your motivation if you're leaning toward force-feeding, or any other heroic end-of-life treatment. Remember that death is not a failure, and denying artificial nourishment is not euthanasia.

4. People often wonder about the relationship of dementia (not delirium) to Alzheimer's disease. Dementia is mental deterioration due to physical changes in the brain, resulting in poor memory. The most common disease causing dementia is Alzheimer's. Signs of dementia include getting lost, misplacing things, poor judgment, difficulty in dressing or grooming, forgetting or using wrong words, problems with numbers, paranoia, and mood swings or personality changes.

5. Dr. Gershten: "Narcotics directly suppress respiratory drive and can decrease the rate and depth of breathing. Benzodiazepines in high doses can induce similar effects. The net effect is that prolonged or high doses of these agents can lead to hypoventilation, hypoxia, and hypercarbia, all of which have the potential to shorten life." Dr. Matlock: "In the case of palliative sedation or terminal seda-

tion, where someone is in so much pain or having so much agitation that the only way to relieve the symptom is through sedation, then they might die more quickly because they have no opportunity to eat or drink. In court cases, the principle of 'double effect' was used to argue that the *intent* is to relieve suffering, distinguishing it from physician-assisted suicide, where the *intent* is to actually kill."

6. Doctors often don't appreciate being told what to prescribe, or for that matter what they should do for the care of someone, so make any suggestions to the attending physician gently.

7. Hospice volunteers are not allowed to provide hands-on care, things like feeding, giving medication, toileting, or deep massage. They provide valuable companionship to the person and the family. Activities might include reading aloud to the person, staying with them so that family can take a break or run errands, helping letters get written, playing cards or games, playing music, giving a manicure or pedicure, arranging or fixing up the patient's hair, discussing end of life issues (or most anything else), and mostly just being there and listening. Hospice volunteers are an integral part of the hospice team.

8. If you do use home health care services, be sure they are bonded and insured, which means they must comply with local and state regulations. Make sure they have a good reputation. Horror stories of theft and even physical abuse of the dying are not uncommon.

9. The (hopefully) dead have been subjected to smelling salts, electric shock, flashlights in eyes, ice water in ears, rubber hammers, sharp pricks to fingers, caustic chemicals to the skin to see if it blisters, yanks on limbs, and other macabre and humorous tests. The Greeks cut off a finger; the Hebrews considered putrefaction the only fail-safe indicator of death. In 1981, the Uniform Determination of Death Act was passed. Section 1 defines death as (1) irreversible cessation of circulatory and respiratory functions, or (2) irreversible cessation of all functions of the entire brain, including the brain stem. See *The Undead: Organ Harvesting, the Ice-Water Test, Beating-Heart Cadavers—How Medicine Is Blurring the Line Between Life and Death* (New York: Pantheon Books, 2012) by Dick Teresi.

10. Contrary to what many medical scientists and doctors assert, the mind is not the brain. There is obviously a deep connection, but the equation of mind and brain—that mind is merely an epiphenomenon, an epigenetic expression of the brain—is a reductionist assumption based on a myopic and materialistic world view. Philosopher Colin McGinn said, "The problem with materialism is that it tries to construct the mind out of properties that refuse to add up to mentality." The philosopher Alfred North Whitehead wrote about "the fallacy of misplaced concreteness." This tendency to pigeonhole and identify a person with/as the disease, or the mind with the brain, are instances of what we could call "the fallacy of misplaced identification."

One way to resolve this is that at gross levels of mind, the connection between the mind and the brain, the mental and the physical, is intimate. Since most of science works at these gross levels, it is not surprising to find most scientists equating mind with brain. But at subtle levels of mind, that connection starts to unravel. According to the Buddhist view, at very subtle levels of formless awareness, mind becomes independent of body and brain. The clear light mind of death, the dharmakaya, as form-less and therefore brain-less awareness, is not contingent upon the body, the form kayas.

11. But I have worked in hospitals, and been around the medical world for over thirty years, and there are doctors who abuse the power unconsciously invested in them by their patients, almost seducing their patients into believing that the diagnosis is now who they are. There is also evidence that succumbing to a diagnosis can induce a negative placebo effect. Instead of curing an ailment, as positive placebos have been shown to do, negative placebo effects fulfill the prophecy of the diagnosis.

12. And of prognosis. Patients and families often want to know the prognosis, the outlook, for an illness. While an average estimate can be given for a particular terminal illness, the range around this average can vary enormously. Dr. Berman says, "Some patients I would expect to live for many months die rapidly. Other patients who I have expected to live for a short period have gone on for years."

13. Candace Pert, *Molecules of Emotion: The Science Behind Mind-Body Medicine* (New York: Scribner, 1997), 323. This is a penetrating book on psychoneuro-immunology (PNI), or mind-body medicine. It explores the two-way street of how mind affects body (downward causation) and body affects mind (upward causation).

14. Chögyam Trungpa, *Shambhala: The Sacred Path of the Warrior* (Boston: Shambhala Publications, 1984), 155.

15. B. K. S. Iyengar, *Concise Light on Yoga*, 20, 30.

16. Of the many books on emptiness, see Khenpo Tsültrim Gyamtso Rinpoche, *Progressive Stages of Meditation on Emptiness* (Oxford: Longchen Foundation, 1986), and *The Sun of Wisdom* (Boston: Shambhala Publications, 2003). Echoes of emptiness are also found in general systems theory, ecology, deep ecology, quantum mechanics, chaos and complexity theory, deconstructionism, and any other discipline that deals with dependent origination. In many ways, emptiness is the heart of Buddhism, as represented in the *Heart Sutra*. Emptiness is echoed in other spiritual paths. The Sufi mystic Ibn 'Arabi, says: "For knowledge of God does not presuppose the ceasing of existence nor the ceasing of that ceasing. For things have no existence, and what does not exist cannot cease to exist . . . Then if thou know thyself without existence or ceasing to be, then thou knowest God; and if not, then not" (Ibn 'Arabi, *Whoso Knoweth Himself*, trans. T. H. Weir [Gloucestersire, England: Beshara Publications, 1976], 5).

17. Khenpo Tsültrim Gyamtso Rinpoche, "Illness as Path," talk in Boulder, Colorado, October 11, 1994, translated by Michele Martin.

18. Which would be the error of solipsism. If we are careful, we can proclaim the New Age adage "you create your own reality." Being careful means we first have to define "you," "create," "your," and "reality." Thought *affecting* reality is at the heart of mind-body medicine. But even here it's just one ingredient in the complex play of etiology.

19. John Welwood, "Intimate Relationship as Spiritual Crucible," *Shambhala Sun* magazine 17, no. 2 (2008), 112.

20. Ibid., 112.

21. Enlightenment is identifying with the trikaya, not just the dharmakaya. In order for your identity to be complete, to encompass all of reality, it must include the union of form and emptiness, the rupakayas with the dharmakaya, the relative with the absolute. This, of course, is the great irony of a complete understanding of emptiness: by becoming no-thing (empty, the dharmakaya) you simultaneously become everything (the form kayas). Real emptiness means fullness.

CHAPTER 9: AFTER DEATH

1. With Karen Van Vuuren's permission, I have inserted all the endnotes for her contribution to this chapter.

    Not everyone will feel comfortable bathing the body of a loved one after death, or engaging in other practical matters and spiritual rituals that surround death. This section offers possibilities that many people are not even aware of; it does not mandate the application of these possibilities. If bathing the body doesn't feel right to you, for example, then don't do it. [Andrew Holecek]

2. Artist Jae Rhim Lee is blending art, science, and culture in a highly innovative way when it comes to dealing with dead bodies. In her "Infinity Burial Project," Lee is cultivating "infinity mushrooms" that are seeded in a "mushroom death suit," a hooded garment that is like a snowmobile suit. These special mushrooms are designed to eat the body and remove the environmental toxins that are stored within it—toxins that would otherwise be released into the air with cremation, or into the soil with burial. She takes the idea of a green funeral to new frontiers. With her "Decompiculture Society," she is finding ways to keep impermanence in mind, reduce our impact on the environment, and chuckle while you do so. [Andrew Holecek]

3. There are currently a handful of states that make it difficult to work without a funeral director—see the Funeral Consumers Alliance website, www.funerals. org, for the latest on state requirements listed in Carlson's book *Caring for the Dead: Your Final Act of Love* (Hinesburg, VT: Upper Access, 1998).

4. If you're working with a funeral home, they often get the death certificate, have it signed by the doctor and medical examiner, and file it with the county clerk.

    Most states have either a coroner or a medical examiner. Coroners and medical examiners both deal with death, and therefore the two titles are often used interchangeably. This usage is technically incorrect, since the job descriptions are very different. The qualifications for becoming a medical examiner are more strenuous than those for becoming a coroner, and the two go about their jobs in different ways.

A medical examiner is a licensed physician who specializes in forensic pathology. When a death merits an autopsy, a medical examiner performs the autopsy and records the findings. Although medical examiners form an important part of a law enforcement team, they do not necessarily decide the course of an investigation or prosecution of a suspect—but they can make recommendations to law enforcement about whether to proceed with an investigation. A medical examiner's job is based on professional skill, and he or she is an appointed official. Some states do not have any specifications around who can be elected coroners while others require a coroner to be a physician (which makes the position a medical examiner in all but name). Coroners are generally elected and do not need a medical background. [Andrew Holecek]

5. The signs in the Tibetan tradition are discussed above in the section on tukdam—see page 82.

6. You may also want to consider removing your loved one's gold dental work before cremation. It's easy to remove a gold crown and take it to a jeweler for cash. If grandma had gold crowns, discuss this issue with your family and the funeral director. There have been a number of cases of morticians pulling out the gold dental work from corpses under their care and selling it without the knowledge of the deceased's family. [Andrew Holecek]

7. Embalming, and autopsy, should be avoided if possible. Refrigeration of the body (discussed below) is the preservation of choice. [Andrew Holecek]

8. From the Buddhist perspective, autopsies are to be avoided, as discussed earlier. [Andrew Holecek]

9. To give you some idea of costs, as of this writing (2009): funeral service with casket, vault, and gravestone: $4,400; cremation service with rental casket and marble urn: $3,400; direct cremation, including simple plastic urn: $900; direct, or green, burial, including simple cloth and fiberboard casket: $1,500; veterans service package with wood or metal casket: $3,700; cremation with memorial service, including register book and thank-you cards: $1,200. [Andrew Holecek]

10. From a Buddhist perspective, cryogenics, or any attempt to preserve the body for future vivification, is not good. It can foster serious attachment to the body and adversely affect our journey through the bardo. At death, we must let go. Preserving the body in this way makes letting go much harder. [Andrew Holecek]

11. As part of Trungpa Rinpoche's training and upbringing, he was exposed to dead bodies at an early age and continued to witness death throughout his childhood years. This is standard in many parts of Asia, where death is an honest and open affair. For Buddhists, being around death is a powerful reminder of the truths of

reality. If children are exposed to it early on, and with sensitive guidance, they can develop a mature and healthy relationship to a major part of life. [Andrew Holecek]

12. The following organizations provide further information on home funerals and arranging transport of the body to and from the hospital or home: Crossings: Caring for Our Own at Death (www.crossings.net); Final Passages (www.finalpassages.org); Karen's wonderful organization, Natural Transitions (www.naturaltransitions.org); and Undertaken with Love (www.undertakenwithlove.org).

13. Weeks after I was asked to write this, both my mother and my mother-in-law died within a week of each other. These deaths have made this entire project—gathering my thoughts, not knowing if they make sense, forgetting to write, forgetting where I left my notes, having emotional outbreaks at the closeness of the subject, questioning my ability to offer anyone anything of value—very challenging. But the severe reality of living without these two precious women has placed this passage in front of me every day with every word I say, think, and write. While my own process feels too new and too private to share, the voice I can offer right now is seated inside a broken-open heart with many years of watching and helping behind me. I hope it is useful.

14. Christine Longaker, *Facing Death and Finding Hope*, 166.

15. Karma and the samskaras are the residue of unlived experience, of events that were not related to properly. If we do not relate to experiences properly, especially painful ones, we reincarnate until we learn how to do so. The residue becomes seeds that blossom into future experiences. Many experiences are too "hot," so we cool life down in an effort to handle it, unknowingly planting the seeds for countless future lives by our inability, or unwillingness, to live this one fully. A fundamental ingredient of proper relationship, of course, is equanimity.

16. Christine Longaker, *Facing Death and Finding Hope*, 161.

17. We should avail ourselves of both supports. It is beyond our scope, but grief can get difficult: there is traumatic grief; disenfranchised grief; delayed, avoided, or distorted grief; prolonged grief; and complicated grief, to name some of the most common.

    Many of us feel sad thoughts that don't slide into depression. People biochemically or emotionally predisposed to depression will let those thoughts take them over the edge into a deep abyss of negative thinking—an abyss dug through repetitive negative thinking.

18. For a more complete discussion of grief and depression, see appendix 3. Here is one way to look at the roots of depression: look below depression and you will find anger; look below anger and you will find sadness; look below sadness and you will find fear; and look below fear to discover its root in existential anxiety. In other words, the basis of all these emotions is the fear of our nonexistence, our inherent egolessness—the fear of death.

Once we crystalize the sense of self out of space (the first skandha), we automatically crystalize the sense of other. With the birth of other comes the birth of fear.

19. Grieving for a pet has all the same factors as grieving for a human being. It's the *relationship* that's under consideration, not the object of that relationship. One could grieve the loss of a house, or any other object. See the section on death of a pet in chapter 10 below.

20. Yoga, t'ai chi, or any form of mindful exercise invites us into the natural wisdom and healing power of the body. There is evidence that if you can get someone with depression to exercise, the depression lifts. Any form of body work is healthy, but especially when thoughts and emotions overwhelm us. There is wisdom, literally and metaphorically, in "coming to our senses."

21. Arnaud Maitland, *Living Without Regret: Growing Old in the Light of Tibetan Buddhism* (Berkeley: Dharma Publishing, 2006), 268.

22. Thrangu Rinpoche said that compassion and devotion enhance the experience of mahamudra (enlightenment), and are simultaneously expressions of it.

23. Kathleen Willis Morton, quoted in a review of her book *The Blue Poppy and the Mustard Seed: A Mother's Story of Loss and Hope* (Somerville, MA: Wisdom Publications, 2008) by Sarah Todd in *Tricycle* magazine, Summer 2009.

24. Judy Tatelbaum, *The Courage to Grieve: Creative Living, Recovery, and Growth Through Grief* (New York: Harper and Row, 1980), 107.

25. In many ways, the entire Buddhist path is about purifying reality of existence and discovering the illusory nature (the emptiness) of things. Enlightenment is a great irony. It is waking up *from* the nightmare of existence—of seeing things as solid, lasting, and independent—and *into* a dreamlike world.

26. Sogyal Rinpoche, quoted in Christine Longaker, *Facing Death and Finding Hope*, x.

27. The body can be viewed as a mandala, which is literally an "essence" (*manda*) "container" (*la*). When the mandala dissolves at death, the deathless essence once contained by the body now spills out into space, and eventually into countless new mandalas.

28. Thich Nhat Hanh, "The Heart of the Matter," in *Tricycle* magazine, Winter 2009.

29. To put this from the perspective of the bardos: the luminosity that arises out of emptiness (and is inseparable from it) first manifests as five principal qualities of enlightenment, the five Buddha families. From those primordial qualities are born the infinite forms of this world. In other words, the luminous bardo of dharmata is pure quality. From that arises the solid forms of the bardo of this life, which are just reified qualities. For more on the five Buddha families, see *Journey Without Goal*, 77–87, by Trungpa Rinpoche, and *The Five Wisdom Energies* by Irini Rockwell.

30. According to Wikisource, the passage was published anonymously: see http://

en.wikisource.org/wiki/Gone_From_My_Sight, accessed July 25, 2012. It appeared with no title in *Record of Christian Work*, vol. 23, edited by Alexander McConnell, William Revell Moody, and Arthur Percy Fitt (Record of Christian Work, Co., 1904), 349–350.

CHAPTER 10: DIFFICULT ISSUES

1. The death of a child is also one of the most difficult experiences. See Christine Longaker, *Facing Death and Finding Hope*, 202–216.
2. Judith Simmer-Brown, personal correspondence.
3. Scott Edelstein, in *Buddhadharma* magazine, Summer 2011, p. 15.
4. Khenpo Tsültrim Gyamtso Rinpoche, personal correspondence, translated by Ari Goldfield. Masters often manifest tukdam for the benefit of their students, to inspire them that enlightenment is possible.
5. This is because they have not yet been introduced to, or become familiar with, the subtle levels of enlightened mind that are laid bare at the end of the bardo of dying. The child will not recognize the mother, and therefore their reunion (tukdam) doesn't occur.
6. *Vajradhatu Practice Manual*, p. 7, accessed on May 18, 2009 at http://www. halifax.shambhala.org/aging.php.
7. Organ donation is expanding dramatically in its scope. In addition to full face transplants, people can donate feet, ankles, legs, fingers, windpipes, voice boxes, the abdominal wall, and even a uterus or penis. Dr. Bohdan Pomahac, who has done four face transplants, says, "When you think about the human body, there is really nothing that could not be replaced by transplantation. Almost nothing" (*The Denver Post*, January 1, 2011).
8. If possible, leave the body undisturbed for twenty minutes after breathing has stopped, for the inner dissolution to transpire. If that's not possible, then don't worry.
9. See chapter 1, note 93, for more on the brahmarandhra.
10. You can also mix some *mani* pills with water from Mt. Kailash. According to Lama Zopa, this is Vajrayogini water, and "anyone who drinks this, it is said, goes to a pure land. . . . when you think you are dying, at that time you drink it" (Lama Zopa Rinpoche, *Advice and Practices for Death and Dying*, 42).
11. Similar considerations apply in the case of autopsy. Dr. Levy writes:

> Trungpa Rinpoche said that autopsies are to be avoided by Buddhists because the consciousness is still very close to the body immediately after death. Thus the consciousness experiences and witnesses what happens to the body. Even when death is anticipated, the confusion and panic that arises because of identification with the body will be heightened by the autopsy experience. For these reasons, autopsies are discouraged. There are situations in which autopsies are required by law. In these instances,

it should be made clear to the authorities that autopsy is contrary to your religious belief.

> See *Vajradhatu Practice Manual*, p. 15, accessed on May 18, 2009 at http://www.halifax.shambhala.org/aging.php.

12. For a detailed discussion of euthanasia, suicide, and a host of related topics, see *Into the Jaws of Yama, Lord of Death: Buddhism, Bioethics, and Death*, by Karma Lekshe Tsomo.

13. Most of the teachings on the bardo for humans also applies to pets. They are sentient beings like us. But in terms of actively euthanizing a pet, Khenpo Tsültrim Gyamtso Rinpoche said, "If your motivation is great compassion for your pet, and you make aspiration prayers for it, then administering euthanasia to a suffering pet is okay."

14. The increase of suffering after death may seem to be contradicted by those who come back from near-death and relate blissful experiences. This is because they haven't completely died, and therefore have not entered the karmic bardo of becoming. They are perhaps experiencing the bliss, clarity, and nonthought of the inner dissolution, or maybe even glimpsing something of the luminous bardo of dharmata. In these first two bardos, there is bliss and light as karma is temporarily suspended. But karma reignites with a vengeance in the karmic bardo of becoming, which is where the nightmarish consequences of our final actions and states of mind re-arise. We may temporarily fall into blissful deep sleep, but then the nightmares kick in when we start to dream.

15. The Dalai Lama, quoted in Sogyal Rinpoche, *The Tibetan Book of Living and Dying*, 375.

16. Kalu Rinpoche, *The Gem Ornament* (Ithaca, NY: Snow Lion Publications, 1986), 194.

17. About 2,300 suicides occur every day (18.4 suicides per 100,000 people). Suicide is often in the top ten causes of death. Michelle Linn-Gust, president of the American Association of Suicidology, offers this word of advice: "When someone dies like that, all anyone can think about is how the person died. Let go of how that person died and remember how they were in life. A life shouldn't be defined by a suicide." In other words, don't reify the event, making it the defining moment of a person's life.

Parents Surviving Suicide, a support group, recommends the following books. I list all these to show that suicide survivors are not alone: *My son . . . My son . . .* by Iris Bolton; *Touched by Suicide: Hope and Healing After Loss*, by Michael F. Myers and Carle Fine; *Life After Suicide: A Ray of Hope for Those Left Behind*, by E. Betsy Ross; *Night Falls Fast*, by Kay Redfield Jamison; *Why Suicide?* by Eric Marcus; *Do They Have Bad Days in Heaven?* by Michelle Linn-Gust; *Survivors of Suicide*, by Rita Robinson; *When Nothing Matters Anymore: A Survival Guide for Depressed Teens*, by Bev Cobain; *Healing After the Suicide of a Loved One*, by Ann Smolin and John Guinan; *Suicide: The Forever Decision*, by Paul Quinnett; *No Time to Say Goodbye*, by Carla Fine; *After Suicide Loss: Coping With Your Grief*, by Bob Baugher; *Recovering From Your Child's Suicide*, by Mort Schrag; *The Power to Prevent Suicide*, by Richard E. Nelson and Judith C. Galas; *The Silent Cry: Teen Suicide and Self-Destructive Behaviors*, by Joan Esherick.

18. Khenpo Karthar Rinpoche says that a person who commits suicide will spend all the time they would have naturally lived (had they not committed suicide) in the bardo, and that during this time they will re-experience their suicide five hundred times each day. His Holiness Khyentse Rinpoche says: "When a person commits suicide, the consciousness has no choice but to follow its negative karma, and it may well happen that a harmful spirit will seize and possess its life force. In the case of suicide, a powerful master must perform special kinds of practices, such as fire ceremonies and other rituals, in order to free the dead person's consciousness" (Khyentse Rinpoche, quoted in Sogyal Rinpoche, *The Tibetan Book of Living and Dying*, 376). See pages 152 and 296 above on the practice of *dur* in dealing with these harmful spirits. Bokar Rinpoche said:

> Buddha said that suicide is an extremely negative act ... it is said that committing suicide is far more serious than killing another person. Committing suicide means killing the deities that are the essence of our body. That which motivates a person to commit suicide, and consequently to kill his or her own deities, is karmically more serious than the motivation leading to killing someone else.
>
> QUESTION [to Bokar Rinpoche]: Is it not said that a person who commits suicide will do it again five hundred times in future lives?
>
> ANSWER: Yes, that is correct, and yet this does not happen systematically. (Bokar Rinpoche, *Death and the Art of Dying in Tibetan Buddhism* [San Francisco: ClearPoint Press, 1993], 40)

Lama Lodo says, "It is impossible for beings to kill themselves while in a positive state of mind. This is a contradiction in terms.... Buddhas never kill themselves." Karma Lekshe Tsomo says, "To die with a bad conscience is karmically lethal."

19. Carl B. Becker, *Breaking the Circle*, 136, 137, 139.

20. Jean-François Revel and Matthieu Ricard, *The Monk and the Philosopher: A Father and Son Discuss the Meaning of Life* (New York, Schocken Books Inc., 1998), 238.

21. See "Buddhism and Suicide: The Case of Channa," by Damien Keown, *Journal of Buddhist Ethics* 3 (1996). This article is notable for its many references on the topic. Recall that *mrtyu-mara* (the Lord of Death) is the second of the four maras.

22. It is beyond our scope to explore the complex reasons why people commit

suicide. A close study would suggest it is largely because of a highly inappropriate relationship to the contents of one's mind. The heart of inappropriate relationship is taking thoughts and emotions to be truly existent. In other words, reification is the root problem. If you take your thoughts and emotions to be real, you will act upon that imputed reality.

But look closely at your mind, which is what meditation invites, and you will discover the empty nature of whatever arises within it. You will no longer be so affected by thought and emotion. Meditation teaches you to relate *to* your mind instead of *from* it, as Stephen Levine put it. This simple maxim has enormous implications for relieving suffering and ending karma. It summarizes the fundamental difference between samsara and nirvana. This is the essence of enlightenment. This is also a reason why people drink or take drugs—to alter (soften) the relationship to the contents of their mind.

Dilgo Khyentse Rinpoche says, "Once you have the View, although the delusory perceptions of samsara may arise in your mind, you will be like the sky; when a rainbow appears in front of it, it's not particularly flattered, and when the clouds appear it's not particularly disappointed either. There is a deep sense of contentment. You chuckle from inside as you see the facade of samsara and nirvana; the View will keep you constantly amused, with a little inner smile bubbling away all the time" (Dilgo Khyentse Rinpoche, quoted in Sogyal Rinpoche, *Glimpse After Glimpse*, February 22).

Patrul Rinpoche says, "The practitioner of self-liberation is like an ordinary person as far as the way in which the thoughts of pleasure and pain, hope and fear, manifest themselves as creative energy. However, the ordinary person, taking these really seriously and judging them as acceptable or rejecting them, continues to get caught up in situations and becomes conditioned by attachment and aversion. Not doing this, a practitioner, when such thoughts arise, experiences freedom: initially, by recognizing the thought for what it is, it is freed ..." (quoted in Longchenpa, *You Are the Eyes of the World*, trans. Kennard Lipman and Merrill Peterson [Ithaca, NY: Snow Lion Publications, 2000], 77).

The translator and scholar Kennard Lipman says, "[F]reeing or liberating thought does not mean ignoring, letting go of, being indifferent to, observing, or even not having thoughts. It means being present in hope and fear, pain and pleasure, not as objects before us, but as the radiant clarity of our natural state. Thus anger, for example, when experienced dualistically, is an irritation which we may indulge in or reject, depending on our conditioning. Either way we are caught up in it and act out of it. But when aware of anger as a manifestation of clarity, its energy is a very fresh awareness of the particulars of the situation. However, these particulars are no longer irritating" (ibid., 77–78).

23. See Tsomo, *Into the Jaws of Yama, Lord of Death*, 139 for other instances of religious suicide (the self-immolation of Vietnamese monks in protest of the war), and related issues.

24. According to the teachings on emptiness, there are no "things" in reality. Because there is no-thing to be created, there is no need for a creator of these things.

25. The teaching on the *trishiksha*, or three trainings, empowers the value of good karma. These three trainings are *shila* (discipline, morality, conduct, character); *samadhi* (meditative absorption, stability); and *prajna* (insight, wisdom). Each training builds on its predecessor. So without the ground of good actions, meditative stability and wisdom will not arise. Without these trainings, enlightenment is not possible. Morality, ethics, and good conduct (karma) are the basis out of which the entire path evolves.

26. See *Into the Jaws of Yama, Lord of Death*, 145–155, for a discussion on the issue of Buddhist ethics around abortion.

27. This is a loaded statement, often quoted and misconstrued. The Dalai Lama is not categorically acceding to the dominance of physical science. He is recognizing that some ancient teachings in Buddhism that relate to the domains of reality where science has a superior empirical methodology (the domain of the physical) can be modified by discoveries made by that methodology. In spiritual domains (where Buddhism, a science of mind with a methodology as rigorous as any in the West), the timeless truths of Buddhism remain steadfast.

   In a reciprocating fashion, the first-person science of meditation, as put forth in Buddhism, can shed light on the less sophisticated third-person empirical methods of science (when those methods are applied to meditation). In the domain of matter, spiritual traditions can learn from the sciences of matter; in the domain of mind, material traditions can learn from the contemplative sciences of mind.

28. Dilgo Khyentse Rinpoche, quoted in Sogyal Rinpoche, *The Tibetan Book of Living and Dying*, 376.

29. Lama Yeshe writes: "[I]f the child is aborted out of self-cherishing, that's heavy karma. Nevertheless, heavy karma can still be completely purified; you can change it.... You should not think, 'I created bad karma; my life is over. The rest of my life's going to be a disaster.' That's wrong" (*Life, Death, and After Death*, 111).

30. Sogyal Rinpoche, *The Tibetan Book of Living and Dying*, 376.

31. Robert Aitken, *The Mind of Clover: Essays in Zen Buddhist Ethics* (San Francisco: North Point Press, 1984).

32. Yvonne Rand, "Abortion: A Respectful Meeting Ground," in *Buddhism Through American Women's Eyes*, ed. Karma Lekshe Tsomo (Ithaca, NY: Snow Lion Publications, 1995).

33. According to a Kelton Research survey, 81 percent regard their pets as full members of the family; 58 percent call themselves their pets' "mommy" or "daddy"; 77 percent buy pets birthday gifts; more than half of pet owners say they talk about pets more than politics or sex (*USA Today*, December 19, 2011). See also

"Bones of Contention: Custody of Family Pets," by Ann Hartwell Britton, in *The Journal of the American Academy of Matrimonial Lawyers* 20 (2006).

34. Anyen Rinpoche, *Dying With Confidence*, 109.

35. One definition of karma is that you can't get away with anything. This is good or bad, depending on whether your actions are good or bad. Good actions immutably lead to good results; bad actions immutably lead to bad results. One can purify karma using the four opponent powers discussed earlier. Outside of that, there's no way to bend or break these fundamental laws, just like there's no way to fudge the laws of gravity and electromagnetism.

36. It's often argued that statements like this by the Buddha were made at the provisional level and weren't his definitive teachings. What the Buddha, or any teacher, says at the level of the Hinayana may not apply to the Mahayana or Vajrayana—or vice versa.

37. The Dalai Lama, *The Path to Enlightenment*, 129.

38. The idea of questioning the guru is difficult at the level of tantra, where surrender to the guru is a central theme. The Dalai Lama acknowledges this: "This task becomes somewhat more sensitive in Highest Tantra, where total surrender to the guru is a prerequisite; but even here this surrender must be made only in a particular sense" (*Snow Lion Newsletter and Magazine*, Spring 2009). I can't speak for His Holiness, but "particular sense" probably refers to the surrender to wisdom, to a higher power. We surrender to something that is utterly good, always and only beneficent, forever saturated with love and compassion. Hence, while it may not be safe to our ego to surrender in this way, it is safe for our spirit. This is why surrender to a guru only comes at the highest stages, when we have tested the teachings. We have proven to ourselves that it's safe to surrender. Only then, when we know in our heart that surrender is in our best spiritual interest, do we finally give up.

HEART ADVICE FROM SPIRITUAL MASTERS

1. This is a play on the famous dzogchen text, *The Three Words That Strike the Vital Point*.

2. When the Dalai Lama is asked, "What is Buddhism?" he responds, "My religion is kindness."

3. The "five strengths" are part of Part Four in the slogans: Showing the Utilization of Practice in One's Whole Life, specifically, slogans seventeen and eighteen: "Practice the five strengths, the condensed heart instructions" and "The Mahayana instruction for ejection of consciousness at death is the five strengths: how you conduct yourself is important." See Chögyam Trungpa, *Training the Mind and Cultivating Loving-Kindness* (Boston: Shambhala Publications, 2003), 131–146.

4. Bardo practice is becoming familiar with the death bardos, studying the map.

5. In a follow-up discussion with Lama Pegyul about *shendur*, he said this practice comes from Karma Chagme and originated in Tibet when there was a problem with *rolangs*, a Tibetan-style zombie that is believed to be caused by a spirit force that occupies a dead body. As a way to remove the malevolent spirit that was creating the *rolang*, *shendur* came about. See *Rainbow Painting*, 183, and *Blazing Splendor*, 245–246, by Tulku Urgyen Rinpoche.

6. Bound volumes of prayers and practices are available from the Phowa Foundation (www.phowafoundation.org). These include, but are not limited to, "The Prayer of Excellent Conduct," "The Amitabha Aspiration Prayer to be Reborn in Sukhavati," "The Prayer of Kuntuzangpo," and "Meditation on the Great Compassionate One (Chenrezig)."

7. See above, page 142, on the minor death that occurs every seven days in the bardo.

APPENDIX 1: CHECKLISTS

1. I used these lists to create my dharma will, and other directives that I placed in my dharma box. Under each bullet point, I wrote out what I wanted or did not want. It made the otherwise intimidating process of writing my dharma will easy.

2. Richard Reoch, *To Die Well: A Holistic Approach for the Dying and Their Caregivers* (New York: HarperPerennial, 1997), 130.

3. Ibid., 173.

4. See Francesca Fremantle, *Luminous Emptiness*, 51–52.

5. The package includes more detailed descriptions and instructions, and can be ordered from Karma Triyana Dharmachakra, or via bardopackage@yahoo.com.

6. See Lama Zopa Rinpoche, *Advice and Practices for Death and Dying*, 17.

7. A smaller-size *takdrol* is included as an amulet, to be worn during life. Takdrol is discussed in chapter 14 of Gyurme Dorje's translation of *The Tibetan Book of the Dead* (what we know as the *Bardo Thödrol* is just the eleventh chapter of the complete text). For more on takdrol, see Anyen Rinpoche, *Dying with Confidence*, chapter 13. The takdrol can also be procured from the Phowa Foundation, at www.phowafoundation.org/PFmandala.php.

8. All kinds of unusual and difficult situations can arise around death. A friend told me that when his beloved mother died after being in the hospital for a week, he almost came to blows with the hospital staff. Because his mother had a record of being hospitalized for a number of bruises and broken bones, all the result of repeated falls, the nurse on staff at the time of her death suddenly told the family that an autopsy would be required. The family was stunned, partly because there wasn't the slightest hint of this during the week they were in the hospital, and partly because their religious beliefs forbade autopsies unless

absolutely necessary. Upon furious questioning, it turned out that several of
the hospital staff became suspicious of elder abuse, based on the recent hospital admissions for "alleged falls." To have this information delivered just after
the shock of death, and in a contentious manner, left the family in even more
shock. The nurse threatened to call the police, the family threatened to physically resist. Finally a reasonable doctor came in, assessed the situation, and the
situation was resolved before it became violent. Unfortunately, psychological
violence had already occurred.

9. Here is sample obituary information for a normal newspaper: Obituaries are
placed by funeral homes or private individuals, they are available online, and
you may click on the "guest book" to enter a message or view messages from
friends and family. Include the name and phone number of the funeral home or
crematory for verification. Include the name, address, and phone number of the
person responsible for placing the obituary. Indicate the date(s) the obituary
or "In Memoriam" should be published. Prepay by credit card or phone check.
The "In Memoriam" section includes memorials that mark the anniversary of
a deceased person's birth, death, or other important date. Submissions should
follow obituary guidelines, although no funeral home information is required.

10. See Joshua Slocum and Lisa Carlson, *Final Rights: Reclaiming the American
Way of Death* (Hinesburg, VT: Upper Access, 2011). Karen Van Vuuren says,
"Lisa Carlson of the Funeral Ethics Organization and Joshua Slocum of the
Funeral Consumers Alliance call their book on funeral law 'The book the
funeral industry doesn't want you to read.' *Final Rights* covers all US states,
outlining funeral consumers' rights and also documenting abuse by the funeral
industry." This book is a follow-up to the classic exposé *The American Way of
Death*, first published in 1963 by Jessica Mitford. Both books reveal numerous
instances of consumer abuse and financial exploitation of the bereaved.

11. Steve Prastka's Capsule Urn project offers stylish funeral urns for the ashes of
your loved one. Instead of the usual somber urn, these modern urns bring a sense
of art to the ash.

12. Bereavement discounts from airlines often don't save you very much but are still
worth asking for. Give the airline the name of the mortuary handling the death
and the contact information for it. They will confirm the death, and you will
receive discounts for your flight.

13. In a poorly regulated business, all sorts of shady undertakings have been discovered. The owners of cemeteries have been known to double-sell burial plots,
sometimes exhuming the original coffin and throwing it into a landfill. In a
notorious case in Illinois, hundreds of bones and skulls were found next to a
cemetery, dug up and removed to make room for new graves. In other cases,
plots are sometimes jammed so close together that workers report breaking into
previously buried coffins as they dig a new grave. In big cities, where land is precious, cemeteries comprise some of the most valuable real estate in the country.

Appendix 3: Depression and Grief

1. I wish to thank Kim Mooney and HospiceCare of Boulder for much of this information.
2. I want to thank the Denver Hospice for this valuable information.

Selected Bibliography

Aitken, Robert. *The Mind of Clover: Essays in Zen Buddhist Ethics*. San Francisco: North Point Press, 1984.

Anam Thubten. *No Self, No Problem*. Ithaca, NY: Snow Lion Publications, 2009.

Anyen Rinpoche. *Dying with Confidence: A Tibetan Buddhist Guide to Preparing for Death*. Trans. Allison Graboski. Boston: Wisdom Publications, 2010.

Becker, Ernest. *The Denial of Death*. New York: Free Press, 1973.

Becker, Carl B. *Breaking the Circle: Death and the Afterlife in Buddhism*. Carbondale: Southern Illinois University Press, 1993.

Blackman, Sushila, comp. and ed. *Graceful Exists: How Great Beings Die: Death Stories of Tibetan, Hindu, and Zen Masters*. New York: Weatherhill, 1997.

Bloom, Alfred, ed. *The Essential Shinran: A Buddhist Path of True Entrusting*. Bloomington, IN: World Wisdom, 2007.

———. *Living in Amida's Universal Vow: Essays in Shin Buddhism*. Bloomington, IN: World Wisdom, 2004.

Blum, Mark L. *The Origins and Development of Pure Land Buddhism: A Study and Translation of Gyonen's Jodo Homon Genrusho*. Oxford and New York: Oxford University Press, 2002.

Bokar Rinpoche. *Death and the Art of Dying in Tibetan Buddhism*. San Francisco: ClearPoint Press, 1993.

Boldman, Robert. *Sacred Life, Holy Death: Seven Stages of Crossing the Divide*. Santa Fe, NM: Heartsfire Books, 1999.

Brazier, Caroline. *The Other Buddhism: Amida Comes West*. Winchester, UK: O Books, 2007.

Britton, Ann Hartwell. "Bones of Contention: Custody of Family Pets." *The Journal of the American Academy of Matrimonial Lawyers* 20 (2006).

Brown, Gordon. *Courage: Portraits of Bravery in the Service of Great Causes*. New York: Weinstein Books, 2008.

Brown, Mick. *The Dance of 17 Lives: The Incredible True Story of Tibet's 17th Karmapa*. New York: Bloomsbury Publishing, 2004.

Brunnhölzl, Karl. *Luminous Heart: The Third Karmapa on Consciousness, Wisdom, and Buddha Nature*. Ithaca, NY: Snow Lion Publications, 2009.

Callahan, Maggie, and Patricia Kelley. *Final Gifts: Understanding the Special Awareness Needs and Communications of the Dying.* New York: Bantam Books, 1997.

Carlson, Lisa. *Caring for the Dead: Your Final Act of Love.* Hinesburg, VT: Upper Access, 1998.

Carr, Nicholas. *The Shallows: What the Internet Is Doing to Our Brains.* New York: W.W. Norton, 2010.

Chagdud Khadro. *P'howa Commentary: Instructions for the Practice of Consciousness Transference as Revealed by Rigdzen Longsal Nyingpo.* Junction City, CA: Padma Publishing, 1998.

———. *Red Tara Commentary: Instructions for the Concise Practice Known as Red Tara: An Open Door to Bliss and Ultimate Awareness.* Junction City, CA: Padma Publishing, 1999.

Chagdud Tulku. *Life in Relation to Death.* 2nd ed. Junction City, CA: Padma Publishing, 1987.

———. *Lord of the Dance: The Autobiography of a Tibetan Lama.* Junction City, CA: Padma Publishing, 1992.

Chitkara, M. G. *Buddhism, Reincarnation, and Dalai Lamas of Tibet.* New Delhi: A. P. H. Publishing Corporation, 1998.

Chödrön, Pema. *Start Where you Are: A Guide to Compassionate Living.* Boston: Shambhala Publications, 1994.

Chögyam Trungpa. *The Collected Works of Chögyam Trungpa, Volume Six.* Ed. Carolyn Gimian. Boston: Shambhala Publications, 2004.

———. *Crazy Wisdom.* Boston: Shambhala Publications, 1991.

———. *Glimpses of Abhidharma.* Boston: Shambhala Publications, 1987.

———. *The Heart of the Buddha.* Boston: Shambhala Publications, 1991.

———. *Illusion's Game: The Life and Teaching of Naropa.* Edited by Sherab Chödzin. Boston: Shambhala Publications, 1994.

———. *Journey Without Goal: The Tantric Wisdom of the Buddha.* Boston: Shambhala Publications, 1981.

———. *Shambhala: The Sacred Path of the Warrior.* Boston: Shambhala Publications, 1984.

———. *Training the Mind and Cultivating Loving-Kindness.* Boston: Shambhala Publications, 2003.

———. *Transcending Madness: The Experience of the Six Bardos.* Boston: Shambhala Publications, 1992.

———. *The Truth of Suffering and the Path of Liberation.* Ed. Judith L. Lief. Boston: Shambhala Publications, 2009.

Chökyi Nyima Rinpoche. *The Bardo Guidebook.* Trans. Erik Pema Kunsang. Ed. Marcia Schmidt. Kathmandu: Rangjung Yeshe Publications, 1991.

Chopra, Deepak. *Life After Death: The Burden of Proof.* New York: Three Rivers Press, 2006.

Coleman, Graham, and Thupten Jinpa, eds. *Meditations on Living, Dying, and Loss: Ancient Knowledge for a Modern World, from the first complete transla-*

tion of *The Tibetan Book of the Dead.* Trans. Gyurme Dorje. London: Penguin Books, 2005.

Csikszentmihalyi, Mihaly. *Flow: The Psychology of Optimal Experience.* New York: HarperCollins, 1990.

Cuevas, Bryan J. *The Hidden History of the Tibetan Book of the Dead.* New York: Oxford University Press, 2003.

Dalai Lama XIV, Tenzin Gyatso. *Advice on Dying and Living a Better Life.* Trans. and ed. Jeffrey Hopkins. London: Random House, 2002.

———. *Consciousness at the Crossroads: Conversations with The Dalai Lama on Brain Science and Buddhism.* Ed. Zara Houshmand, Robert B. Livingston, and B. Alan Wallace. Ithaca, NY: Snow Lion Publications, 1999.

———. *Kindness, Clarity, and Insight.* Trans. and ed. Jeffrey Hopkins. Ithaca, NY: Snow Lion Publications, 1984.

———. *The Path to Enlightenment.* Ed. and trans. Glenn H. Mullin. Ithaca, NY: Snow Lion Publications, 1995.

———. *Sleeping, Dreaming, and Dying: An Exploration of Consciousness with the Dalai Lama.* Ed. Francisco J. Varela. Boston: Wisdom Publications, 1997.

———. *Stages of Meditation.* By Kamalashila. Trans. Geshe Lobsang Jordhen, Losang Choephel Ganchenpa, and Jeremy Russell. Ithaca, NY: Snow Lion Publications, 2001.

Delog Dawa Drolma. *Delog: Journey to Realms Beyond Death.* Junction City, CA: Padma Publishing, 1995.

Dilgo Khyentse Rinpoche. *Pure Appearance: Development and Completion Stages in Vajrayana Practice.* Trans. Ani Jimba Palmo. Halifax: Vajravairochana Translation Committee, 1992.

Dimidjian, Victoria Jean. *Journeying East: Conversations on Aging and Dying.* Berkeley: Parallax Press, 2004.

Doka, Kenneth J., and Amy S. Tucci, eds. *Living With Grief: Spirituality and End-of-Life Care.* Washington, DC: Hospice Foundation of America, 2011.

Doore, Gary, ed. *What Survives? Contemporary Explorations of Life After Death.* Los Angeles: Jeremy P. Tarcher, 1990.

Du Boulay, Shirley. *Cicely Saunders: Founder of the Modern Hospice Movement.* London: Hodder and Stoughton, 1984.

Dudjom Rinpoche, Jikdrel Yeshe Dorje. *The Nyingma School of Tibetan Buddhism. Volume One: The Translations.* Trans. and ed. by Gyurme Dorje with the collaboration of Matthew Kapstein. Boston: Wisdom Publications, 1991.

Dzogchen Ponlop. *Mind Beyond Death.* Ithaca, NY: Snow Lion Publications, 2006.

———. *Rebel Buddha: On the Road to Freedom.* Boston: Shambhala Publications, 2010.

Evans-Wentz, W. Y. *The Tibetan Book of the Dead.* London: Oxford University Press, 1960.

Faulkner, Raymond O., trans. *Ancient Egyptian Book of the Dead.* New York: Barnes & Noble, 2005.

Fremantle, Francesca. *Luminous Emptiness: Understanding the Tibetan Book of the Dead.* Boston: Shambhala Publications, 2001.

Garces-Foley, K. "Buddhism, Hospice and the American Way of Dying." *Review of Religious Research* 44, no. 4 (2003).

Gold, E. J. *The American Book of the Dead.* Nevada City: Gateways Books & Tapes, 1999.

Gómez, Luis O. *The Land of Bliss: The Paradise of the Buddha of Measureless Light.* Honolulu: University of Hawaii Press, 1996.

Grof, Stanislav. *The Ultimate Journey: Consciousness and the Mystery of Death.* Ben Lomond, CA: MAPS, 2006.

Gyatrul Rinpoche. *Ancient Wisdom: Nyingma Teachings on Dream Yoga, Meditation, and Transformation.* Trans. B. Alan Wallace and Sangye Khandro. Ithaca, NY: Snow Lion Publications, 1993.

Halifax, Joan. *Being with Dying: Cultivating Compassion and Fearlessness in the Presence of Death.* Boston: Shambhala Publications, 2008.

Harris, Sam. *The End of Faith: Religion, Terror, and the Future of Reason.* New York: W. W. Norton, 2004.

Hisao Inagaki. *The Three Pure Land Sutras.* Berkeley: Numata Center for Buddhist Translation and Research, 1995.

Hodge, Stephen, and Martin Boord. *The Illustrated Tibetan Book of the Dead.* New Arlesford: Godsfield Press, 2000.

Hookham, Lama Shenpen. *There's More to Dying Than Death: A Buddhist Perspective.* Birmingham: Windhorse Publications, 2006.

Horgan, John. *Rational Mysticism: Spirituality Meets Science in the Search for Enlightenment.* New York: Houghton Mifflin, 2003.

Ibn 'Arabi, Muhyiddin. *Whoso Knoweth Himself.* Trans. T. H. Weir. Gloucestershire, England: Beshara Publications, 1976.

Iyengar, B. K. S. *The Concise Light on Yoga.* New York: Schocken Books, 1980.

Jamgön Kongtrul. *Creation and Completion: The Essential Points of Tantric Meditation.* Trans. Sarah Harding. Boston: Wisdom Publications, 1996.

———. *Enthronement: The Recognition of the Reincarnate Masters of Tibet and the Himalayas.* Trans. Ngawang Zangpo. Ithaca, NY: Snow Lion Publications, 1997.

———. *The Treasury of Knowledge: The Elements of Tantric Practice.* Trans. Elio Guarisco and Ingrid McLeod. Ithaca, NY: Snow Lion Publications, 2008.

———. *The Treasury of Knowledge: Esoteric Instructions.* Trans. Sarah Harding. Ithaca, NY: Snow Lion Publications, 2007.

———. *The Treasury of Knowledge: Systems of Buddhist Tantra.* Trans. Elio Guarisco and Ingrid McLeod. Ithaca, NY: Snow Lion Publications, 2005.

Johnson, Christopher Jay, and Marsha G. McGee, eds. *How Different Religions View Death and Afterlife.* Philadelphia: The Charles Press, 1998.

Kabat-Zinn, Jon. *Full Catastrophe Living: Using the Wisdom of Your Body and Mind to Face Stress, Pain, and Illness.* New York: Delacorte Press, 1990.

————. *Wherever You Go, There You Are: Mindfulness Meditation in Everyday Life.* New York: Hyperion, 1994.

Kalu Rinpoche. *The Dharma That Illuminates All Beings Impartially Like the Light of the Sun and the Moon.* Albany: State University of New York Press, 1986.

————. *The Gem Ornament.* Ithaca, NY: Snow Lion Publications, 1986.

————. *Secret Buddhism: Vajrayana Practices.* Trans. Christiane Buchet. San Francisco: ClearPoint Press, 1995.

Kapleau, Philip. *The Wheel of Death: A Collection of Writings and Zen Buddhist and Other Sources on Death, Rebirth, Dying.* New York: Harper and Row, 1971.

————. *The Wheel of Life and Death: A Practical and Spiritual Guide.* New York: Doubleday, 1989.

————. *The Zen of Living and Dying.* Boston: Shambhala Publications, 1989.

Karma Lekshe Tsomo. *Into the Jaws of Yama, Lord of Death: Buddhism, Bioethics, and Death.* Albany: State University of New York Press, 2006.

Karthar Rinpoche, Khenpo. *Bardo: Interval of Possibility.* Trans. Yeshe Gyamtso. Woodstock, NY: KTD Publications, 2007.

Katz, Michael. *Tibetan Dream Yoga: The Royal Road to Enlightenment.* New York: Bodhi Tree Publications, 2011.

Kelsang Gyatso, Geshe. *Clear Light of Bliss: The Practice of Mahamudra in Vajrayana Buddhism.* London: Tharpa Publications, 1995.

Keown, Damien. "Buddhism and Suicide: The Case of Channa." *Journal of Buddhist Ethics* 3 (1996).

Khedrup Norsang Gyatso. *Ornament of Stainless Light: An Exposition of the Kalacakra Tantra.* Trans. Gavin Kilty. Boston: Wisdom Publications, 2004.

Klein, Anne Carolyn. *Heart Essence of the Vast Expanse: A Story of Transmission.* Ithaca, NY: Snow Lion Publications, 2009.

Kornfield, Jack. *A Path With Heart: A Guide Through the Perils and Promises of Spiritual Life.* New York: Bantam Books, 1993.

Kübler-Ross, Elisabeth. *Death: The Final Stages of Growth.* New York: Simon and Schuster, 1975.

LaBerge, Stephen, and Howard Rheingold. *Exploring the World of Lucid Dreaming.* New York: Ballantine Books, 1990.

Lama Kunsang, Lama Pemo, and Marie Aubèle. *History of the Karmapas: The Odyssey of the Tibetan Masters with the Black Crown.* Trans. Jonathan C. Bell. Ithaca, NY: Snow Lion Publications, 2012.

Lati Rinbochay and Jeffrey Hopkins. *Death, Intermediate State, and Rebirth in Tibetan Buddhism.* Ithaca, NY: Snow Lion Publications, 1979.

Lauf, Detlef Ingo. *Secret Doctrines of the Tibetan Books of the Dead.* Boston: Shambhala Publications, 1989.

Levine, Stephen. *A Year to Live: How to Live This Year As If It Were Your Last.* New York: Bell Tower, 1997.

————. *Meetings at the Edge: Dialogues with the Grieving and the Dying, the Healing and the Healed.* New York: Anchor Books, 1984.

———. *Who Dies? An Investigation of Conscious Living and Conscious Dying.* New York: Anchor Books, 1982.

Lief, Judith L. *Making Friends with Death: A Buddhist Guide to Encountering Mortality.* Boston: Shambhala Publications, 2001.

Lodö, Venerable Lama. *Bardo Teachings: The Way of Death and Rebirth.* Ithaca, NY: Snow Lion Publications, 1982.

Longaker, Christine. *Facing Death and Finding Hope: A Guide to the Emotional and Spiritual Care of the Dying.* New York: Broadway Books, 1997.

Longchenpa. *Now That I Come to Die: Intimate Guidance from one of Tibet's Greatest Masters.* Berkeley: Dharma Press, 2007.

———. *You Are the Eyes of the World.* Trans. Kennard Lipman and Merrill Peterson. Ithaca, NY: Snow Lion Publications, 2000.

Lopez, Donald S., Jr. *The Tibetan Book of the Dead: A Biography.* Princeton: Princeton University Press, 2011.

Mackenzie, Vicki. *Reborn in the West: The Reincarnation Masters.* New York: Marlowe, 1996.

———. *Reincarnation: The Boy Lama.* Boston: Wisdom Publications, 1988.

Maitland, Arnaud. *Living Without Regret: Growing Old in the Light of Tibetan Buddhism.* Berkeley: Dharma Publishing, 2006.

Maitreyanatha/Aryasanga. *The Universal Vehicle Discourse Literature.* Trans. by L. Jamspal et al. New York: American Institute of Buddhist Studies, 2004.

Master Chu-hung and Master Tsun-pen. *Pure Land, Pure Mind: The Buddhism of Masters Chu-hung and Tsun-pen.* Trans. J. C. Cleary. New York: Sutra Translation Committee of the United States and Canada, 1994.

Montaigne, Michel de. *The Essays of Michel de Montaigne.* Trans. and ed. by M. A. Screech. London: Allen Lane, 1991.

Mullin, Glenn H. *Death and Dying: The Tibetan Tradition.* Boston: Arkana Paperbacks, 1986.

———. *Living in the Face of Death: The Tibetan Tradition.* Ithaca, NY: Snow Lion Publications, 1998.

———. *Readings on the Six Yogas of Naropa.* Ithaca, NY: Snow Lion Publications, 1997.

———. *Tsongkhapa's Six Yogas of Naropa.* Ithaca, NY: Snow Lion Publications, 1996.

Nairn, Rob. *Living, Dreaming, Dying: Practical Wisdom from the Tibetan Book of the Dead.* Boston: Shambhala Publications, 2004.

Namkhai Norbu. *Dream Yoga and the Practice of Clear Light.* Ithaca, NY: Snow Lion Publications, 1992.

Nawang Gehlek, Rimpoche. *Good Life, Good Death: Tibetan Wisdom on Reincarnation.* New York: Riverhead Books, 2001.

Nebesky-Wojkowitz, René de. *Oracles and Demons of Tibet: The Cult and Iconography of the Tibetan Protective Deities.* New Delhi: Paljor Publications, 1998.

Ngawang Dhargyey, Geshe. *Kalacakra Tantra.* Dharamsala: Library of Tibetan Works and Archives, 1985.

Nuland, Sherwin B. *How We Die: Reflections on Life's Final Chapter.* New York: Vintage Books, 1995.

Padmasambhava. *Natural Liberation: Padmasambhava's Teachings on the Six Bardos.* Commentary by Gyatrul Rinpoche. Trans. B. Alan Wallace. Boston: Wisdom Publications, 1998.

Pandey, Alok. *Death, Dying, and Beyond; The Science and Spirituality of Death.* New Delhi: Wisdom Tree, 2009.

Patrul Rinpoche. *The Words of My Perfect Teacher.* Trans. Padmakara Translation Group. San Francisco: HarperCollins, 1994.

Payne, Richard K., and Kenneth K Tanaka. *Approaching the Land of Bliss: Religious Praxis in the Cult of Amitabha.* Honolulu: University of Hawaii Press, 2004.

Peacock, John. *The Tibetan Way of Life, Death, and Rebirth: The Illustrated Guide to Tibetan Wisdom.* London: Element, 2003.

Pert, Candace. *Molecules of Emotion: The Science Behind Mind-Body Medicine.* New York: Scribner, 1997.

Pertik, Maria, and Zora de Bodisco. *Shaking Hands with Alzheimer's Disease: A Guide to Compassionate Care for Caregivers.* Seattle: CreateSpace, 2011.

Powers, John. *Introduction to Tibetan Buddhism.* Ithaca, NY: Snow Lion Publications, 1995.

Ram Dass and Paul Gorman. *How Can I Help? Stories and Reflections on Service.* New York: Alfred Knopf, 1986.

Rand, Yvonne, "Abortion: A Respectful Meeting Ground." In *Buddhism Through American Women's Eyes.* Ed. Karma Lekshe Tsomo. Ithaca, NY: Snow Lion Publications, 1995.

Ray, Reginald A. *Indestructible Truth: The Living Spirituality of Tibetan Buddhism.* Boston: Shambhala Publications, 2000.

———. *Secret of the Vajra World: The Tantric Buddhism of Tibet.* Boston: Shambhala Publications, 2001.

Reoch, Richard. *To Die Well: A Holistic Approach for the Dying and Their Caregivers.* New York: HarperPerennial, 1997.

Revel, Jean-François, and Matthieu Ricard. *The Monk and the Philosopher: A Father and Son Discuss the Meaning of Life.* New York: Schocken Books, 1998.

Roach, Mary. *Spook: Science Tackles the Afterlife.* New York: W.W. Norton and Co., 2005.

Roach, Mary. *Stiff: The Curious Lives of Human Cadavers.* New York: W. W. Norton, 2003.

Rockwell, Irini. *The Five Wisdom Energies; A Buddhist Way of Understanding Personalities, Emotions, and Relationships.* Boston: Shambhala Publications, 2002.

———. *Natural Brilliance: A Buddhist System for Uncovering Your Strengths and Letting Them Shine.* Boston: Shambhala Publications, 2012.

Sakyong Mipham. *Turning the Mind into an Ally.* New York: Riverhead Books, 2003.

Sayadaw, Mahasi. *A Discourse on Dependent Origination.* Bangkok: Buddhadhamma Foundation, 1999.

Shardza Tashi Gyaltsen. *Heart Drops of Dharmakaya: Dzogchen Practice of the Bon Tradition.* Ithaca, NY: Snow Lion Publications, 1993.

Shinran. *The Collected Works of Shinran: Volumes One and Two.* Trans. Dennis Hirota et al. Kyoto: Jodo Shinshu Hongwanji-ha, 1997.

Slocum, Joshua, and Lisa Carlson. *Final Rights: Reclaiming the American Way of Death.* Hinesburg, VT: Upper Access, 2011.

Smith, Rodney. *Lessons from the Dying.* Boston: Wisdom Publications, 1998.

Snelling, John. *The Buddhist Handbook: A Complete Guide to Buddhist Schools, Teaching, Practice, and History.* Rochester, VT: Inner Traditions International, 1991.

Sogyal Rinpoche. *Glimpse After Glimpse: Daily Reflections on Living and Dying.* New York: HarperOne, 1995.

———. *The Tibetan Book of Living and Dying.* San Francisco: HarperCollins, 1993.

Story, Francis. *Rebirth as Doctrine and Experience.* Kandy, Sri Lanka: Buddhist Publication Society, 1975.

Strassman, Rick. *DMT: The Spirit Molecule: A Doctor's Revolutionary Research into the Biology of Near-Death and Mystical Experiences.* Rochester, VT: Park Street Press, 2001.

Suzuki, D. T. *Buddha of Infinite Light.* Boston: Shambhala Publications, 2002.

Tatelbaum, Judy. *The Courage to Grieve: Creative Living, Recovery, and Growth Through Grief.* New York: Harper and Row, 1980.

Tenga Rinpoche. *Transition and Liberation: Explanations of Meditation in the Bardo.* Ed. Susanne Schefczyk. Trans. Alex Wilding. Osterby: Khampa Buchverlag, 1996.

Tenzin Wangyal. *Tibetan Yogas of Body, Speech, and Mind.* Ithaca, NY: Snow Lion Publications, 2011.

———. *The Tibetan Yogas of Dream and Sleep.* Ithaca, NY: Snow Lion Publications, 1998.

———. *Wonders of the Natural Mind: The Essence of Dzogchen in the Native Bon Tradition of Tibet.* Barrytown, NY: Station Hill Press, 1993.

Teresi, Dick. *The Undead: Organ Harvesting, the Ice-Water Test, Beating-Heart Cadavers—How Medicine Is Blurring the Line Between Life and Death.* New York: Pantheon Books, 2012.

Terhune, Lea. *Karmapa: The Politics of Reincarnation.* Boston: Wisdom Publications, 2004.

Thich Nhat Hanh. *No Death, No Fear: Comforting Wisdom for Life.* New York: Riverhead Books, 2002.

Thich-Thien-Tham. *Buddhism of Wisdom and Faith: Pure Land Principles and Practice.* New York: The Corporate Body of the Buddha Education Foundation, 1991.

———. *Pure Land Zen, Zen Pure Land: Letters from Patriarch Yin Kuang.* Taipei: The Corporate Body of the Buddha Education Foundation, 1993.

Thondup, Tulku. *Incarnation: The History and Mysticism of the Tulku Tradition of Tibet.* Boston: Shambhala Publications, 2011.

———. *Peaceful Death, Joyful Rebirth: A Tibetan Buddhist Guidebook*. Boston: Shambhala Publications, 2005.

Thrangu Rinpoche. *Everyday Consciousness and Buddha Awakening*. Trans. Susanne Schefczyk. Ithaca, NY: Snow Lion Publications, 2002.

———. *The Four Foundations of Buddhist Practice*. Boulder, CO: Namo Buddha Publications, 2001.

———. *Journey of the Mind: Putting the Teachings on the Bardo into Effective Practice*. Vancouver, B.C.: Karme Thekchen Choling, 1997.

———. *An Ocean of the Ultimate Meaning: Teachings on Mahamudra*. Boston: Shambhala Publications, 2004.

———. *Pointing Out the Dharmakaya*. Intro. by Lama Tashi Namgyal. Ithaca, NY: Snow Lion Publications, 2003.

———. *Transcending Ego: Distinguishing Consciousness from Wisdom*. Boulder: Namo Buddha Publications, 2001.

———. *Vivid Awareness: The Mind Instructions of Khenpo Gangshar*. Boston: Shambhala Publications, 2011.

Thubten Loden, Geshe Acharya. *Great Treasures of the Six Yogas of Naropa*. Melbourne: Tushita Publications, 2005.

The Tibetan Book of the Dead: The Great Liberation by Hearing in the Intermediate States. By Padmasambhava. Revealed by Terton Karma Lingpa. Ed. Graham Coleman and Thubten Jinpa. Trans. Gyurme Dorje. New York: Viking, 2006.

The Tibetan Book of the Dead: The Great Liberation Through Hearing in the Bardo. By Guru Rinpoche, according to Karma Lingpa. Trans. Francesca Fremantle and Chögyam Trungpa. Berkeley: Shambhala Publications, 1975.

The Tibetan Book of the Dead: Liberation Through Understanding in the Between. By Padmasambhava. Discovered by Karma Lingpa. Trans. Robert A. F. Thurman. New York: Bantam Books, 1994.

Tolle, Eckhart. *A New Earth: Awakening to Your Life's Purpose*. New York: Penguin Group, 2005.

Traleg Rinpoche. *Mind at Ease: Self-Liberation Through Mahamudra Meditation*. Boston: Shambhala Publications, 2003.

Tsele Natsok Rangdrol. *The Mirror of Mindfulness: The Cycle of the Four Bardos*. Trans. Erik Pema Kunsang. Boston: Shambhala Publications, 1989.

Tsültrim Gyamtso Rinpoche, Khenpo. *Progressive Stages of Meditation on Emptiness*. Trans. Shenpen Hookham. Oxford: Longchen Foundation, 1986.

Urgyen, Tulku. *Blazing Splendor: The Memoirs of the Dzogchen Yogi Tulku Urgyen Rinpoche*. As told to Erik Pema Kunsang and Marcia Binder Schmidt. Boudhanath: Rangjung Yeshe Publications, 2005.

———. *Rainbow Painting*. Hong Kong: Rangjung Yeshe Publications, 1995.

Unno, Taitetsu. *River of Fire, River of Water*. New York: Doubleday, 1998.

Vajradhatu Practice Manual. Accessed at http://www.halifax.shambhala.org/aging.php.

Van Itallie, Jean-Claude. *The Tibetan Book of the Dead for Reading Aloud.* Berkeley: North Atlantic Books, 1998.

Vasubandhu. *Abhidharmakosabhasyam.* Trans. Louis de La Vallée Poussin and Leo M. Pruden. 4 vols. Berkeley: Asian Humanities Press, 1988.

Wallace, B. Alan. *The Attention Revolution: Unlocking the Power of the Focused Mind.* Boston, MA: Wisdom Publications, 2006.

———. *Dreaming Yourself Awake: Lucid Dreaming and Tibetan Dream Yoga for Insight and Transformation.* Boston and London: Shambhala Publications, 2012.

———. *Mind in the Balance: Meditation in Science, Buddhism, and Christianity.* New York: Columbia University Press, 2009.

———. *Stilling the Mind: Shamatha Teachings from Düdjom Lingpa's Vajra Essence.* Boston, MA: Wisdom Publications, 2011.

Wallace, Vesna A. *The Inner Kalacakratantra: A Buddhist Tantric View of the Individual.* New York: Oxford University Press, 2001.

Ware, Bronnie. *The Top Five Regrets of the Dying: A Life Transformed by the Dearly Departing.* Bloomington, IN: Balboa Press, 2011.

Ways of Enlightenment: Buddhist Studies at Nyingma Institute. Berkeley: Dharma Publishing, 1993.

Welwood, John. "Intimate Relationship as Spiritual Crucible." *Shambhala Sun* 17, no. 2 (2008).

Wilber, Ken. *A Brief History of Everything.* Boston: Shambhala Publications, 1996.

———. *Sex, Ecology, Spirituality: The Spirit of Evolution.* Boston: Shambhala Publications, 1995.

Willis, Janice Dean. *On Knowing Reality: The Tattvartha Chapter of Asanga's Bodhisattvabhumi.* Delhi: Motilal Banarsidass, 1979.

Yamasaki, Taiko. *Shingon: Japanese Esoteric Buddhism.* Trans. Richard and Cynthia Peterson. Boston: Shambhala Publications, 1988.

Yeshe, Lama Thubten. *The Bliss of Inner Fire: Heart Practice of the Six Yogas of Naropa.* Boston: Wisdom Publications, 1998.

———. *Life, Death, and After Death.* Boston: Lama Yeshe Wisdom Archive, 2011.

Young, Serinity. *Dreaming in the Lotus.* Boston: Wisdom Publications, 1999.

Zajonc, Arthur. *Catching the Light: The Entwined History of Light and Mind.* Oxford: Oxford University Press, 1993.

Zaleski, Philip, and Paul Kaufman. *Gifts of the Spirit: Living the Wisdom of the Great Religious Traditions.* San Francisco: HarperCollins, 1998.

Zopa Rinpoche, Lama Thubten. *Advice and Practices for Death and Dying for the Benefit of Self and Others.* Portland: FPMT, 2003.

———. *Heart Advice for Death and Dying.* Portland: FPMT Education Publications, 2008.

Zopa Rinpoche, Lama Thubten, and Kathleen McDonald. *Wholesome Fear: Transforming Your Anxiety about Impermanence and Death.* Boston: Wisdom Publications, 2010.

CONTRIBUTORS

MITCHELL GERSHTEN practices internal medicine at St. Mary's Hospital in Grand Junction, Colorado. He lives and helps his wife farm in Paonia. A Buddhist practitioner, he is a student of Lhoppon Rechung and Anyen Rinpoche.

ALEX HALPERN has been a practicing attorney in Boulder, Colorado, since 1976, specializing in nonprofit law and estate planning. He has been a member of the Shambhala Buddhist community since 1972. Alex serves as general counsel to Shambhala International and provides legal services for several other Buddhist teachers in the United States. He has been a member of the board of directors of Shambhala, Naropa University, and several other nonprofit organizations. His website is www.halpernllc.com.

CHRISTINE LONGAKER is the author of *Facing Death and Finding Hope: A Guide to the Emotional and Spiritual Care of the Dying*. She is former director and staff trainer of the Hospice of Santa Cruz County, and has provided hospice trainings internationally since 1978. Christine helped found Rigpa Fellowship in the United States in 1980, and in 1993 was instrumental in developing Rigpa's Spiritual Care Education Program, an international organization for those interested in improving end-of-life care. Christine currently serves as the program's International Education Director and as core faculty in the accredited "Contemplative End-of-Life Care" training offered through Naropa University in Colorado.

KIM MOONEY has been working personally and professionally with grief for the last twenty years. She has worked extensively with end-of-life issues, grief, and crisis intervention, and has provided education and support for faith communities, community organizations, school districts, health care organizations, and corporations, as well as disenfranchised loss groups such as cult survivors. She is a writer and national speaker. Kim is the Director of Community Education for HospiceCare of Boulder and Broomfield Counties and a member of their Ethics Committee. She is on the Education Committee for the Colorado Organization for Hospice and Palliative Care, and on the board of the Association for Death Education and Counseling. See her website at www.kimmooney.net.

After many years as an entertainment attorney in New York City, BETH PATTERSON moved to Colorado in 2002 to attend Naropa University. She received a Master of Arts in Transpersonal Counseling Psychology from Naropa in 2006. Beth is a psychotherapist in Denver, specializing in grief, loss, and life transitions, as well as trauma and depression (www.bethspatterson.com). She is also the Life Care Coordinator and Bereavement Coordinator for SolAmor Hospice of Denver, and maintains a small law practice working with musicians. Beth is a long-time Buddhist practitioner and meditation instructor, and a student of Dzogchen Ponlop Rinpoche.

KAREN VAN VUUREN is founder and director of Natural Transitions, a Colorado-based nonprofit providing education and support to families on caring for their own dead. Karen has a bachelor's degree in linguistics and international studies, and a postgraduate diploma in broadcast journalism. Following a hiatus from journalism, Karen began work at an assisted living home where she cared for the elderly, organized activities, and laid out the dead. Since starting Natural Transitions in 2003, she has provided direct support to families, conducted community outreach, and organized national conferences on green and home funerals. In 2007, she formed Wordwise Productions, to produce educational end-of-life media. She is the director of the documentary *Dying Wish*, about a dying doctor's decision to forgo food and fluids at the end of a terminal illness. Her website is www.naturaltransitions.org, and her magazine about holistic approaches to end of life is at www.naturaltransitionsmagazine.com.

INDEX

abortion, 268–70
Abraham a Sancta Clara, 60
advance directive, 165, 169–73
after-death care, 223–39; bathing the
    deceased, 229, 383n1; burial, 234–
    35; caskets, 232; cremation, 156, 236–
    38, 384n6, 394n11; disposition of
    remains, options for, 238–39, 383n2;
    dressing the deceased, 230; dry
    ice, 231; expected death, first steps
    after, 226–27; funeral costs, 384n9;
    funeral directors, role of, 225–26,
    383–84n4; home funerals, 223–24,
    385n12; legality of caring for own
    dead, 224; odors and bodily changes,
    233–34; rigor mortis, 227; temporary
    preservation methods, 230–31, 384n7,
    384n10; unexpected death, 232–33
Aitken, Robert, 270
Allen, Woody, 19, 362n20
Alzheimer's disease, 380n4
The American Way of Death (Mitford),
    230
Amitabha Buddha, 34–37, 144, 289, 294,
    342n47, 344n60
Anam Thubten Rinpoche, 43, 60, 275–76
Anyen Rinpoche, 3, 54–55, 61, 62, 73,
    270, 277
Asanga, 43
aspiration prayers, 147–48
attachment: and grief, 252–53; and love,
    108, 112, 250, 253; as mark of samsara,
    23, 69; at moment of death, 64, 89,
    112, 283, 285; and rebirth, 52, 134, 136,

284; and transference, 55, 163–64. See
    also letting go
Atisha, 23
Atse, Lama, 152
autopsy, 178, 232–33, 384n7, 387–88n11,
    393n8

Baker Roshi, 20–21
bardo of becoming, 117–38; advice from
    Tibetan Book of the Dead, 127–32, 135–
    36; advice from Tulku Thondup, 125,
    134, 138; bright and soft lights, 132–33;
    choosing best rebirth, 133–37; defined,
    6; experiences in, 117–18, 357n40,
    365n4; familiarity with confusion,
    118–19; finding our true nature, 119;
    hallucinations in, 120–21; practices
    during, 125–26, 127; preparation for,
    49, 51–61; recognizing death, 121–25
bardo of dharmata, 45–49, 82–90;
    defined, 6, 336–37n12, 358nn42–
    43; emptiness in, 339n29; as fourth
    moment, 20, 336–37n12, 337n14;
    hourglass, 85–89, 86 fig. 3, 336–37n12;
    instruction from Tibetan Book of
    the Dead, 89–90; light and sound
    of, 47–49; peaceful and wrathful
    deities, 42, 50 fig. 2, 57, 84–85,
    362n17; preparation for, 46–49,
    57; recognition of, 45–46; tukdam,
    82–83, 261, 356–57n37, 357n39; visions
    of, 47
bardo of dying, 68–82; as analog to
    Big Crunch, 359–60n52; death

of confusion, 86 fig. 3; defined, 6;
dissolution, 70–82, 77 table 2, 352–
53n17, 353n25, 353–54n27, 355n35,
388n14; letting go, 68–69, 163–64
bardo package, 115, 314
Bardor Tulku Rinpoche, 277–79
bardo(s): cultural differences and, 6–7,
84–85, 334n8; defined, 3, 6, 333n1; of
life, 350n117; recognition of, 121–23;
studying, importance of, 26–28; yoga,
51. *See also* bardo of becoming; bardo
of dharmata; bardo of dying
Becker, Carl, 7, 265
bindu(s) (drops), 69, 79–81;
indestructible, 83, 89, 348n92, 355n34;
red and white, 79, 83, 354n32, 357n40
blocking, 129–32
bodhichitta, 16, 55, 87, 162, 335n2
bodies: outer and inner, 69, 86 fig. 3,
88, 348n92; subtle, 69–70, 79, 88,
359n48; very subtle, 69, 102, 351n5. *See
also* bindu(s), central channel, nadis,
prana
brahmarandhra, 54, 348n93
Buddha families, five, 1, 386n29
buddhahood, defined, 45
Buddha Shakyamuni, 16, 24, 25, 43, 148,
272, 337–38n19, 392n36
burial, 234–35
butterfly effect, 354n28

Caring for the Dead (Carlson), 225
Carlson, Lisa, 225
Carr, Jesse, 230
caskets, 232
central channel, 54, 73, 79, 81, 348n95,
354n32
Chagdud Khadro, 155–56
Chagdud Tulku Rinpoche, 18, 152, 156
Chah, Ajahn, 250
chakras, 73, 348n93, 352n15
Chandogya Upanishad, 119
chang chok (effigy ritual), 153–54, 292
checklists, 311–18
Chenrezig, 37–38, 130, 133
children: exposure to death, 11, 239–41,
384–85n11; guardian for, 176

Chökyi Nyima Rinpoche, 23, 127, 279–80
Coleman, Graham, 17
compassion, 114, 251
completion stage, 46, 64, 290, 348n74,
358n43
consciousness: death of, 78–79; exit point
of, 54, 115, 143, 347–48nn91–94;
transference of, 54–57, 262
CPR (cardio-pulmonary resuscitation):
directive, 170; survival rate, 376n5
cremation, 156, 236–38, 384n6, 394n11

Dalai Lama: on cultural differences,
84–85; on enlightenment, 55; on
euthanasia, 263–64; on facilitating
transference of consciousness, 262; on
meditation, 70; on preparation for
death, 15, 16–17, 18; on questioning
one's guru, 272; on science and
Buddhism, 268
dark retreat, 47, 346n75
dead person: help for, 139–58; gathering
and dedicating merit, 144–48,
363n41; Gelugpa rituals, 156–58;
monastic rituals and ceremonies, 151–
56; reasons for helping, 140–44; *sur*
(burnt) offering, 149–50, 374n26;
when to help, 142–44
death: acknowledgment of, 22–26; best
things to do, 43; cultural differences
and, 6–7, 84–85, 334n8; expectations
about, 4–5, 41, 69, 92–93; exposing
children to, 11, 239–41, 384–85n11;
familiarity with, 10; fears about, 106–
7; feelings about, 3–4; helping others
understand, 65–66; as inspiration,
117; legal definition of, 381n9; point
of death, 69, 81–82; prayer at moment
of, 113; as return to infinity, 255–
57; seduction of, 360n1; signs for
verification of, 123–24; sleep and,
346n81; state of mind at, 39–40;
sudden, 37–38, 207, 232–33, 320, 343–
44n57, 343n56; truths about, 39–42;
when to help deceased person, 142–
44. *See also* dying, physical signs and
symptoms of

deities, peaceful and wrathful, 42, 50 fig. 2, 57, 84–85, 362n17

deity yoga, 46–47, 52–53, 58, 345n74, 353n20

dementia, 380n4

depression, 249, 327–29, 385–86n18, 386n20

devotion, 42–43, 251

dharma box, 62–63, 100

dharma friends, 61–62, 158

dharmakaya, 43, 44, 45–46, 119, 360n54

dharmata. *See* bardo of dharmata

dharma will, 62

Dilgo Khyentse Rinpoche, 269

Dilyak Drupon Rinpoche, 280–82

disease, emptiness of, 219–21

dissolution, 18, 304, 352n15, 352n17, 353n27; inner, 69–73, 78–82, 85–88, 143, 295, 353n25, 355n35, 387n8; outer, 69–78, 85–88, 110, 353n24

distraction, 18, 22, 32–33, 120–21, 123, 338n20, 365–66n9

Dodrupchen Rinpoche, 59–60, 148

do not resuscitate directive (DNR), 170–72

dream yoga, 51, 124, 337n18, 346–47n83

dry ice, as temporary preservation method, 231

duality, 76, 79, 80, 85, 87

dur, 152–53, 375n35

durable power of attorney, 167

dying, physical signs and symptoms of, 206–14; biological changes, 200–203; body temperature, 209; breathing, 212–13; circulation, 210, 212; death rattle, 201, 208, 212, 217, 353n18; discoloration of extremities, 210; disorientation, 210; eating and drinking, 207–8; fever, 209; hallucinations, 211; incontinence, 213; increase in pain, 207; indications of impending death, 215–17; secret signs, 71–76, 79, 81, 352n10; strange dreams, 211; waste elimination, 209; withdrawal from world, 209–10

dying person, 93–115, 189–206; behavior toward, 93–96, 101–5; dedication of death, 111–12; esoteric practices for, 115; finding forgiveness, 108; giving hope to, 107; home health care services for, 213, 381n8; hopes and fears of, 96–97; hydration, 204, 207–8; loved ones, psychological stages in, 200; needs of, 191–97; nutrition, 204–5; pain management, 189–90, 205–6, 207; proper holding environment for, 97–101, 109–10; psychological stages, 197–99; regrets of, 334–35n11; saying goodbye to, 108–9, 112; spiritual context, 217–19; spiritual practice of, 110–11, 113–14; telling truth to, 105–6; unfinished business, resolution of, 107. *See also* after-death care

Dzigar Kongtrul Rinpoche, 124, 283–86

dzogchen, 60, 281, 293, 304, 340n35, 343n56

Dzogchen Ponlop Rinpoche, 19, 30–32, 97, 131, 135, 297–99

dzogchen tantras, 84, 131, 154

Dzongsar Khyentse Rinpoche, 139, 154, 286–87

Edelstein, Scott, 260

embalming, 225, 230

Emerson, Ralph Waldo, 246

emptiness, 47, 51, 58, 219, 221, 253–55, 339n29, 382n16, 391n24

enlightenment, 35, 55, 76, 82, 383n21, 386n25

estate planning, 162, 377n6

ethical will, 167–68

euthanasia, 262–65

"Family Love Letter" (Scroggin), 162

fear, 27, 33, 47, 58, 362–63n31, 370n55

financial responsibilities, 319–20

Ford, Henry, 161

four reminders, 22–26, 337–38n19, 338–39n28

fourth moment, 20, 336–37n12, 337n14

Franzen, Jonathan, 114

Fremantle, Francesca, 57, 89, 130, 134, 137–38

funerals: cemetery scams, 394n13; costs, 384n9, 394n12; Funeral Consumers' Alliance, 226; funeral directors, role of, 225–26, 383–84n4; funeral homes, dealing with, 321–24; home funerals, 223–24, 385n12; prepayment, 226; written directive for, 177–78

gandharva (scent eater), 149, 374n25
Gangshar, Khenpo, 48
garuda, 84
Gelugpa rituals, 156–58
generation stage practice, 58, 124–25, 343n57
Gershten, Mitchell, 197–206
Gibran, Kahlil, 94
Gómez, Luis, 144
Gotsangpa, 94, 101
grief, 241–46, 250–51, 328–31; Buddhist perspective, 246–48, 253–55, 385n17
Guru Rinpoche. See Padmasambhava
guru yoga, 43

Halifax, Roshi Joan, 92–93, 94–95, 104, 186
Halpern, Alex, 173
Harris, Sam, 24
Haub, Carl, 67
health care agent, 166–67
Hennezel, Marie de, 98
home health care services, 213, 381n8
horror movies, reverse meditation and, 33, 340n41
hospice, 184–90, 213, 361n11, 381n7
hourglass, 85–89, 86 fig. 3, 336–37n12

illusory form, 51–52, 347n85
immeasurables, four, 147
impermanence, 253–55, 338n22
inner yogas, 69–70
insomnia yoga, 137
Iron Hook of Compassion, 151–52, 371n6
Iyengar, B. K. S., 20, 191, 219

Jamgön Kongtrul, 142–43
Jobs, Steve, 161
Johnson, Samuel, 23

Joplin, Janis, 79
Julian of Norwich, 245

Kalachakra Tantra, 144
Kalu Rinpoche, 34, 54, 75, 118, 122, 142, 264–65
karma: in bardo of becoming, 6, 31, 53, 117, 364n2; defined, 392n35; good, 15–16, 67, 144, 344–45n66, 391n25; law of proximate, 263, 344n60; merit and, 144; negative, 55, 58; purification of, 154, 349nn106–7; rebirth and, 134, 136; relationship to death, 15–16, 39–41, 53, 67; as result of not experiencing fully, 385n15; suicide and, 266; winds of, 52, 54, 83, 117–18, 270
Karma Chagme Rinpoche, 35
Karma Lingpa, 51, 290
Karmapa, Seventeenth, 271
Karmapa, Sixteenth, 69
kayas. See bodies, dharmakaya, nirmanakaya, sambhogakaya, trikaya
Keown, Damien, 266
Khandro Rinpoche, Jetsun, 287–88
Khenpo Karthar Rinpoche, 33–34, 41, 51, 98, 137, 146, 288–89
The King of Aspiration Prayers (Samantabhadra), 147
Klein, Anne Carolyn, 24
Kübler-Ross, Elisabeth, 104, 105–6, 185, 190, 198

Lack, Sylvia, 186
LaLanne, Jack, 25
lama dances, 49
Lao-Tzu, 139
legal terms, explanation of, 165–68
letting go, 55, 68–70, 109, 112, 163–64, 249–50, 253
Levine, Stephen, 218–19, 244
Levy, Mitchell, 261
liberation, 44–45, 44 table 1, 345n71, 348n99, 353n21, 353n26, 376n46
living wills, 165, 169–73, 180–84, 380n3
lojong (mind training), 51, 281, 283, 300, 302

Longaker, Christine, 98, 108, 191–97, 246–48
Longer Sukhavati Sutra, 35
longevity practices, 349–50n108
lucid dreaming, 21, 121–22, 346n83
luminosities, mother and child, 45, 46, 82
luminosity yogas, 46, 355–56n36

Madhyamaka, 46, 345n73
Mahabharata, 24
mahamudra, 46, 60, 299, 300, 345n73, 368n31
Mahanama Sutta, 16
mandala, 57, 76, 156, 270, 386n27
Manjushri, 27
mantras: Amitabha, 35, 343nn54–55; in bardo of becoming, 127; for blocking, 131; Chenrezig, 37–38; for liberation, 353n21, 376n46; as protection, 60; for purification and healing, 155; Vajra Guru, 115; Vajrasattva, 57–58, 155, 269
Mara, 266, 333n3
maras, 152
marigpa (ignorance), 80, 354n29
Marpa, 254
Matlock, Daniel, 212
Medicaid, 379n12
medical order for scope of treatment (MOST), 172
medical power of attorney (MPOA), 165–66, 180–84, 377n7, 380n3
Medicare, 186–88, 216, 377–79n12
meditation: creating many thoughts, 31–32; meditation day, 83; in overly stimulating environment, 32–33; path of, 119; as preparation for death, 78; purpose of, 26–27, 57; unconditional presence, development of, 98; *vipashyana*, 21–22
meditations: deity yoga, 46–47, 52–53, 58, 136; dream yoga, 51; formless, 46; illusory form, 51–52; Pure Land, 34–35; Red Tara, 155–56; reverse, 29–33, 340n40; shamatha, 18–21, 121; thögal, 47–49; Vajrasattva, 57–58; visualization practice, 49
Meditation Sutra, 35

meditative absorption, 21, 82
merit, 144–48, 342n47, 363n41, 371n11, 372–73n12, 373n15, 374n21
Milarepa, 40, 56
mind: in the bardo, 371n5; familiarizing with, 57, 366–67n11; brain and, 367n24, 381–82n10; breath of, 79–80; elemental qualities of, 86, 358n47; as reality, 53
mindfulness, 18–21, 336n10
Mingyur Rinpoche, 291–92
miscarriage, 268–69
Mitford, Jessica, 230
monasteries, commissioning rituals for the dead, 150–56
Montaigne, Michel de, 8
Mooney, Kim, 241–46, 248, 249
Morton, Kathleen Willis, 251
Mullin, Glenn, 164

nadis (channels), 69, 79, 348n92
Nagarjuna, 144
Namkha Drimed Rinpoche, 100, 292–97
narcotics, 380–81n5
Naropa, 21, 56
né dren ("leading to places"), 153–54, 291
neti neti, 119
New Age philosophy, 219–20, 383n18
nirmanakaya, 44, 44 table 1, 49–53
nirvana, 15, 80, 81, 130, 133, 306, 357–58n41
Nisargadatta Maharaj, 31
Noble Truths, 38–39, 344n58
nonduality, 76, 79, 85

obituary/eulogy, 325–26, 394n9
Oedipus complex, 368n35
On Death and Dying (Kübler-Ross), 185
organ donation, 143, 173, 214, 261–62, 387n7, 387n10
Ostaseski, Frank, 93

Padmasambhava (Guru Rinpoche), 20, 45–46, 51, 56, 100, 115
pain: management, 189–90, 205–6, 207; meditation, 30–31
palliative care, 264, 361n16, 380n2

paramitas, five, 147
Pascal, Blaise, 18
path of seeing, 119, 365nn5–6
Patrul Rinpoche, 56
Patterson, Beth, 184
Pert, Candace, 218
pets, death of, 270–71, 386n19, 388n13
phowa (transference of consciousness), 37, 43, 54–57, 78, 110–11, 151–52, 293, 348n95, 353n24, 375n31
physician orders for life-sustaining treatment (POLST), 172–73
Plato, 65
post-death practices, 139–41
practitioner, levels of, 68
prajna (wisdom), 147, 391n25
prajnaparamita sutras, 46, 345n73
prana (wind), 69, 73, 79–81, 89, 348n92, 355n34
preservation methods, temporary, 230–31, 384n7, 384n10
prognosis, estimates of, 214–15, 382n12
proof of ownership document, 167
property, disposition of, 178
psychedelic therapy, 351n3
Pure Land Buddhism, 33–37, 54, 60, 122, 144, 265, 282, 306, 340–41n42, 342n47, 342n52, 344n60, 372n12
pure lands, 34, 52–54, 102, 112, 133–34, 146, 152, 154, 306–07, 341n44, 352–53n17. *See also* Sukhavati
Purification of the Six Realms, 154
purification practices, 58, 154–56, 269

Rangdrol, Tsele Natsok, 135
reality: facing, 25, 41, 70, 106, 132–33; levels of, 44; mind as, 53, 79, 133
rebirth, 129–30, 133–37, 306–7, 369n45, 369n49, 370n54, 371n10, 379–80n1
Red Tara meditation, 155–56
reincarnation, 42, 48, 121, 350n1
remains, disposition of, 176–77
renunciation, 46
reverse meditations, 29–33, 340n40
Ricard, Matthieu, 265–66
rigor mortis, 83, 153, 177, 227, 357n39

rigpa, 114
Rumi, 82

sacred listening, 94–96, 103–4
Sakyong Mipham Rinpoche, 15, 17, 25, 53, 55, 125
samadhi, 21
Samantabhadra, 147
sambhogakaya, 44, 44 table 1, 46–49
samsara: basis of, 69, 354n30; blocking door to, 130–32; fear and, 58; ignorance and, 80; realms of, 53, 340–41n42, 347n88; root poisons of, 35, 37
Saunders, Dame Cicely, 184–85, 189
science, Buddhism and, 268, 391n27
Scroggin, John, 162
secret names, 128, 368n31
Seneca, 95
Shakespeare, William, 3
shamatha meditation, 18–21, 121
Shambhala Buddhism, 132, 177, 341n44
Shantideva, 29
Simmer-Brown, Judith, 259
Simon, Paul, 24
Six Yogas of Naropa, 52, 290
skandhas, 73, 352n12
Smith, Huston, 263
Sogyal Rinpoche: on abortion, 269; on best things to do upon dying, 43; on buddhahood, 84; on crematorium practices, 156; on death as inspiration, 117; on death as triumph, 15; on dedicating one's pain, 111, 112; on emptiness, 253–54; on Essential Phowa, 110–11; on expectations about death, 41, 69; on fear of death, 119–20; on helping the dying, 91, 96; on letting go, 68, 109; on the mind, 53; on *né dren* and *chang chok*, 153–54; on physical rebirth, 130–31; on positive thoughts, 60, 64; on preparation for eternity, 126; on purification, 154–55; on state of mind at death, 39; on teaching about dying, 11
spiritual bypassing, 220
spiritual masters, consulting, 259–61
suffering, 19, 334n7, 336n11, 338n28

suicide, 147, 265–68, 388n17, 389n18, 389–90n22, 390n23
Sukhavati (Land of Bliss), 33–37, 54, 122, 127, 134, 144, 306, 341n44, 342n53
Sukhavati ritual, 153, 269. *See also* Amitabha, phowa
Sukhavati Aspiration Prayer (Karma Chagme), 35
sur (burnt) offering, 149–50, 374n26
Suzuki Roshi, 247

Tagore, Rabindranath, 67, 82
takdrol (liberation blanket), 270, 295, 314, 393n7
tantric iconography, 49
Tara, 155–56
Tatelbaum, Judy, 252
tathagatagarbha, 89
tat tvam asi, 119
Tenga Rinpoche, 16, 131, 299–300
Tenzin Wangyal Rinpoche, 149, 300–301
thangkas, 49
Tharchin Rinpoche, Lama, 289–91
Thich Nhat Hanh, 35, 255, 256
thögal (leaping over), 46, 47–49
Thrangu Rinpoche: on bardo instructions, 27; on choosing fortunate rebirth, 129–30, 134; on controlling sexual desire, 59; interview with, 302–3; on preparation for death, 48–49, 57, 120–21, 123; on Pure Land practice, 33
Thurman, Robert, 3
The Tibetan Book of Living and Dying (Sogyal Rinpoche), 102–8, 187
The Tibetan Book of the Dead: on blocking, 130–32; on choosing best rebirth, 135–37; on death, 4, 18; on distraction, 123; on emptiness, 58; on experiences in the bardo, 124; on helping the deceased, 140; instruction for bardos, 89–90; main themes in, 18, 21; original length of, 336n7; on preparation for death, 63–64; on pure perception, 133; purpose of, 122; reading aloud to the deceased, 148–49; on sound of dharmata, 49

three poisons, 35, 37, 120, 355n33; aggression, 35–36, 80, 86, 130–32, 136–37, 354n31; ignorance, 80, 354n29; passion, 58–59, 354n31, 359n50
Tilopa, 56
Tolle, Eckhart, 72
tonglen (sending and taking), 28–29, 111, 112, 148, 265, 340nn35–36
Toynbee, Arnold, 25
trekchö (cutting through), 46, 47, 345n73
trikaya (three bodies), 44–45, 359n48, 365n6, 383n21, 345nn70–71
Trungpa Rinpoche: on death, 39; on disease, 218; on the four reminders, 22–23; on grief, 254, 256; on groundlessness, 93; on letting go, 164; on mindfulness, 20; on mortality, 24; on organ donation, 261–62; on pain, 30; on reading aloud to the dead, 149; on reality of death, 42; on relating to dying person, 99; on *tonglen,* 29
trusts, 165, 178–80
tsatsa, 154, 156
Tsoknyi Rinpoche, 101, 303–6
Tsültrim Gyamtso Rinpoche, Khenpo, 33, 51, 52, 108, 147, 219, 261
tukdam, 82–83, 261, 356–57n37, 357n39
Tulku Nyima Rinpoche, 35
Tulku Thondup Rinpoche: advice for the bardo, 125, 134, 138; on attaining the human realm, 135; on enlightenment, 35; on merit, 145–46; on the mind in the bardo, 126; on preparation for death, 67; on rebirth in a pure land, 306–7; on *sur* ceremonies, 149–50
Tulku Urgyen Rinpoche, 32, 45, 152

Upanishads, 47

Vajradhara, 55
Vajra Guru mantra, 115
Vajrasattva, 57–58, 155, 269
van Dyke, Henry, 256
Van Vuuren, Karen, 223–41
via positiva, 119

vipashyana (insight) meditation, 21–22, 280, 337n18
visualization practice, 49

Wallace, B. Alan, 41, 126, 146–47
Weitzel, Lynn, 212
Welwood, John, 220
Wheel of Life, 87, 342n51
Wilber, Ken, 220
wills, 163–65, 175–78
Winnicott, Donald, 97
wisdom, 57, 76, 79, 84, 133, 374n21; five, 73; lights, five, 133

Wittgenstein, Ludwig, 20

Yama, Lord of Death, 87, 368n30
Yamantaka, 27
Yeshe, Lama, 56–57, 69, 78
Yogachara, 73
Yudisthira, 24

Zopa Rinpoche, Lama, 4, 16, 25, 29, 39, 156–58, 262